Bandy Kiki

Cameroon's LGBTQ Digital Advocate – Unauthorized

Chike Zhang

ISBN: 9781779696892
Imprint: Telephasic Workshop
Copyright © 2024 Chike Zhang.
All Rights Reserved.

Contents

The Masked Activist	13
The Struggles of LGBTQ Community in Cameroon	24
Bibliography	**33**
Bibliography	**37**
Activism in the Digital Age	37
The Impact of Bandy Kiki's Work	48
A Journey to Self-Acceptance	**61**
A Journey to Self-Acceptance	61
Discovering Sexuality and Gender Identity	63
Coming out in a Hostile Environment	75
A Quest for Authenticity	87
Bibliography	**93**
Battling Self-Doubt and Insecurities	99
Cultivating Self-Love and Self-Care	111
The Fight for Equality	**123**
The Fight for Equality	123
Taking a Stand against Discrimination	125
Raising Global Awareness	137
Navigating Activism in a Hostile Climate	148
Building Allies and Coalitions	159
Towards a Brighter Future	171
Bibliography	**177**
A Legacy of Courage	**185**

A Legacy of Courage 185
Inspiring Future Activists 187
Personal Growth and Evolution 200
Bandy Kiki: The Woman Behind the Mask 210
Leaving a Lasting Impact 222
The Future of LGBTQ Activism 233

The Unapologetic Activist 247
The Unapologetic Activist 247
Facing Adversity with Resilience 249
The Power of Authenticity 260
Redefining Activism in the Digital Age 272
Bandy Kiki's Vision for the Future 284

Epilogue - The Unstoppable Spirit 297
Epilogue - The Unstoppable Spirit 297
Bandy Kiki's Continuing Impact 299
The Evolution of LGBTQ Rights in Cameroon 308

Bibliography 319
Celebrating Diversity and Queerness 319
The Fight Goes On 329

Bibliography 339

Index 341

The Birth of Bandy Kiki

The story of Bandy Kiki begins in the vibrant, bustling city of Douala, Cameroon. Nestled between the Atlantic Ocean and the lush green hills, Douala is a city that pulsates with life, culture, and contradictions. It is here, in the heart of this complex tapestry, that Bandy Kiki was born—an identity forged in the fires of adversity and resilience.

1.1.1 Growing Up in Douala

Growing up in Douala was both a blessing and a challenge for young Bandy. The city is a melting pot of cultures, languages, and traditions, yet it is also a place where conservative values often clash with the realities of modern life. As a child, Bandy was surrounded by the vibrant sounds of market vendors, the aroma of local delicacies, and the laughter of children playing in the streets. However, beneath this colorful surface lay a society that was deeply entrenched in patriarchal norms and rigid gender expectations.

1.1.2 Early Signs of Activism

From an early age, Bandy exhibited signs of a budding activist. While other children played with dolls or toy cars, she found herself drawn to the stories of those who were marginalized and oppressed. She often questioned the status quo, asking why certain people were treated differently based on their sexual orientation or gender identity. These early inklings of activism were nurtured by her family, who encouraged her to speak her mind and stand up for what she believed in.

1.1.3 Discovering Her Identity

As Bandy entered her teenage years, she began to grapple with her own identity. Like many young people, she experienced confusion and uncertainty about her sexuality. Growing up in a society that often demonizes LGBTQ identities made this journey particularly challenging. Bandy's exploration of her identity was marked by moments of joy and despair, as she navigated the complexities of self-discovery.

$$I_{identity} = f(I_{self}, S_{society}, C_{culture}) \tag{1}$$

Where:

- $I_{identity}$ is the individual's identity.
- I_{self} is the internal understanding of oneself.

- $S_{society}$ is the societal norms and expectations.
- $C_{culture}$ is the cultural context influencing identity formation.

This equation illustrates that identity is a function of both internal self-perception and external societal pressures, a theme that would resonate throughout Bandy's life.

1.1.4 Coming to Terms with Her Truth

Coming to terms with her truth was not an easy feat. Bandy faced the daunting task of reconciling her authentic self with the expectations of her family and society. In a culture where LGBTQ identities are often stigmatized, the fear of rejection loomed large. Yet, she found solace in the stories of other activists and the burgeoning global LGBTQ movement. These narratives became a source of strength, inspiring her to embrace her identity fully.

1.1.5 The Decision to Fight for LGBTQ Rights

The pivotal moment in Bandy's journey came when she realized that her struggle was not just personal; it was part of a larger fight for justice and equality. The oppressive legal framework in Cameroon, which criminalizes same-sex relationships, fueled her determination. Bandy made the courageous decision to become an advocate for LGBTQ rights, recognizing that her voice could be a beacon of hope for others facing similar challenges.

$$F_{activism} = \sum_{i=1}^{n}(V_i + E_i + C_i) \qquad (2)$$

Where:

- $F_{activism}$ is the force of activism.
- V_i is the voice of each individual in the community.
- E_i is the emotional impact of shared experiences.
- C_i is the collective action taken by the community.

This equation encapsulates the essence of activism as a collective force, driven by the voices and experiences of individuals united for a common cause.

In conclusion, the birth of Bandy Kiki is a tale of self-discovery, resilience, and the unwavering spirit of activism. It sets the stage for a journey that would challenge societal norms and inspire countless others to embrace their true selves. As we delve deeper into Bandy's life, we will witness how her early experiences in Douala shaped her into a powerful advocate for change, armed with the courage to stand up for her community and fight for a brighter future.

The Birth of Bandy Kiki

The story of Bandy Kiki begins in the vibrant coastal city of Douala, Cameroon, where the sun kisses the Atlantic Ocean and the rhythms of life pulse through the streets. Born into a society that often views LGBTQ identities as taboo, Bandy's journey is marked by both struggle and resilience. This section explores the early life of Bandy Kiki, the foundational experiences that shaped her identity, and the awakening of her activist spirit.

1.1.1 Growing Up in Douala

In the heart of Douala, Bandy Kiki was born into a family filled with love but also steeped in traditional values. Douala, known for its bustling markets and rich cultural tapestry, is a city that embodies the duality of modernity and conservatism. Here, Bandy's childhood was a blend of joyous exploration and the looming shadow of societal expectations.

From a young age, Bandy exhibited traits that set her apart. Whether it was her knack for storytelling, her passion for art, or her fierce sense of justice, it was clear that she was destined for a path less traveled. But growing up in a society that often stigmatizes non-conformity posed significant challenges. The societal norms dictated strict gender roles and expectations, which left little room for deviation.

1.1.2 Early Signs of Activism

Even as a child, Bandy showed signs of her future activism. She would often stand up for her friends who were bullied, using her words like a shield to protect those who were marginalized. This early inclination towards advocacy was not without its consequences; Bandy faced ridicule and backlash from peers and adults alike. Yet, each confrontation only fueled her desire to fight against injustice.

1.1.3 Discovering Her Identity

As Bandy transitioned into her teenage years, the process of self-discovery began in earnest. The realization of her LGBTQ identity came with both clarity and confusion. In a society where being different could lead to ostracism or worse,

Bandy grappled with her feelings in silence. Her journey of self-acceptance was fraught with internalized homophobia, a common struggle among LGBTQ individuals in conservative environments.

$$\text{Self-Acceptance} = \text{Understanding} + \text{Courage} - \text{Fear} \qquad (3)$$

This equation illustrates the delicate balance Bandy had to strike: understanding her identity required courage, but fear of societal rejection was a formidable barrier.

1.1.4 Coming to Terms with Her Truth

The turning point in Bandy's life came when she found solace in literature and online communities. Through reading stories of other LGBTQ individuals, she began to see reflections of her own experiences. These narratives provided a lifeline, allowing her to envision a future where she could embrace her truth without fear.

Bandy's realization that she was not alone was liberating. She began to understand that her identity was not something to be ashamed of but rather a source of strength. This newfound perspective ignited a fire within her, compelling her to take a stand not just for herself but for others who felt similarly trapped.

1.1.5 The Decision to Fight for LGBTQ Rights

Empowered by her journey of self-discovery, Bandy made the pivotal decision to become an advocate for LGBTQ rights. This decision was not made lightly; it came with the understanding that she would face significant risks. The oppressive legal framework in Cameroon criminalizes homosexuality, and the societal stigma surrounding LGBTQ identities often leads to violence and discrimination.

Yet, Bandy was undeterred. She recognized the importance of visibility and representation in the fight for equality. With a heart full of passion and a mind set on change, she began to engage with local LGBTQ organizations, using her voice to amplify the struggles of her community.

In this section, we have traced the early life of Bandy Kiki, from her childhood in Douala to her burgeoning identity as an activist. Each experience, each struggle, laid the groundwork for the fierce advocate she would become. As we continue to explore her journey, we will delve into the complexities of her activism, the challenges she faced, and the impact she has made on the LGBTQ community in Cameroon and beyond.

ERROR. thisXsection() returned an empty string with textbook depth = 3.
ERROR. thisXsection() returned an empty string with textbook depth = 3.
ERROR. thisXsection() returned an empty string with textbook depth = 3.

Early signs of activism

From the bustling streets of Douala, where the sounds of vibrant markets and the scent of street food mingle with the air, Bandy Kiki's early life was a tapestry woven with threads of curiosity and defiance. It was here, amid the vibrant chaos, that the first flickers of her activism began to emerge, illuminating the path she would eventually tread as a digital advocate for LGBTQ rights.

Bandy's childhood was marked by a keen sense of justice, often questioning the societal norms that dictated what was deemed acceptable. She recalls instances in her primary school where discussions about fairness and equality would spark her interest. For instance, during a class debate on gender roles, she found herself passionately defending the idea that everyone, regardless of gender, should have the freedom to choose their path. This early inclination towards social justice was not just a fleeting childhood whim; it was a precursor to the activism that would define her later life.

The seeds of activism were further nurtured by her experiences with discrimination and exclusion. As a young person grappling with her identity in a society rife with rigid gender norms, Bandy often felt the sting of societal expectations. The pressure to conform was palpable, yet it ignited a fire within her. She began to observe how her peers were treated based on their perceived differences, particularly those who dared to step outside the traditional boundaries of gender and sexuality. This observation led her to question the status quo, setting the stage for her future endeavors in advocacy.

Bandy's early signs of activism were also influenced by her exposure to literature and media that challenged societal norms. She discovered books and articles that spoke of LGBTQ rights and the struggles faced by marginalized communities. These narratives resonated deeply with her, providing a sense of validation and solidarity. The writings of renowned activists and authors became her guiding lights, illuminating the path towards understanding her own identity and the broader fight for equality.

In her teenage years, Bandy took her first tangible steps into activism. She began organizing informal gatherings with friends to discuss LGBTQ issues, creating a safe space for dialogue and support. These meetings, held in the comfort of her home, were filled with laughter, tears, and a shared understanding of the challenges they faced. It was here that Bandy honed her ability to communicate effectively, using storytelling as a powerful tool to connect with others. She realized that sharing personal experiences could foster empathy and inspire action, a lesson that would serve her well in her future endeavors.

Moreover, Bandy's involvement in local community events provided her with a platform to voice her concerns. Whether it was participating in youth forums or engaging in discussions about human rights, she seized every opportunity to advocate for change. These experiences not only solidified her commitment to activism but also helped her develop critical skills in public speaking and advocacy. She learned to navigate difficult conversations, often employing humor and relatability to break down barriers and engage her audience.

However, the journey was not without its challenges. Bandy faced pushback from peers and adults who were resistant to change. The societal stigma surrounding LGBTQ issues was deeply entrenched, and her budding activism was often met with skepticism. Yet, rather than deter her, these obstacles fueled her determination. She understood that true change requires resilience and courage, qualities she began to cultivate in abundance.

In summary, the early signs of Bandy Kiki's activism were characterized by a blend of personal experiences, social observations, and a thirst for justice. Her journey from a curious child questioning societal norms to a young advocate organizing discussions among peers laid the groundwork for her future work. It was during these formative years that she began to realize the power of her voice and the impact it could have on those around her. As she navigated the complexities of identity and acceptance, Bandy Kiki was unknowingly preparing herself to become a formidable force in the fight for LGBTQ rights in Cameroon and beyond.

Discovering her identity

The journey of self-discovery is often a complex and multifaceted process, particularly for individuals within marginalized communities. For Bandy Kiki, this journey began in the vibrant yet tumultuous environment of Douala, Cameroon. It was a place where societal norms were rigid, and any deviation from the heteronormative narrative was met with skepticism, fear, and sometimes violence. This section delves into the intricate process through which Bandy began to understand her identity amidst these challenging circumstances.

The Early Signs

From a young age, Bandy exhibited interests and behaviors that diverged from traditional gender roles. These early signs included a preference for activities typically associated with boys, such as playing soccer, and a fascination with fashion that defied conventional expectations. Research in gender studies suggests that children often express their identities through play and social interactions, which can serve as a foundational aspect of their self-concept [?].

However, growing up in a society that rigidly enforces gender binaries made it difficult for Bandy to embrace these early signs. The pressure to conform to societal expectations created a dissonance within her, leading to feelings of confusion and isolation. According to queer theorist Judith Butler, gender is not a fixed identity but rather a performance shaped by societal norms [?]. Bandy's experiences reflect this notion, as she grappled with the performance of gender expected of her while internally questioning its validity.

Navigating Identity and Culture

As Bandy matured, she began to explore the concept of sexuality more deeply. The lack of accessible resources and discussions surrounding LGBTQ identities in Cameroon meant that her exploration was often fraught with uncertainty. The cultural context played a significant role; Cameroon is known for its stringent anti-LGBTQ laws, which further complicated her journey. The societal narrative often portrayed homosexuality as a Western imposition, leading to internalized homophobia among individuals questioning their identities [?].

During this time, Bandy sought solace in online communities, where anonymity provided a safe space for exploration. The digital age has opened avenues for individuals to connect and share experiences, particularly for those in oppressive environments. Bandy found herself drawn to blogs and forums that celebrated diverse sexualities and gender identities, allowing her to see reflections of her own experiences in the stories of others. This exposure was pivotal; it not only validated her feelings but also introduced her to the lexicon of queer identities.

The Moment of Realization

The turning point in Bandy's journey came when she encountered the concept of bisexuality. For many, the realization of one's sexual orientation is often accompanied by a profound sense of relief and clarity. Bandy's understanding of bisexuality as a legitimate identity helped her reconcile her feelings of attraction to multiple genders. This moment of realization was significant; it marked the transition from confusion to acceptance.

However, this newfound identity was not without its challenges. Bandy faced the dual burden of navigating her bisexuality in a society that often invalidates such identities. Research shows that bisexual individuals frequently experience discrimination from both heterosexual and homosexual communities, leading to a phenomenon known as "biphobia" [?]. Bandy's experiences echoed this reality, as she often felt marginalized within the LGBTQ community itself, being perceived as "not queer enough" or "just confused."

Embracing Her Truth

As Bandy continued to explore her identity, she began to embrace the concept of being non-binary. This realization was not an overnight occurrence but rather a gradual process of understanding that gender is not strictly binary. Bandy's journey aligns with the theories posited by gender theorists who advocate for a spectrum of gender identities, challenging the traditional male-female dichotomy [?].

Embracing her non-binary identity allowed Bandy to reclaim her narrative. She began to express herself through fashion and personal style that defied gender norms, using clothing as a form of self-expression. This act of defiance was not merely a personal choice but a political statement against the oppressive societal structures that sought to confine her.

The Decision to Fight for LGBTQ Rights

The culmination of Bandy's journey of self-discovery was the realization that her identity was not just a personal matter; it was a political one. The struggles she faced were reflective of a larger systemic issue affecting countless individuals in Cameroon. This understanding ignited a passion within her to advocate for LGBTQ rights, transforming her personal journey into a collective fight for justice.

In conclusion, Bandy Kiki's journey of discovering her identity was characterized by exploration, struggle, and ultimately, empowerment. Her experiences highlight the importance of representation and support for individuals navigating their identities in oppressive environments. Through her journey, Bandy not only found herself but also became a beacon of hope for others seeking to embrace their truth.

Coming to terms with her truth

Coming to terms with one's truth is often a tumultuous journey, particularly for individuals navigating the complexities of identity within a society that may not always be accepting. For Bandy Kiki, this process was marked by both internal struggles and external pressures that shaped her understanding of self and her place in the world.

The Internal Struggle

Initially, Bandy found herself grappling with conflicting emotions. The realization of her identity as a member of the LGBTQ community clashed with the societal norms instilled in her from a young age. This internal conflict can be understood through the lens of *Cognitive Dissonance Theory*, which posits that individuals experience psychological discomfort when holding two or more contradictory beliefs or values [?]. In Bandy's case, her burgeoning understanding of her identity contradicted the expectations of her family and society, leading to a profound sense of dissonance.

To illustrate, Bandy often recalled moments of self-doubt when she would overhear conversations laden with homophobic rhetoric. These instances reinforced her fear of rejection and isolation, making it difficult for her to embrace her truth fully. The pain of living a double life—one that conformed to societal expectations and another that was true to her identity—took a toll on her mental health.

Seeking Acceptance

As Bandy began to explore her identity more openly, she sought acceptance not only from herself but also from those around her. This quest for acceptance is a common theme in LGBTQ narratives, often described in the context of *Coming Out Theory*. According to *Cass's Model of Sexual Identity Formation*, the journey to self-acceptance typically involves several stages, including identity confusion, identity comparison, identity tolerance, identity acceptance, and ultimately, identity pride [?].

For Bandy, the stage of identity acceptance was particularly pivotal. She started to surround herself with like-minded individuals who shared similar experiences. This community provided a safe space for her to express her thoughts and feelings without fear of judgment. The support she received helped her navigate the complexities of her identity, fostering a sense of belonging that was previously absent.

Confronting Societal Norms

However, the journey towards self-acceptance was not without its challenges. Bandy faced the harsh reality of societal norms that dictated what was deemed acceptable. The pervasive stigma surrounding LGBTQ identities in Cameroon created an environment rife with hostility and discrimination. According to a report by the International Lesbian, Gay, Bisexual, Trans and Intersex Association

(ILGA), same-sex relationships are criminalized in Cameroon, leading to widespread violence and persecution of LGBTQ individuals [?].

Bandy's decision to embrace her truth required not only personal courage but also an understanding of the broader societal context. She realized that her journey was intertwined with the fight for LGBTQ rights in Cameroon. This realization propelled her to not only accept her identity but to also advocate for others who faced similar struggles.

The Role of Intersectionality

In her quest for self-acceptance, Bandy also recognized the importance of intersectionality—the interconnected nature of social categorizations such as race, class, and gender, which can create overlapping systems of discrimination or disadvantage [?]. As a queer individual in Cameroon, Bandy's identity was shaped by multiple layers of oppression, making her journey towards acceptance even more complex.

For example, Bandy often reflected on the experiences of her peers who faced discrimination not only for their sexual orientation but also for their economic status or ethnic background. This understanding deepened her resolve to fight for a more inclusive society where all identities could coexist without fear.

Embracing Self-Truth

Ultimately, coming to terms with her truth was a transformative experience for Bandy. It involved embracing her identity as a bisexual, non-binary individual and recognizing the beauty in her uniqueness. This journey was not linear; it was filled with setbacks and triumphs. However, each step brought her closer to self-acceptance and empowerment.

Bandy's story serves as a powerful reminder of the importance of authenticity in a world that often demands conformity. By embracing her truth, she not only liberated herself but also inspired others to embark on their journeys of self-discovery. Her advocacy work became a testament to the resilience of the human spirit, demonstrating that love and acceptance can flourish even in the most challenging environments.

Conclusion

In conclusion, coming to terms with her truth was a multifaceted journey for Bandy Kiki. It involved navigating the complexities of identity, confronting societal norms, and embracing the power of community. Through her experiences, Bandy not only found acceptance within herself but also became a beacon of hope for others in the LGBTQ community. Her story underscores the significance of authenticity and the ongoing fight for equality, reminding us all that the journey towards self-acceptance is a vital step in the broader struggle for human rights.

The decision to fight for LGBTQ rights

The journey to activism is often a complex and deeply personal one, shaped by experiences of self-discovery, societal pressures, and the stark realities faced by marginalized communities. For Bandy Kiki, the decision to fight for LGBTQ rights in Cameroon was not merely a choice; it was a necessity born out of a profound understanding of the injustices that plagued her community.

Understanding the Context

To fully appreciate the gravity of Bandy's decision, it is crucial to understand the socio-political landscape of Cameroon, where homosexuality is criminalized under Section 347 of the Penal Code, which states that anyone engaging in same-sex relations can face imprisonment for up to five years. This oppressive legal framework not only legitimizes discrimination but also fosters a culture of fear and violence against LGBTQ individuals. The pervasive stigma surrounding non-heteronormative identities creates an environment where many are forced to conceal their true selves, often leading to internalized homophobia and a sense of isolation.

Personal Experiences and Realizations

Bandy's journey toward activism was catalyzed by her personal experiences of discrimination and exclusion. Growing up in Douala, she witnessed firsthand the struggles of her peers who faced harassment and violence due to their sexual orientation. One poignant example was her friend, who was brutally attacked after being outed, an incident that left a lasting scar on Bandy's psyche. This event, coupled with her own struggles to accept her identity, ignited a fire within her—a desire to not only advocate for herself but also for those who could not speak out.

The decision to fight for LGBTQ rights was also influenced by her exposure to global movements and the power of digital activism. The internet became a lifeline for Bandy, allowing her to connect with like-minded individuals and gain insights into successful advocacy strategies employed by activists worldwide. This realization that change was possible, even in the face of overwhelming odds, was a pivotal moment for her.

Theoretical Framework: Social Identity Theory

Bandy's decision can be examined through the lens of Social Identity Theory, which posits that individuals derive a significant part of their self-concept from their group memberships. For Bandy, embracing her LGBTQ identity meant not only acknowledging her individuality but also recognizing the collective struggles of her community. This understanding fostered a sense of solidarity and responsibility, compelling her to take action.

$$\text{Social Identity} = \text{Personal Identity} + \text{Group Identity} \qquad (4)$$

Where: - Social Identity represents the individual's self-concept derived from group affiliations. - Personal Identity pertains to unique personal attributes and experiences. - Group Identity encapsulates the shared characteristics and experiences of the LGBTQ community.

The Call to Action

Fueled by her experiences and theoretical insights, Bandy began to formulate her vision for change. She recognized that fighting for LGBTQ rights was not just about advocating for legal reforms; it was about challenging the societal norms that perpetuated discrimination and violence. She envisioned a Cameroon where LGBTQ individuals could live freely and authentically, without fear of retribution.

This vision crystallized into a call to action, prompting her to leverage her skills in digital communication to raise awareness and mobilize support. Bandy understood that the fight for rights was inherently linked to the fight for visibility. By sharing her story and those of others, she aimed to humanize the LGBTQ experience, dismantling stereotypes and fostering empathy among the broader population.

Challenges and Resilience

However, Bandy's decision was not without challenges. The fear of backlash loomed large, as she navigated the treacherous waters of activism in a hostile environment. The potential for legal repercussions, social ostracism, and personal danger weighed heavily on her. Yet, it was precisely this fear that galvanized her resolve.

Bandy's experiences echoed the sentiments expressed by many activists who have faced similar dilemmas. The renowned LGBTQ activist Marsha P. Johnson once said, "No pride for some of us without liberation for all of us." This mantra resonated deeply with Bandy, reinforcing her belief that her fight was part of a larger struggle for justice and equality.

activist's identity, leading to dire consequences. Bandy Kiki navigated this landscape by employing various digital security measures and being mindful of the information she shared.

Empowerment through Pseudonymity

Ultimately, the act of creating a pseudonym is an empowering process. It allows activists like Bandy Kiki to reclaim their narratives and assert their identities on their own terms. By stepping into the role of Bandy Kiki, she not only fought for her rights but also for the rights of countless others who felt voiceless in a society that often silenced them.

In conclusion, the creation of a pseudonym is a multifaceted decision that encompasses safety, identity, and empowerment. For Bandy Kiki, it was a necessary step in her journey as an LGBTQ advocate in Cameroon, allowing her to navigate the complexities of activism while staying true to her mission. The pseudonym became more than just a name; it became a symbol of hope and resilience for a community in need of representation and change.

Spreading awareness through social media

In the age of digital connectivity, social media has emerged as a powerful tool for activism, enabling individuals to raise awareness about critical issues, mobilize support, and foster community engagement. For Bandy Kiki, social media served as a lifeline, a platform where she could amplify the voices of the LGBTQ community in Cameroon, a place where such expressions are often met with hostility and repression.

Theoretical Framework

The use of social media in activism can be understood through various communication theories, including the *Diffusion of Innovations Theory* (Rogers, 1962), which explains how new ideas and technologies spread within a society. According to this theory, social media acts as a catalyst for the diffusion of information, allowing activists to reach a wider audience more quickly than traditional methods. This rapid dissemination is crucial in contexts where LGBTQ rights are under threat, as it allows for real-time updates and mobilization in response to emerging crises.

Moreover, the *Networked Publics Theory* (boyd, 2008) posits that social media creates new forms of public discourse, enabling marginalized voices to participate in conversations that were previously inaccessible. Bandy Kiki utilized this framework to create a digital space for LGBTQ individuals in Cameroon, fostering a sense of belonging and solidarity among those who felt isolated by societal norms.

Challenges of Social Media Activism

Despite its advantages, social media activism is not without challenges. One significant issue is the threat of censorship and surveillance. In Cameroon, where the government has a history of cracking down on dissent, activists face the constant risk of being monitored online. This reality necessitates a careful approach to content creation and sharing. Bandy Kiki often employed strategies such as using encrypted messaging apps and private groups to discuss sensitive topics, ensuring that her activism could continue without immediate repercussions.

Additionally, the phenomenon of *slacktivism* poses a challenge. Slacktivism refers to the practice of supporting a cause through minimal effort, such as liking or sharing a post, without engaging in more substantial actions. While Bandy Kiki recognized the potential for social media to raise awareness, she also understood the importance of translating online support into real-world action. To combat slacktivism, she encouraged her followers to participate in local events, engage in discussions, and support grassroots organizations actively.

Examples of Impact

Bandy Kiki's social media presence was marked by a series of strategic campaigns aimed at raising awareness about LGBTQ issues in Cameroon. One notable campaign involved the hashtag #CameroonLovesAll, which she launched to counteract the pervasive stigma against LGBTQ individuals. This campaign not only highlighted personal stories of resilience but also educated the broader public about the challenges faced by the community. The hashtag quickly gained traction, drawing attention from international media and human rights organizations, which further amplified the message.

Another example of her impactful use of social media was the creation of a digital support group for LGBTQ youth. Through platforms like Facebook and Instagram, Bandy Kiki facilitated discussions on topics ranging from mental health to coming out experiences. By providing a safe space for individuals to share their stories, she fostered a sense of community and belonging, which is vital in a society that often ostracizes LGBTQ individuals.

Conclusion

In conclusion, Bandy Kiki's strategic use of social media exemplifies the potential of digital platforms to effect change and raise awareness about LGBTQ issues in Cameroon. By harnessing the power of social media, she not only created a space for dialogue and support but also challenged the oppressive narratives that dominate public discourse. As she navigated the complexities of online activism, Bandy Kiki demonstrated that while social media presents challenges, it also offers unprecedented opportunities for connection, empowerment, and advocacy in the ongoing fight for equality.

The Power of Anonymity

Anonymity in activism, especially within the LGBTQ community in oppressive environments, serves as a double-edged sword. On one hand, it provides a shield against persecution; on the other, it can complicate the pursuit of tangible change. This section delves into the multifaceted power of anonymity, exploring its theoretical foundations, practical implications, and the paradoxes it presents.

Theoretical Foundations of Anonymity

Anonymity can be understood through several theoretical lenses, including social identity theory, which posits that individuals derive a sense of self from their group memberships. In contexts where LGBTQ identities are marginalized, anonymity allows activists to dissociate their personal identities from their political actions, thereby reducing the risk of social ostracism and legal repercussions. As Tajfel and Turner (1979) suggest, individuals often seek to protect their in-group identity when faced with discrimination, and anonymity becomes a tool for maintaining this identity while advocating for change.

Advantages of Anonymity

The advantages of anonymity in activism are particularly pronounced in hostile environments like Cameroon, where LGBTQ individuals face severe legal and social consequences. Some key benefits include:

- **Safety and Security:** Anonymity allows activists to express their views without the fear of retribution. For instance, the case of Bandy Kiki illustrates how operating under a pseudonym provided a layer of protection, enabling her to mobilize support and raise awareness without exposing her personal life to danger.

- **Freedom of Expression:** Activists can communicate more freely and boldly when their identities are concealed. This freedom can lead to more impactful advocacy, as individuals feel empowered to voice their truths without the weight of societal expectations. For example, online platforms have allowed many activists to share their stories anonymously, fostering a sense of community and solidarity.

- **Focus on Message Over Identity:** Anonymity shifts the focus from the individual to the cause. This can help to cultivate a collective identity among activists, emphasizing shared goals rather than personal histories. Research has shown that collective movements often gain momentum when individuals can unite under a common banner without the constraints of personal identity.

Challenges and Paradoxes

However, the power of anonymity is not without its challenges. The very act of concealing one's identity can lead to a number of complications:

- **Lack of Accountability:** Anonymity can sometimes foster a sense of detachment, leading to less accountability for one's actions. This can create a culture of irresponsibility where individuals may engage in harmful rhetoric or actions without facing consequences. The anonymity of online platforms has been linked to instances of cyberbullying and harassment, which can detract from the overall message of the movement.

- **Difficulty in Building Trust:** In any movement, trust is paramount. Anonymity can hinder the establishment of genuine relationships among activists and supporters. Without knowing who is behind a pseudonym, individuals may be hesitant to collaborate or share resources, which can stifle the growth of a movement.

- **Potential for Misrepresentation:** When activists hide behind pseudonyms, there is a risk of misrepresentation. Individuals may exploit anonymity to spread misinformation or promote agendas that do not align with the core values of the LGBTQ movement. This can lead to fragmentation within the community, as differing factions emerge based on conflicting narratives.

THE MASKED ACTIVIST

Examples of Anonymity in Action

Throughout history, anonymity has played a crucial role in various activist movements. In the context of LGBTQ advocacy, notable examples include:

- **Online Forums and Social Media:** Platforms like Twitter and Reddit have provided spaces for anonymous discussion and activism. Users can share their experiences and seek support without fear of judgment. For instance, the hashtag #WeAreHere has been used to amplify LGBTQ voices while allowing individuals to remain anonymous, fostering a sense of belonging and community.

- **Anonymous Whistleblowers:** Many activists have utilized anonymity to expose injustices within their societies. The case of an anonymous whistleblower in Cameroon who revealed police abuses against LGBTQ individuals highlights how anonymity can empower individuals to speak out against systemic oppression without risking their safety.

- **Pseudonymous Activism:** The use of pseudonyms by activists like Bandy Kiki demonstrates how anonymity can facilitate impactful advocacy. By creating a distinct persona, she was able to engage with a wider audience and challenge societal norms without the constraints of her real identity.

Conclusion

The power of anonymity in LGBTQ activism is a complex interplay of safety, expression, and the pursuit of justice. While it offers essential protection in hostile environments, it also presents challenges that activists must navigate carefully. As the landscape of activism continues to evolve, understanding the implications of anonymity will be crucial for fostering effective and inclusive movements. Ultimately, the choice to remain anonymous or reveal one's identity is deeply personal and can significantly shape the trajectory of activism in the fight for equality and acceptance.

Balancing personal and public life

In the realm of activism, especially for those who operate under a pseudonym like Bandy Kiki, the delicate dance between personal and public life becomes an intricate choreography of identity, responsibility, and self-preservation. This balancing act is not merely a matter of personal preference; it is a necessity shaped by the realities of living in a society where LGBTQ individuals face significant discrimination and violence.

The Dichotomy of Identity

For many activists, particularly those in marginalized communities, the public persona often starkly contrasts with their private self. Bandy Kiki, as a digital advocate, had to navigate this dichotomy with care. The pseudonym allowed her to speak freely and boldly about LGBTQ rights without immediately exposing her personal life to potential repercussions. However, this anonymity came with its own set of challenges.

The theory of *social identity* posits that an individual's self-concept is derived from perceived membership in social groups. For Bandy, her public identity as an activist was a source of strength and empowerment, yet it also created a barrier to her personal relationships. Friends and family often struggled to reconcile the public figure with the person they knew. This dichotomy can lead to feelings of isolation, as the activist must constantly manage how much of their true self to reveal to those close to them.

Emotional Toll and Self-Care

The emotional toll of maintaining a dual identity cannot be overstated. Research indicates that activists often experience higher levels of stress and burnout due to the constant demands of their public roles. Bandy Kiki had to be vigilant not only in her activism but also in her mental health. This necessitated a robust self-care routine, which included setting boundaries around her public persona.

For instance, she established specific times for engaging with her online community and times for personal reflection and relaxation. This practice is supported by the *Self-Care Theory*, which emphasizes the importance of individuals taking responsibility for their own well-being, particularly in high-stress environments. By prioritizing her mental health, Bandy could continue her advocacy without succumbing to burnout.

Navigating Relationships

Balancing personal and public life also meant navigating relationships with friends, family, and romantic partners. The fear of exposure and the potential for backlash from society often made Bandy cautious about who she allowed into her inner circle. This was compounded by the reality that many of her loved ones might not fully understand the complexities of her activism or the risks involved.

To mitigate this, Bandy employed *communication strategies* that allowed her to share her experiences and the importance of her work without fully disclosing her identity. For example, she might discuss the challenges faced by the LGBTQ community in Cameroon in a general sense, helping her loved ones grasp the gravity of the situation while still protecting her anonymity. This approach not only fostered understanding but also strengthened her relationships, as those around her could see the passion and dedication behind her activism.

The Role of Technology

In the digital age, technology plays a crucial role in managing the balance between personal and public life. Social media platforms provide a space for activists to connect, share their experiences, and mobilize support while maintaining a degree of anonymity. Bandy Kiki utilized various tools to curate her online presence, ensuring that her personal life remained separate from her activist work.

For instance, she might use different accounts for personal and public interactions, allowing her to engage with followers on issues of LGBTQ rights while keeping her private life under wraps. This strategy aligns with the *Boundary Management Theory*, which suggests that individuals create and maintain boundaries between different aspects of their lives to reduce conflict and stress.

The Challenge of Authenticity

Despite the benefits of maintaining a pseudonym, Bandy faced the challenge of authenticity. The pressure to present a polished public image can often lead to a disconnect between one's true self and the persona projected online. This struggle is particularly pronounced in activism, where the stakes are high, and the need for a strong, unwavering voice is paramount.

To counteract this, Bandy embraced vulnerability as a strength. By sharing her struggles and imperfections, she humanized her activism, making it relatable to her audience. This approach is supported by the *Authenticity Theory*, which posits that individuals who express their true selves, including their vulnerabilities, are more likely to foster genuine connections with others.

Conclusion

In conclusion, balancing personal and public life as an activist like Bandy Kiki requires a nuanced understanding of identity, emotional well-being, and the dynamics of relationships. By employing strategies such as boundary management, effective communication, and embracing vulnerability, Bandy navigated the complexities of her dual existence. The journey is not without its challenges, but through careful consideration and intentionality, she forged a path that allowed her to advocate for LGBTQ rights while preserving her personal integrity and mental health. This balance is not just a personal achievement; it serves as a blueprint for future activists navigating similar terrains in their quest for justice and equality.

Navigating the challenges of staying anonymous

In the digital age, anonymity can be both a shield and a double-edged sword, especially for activists like Bandy Kiki, who operate in environments fraught with danger. The choice to remain anonymous stems from a necessity to protect oneself from potential repercussions, including violence, harassment, and social ostracism. However, navigating the challenges of maintaining that anonymity is a complex endeavor filled with its own set of obstacles.

The Psychological Toll of Anonymity

Maintaining anonymity can lead to significant psychological stress. Activists may experience feelings of isolation, anxiety, and fear of exposure. This is particularly true for Bandy, who, while advocating for LGBTQ rights in a hostile environment, must constantly balance her public persona with her private life. Research indicates that the psychological burden of living a dual life can lead to increased levels of stress and burnout among activists [?].

Digital Footprint and Surveillance

One of the primary challenges of staying anonymous is the omnipresence of digital surveillance. In Cameroon, where the government actively monitors online activities, the risk of being tracked is high. Activists must employ various strategies to minimize their digital footprint. This includes using encrypted communication tools, employing Virtual Private Networks (VPNs), and regularly changing their online identities.

Let D represent the risk of digital exposure, which can be modeled as follows:

$$D = \frac{S}{E}$$

where S is the level of surveillance by authorities and E is the effectiveness of the anonymity measures employed. As S increases, the risk D escalates unless E is simultaneously enhanced through better anonymity practices.

Social Connections and Support Systems

While anonymity provides a layer of protection, it can also hinder the formation of supportive social networks. Bandy Kiki's activism relies heavily on collaboration with other activists and organizations. However, the fear of exposure can lead to mistrust, making it difficult to build meaningful alliances. Activists often face the dilemma of whether to reveal their identities to foster deeper connections or to maintain their anonymity for safety.

The equation representing the balance between anonymity A and social connection C can be expressed as:

$$C = \frac{A}{R}$$

where R represents the risk of exposure. As the need for social connection increases, activists must carefully evaluate how much anonymity they can afford to sacrifice.

The Dilemma of Disclosure

At times, the pressure to disclose one's identity can be overwhelming. Activists may feel that revealing their true selves could lend credibility to their cause, yet the risks associated with such disclosure are substantial. Bandy Kiki faces this dilemma regularly; while her pseudonym allows her to speak freely, it also prevents her from fully engaging with the movement and sharing her personal story.

Legal Implications

In many countries, including Cameroon, the legal landscape is hostile towards LGBTQ individuals. The fear of legal repercussions can deter activists from taking bold actions. Bandy Kiki must navigate a precarious legal environment, where even the slightest misstep could lead to arrest or violence. This reality complicates her activism, as she must weigh the potential benefits of visibility against the very real dangers of being identified.

The Role of Technology

Technology plays a crucial role in enabling anonymous activism. Social media platforms, while often scrutinized, can provide a space for activists to share their messages without revealing their identities. However, the same platforms can also be a source of exposure. Bandy Kiki utilizes various tools to maintain her anonymity, such as pseudonymous accounts and encrypted messaging apps.

The effectiveness of these tools can be modeled by the equation:

$$T = \frac{U}{E}$$

where T is the effectiveness of technology in maintaining anonymity, U represents user savvy in employing these tools, and E stands for external threats to anonymity.

Conclusion

Navigating the challenges of staying anonymous is a multifaceted endeavor that requires constant vigilance, strategic planning, and emotional resilience. For Bandy Kiki, the journey of anonymity is not just about protecting herself; it is about ensuring that her voice continues to resonate within the LGBTQ movement in Cameroon. As she continues to advocate for change, the struggle for anonymity remains an integral part of her story, shaping her activism and influencing the broader fight for LGBTQ rights in a society that often seeks to silence dissent.

The Struggles of LGBTQ Community in Cameroon

The oppressive legal system

In Cameroon, the legal framework surrounding LGBTQ rights is not only restrictive but also deeply rooted in colonial-era laws that continue to perpetuate discrimination and violence against individuals based on their sexual orientation and gender identity. The Penal Code of Cameroon, specifically Articles 347 bis and 347 ter, criminalizes same-sex relationships, imposing harsh penalties that can include imprisonment for up to five years. This legal oppression serves as a tool of social control, reinforcing a culture of fear and silence among LGBTQ individuals.

The oppressive nature of the legal system can be understood through the lens of critical legal studies, which posits that laws are not neutral but rather serve to uphold existing power structures and social hierarchies. In this context, the Cameroonian legal system functions to marginalize LGBTQ individuals, denying them the fundamental rights that are afforded to others. The legal discrimination is compounded by societal attitudes that view homosexuality as a taboo, leading to a pervasive climate of hostility.

Legal Oppression = Discriminatory Laws + Social Stigmatization   (7)

This equation illustrates the interplay between legal frameworks and societal attitudes, highlighting how discriminatory laws exacerbate social stigmatization, which in turn fosters an environment where violence and discrimination are normalized.

The ramifications of this oppressive legal system are profound. Many LGBTQ individuals in Cameroon live in constant fear of persecution, not only from the state but also from their families and communities. Reports of police harassment, arbitrary arrests, and violence against LGBTQ individuals are alarmingly common. For instance, in 2019, a group of LGBTQ activists was arrested during a peaceful gathering, highlighting the risks associated with any form of public expression of their identities.

Furthermore, the legal system's failure to protect LGBTQ individuals from violence and discrimination is evident in the lack of legal recourse available to victims. When hate crimes occur, they are often dismissed or inadequately addressed by law enforcement, leaving victims without justice. This systemic failure reinforces a cycle of violence and oppression, where LGBTQ individuals are left vulnerable and marginalized.

The oppressive legal system also impacts mental health and well-being. The constant threat of legal repercussions can lead to internalized homophobia, where individuals internalize society's negative attitudes towards their identities. This internal conflict can result in anxiety, depression, and a sense of isolation, further complicating the already challenging journey of self-acceptance and activism.

In conclusion, the oppressive legal system in Cameroon serves as a formidable barrier to the rights and freedoms of LGBTQ individuals. It perpetuates a cycle of fear, violence, and discrimination that not only affects the individuals directly targeted but also has broader implications for society as a whole. To challenge this oppressive system, it is essential to advocate for legal reforms that promote equality and protect the rights of all individuals, regardless of their sexual orientation or gender identity. Only through a concerted effort to dismantle these oppressive structures can true progress be made towards a more inclusive and accepting society.

Social stigmatization and discrimination

Social stigmatization and discrimination are pervasive issues that significantly affect the LGBTQ community in Cameroon. These phenomena manifest in various forms, from overt hostility to subtle biases, creating an environment where individuals face immense challenges in their daily lives. Stigmatization refers to the negative attitudes and beliefs that society holds towards individuals who belong to marginalized groups, while discrimination involves actions that treat these individuals unfairly based on their identity.

Theoretical Framework

To understand the dynamics of social stigmatization and discrimination, we can refer to Goffman's theory of stigma, which identifies three types of stigma: *abominations of the body, blemishes of individual character,* and *tribal stigma of race, nation, and religion* [?]. In the context of LGBTQ individuals in Cameroon, the stigma primarily falls under the second category, as being part of the LGBTQ community is often viewed as a moral failing or a character flaw. This perception is deeply rooted in cultural, religious, and societal norms that prioritize heteronormativity.

The impact of stigma can be quantified using the following equation:

$$S = \frac{D}{P}$$

Where: - S is the level of stigma experienced, - D is the degree of discrimination faced, - P represents the prevailing public perception of LGBTQ identities.

As the degree of discrimination increases, the level of stigma experienced by individuals also escalates, creating a vicious cycle that perpetuates their marginalization.

Forms of Discrimination

In Cameroon, LGBTQ individuals face various forms of discrimination, including:

- **Legal Discrimination:** Homosexuality is criminalized under Cameroonian law, with penalties that include imprisonment and fines. This legal framework legitimizes discrimination and creates an environment where LGBTQ individuals are constantly at risk of arrest and persecution.

- **Employment Discrimination:** Many LGBTQ individuals encounter barriers in the job market, as employers often refuse to hire or promote them based on their sexual orientation or gender identity. This discrimination can lead to economic instability and increased vulnerability.

- **Social Exclusion:** LGBTQ individuals often face rejection from their families, friends, and communities. This social exclusion can result in isolation, mental health issues, and a lack of access to essential resources and support systems.

- **Violence and Harassment:** Reports of violence against LGBTQ individuals in Cameroon are alarmingly high. Hate crimes, including physical assaults and sexual violence, are common, often perpetrated by both individuals and state actors.

Examples of Stigmatization

The experiences of LGBTQ individuals in Cameroon illustrate the profound effects of social stigmatization. For instance, a study conducted by the International Lesbian, Gay, Bisexual, Trans and Intersex Association (ILGA) highlighted the story of a young gay man who was expelled from his home after coming out to his family. His experience reflects the harsh reality faced by many LGBTQ individuals who are often forced to choose between their identities and their familial ties.

Another example can be seen in the media portrayal of LGBTQ individuals in Cameroon, which is frequently negative and sensationalized. This portrayal not only reinforces harmful stereotypes but also contributes to the societal belief that LGBTQ identities are deviant or immoral. Such representations can lead to increased hostility and discrimination, as individuals feel justified in their prejudiced attitudes.

Consequences of Stigmatization and Discrimination

The consequences of social stigmatization and discrimination are far-reaching. They can lead to:

- **Mental Health Issues:** LGBTQ individuals in Cameroon often experience high levels of anxiety, depression, and suicidal ideation due to the pervasive stigma and discrimination they encounter.

- **Reduced Access to Healthcare:** Fear of discrimination in healthcare settings can prevent LGBTQ individuals from seeking necessary medical care, exacerbating health disparities within the community.

- **Increased Vulnerability:** The combination of social exclusion, economic instability, and legal discrimination leaves LGBTQ individuals vulnerable to exploitation and violence, further entrenching their marginalization.

Conclusion

In conclusion, social stigmatization and discrimination are critical issues that significantly impact the lives of LGBTQ individuals in Cameroon. Understanding the theoretical underpinnings of stigma, recognizing the various forms of discrimination, and acknowledging the real-life consequences of these issues are essential for fostering a more inclusive and equitable society. By addressing these challenges head-on, activists like Bandy Kiki aim to create a future where LGBTQ individuals can live authentically and without fear of persecution.

Fear and danger in everyday life

Living as a member of the LGBTQ community in Cameroon is fraught with fear and danger, a reality that Bandy Kiki and many others face daily. The oppressive legal framework, which criminalizes same-sex relationships, creates a pervasive atmosphere of fear that permeates every aspect of life. This section delves into the multifaceted nature of fear and danger experienced by LGBTQ individuals in Cameroon, examining the psychological, social, and legal dimensions that contribute to their daily struggles.

Psychological Impact of Fear

The constant threat of violence and persecution leads to significant psychological distress among LGBTQ individuals. Studies have shown that individuals who live in hostile environments often experience higher rates of anxiety, depression, and post-traumatic stress disorder (PTSD) [Meyer(2003)]. The fear of being outed, harassed, or physically assaulted creates a perpetual state of hyper-vigilance. Bandy Kiki, for instance, frequently describes the anxiety that accompanies the simple act of stepping outside her home. This anxiety is compounded by the knowledge that her identity could lead to severe repercussions, including imprisonment or violence.

Social Isolation

Fear also breeds social isolation. Many LGBTQ individuals feel compelled to hide their identities from family, friends, and colleagues, leading to a lack of support systems. This isolation can exacerbate feelings of loneliness and despair. Bandy

Kiki's early experiences in Douala exemplify this phenomenon. Growing up, she often felt she had to choose between her safety and her authenticity, leading her to suppress her true self in social situations. The absence of a supportive community can leave individuals feeling abandoned and vulnerable.

Legal and Institutional Threats

The legal framework in Cameroon not only criminalizes homosexuality but also emboldens societal discrimination and violence. Article 347 bis of the Cameroon Penal Code states that individuals found guilty of engaging in same-sex relations can face up to five years in prison. This legal backdrop creates a chilling effect on activism, as individuals fear legal repercussions for speaking out against discrimination. Bandy Kiki has witnessed firsthand the consequences of this legal environment, as friends and fellow activists have been arrested simply for expressing their identities or advocating for their rights.

Violence and Harassment

The fear of violence is a daily reality for many LGBTQ individuals in Cameroon. Reports of physical assaults, verbal harassment, and even murder based on sexual orientation or gender identity are alarmingly common. Bandy Kiki recalls a harrowing incident where a close friend was attacked by a mob after being outed in their community. Such incidents serve as a grim reminder of the dangers that LGBTQ individuals face and the urgent need for change. The pervasive threat of violence not only affects individuals but also silences communities and stifles activism.

Coping Mechanisms

In the face of such overwhelming fear and danger, many LGBTQ individuals develop coping mechanisms to navigate their realities. Some find solace in online communities, where anonymity offers a degree of safety and connection. Bandy Kiki herself has utilized social media as a platform to share her experiences and connect with others facing similar challenges. However, this reliance on digital spaces is not without its own risks, as surveillance and censorship can threaten the very platforms that provide refuge.

Conclusion

The fear and danger that LGBTQ individuals face in Cameroon is a complex interplay of psychological, social, and legal factors. For Bandy Kiki and her peers, the struggle is not just for legal recognition but for the fundamental right to live without fear. Understanding these dynamics is crucial for fostering empathy and support for the LGBTQ community, as well as for driving the necessary changes in policy and societal attitudes.

Stories of resilience and survival

In the face of oppression, the LGBTQ community in Cameroon has demonstrated remarkable resilience and an unyielding spirit of survival. These narratives are not merely tales of hardship; they are testaments to the strength of the human spirit, showcasing how individuals navigate a landscape fraught with danger and discrimination while forging paths toward acceptance and equality.

Theoretical Framework

The concept of resilience can be understood through various psychological and sociological lenses. According to Rutter (1987), resilience is defined as the ability to overcome adversity and emerge stronger from challenges. This notion is particularly relevant in the context of marginalized communities, where systemic oppression can lead to significant psychological distress. Resilience theory posits that individuals possess inherent strengths that can be activated in the face of adversity, allowing them to cope effectively and thrive despite their circumstances.

In the context of LGBTQ activism in Cameroon, resilience is often cultivated through community support, shared experiences, and the pursuit of a common goal—namely, the fight for equality and acceptance. This collective resilience serves as a buffer against the psychological toll of discrimination and violence, enabling individuals to maintain hope and motivation.

Personal Narratives

1. The Story of Amina

Amina, a young bisexual woman from Yaoundé, faced severe backlash after coming out to her family. Initially met with rejection and violence, she found solace in a local LGBTQ support group. This network not only provided emotional support but also equipped her with the tools to advocate for her rights. Amina's activism began with small community gatherings, where she shared her story and encouraged others to speak out. Her resilience became a beacon of hope for many, demonstrating that personal pain could be transformed into a collective movement for change.

2. The Journey of Samuel

Samuel, a gay man from Douala, experienced direct threats to his safety due to his sexual orientation. After being attacked by a group of men, he sought refuge in a safe house run by an LGBTQ organization. While there, Samuel became involved in advocacy work, using his experiences to educate others about the realities of living as an LGBTQ individual in Cameroon. His story highlights the importance of safe spaces and community support in fostering resilience. Samuel's transformation from victim to advocate illustrates how individuals can reclaim their narrative and empower others.

3. The Resilience of Marie

Marie, a transgender woman, faced systemic discrimination in her workplace. After being fired due to her gender identity, she decided to take action. Marie documented her experiences, creating a blog that detailed her journey and the challenges faced by transgender individuals in Cameroon. Her writings gained traction and sparked conversations about gender identity and rights, thereby amplifying the voices of many who felt silenced. Marie's story underscores the power of storytelling as a tool for resilience and advocacy, illustrating how personal narratives can challenge societal norms and inspire change.

Collective Resilience

The LGBTQ community in Cameroon has also demonstrated resilience through collective action. Grassroots organizations have emerged, providing safe spaces for individuals to gather, share their stories, and strategize for change. Events such as pride marches, although often met with hostility, serve as powerful symbols of resistance and solidarity. These gatherings not only foster a sense of belonging but also empower individuals to stand up against discrimination.

Moreover, the use of digital platforms has allowed for broader outreach and connection, enabling activists to share their experiences and mobilize support on a global scale. The collective resilience of the LGBTQ community is evident in their ability to adapt and innovate in the face of adversity, utilizing technology to amplify their voices and advocate for their rights.

Conclusion

The stories of resilience and survival within the LGBTQ community in Cameroon are not just individual tales; they represent a larger narrative of strength, hope, and the relentless pursuit of justice. These narratives challenge the pervasive stigma and discrimination that exist in society, illustrating that resilience can be cultivated through community support, shared experiences, and a commitment to advocacy. As these stories continue to unfold, they remind us that even in the darkest of times, the human spirit can shine brightly, illuminating the path toward a more inclusive and accepting future.

Bibliography

[1] Rutter, M. (1987). *Psychosocial resilience and protective mechanisms.* American Journal of Orthopsychiatry, 57(3), 316-331.

Advocating for Change

Advocating for change in the LGBTQ community in Cameroon is not merely an act of defiance; it is a profound commitment to human rights, dignity, and the relentless pursuit of equality. In a country where laws and societal norms are heavily skewed against sexual minorities, the challenges are immense. Yet, the urgency for advocacy has never been clearer.

Understanding the Context

The legal framework in Cameroon is particularly oppressive, with laws that criminalize same-sex relationships under Articles 347 bis and 347 ter of the Penal Code. These laws create an environment of fear, where LGBTQ individuals face harassment, violence, and discrimination. The societal stigma surrounding non-heteronormative identities further exacerbates these issues, leading to isolation and a lack of support for those who dare to live authentically.

To understand the necessity of advocacy, we must consider the theory of social change, which posits that collective action can lead to significant shifts in societal norms and legal frameworks. According to the *Theory of Planned Behavior* (Ajzen, 1991), the intention to engage in a behavior is influenced by attitudes, subjective norms, and perceived behavioral control. In the context of LGBTQ advocacy, changing societal attitudes towards sexual minorities is crucial for fostering an environment where individuals feel empowered to advocate for their rights.

Strategies for Advocacy

1. **Grassroots Mobilization**: Grassroots movements are vital for effecting change at the community level. Bandy Kiki has utilized social media platforms to mobilize support and raise awareness about LGBTQ issues. By sharing personal stories and highlighting the struggles faced by LGBTQ individuals, she has created a sense of community and solidarity among those who feel marginalized.

2. **Education and Awareness Campaigns**: Educating the public about LGBTQ rights and issues is essential for dismantling stereotypes and misconceptions. Bandy Kiki has organized workshops and seminars aimed at informing both the LGBTQ community and the broader society about human rights. This approach aligns with the *Social Learning Theory* (Bandura, 1977), which emphasizes the role of observational learning in behavior change.

3. **Legal Advocacy**: Engaging with legal frameworks to challenge discriminatory laws is a critical aspect of advocacy. Although the legal system in Cameroon poses significant challenges, strategic litigation can create precedents that promote equality. Bandy Kiki collaborates with local and international human rights organizations to advocate for legal reforms that protect LGBTQ individuals.

4. **Building Alliances**: Forming coalitions with other marginalized groups is essential for creating a unified front against discrimination. By building alliances with women's rights organizations, disability rights activists, and other social justice movements, Bandy Kiki has expanded the reach of her advocacy efforts and emphasized the intersectionality of oppression.

5. **Utilizing Media**: The media serves as a powerful tool for advocacy. By leveraging both traditional and digital media, Bandy Kiki has been able to amplify the voices of LGBTQ individuals and bring attention to their struggles. Campaigns that feature personal narratives can humanize the issues and foster empathy among the general public.

Challenges in Advocacy

Despite the progress made, advocating for change in Cameroon is fraught with challenges. The pervasive climate of fear often silences voices of dissent, making it difficult for activists to operate openly. Additionally, backlash from conservative groups can lead to violent repercussions for those involved in advocacy efforts.

The concept of *Collective Efficacy* (Bandura, 2000) suggests that communities with a strong sense of shared purpose and mutual support are more likely to succeed in their advocacy efforts. However, in Cameroon, the lack of support from both the government and society at large undermines collective efficacy, making it imperative for activists to find innovative ways to mobilize support while minimizing risk.

Examples of Successful Advocacy

One notable example of successful advocacy is the campaign led by Bandy Kiki to raise awareness about the plight of LGBTQ refugees in Cameroon. By collaborating with international NGOs, she was able to secure funding and resources to provide safe havens for those fleeing persecution. This initiative not only highlighted the intersectionality of LGBTQ rights and refugee issues but also galvanized international support for change.

Another example is the social media campaign #LoveIsLoveCameroon, which aimed to challenge societal norms by showcasing diverse representations of love and relationships. This campaign received significant attention and sparked conversations about LGBTQ rights, demonstrating the power of digital activism in effecting change.

Conclusion

Advocating for change within the LGBTQ community in Cameroon requires courage, creativity, and resilience. As Bandy Kiki continues her fight for equality, she embodies the spirit of activism that refuses to be silenced. Through grassroots mobilization, education, legal advocacy, and coalition-building, she is not only challenging oppressive systems but also inspiring a new generation of activists to join the struggle for justice and equality. The road ahead may be fraught with challenges, but the collective efforts of advocates like Bandy Kiki illuminate the path toward a more inclusive and accepting society.

Bibliography

[1] Ajzen, I. (1991). *The Theory of Planned Behavior*. Organizational Behavior and Human Decision Processes, 50(2), 179-211.

[2] Bandura, A. (1977). *Social Learning Theory*. Prentice Hall.

[3] Bandura, A. (2000). *Exercise of Human Agency Through Collective Efficacy*. Current Directions in Psychological Science, 9(3), 75-78.

Activism in the Digital Age

Using the internet as a platform for change

In the digital age, the internet has emerged as a powerful tool for social change, especially for marginalized communities. Bandy Kiki recognized early on that the online world could amplify her voice and the voices of those in the LGBTQ community in Cameroon, a country where open expression of sexual orientation can lead to severe repercussions. The internet serves as a platform for activism, enabling individuals to share their stories, mobilize support, and challenge oppressive systems.

Theoretical Framework

The use of the internet for activism can be understood through several theoretical lenses, including *networked individualism* and *digital activism*. Networked individualism describes how individuals are connected through social networks, allowing for the dissemination of information and the creation of communities without geographic limitations. This phenomenon is particularly relevant for LGBTQ activists in regions where physical gatherings may be dangerous.

Digital activism refers to the use of digital tools and platforms to promote social change. This form of activism can include social media campaigns, online petitions, and the use of hashtags to raise awareness about specific issues. The effectiveness of digital activism lies in its ability to bypass traditional media channels, which may be hostile or unresponsive to LGBTQ issues.

Challenges and Limitations

While the internet provides an unprecedented opportunity for advocacy, it is not without challenges. One major issue is the prevalence of *censorship* and *surveillance* in many countries, including Cameroon. The government often monitors online activities, making it risky for activists to express their views openly. This reality necessitates the use of pseudonyms and encrypted communication to protect the identities of activists.

Moreover, the digital divide remains a significant barrier. Access to the internet is not uniform; many individuals in Cameroon may lack the necessary resources or skills to engage with online activism. This disparity can lead to the marginalization of voices within the LGBTQ community that are already underrepresented.

Examples of Digital Activism

Bandy Kiki's journey exemplifies the power of the internet in creating change. Through her pseudonymous social media presence, she has been able to share her experiences and those of others in the LGBTQ community, fostering a sense of solidarity and support. One notable campaign involved the use of the hashtag #StandWithCameroon, which garnered international attention and support for LGBTQ rights in the country. This campaign highlighted the severe human rights abuses faced by LGBTQ individuals and spurred global advocacy efforts.

Another example is the online petition platform Change.org, where Bandy initiated petitions calling for the repeal of discriminatory laws against LGBTQ individuals in Cameroon. These petitions not only mobilized local support but also attracted international attention, leading to increased pressure on the Cameroonian government to address human rights violations.

The Role of Global Networks

Bandy Kiki's activism is also bolstered by her connections with global LGBTQ networks. By engaging with international organizations, she has been able to share resources, strategies, and support. These collaborations have proven crucial in amplifying her message and providing a safety net for activists operating in hostile environments.

For instance, partnerships with organizations like ILGA (International Lesbian, Gay, Bisexual, Trans and Intersex Association) have allowed Bandy to participate in global forums, where she can advocate for her community and share the unique challenges faced by LGBTQ individuals in Cameroon. This cross-border solidarity is vital for fostering a more inclusive and understanding global community.

Conclusion

In conclusion, the internet serves as a vital platform for change, particularly for marginalized groups like the LGBTQ community in Cameroon. While challenges such as censorship and the digital divide persist, the potential for digital activism to foster awareness, solidarity, and advocacy is immense. Bandy Kiki's story exemplifies how the internet can be harnessed to create a powerful movement for change, inspiring others to leverage digital tools in their fight for equality and justice. As the landscape of activism continues to evolve, it is crucial for advocates to adapt and innovate, ensuring that their voices are heard in both the digital and physical realms.

Navigating censorship and surveillance

In the digital age, activists like Bandy Kiki face the dual challenges of censorship and surveillance, particularly in oppressive regimes where freedom of expression is curtailed. These challenges necessitate innovative strategies and a deep understanding of the digital landscape. The intersection of technology, activism, and human rights creates a complex environment where the stakes are high, and the margins for error are slim.

Theoretical Framework

Censorship can be understood through the lens of *control theory*, which posits that authorities seek to regulate information to maintain power and suppress dissent. This is often achieved through legal frameworks that criminalize certain expressions, as well as through technological means, such as internet filtering and surveillance.

Surveillance, on the other hand, can be analyzed using *panopticism*, a concept introduced by Michel Foucault, which describes a society where individuals regulate their behavior due to the constant possibility of being watched. In the context of LGBTQ activism, this means that the fear of surveillance can inhibit free expression and limit the effectiveness of advocacy efforts.

Challenges Faced

1. **Censorship Mechanisms**: In many countries, governments employ sophisticated censorship techniques, including:

- **Internet Filtering:** Blocking access to websites that promote LGBTQ rights or provide supportive resources.

- **Content Removal:** Actively monitoring and removing social media posts that challenge the status quo.

- **Legal Repercussions:** Enforcing laws that criminalize LGBTQ expression, which can lead to arrests and persecution.

2. **Surveillance Tactics**: Activists must navigate a landscape where their online activities may be monitored. Common surveillance tactics include:

- **Data Collection:** Governments and corporations may collect data on users' online behavior, making it easier to identify and target activists.

- **Social Media Monitoring:** Authorities often monitor social media platforms for dissenting voices, creating a chilling effect on free speech.

- **Physical Surveillance:** In some cases, activists may face physical surveillance, where their movements are tracked by authorities.

Strategies for Resistance

Activists like Bandy Kiki have developed strategies to counteract censorship and surveillance, ensuring that their voices remain heard despite the risks:

1. **Use of Pseudonyms**: By creating a pseudonym, activists can maintain a degree of anonymity while advocating for change. This allows them to express their views without the fear of immediate repercussions.

2. **Encrypted Communication**: Utilizing encrypted messaging apps, such as Signal or Telegram, can protect conversations from being intercepted. This is crucial for organizing and mobilizing efforts while minimizing risks.

3. **Circumventing Censorship**: Activists often employ virtual private networks (VPNs) to bypass internet restrictions. VPNs encrypt internet traffic and mask the user's IP address, making it more challenging for authorities to monitor online activities.

4. **Digital Literacy and Education**: Training activists in digital security practices is essential. Understanding how to protect personal information and

recognizing potential threats can empower activists to navigate the digital landscape more effectively.

5. **Building Coalitions**: Collaborating with international organizations can provide additional support and resources. Global solidarity can amplify local voices and apply pressure on oppressive regimes.

Case Studies and Examples

Several notable examples illustrate the effectiveness of these strategies:

- In countries like Iran and Russia, LGBTQ activists have successfully used pseudonyms and encrypted communication to organize protests and share information, despite facing severe repercussions.
- The #FreeTheNipple campaign, which advocates for gender equality in social media policies, has shown how collective action can challenge censorship. Activists utilized multiple platforms to bypass restrictions, gaining international attention and support.
- In Cameroon, where LGBTQ rights are heavily suppressed, activists have employed VPNs to access blocked resources and connect with global networks, allowing them to share their stories and advocate for change.

Conclusion

Navigating censorship and surveillance is an ongoing battle for LGBTQ activists like Bandy Kiki. By understanding the mechanisms of control and employing innovative strategies, they can continue to fight for their rights and the rights of others. The resilience and creativity displayed by these activists highlight the importance of digital literacy and the need for solidarity in the face of oppression. As the digital landscape evolves, so too must the strategies employed by those committed to justice and equality.

Reaching out to the global community

In an era where digital connectivity transcends geographical boundaries, the power of reaching out to the global community becomes a pivotal strategy for activists like Bandy Kiki. The internet serves as a double-edged sword, offering both a platform for advocacy and a space fraught with challenges. By leveraging social media and online networks, LGBTQ activists can garner international support and solidarity, amplifying their voices and experiences to a wider audience.

The Importance of Global Solidarity

Global solidarity is essential for marginalized communities, particularly in regions where local laws and cultural norms are hostile to LGBTQ rights. Bandy Kiki recognized that the struggles faced by LGBTQ individuals in Cameroon were not isolated; they were part of a larger narrative of oppression and resistance that resonated with activists worldwide. By reaching out to the global community, Bandy Kiki aimed to create a network of allies who could support and amplify the fight for equality.

$$\text{Global Solidarity} = \text{Local Action} + \text{International Support} \qquad (8)$$

This equation illustrates the symbiotic relationship between local activism and global support. Local actions, fueled by international solidarity, can lead to significant change. For instance, campaigns that highlight the plight of LGBTQ individuals in Cameroon can prompt international organizations to apply pressure on local governments, advocating for policy changes and greater protections.

Utilizing Digital Platforms

Bandy Kiki harnessed the power of digital platforms to disseminate information and engage with a global audience. Social media channels such as Twitter, Facebook, and Instagram became vital tools for sharing stories, raising awareness, and mobilizing support. The immediacy of these platforms allowed activists to respond swiftly to incidents of discrimination and violence, creating a real-time dialogue around LGBTQ rights.

- **Twitter** enabled Bandy Kiki to engage with international LGBTQ organizations, share updates on local events, and participate in global conversations about human rights.
- **Facebook** served as a space for community building, where individuals could share personal stories and experiences, fostering a sense of belonging and collective identity.
- **Instagram** allowed for visual storytelling, showcasing the vibrant culture of the LGBTQ community in Cameroon while highlighting the challenges they faced.

Through these platforms, Bandy Kiki not only raised awareness but also built a supportive network that transcended borders. The global community became a source of inspiration and motivation, reminding activists that they were not alone in their fight.

Challenges of Digital Activism

Despite the advantages, reaching out to the global community through digital platforms is not without its challenges. Activists often face censorship, surveillance, and backlash from both local authorities and online trolls. The oppressive legal environment in Cameroon poses significant risks for LGBTQ activists, making anonymity a crucial aspect of their online presence.

$$\text{Risk} = \text{Visibility} \times \text{Oppression} \qquad (9)$$

This equation emphasizes the heightened risk faced by activists as their visibility increases. For many, the decision to engage with a global audience means navigating a complex landscape of safety concerns. Bandy Kiki had to carefully balance the desire for visibility with the need for protection, often employing pseudonyms and encryption tools to safeguard her identity.

Building International Alliances

Bandy Kiki's outreach efforts were also focused on building alliances with international LGBTQ organizations. By collaborating with established groups, she was able to access resources, training, and funding that could bolster local activism. These partnerships provided a platform for knowledge exchange, where activists could learn from each other's experiences and strategies.

For example, organizations like *OutRight Action International* and *ILGA World* have played pivotal roles in supporting LGBTQ activists in hostile environments. They provide not only advocacy tools but also legal assistance and psychological support for those facing persecution. Bandy Kiki's engagement with these organizations exemplifies the potential of international collaboration to effect change.

Case Studies of Successful Global Outreach

Several case studies illustrate the effectiveness of reaching out to the global community. One notable example is the *#FreeTheGays* campaign, which garnered international attention and support for LGBTQ individuals facing persecution in various countries. By utilizing hashtags and viral content, activists were able to mobilize global outrage and demand action from governments.

Another successful initiative was the *Global Day of Action for LGBTQ Rights*, where activists worldwide coordinated protests, social media campaigns, and awareness-raising events. This collective effort not only amplified local struggles but also created a sense of unity among diverse LGBTQ communities.

Conclusion

Reaching out to the global community is a vital component of contemporary LGBTQ activism. Through digital platforms, Bandy Kiki and her allies have been able to share their stories, build international alliances, and mobilize support for their cause. While challenges persist, the power of global solidarity remains an essential force in the fight for equality. As Bandy Kiki continues to navigate the complexities of activism, her commitment to connecting with the global community serves as a beacon of hope for LGBTQ individuals in Cameroon and beyond.

$$\text{Future of LGBTQ Activism} = \text{Local Empowerment} + \text{Global Support} \quad (10)$$

Building connections and alliances

In the realm of activism, especially within the LGBTQ community, building connections and alliances is not merely beneficial—it is essential for sustained impact and change. The theory of social capital, as proposed by Pierre Bourdieu, posits that social networks have value, and the resources available within these networks can be leveraged for collective action. This concept becomes particularly relevant in the context of LGBTQ activism in Cameroon, where societal norms often marginalize queer identities.

The first step in building these connections is the identification of common goals. Activists must look beyond their immediate circles and seek out groups and individuals who share similar objectives, whether that be legal reform, social acceptance, or mental health support. For instance, Bandy Kiki recognized the importance of collaboration with local NGOs that focused on human rights, thereby creating a coalition that could amplify their voices. This coalition not only provided a platform for shared resources but also facilitated a united front against discrimination.

However, building alliances is fraught with challenges. One significant problem is the risk of co-optation, where larger organizations may overshadow smaller, grassroots efforts. This phenomenon can lead to a dilution of the original mission and a loss of authenticity. An example of this can be seen in various international LGBTQ organizations that, while well-intentioned, may inadvertently prioritize Western narratives over local experiences. To combat this, Bandy Kiki emphasized the importance of ensuring that all voices within the coalition are heard and valued, advocating for a model of activism that is inclusive and representative of the diverse experiences within the community.

Moreover, the dynamics of power within these alliances can pose additional challenges. The theory of intersectionality, introduced by Kimberlé Crenshaw, highlights how various forms of identity—such as race, gender, and class—intersect to create unique experiences of oppression. In building alliances, it is crucial to acknowledge these intersections to avoid perpetuating existing inequalities within the movement. Bandy Kiki's activism exemplified this approach, as she actively sought to uplift marginalized voices within the LGBTQ community, including those of transgender individuals and people of color, ensuring that the movement was holistic and representative.

Another critical aspect of building connections is the utilization of digital platforms. In the age of technology, social media has become a powerful tool for activists to connect with a global audience. Bandy Kiki leveraged platforms like Twitter and Instagram to share stories, raise awareness, and mobilize support. This digital activism not only expanded her reach but also facilitated connections with international allies who could provide resources, visibility, and solidarity. For example, during a significant protest against anti-LGBTQ laws in Cameroon, a viral campaign on social media brought together activists from various countries, showcasing a united front that transcended geographical boundaries.

In addition to social media, community engagement through workshops, forums, and events plays a vital role in fostering alliances. These gatherings provide a space for dialogue, education, and collaboration. Bandy Kiki often organized community forums that brought together activists, allies, and the general public to discuss LGBTQ issues, share experiences, and strategize on collective actions. Such initiatives not only build solidarity but also educate the broader community, fostering an environment of understanding and support.

Furthermore, establishing alliances with academic institutions can enhance the credibility and reach of LGBTQ activism. Collaborating with researchers and scholars can provide valuable insights and data to support advocacy efforts. For instance, partnerships with universities in Cameroon allowed Bandy Kiki to access research on LGBTQ issues, which was instrumental in informing policy proposals and raising awareness among lawmakers.

In conclusion, building connections and alliances is a multifaceted process that requires intentionality, inclusivity, and adaptability. By recognizing the value of social capital, addressing the challenges of co-optation and power dynamics, leveraging digital platforms, engaging with the community, and collaborating with academic institutions, activists like Bandy Kiki can create a robust network of support that amplifies their impact. This interconnectedness not only strengthens the movement but also fosters a sense of belonging and empowerment within the LGBTQ community, paving the way for a more inclusive and equitable future.

Leveraging technology for activism

In the contemporary landscape of activism, technology plays a pivotal role in amplifying voices, mobilizing communities, and fostering connections across borders. For LGBTQ activists like Bandy Kiki, leveraging technology is not merely an option; it is a necessity for survival and progress. This section explores the various ways technology has been harnessed for activism, the challenges that accompany its use, and the theoretical frameworks that underpin these digital strategies.

The Role of Social Media

Social media platforms such as Twitter, Facebook, and Instagram serve as powerful tools for LGBTQ activism. They enable activists to share their stories, raise awareness about issues, and mobilize supporters quickly and effectively. According to Castells (2012), social media allows for the creation of "networked movements," where individuals can connect and organize around shared goals without the need for traditional hierarchical structures. This democratization of activism means that anyone with internet access can contribute to the cause, fostering a sense of community and solidarity.

$$\text{Engagement} = \frac{\text{Interactions}}{\text{Total Followers}} \times 100 \qquad (11)$$

This equation illustrates the importance of engagement in measuring the impact of online activism. High engagement rates indicate that content resonates with audiences, leading to increased visibility for LGBTQ issues.

Online Campaigns and Hashtags

Hashtags have become a vital part of online activism, allowing movements to gain traction and visibility. Campaigns like #LoveIsLove and #TransRightsAreHumanRights have galvanized support and spread messages of equality and acceptance. These digital campaigns often lead to real-world action, as seen in the global response to the Pulse nightclub shooting in 2016, where social media served as a platform for mourning and advocacy.

Challenges of Digital Activism

Despite its advantages, leveraging technology for activism is fraught with challenges. Issues such as censorship, surveillance, and online harassment pose significant risks to LGBTQ activists. In many countries, governments monitor social media activity, making anonymity a crucial aspect of online engagement. The need for pseudonyms and encrypted communications has become a standard practice for activists operating in hostile environments.

Moreover, the digital divide remains a pressing issue. Not all individuals have equal access to technology, which can exacerbate existing inequalities within the LGBTQ community. As noted by Wresch (1996), the "digital divide" refers to the gap between those who have easy access to digital technology and those who do not, often along socioeconomic lines. This divide can limit the effectiveness of digital activism, as marginalized voices may remain unheard.

Building Alliances through Technology

Technology also enables activists to build alliances and collaborate across borders. Platforms like Zoom and Discord facilitate virtual meetings and discussions, allowing activists from different regions to share strategies and support one another. This interconnectedness is crucial for movements that face similar challenges, as it fosters a sense of global solidarity.

An example of this is the collaboration between LGBTQ activists in Cameroon and those in the United States during the global push for marriage equality. By sharing resources and strategies, activists were able to amplify their voices and create a more significant impact on a global scale.

Theoretical Frameworks: Networked Activism

The concept of networked activism, as described by Bennett and Segerberg (2012), emphasizes the importance of digital networks in contemporary social movements. This framework posits that technology enables activists to create flexible, decentralized networks that can respond quickly to changing circumstances. The ability to mobilize support through social media allows movements to adapt and evolve, making them more resilient in the face of adversity.

Networked Activism = Connectivity + Collective Action + Digital Tools   (12)

This equation summarizes the essence of networked activism, highlighting the interdependence of connectivity, collective action, and the use of digital tools in fostering effective movements.

Conclusion

In conclusion, leveraging technology for activism presents both opportunities and challenges for LGBTQ advocates like Bandy Kiki. While social media and digital tools facilitate communication and organization, they also require careful navigation of risks such as censorship and online harassment. By understanding the theoretical frameworks that underpin these digital strategies, activists can better harness the power of technology to create meaningful change in their communities and beyond. As the fight for LGBTQ rights continues, the innovative use of technology will remain a cornerstone of effective activism, ensuring that voices are heard and that the struggle for equality persists in the digital age.

The Impact of Bandy Kiki's Work

Inspiring hope and empowerment

In the landscape of LGBTQ activism, the work of Bandy Kiki serves as a beacon of hope and empowerment for individuals navigating the treacherous waters of identity and acceptance. Through her fearless advocacy, she has not only highlighted the struggles faced by the LGBTQ community in Cameroon but has also instilled a sense of resilience and strength among those who feel marginalized and voiceless. This section delves into the mechanisms through which Bandy Kiki inspires hope and empowerment, examining the theories of empowerment, the challenges faced by the community, and the transformative impact of her work.

Theoretical Framework of Empowerment

Empowerment is a multifaceted concept that encompasses the processes through which individuals gain control over their lives, make choices, and develop a sense of agency. According to [?], empowerment involves a critical consciousness that allows individuals to recognize and challenge oppressive structures. This framework is particularly relevant in the context of LGBTQ activism, where societal norms often dictate the terms of acceptance and visibility.

The empowerment theory posits that marginalized groups can achieve greater agency through collective action and support networks. [?] emphasizes the importance of social support systems in fostering resilience and self-efficacy. Bandy Kiki embodies this theory by creating platforms for dialogue and community building, encouraging individuals to share their stories and experiences.

Challenges Faced by the LGBTQ Community

In Cameroon, the LGBTQ community faces a myriad of challenges, including legal discrimination, social stigmatization, and violence. The oppressive legal framework, which criminalizes same-sex relationships, creates an environment of fear and isolation. As noted by [?], the repercussions of being openly LGBTQ can range from harassment to imprisonment, stifling any attempts at self-expression.

This hostile environment can lead to internalized homophobia, where individuals internalize societal prejudices and develop a negative self-image. The psychological toll of such discrimination can be profound, leading to issues such as depression and anxiety. Bandy Kiki's work directly addresses these challenges by providing a counter-narrative that celebrates queer identities and fosters a sense of belonging.

Bandy Kiki's Impact on Hope and Empowerment

Bandy Kiki's advocacy is characterized by her ability to inspire hope in the face of adversity. Through her art, writing, and activism, she communicates a powerful message: that acceptance and love are attainable, even in the most challenging circumstances. Her use of social media platforms has been instrumental in reaching a wider audience, allowing her to connect with individuals who may feel isolated or hopeless.

For instance, during a particularly oppressive period in Cameroon, Bandy Kiki initiated a campaign titled "Voices of the Silenced," where she invited LGBTQ individuals to share their stories anonymously. This initiative not only provided a safe space for self-expression but also highlighted the resilience and diversity within the community. The campaign went viral, garnering international attention and support, which in turn empowered local activists to continue their fight for rights and recognition.

Examples of Empowerment through Advocacy

Bandy Kiki's activism has led to tangible changes in the lives of many individuals. One notable example is her collaboration with local NGOs to provide mental health resources for LGBTQ youth. By addressing the psychological impacts of discrimination, these initiatives have fostered a sense of hope and empowerment among young people who often feel trapped in a hostile environment.

Moreover, Bandy Kiki has been a vocal advocate for legal reforms, challenging discriminatory laws and pushing for greater recognition of LGBTQ rights. Her participation in international forums has not only amplified the voices of Cameroonian activists but has also inspired a new generation of leaders who are committed to the cause. By leveraging her platform, she has shown that change is possible and that collective action can lead to significant advancements in rights and acceptance.

Conclusion

In conclusion, Bandy Kiki's work in inspiring hope and empowerment within the LGBTQ community is a testament to the transformative power of activism. By fostering a culture of resilience, she has not only challenged oppressive structures but has also provided a roadmap for others to follow. The intersection of empowerment theory and Bandy Kiki's advocacy illustrates that, despite the challenges faced, hope remains a powerful catalyst for change. As the fight for equality continues, her legacy serves as a reminder that empowerment is not just about individual agency but also about building a collective movement that uplifts and supports all members of the community.

Creating a support network

In the realm of activism, particularly within marginalized communities, the creation of a robust support network is paramount. For Bandy Kiki, the journey of establishing such a network was not merely a task; it was a lifeline that provided strength, resilience, and a sense of belonging amidst the harsh realities faced by the LGBTQ community in Cameroon.

The Importance of Support Networks

Support networks serve as a foundation for individuals seeking affirmation, guidance, and solidarity. They can significantly impact mental health, providing emotional support and fostering a sense of community. According to *Social Support*

Theory, individuals who perceive themselves as part of a supportive network tend to experience lower levels of stress and greater psychological well-being. This theory posits that social ties can buffer against the negative effects of stressors, making it essential for activists like Bandy to cultivate connections that empower rather than isolate.

Building Connections

Bandy Kiki recognized the importance of building connections not only within her immediate community but also extending her reach to international allies. She utilized social media platforms as a tool for outreach, creating virtual spaces where LGBTQ individuals could share their experiences and provide mutual support. For example, Bandy established online support groups where members could discuss personal challenges and celebrate victories, fostering a sense of unity and shared purpose.

Challenges in Creating a Network

However, the path to creating a support network was fraught with challenges. The oppressive legal and social environment in Cameroon posed significant barriers to open communication and collaboration. Many individuals feared repercussions for their involvement in LGBTQ activism, leading to a pervasive sense of isolation. Bandy had to navigate these treacherous waters carefully, often employing anonymity as a strategy to protect her network's members while still providing them with the support they desperately needed.

Examples of Effective Support Networks

One notable example of an effective support network that Bandy helped to establish was the "Safe Haven Initiative." This initiative focused on creating safe spaces for LGBTQ individuals to gather, share resources, and receive counseling. By partnering with local NGOs and international organizations, Bandy was able to secure funding and resources that allowed for the establishment of physical and virtual safe spaces. The initiative not only provided emotional support but also offered workshops on mental health, legal rights, and self-defense, empowering participants with knowledge and skills.

The Role of Allies

Allies played a crucial role in the support network that Bandy Kiki cultivated. By collaborating with heterosexual individuals and organizations that championed LGBTQ rights, Bandy was able to amplify her message and create a broader coalition for change. Allies provided additional resources, visibility, and legitimacy to the movement, demonstrating that the fight for equality transcended sexual orientation and gender identity. This intersectional approach was vital in challenging the prevailing narratives that sought to marginalize LGBTQ voices.

Creating Lasting Impact

Ultimately, the support network that Bandy Kiki created was not just about immediate assistance; it was about fostering a culture of resilience and empowerment. By encouraging members to take on leadership roles within the network, she cultivated a sense of ownership and agency among participants. This approach aligns with *Empowerment Theory*, which posits that individuals gain confidence and self-efficacy through active participation in their communities. The network became a breeding ground for future activists, equipped with the tools and support necessary to continue the fight for LGBTQ rights in Cameroon.

In conclusion, the creation of a support network was a pivotal aspect of Bandy Kiki's activism. It provided a sanctuary for individuals navigating the complexities of their identities while also serving as a catalyst for broader social change. Through strategic partnerships, the use of technology, and a commitment to inclusivity, Bandy was able to foster a vibrant community that not only survived but thrived in the face of adversity. This legacy of support and empowerment continues to inspire new generations of activists, proving that collective strength can indeed challenge the status quo.

Changing perceptions and challenging stereotypes

The journey of Bandy Kiki as an activist has been marked by a relentless pursuit of changing perceptions and challenging stereotypes surrounding the LGBTQ community in Cameroon. This endeavor is not merely about altering individual opinions but involves a broader cultural shift that addresses deeply ingrained societal norms. The process of changing perceptions can be understood through various theoretical frameworks, including social identity theory, which posits that individuals derive a sense of identity from their group memberships, and stereotype threat theory, which suggests that negative stereotypes can adversely affect performance and self-perception.

Theoretical Frameworks

Social identity theory, as articulated by Henri Tajfel and John Turner, emphasizes the significance of group identity in shaping individual behavior and attitudes. In the context of LGBTQ activism, this theory highlights how societal perceptions of LGBTQ individuals can influence their self-identity and the identities of those around them. Bandy Kiki's activism works to dismantle negative stereotypes associated with LGBTQ identities, thereby fostering a more inclusive social identity that embraces diversity.

Stereotype threat theory, introduced by Claude Steele, underscores the impact of negative stereotypes on individuals' performance and self-esteem. For instance, LGBTQ individuals often face societal stereotypes that label them as deviant or immoral. This creates a hostile environment that can lead to internalized homophobia and self-doubt. Bandy Kiki's efforts aim to counteract these stereotypes by promoting positive representations of LGBTQ individuals, thereby reducing the impact of stereotype threat.

Identifying Problems

One of the primary challenges faced by Bandy Kiki and other activists is the pervasive stigma associated with LGBTQ identities in Cameroon. This stigma is rooted in cultural, religious, and legal frameworks that often demonize non-heteronormative identities. For example, the legal system in Cameroon criminalizes same-sex relationships, reinforcing negative stereotypes and perpetuating discrimination. This legal backdrop serves as a barrier to changing perceptions, as it legitimizes societal prejudices and fosters an environment where LGBTQ individuals are marginalized.

Moreover, the media plays a crucial role in shaping public perceptions. Unfortunately, LGBTQ representations in Cameroonian media are often negative, depicting LGBTQ individuals as immoral or dangerous. This portrayal exacerbates societal stereotypes and hinders efforts to promote understanding and acceptance. Bandy Kiki's activism seeks to challenge these media narratives by highlighting positive stories of LGBTQ individuals, thereby reshaping the public discourse.

Examples of Activism

Bandy Kiki employs various strategies to challenge stereotypes and change perceptions. One notable example is her use of social media platforms to amplify LGBTQ voices and stories. By sharing personal narratives and experiences, Bandy

Kiki humanizes LGBTQ individuals, allowing the public to see them as complex beings rather than mere stereotypes. This approach aligns with the concept of narrative transportation, where individuals become emotionally involved in a story, leading to changes in attitudes and beliefs.

Additionally, Bandy Kiki organizes community workshops and awareness campaigns that educate the public about LGBTQ issues. These initiatives often involve interactive discussions that challenge preconceived notions and encourage empathy. For instance, in one workshop, participants were invited to share their views on LGBTQ identities, followed by a facilitated discussion that addressed misconceptions and provided factual information. This method not only promotes understanding but also fosters a sense of community and solidarity among participants.

Measuring Impact

The impact of Bandy Kiki's work can be measured through various indicators, including shifts in public attitudes, increased visibility of LGBTQ individuals, and changes in media representation. Surveys conducted before and after awareness campaigns often reveal a significant decrease in negative perceptions of LGBTQ individuals. For example, a survey conducted by a local NGO indicated that after participating in Bandy Kiki's workshops, 70% of respondents reported a more positive view of LGBTQ identities compared to only 30% prior to the intervention.

Furthermore, the emergence of LGBTQ-friendly spaces and events in Cameroon, such as pride marches and community gatherings, signifies a cultural shift towards acceptance. These events not only celebrate LGBTQ identities but also challenge the dominant narratives that perpetuate stereotypes. Bandy Kiki's involvement in organizing such events demonstrates her commitment to fostering a more inclusive society.

Conclusion

Changing perceptions and challenging stereotypes is an ongoing struggle that requires sustained effort and resilience. Bandy Kiki's activism exemplifies the power of individual and collective action in reshaping societal attitudes towards LGBTQ identities. By employing theoretical frameworks, addressing systemic problems, and utilizing innovative strategies, Bandy Kiki is paving the way for a more inclusive and accepting Cameroon. Her work not only inspires hope for LGBTQ individuals but also serves as a catalyst for broader societal change, challenging the status quo and fostering a culture of understanding and acceptance.

Celebrating successes and milestones

The journey of Bandy Kiki, a beacon of hope and resilience in the fight for LGBTQ rights in Cameroon, is marked by numerous successes and milestones that not only reflect her personal growth but also signify the collective achievements of the LGBTQ community. Celebrating these victories is crucial, as it fosters a sense of unity, encourages continued activism, and inspires future generations to carry the torch of equality and acceptance.

Recognizing Milestones

Milestones in activism serve as critical markers of progress, allowing individuals and communities to reflect on their achievements and the impact of their efforts. For Bandy Kiki, notable milestones include:

- **The Launch of Online Campaigns:** One of the first major successes was the launch of her online campaigns aimed at raising awareness about LGBTQ issues in Cameroon. These campaigns not only garnered attention but also mobilized support from both local and international communities. The engagement metrics, such as likes, shares, and comments, reflected a growing interest in LGBTQ rights, indicating a shift in public perception.

- **Formation of Support Networks:** Another significant achievement was the establishment of support networks for LGBTQ individuals. These networks provided safe spaces for sharing experiences and resources, fostering a sense of belonging. The success of these networks can be measured by the increasing number of participants and the positive feedback received from community members who found solace and strength in solidarity.

- **Global Recognition and Awards:** Bandy Kiki's activism has not gone unnoticed on the global stage. Receiving awards from international human rights organizations not only validated her efforts but also highlighted the plight of LGBTQ individuals in Cameroon. Such recognition serves as a powerful reminder that the fight for equality transcends borders and resonates with a global audience.

Theoretical Framework: Celebrating Success in Activism

The act of celebrating successes in activism can be understood through various theoretical lenses. One such framework is *Social Movement Theory*, which posits that recognition of achievements can enhance collective identity and motivate further action. According to Tilly and Tarrow (2015), "success breeds success," suggesting that visible accomplishments can galvanize additional support and participation in social movements.

$$P_{\text{success}} = \frac{N_{\text{achievements}}}{N_{\text{goals}}} \qquad (13)$$

Where:

- P_{success} is the probability of success in achieving movement goals,
- $N_{\text{achievements}}$ is the number of milestones reached,
- N_{goals} is the total number of goals set by the movement.

This equation illustrates that as the number of achievements increases, so does the likelihood of sustained activism and engagement within the community.

Examples of Celebrating Success

Celebrating successes can take various forms, from community gatherings to social media campaigns. For instance, Bandy Kiki organized annual pride events that not only celebrated the LGBTQ community but also served as a platform for sharing stories of resilience and triumph. These events became a source of empowerment, where individuals could express their identities freely and proudly.

$$E_{\text{event}} = \sum_{i=1}^{n} S_i \qquad (14)$$

Where:

- E_{event} represents the overall effectiveness of the event,
- S_i is the success score of each individual participant's story, and
- n is the total number of participants.

The sum of individual success stories contributed to a collective narrative of strength and hope, reinforcing the community's resolve in the face of adversity.

Moreover, the use of social media to highlight these successes has proven effective. Bandy Kiki's campaigns often featured testimonials from community members, showcasing their journeys and the positive impact of activism on their lives. This not only humanized the struggle but also created a ripple effect, encouraging others to share their stories and engage in the movement.

Challenges in Celebrating Successes

Despite the importance of celebrating milestones, challenges often arise. In a hostile environment where LGBTQ rights are continuously under threat, public celebrations can sometimes lead to backlash. Activists must navigate the fine line between visibility and safety. Bandy Kiki faced instances where celebrating achievements attracted negative attention, resulting in increased scrutiny from authorities and societal backlash.

To mitigate these risks, Bandy Kiki adopted a strategy of *discreet celebration*, where successes were acknowledged within safe spaces, allowing for reflection and encouragement without drawing undue attention. This approach emphasizes the importance of resilience and strategic planning in activism.

Conclusion

In conclusion, celebrating successes and milestones is an integral part of the activism journey for Bandy Kiki and the broader LGBTQ community in Cameroon. It fosters a sense of identity, encourages continued engagement, and inspires future activists to persist in their pursuit of equality. As the movement progresses, recognizing and honoring these victories will remain essential in building a more inclusive and accepting society, ensuring that the fight for LGBTQ rights continues to thrive amidst challenges.

Through the lens of theory, practical examples, and the acknowledgment of challenges, the celebration of successes emerges not just as a moment of joy but as a powerful catalyst for change, reinforcing the notion that every milestone achieved is a step closer to equality and acceptance for all.

Leaving a lasting legacy

The legacy of Bandy Kiki, an emblematic figure in the fight for LGBTQ rights in Cameroon, resonates far beyond her immediate impact. To understand the depth of this legacy, we must explore several dimensions: the cultural, social, and political ramifications of her activism, as well as the theoretical frameworks that underpin the movements she inspired.

Cultural Impact

Bandy Kiki's work has had a profound cultural impact, challenging entrenched norms and fostering a climate of acceptance. By leveraging social media platforms, she created a space where marginalized voices could be amplified. The cultural legacy of her activism can be analyzed through the lens of cultural hegemony, a theory introduced by Antonio Gramsci. This theory posits that dominant cultural norms are maintained through a combination of coercion and consent. Bandy's efforts to deconstruct these norms represent a counter-hegemonic movement, one that seeks to empower individuals to embrace their identities unapologetically.

$$H = \frac{C + R}{S} \qquad (15)$$

Where H is the level of hegemony, C is the coercive power of the state, R is the resistance from the oppressed, and S is the social consent given to the dominant ideology. Bandy's activism has shifted the balance in favor of R, demonstrating that resistance can lead to significant cultural shifts.

Social Networks and Community Building

One of the most enduring aspects of Bandy Kiki's legacy is her ability to foster community among LGBTQ individuals in Cameroon. She established networks that provided support, resources, and solidarity. This aligns with the Social Capital Theory, which emphasizes the importance of social networks in achieving collective goals. The connections formed through her initiatives have created a resilient community that continues to advocate for rights and recognition.

The equation for social capital can be expressed as:

$$SC = \frac{C + R}{D} \qquad (16)$$

Where SC represents social capital, C is the connections made, R is the resources shared, and D is the division among community members. Bandy's legacy is characterized by a high SC value, indicating a robust network that thrives on collaboration rather than division.

Political Ramifications

Politically, Bandy Kiki's activism has catalyzed discussions around LGBTQ rights in Cameroon, challenging oppressive laws and advocating for policy changes. Her legacy can be examined through the lens of the Political Opportunity Structure (POS) theory, which suggests that the political environment significantly influences the success of social movements. Bandy's ability to navigate the treacherous political landscape of Cameroon has opened doors for dialogue and reform.

The Political Opportunity Structure can be expressed as:

$$POS = \frac{E + A + I}{C} \tag{17}$$

Where POS is the political opportunity structure, E represents the existing political environment, A is the actions taken by activists, I is the interest of the public, and C is the level of state control. Bandy's activism has shifted the equation, creating a more favorable POS for LGBTQ rights.

Inspiring Future Generations

Bandy Kiki's legacy is not only about the changes she enacted but also about the inspiration she provides to future generations of activists. Her story is one of resilience, courage, and unwavering commitment to justice. By documenting her journey and sharing her experiences, she has created a blueprint for others to follow. The concept of intergenerational activism is vital here, as it emphasizes the importance of passing down knowledge, strategies, and hope.

The intergenerational impact of activism can be represented as:

$$IA = \frac{K + S}{T} \tag{18}$$

Where IA is intergenerational activism, K is the knowledge shared, S is the solidarity built, and T is the time taken to effect change. Bandy's legacy ensures that K and S are maximized, thus fostering a strong IA that will continue to thrive.

Conclusion

In conclusion, Bandy Kiki's legacy is a multifaceted tapestry woven from cultural, social, and political threads. Her impact on the LGBTQ community in Cameroon is profound, creating a lasting foundation upon which future activists can build. By understanding the theories that underpin her work, we can appreciate the significance of her contributions and the enduring spirit of resilience that she embodies. As Bandy Kiki herself once stated, "Our fight is not just for today; it is for every tomorrow that follows." Her legacy will undoubtedly continue to inspire and empower generations to come.

A Journey to Self-Acceptance

A Journey to Self-Acceptance

A Journey to Self-Acceptance

The journey to self-acceptance is often fraught with challenges, particularly for individuals navigating the complexities of sexual orientation and gender identity. This section explores the multifaceted experiences of those who embark on this journey, highlighting the emotional and psychological struggles, as well as the triumphs that accompany the quest for authenticity.

Understanding Self-Acceptance

Self-acceptance is defined as the recognition and acknowledgment of one's own worth, abilities, and character. According to [?], self-acceptance is a critical component of self-esteem and emotional well-being. It involves embracing both strengths and weaknesses, and fostering a positive relationship with oneself. In the context of LGBTQ individuals, self-acceptance can be particularly challenging due to societal stigma and internalized homophobia.

Theoretical Framework

The process of self-acceptance can be understood through various psychological theories. One relevant framework is the **Identity Development Theory** proposed by [?]. Cass's model outlines six stages of sexual identity development, which include:
1. **Identity Confusion**: The individual begins to question their sexual orientation or gender identity. 2. **Identity Comparison**: The individual recognizes their identity and compares it to societal norms. 3. **Identity Tolerance**: The individual begins to accept their identity but may still feel

isolated. 4. **Identity Acceptance**: The individual embraces their identity and seeks connections with others. 5. **Identity Pride**: The individual takes pride in their identity and actively engages in LGBTQ communities. 6. **Identity Synthesis**: The individual integrates their identity into their overall self-concept, achieving a sense of wholeness.

This theoretical framework provides insight into the stages individuals may experience on their path to self-acceptance.

Challenges Faced on the Journey

Individuals often encounter numerous obstacles on their journey to self-acceptance. These challenges can manifest as:

- **Internalized Homophobia:** The internal conflict stemming from societal stigma can lead to self-hatred and denial of one's identity.

- **Fear of Rejection:** Concerns about familial and societal rejection can hinder individuals from embracing their true selves.

- **Lack of Support:** The absence of a supportive community can exacerbate feelings of isolation and confusion.

- **Cultural and Religious Pressures:** Many individuals face conflicting messages from cultural and religious contexts that discourage acceptance of diverse sexual orientations and gender identities.

Examples of Self-Acceptance Journeys

To illustrate the journey of self-acceptance, we can explore the stories of notable LGBTQ activists:

- **Mark Tewksbury:** The Canadian Olympic swimmer faced immense pressure to conform to societal norms. His journey included a public coming out, which ultimately led to greater self-acceptance and advocacy for LGBTQ rights.

- **Laverne Cox:** The actress and advocate has spoken openly about her journey as a transgender woman, emphasizing the importance of self-love and acceptance in the face of adversity.

These examples highlight the transformative power of self-acceptance, not only for the individuals themselves but also for the communities they inspire.

Strategies for Cultivating Self-Acceptance

Cultivating self-acceptance involves various strategies, including:

- **Self-Reflection:** Engaging in self-reflection can help individuals understand their feelings and experiences. Journaling is a helpful tool for processing emotions.

- **Seeking Support:** Connecting with supportive friends, family, or LGBTQ organizations can provide a sense of belonging and affirmation.

- **Education and Awareness:** Learning about LGBTQ history and the experiences of others can foster a sense of pride and acceptance.

- **Mindfulness Practices:** Techniques such as meditation and mindfulness can enhance self-compassion and reduce negative self-talk.

Conclusion

The journey to self-acceptance is deeply personal and complex, shaped by individual experiences, societal influences, and cultural contexts. While challenges abound, the pursuit of authenticity and self-love is a powerful catalyst for personal growth and empowerment. As individuals navigate this journey, they not only embrace their identities but also pave the way for future generations to live openly and authentically.

Discovering Sexuality and Gender Identity

Early experiences and confusion

The journey of self-discovery, particularly within the LGBTQ community, is often marked by a series of complex and sometimes conflicting emotions. For many, these early experiences can be a tumultuous blend of curiosity, fear, and confusion. In the case of Bandy Kiki, her formative years in Douala were characterized by an environment that was not only culturally rich but also steeped in traditional norms that often clashed with her emerging sense of self.

From a young age, Bandy exhibited a keen awareness of her differences compared to her peers. This awareness often manifested in moments of introspection, where she grappled with her feelings towards both boys and girls. The internal conflict was exacerbated by societal expectations that dictated a strict binary understanding of gender and sexuality. Theories such as the **Gender Schema Theory** (Bem, 1981) suggest that individuals develop cognitive frameworks to categorize gender-related information, which can lead to confusion when one's experiences do not align with these schemas.

Bandy's early experiences were marked by a profound sense of isolation. In a society where traditional gender roles were rigidly enforced, her burgeoning identity felt like a secret she could not share. This secrecy often led to a sense of shame, which is a common emotional response among LGBTQ individuals during their formative years. According to **Erikson's Stages of Psychosocial Development**, the stage of identity versus role confusion is crucial during adolescence. Bandy found herself in a state of confusion as she navigated her identity amidst societal pressures that demanded conformity.

For instance, during her early teenage years, Bandy experienced her first crush on a close friend. This infatuation was both exhilarating and terrifying. She recalled moments of daydreaming about their friendship evolving into something more, yet the fear of rejection and societal backlash loomed large. These feelings are echoed in the works of researchers such as **Savin-Williams (2005)**, who noted that adolescents often experience heightened anxiety regarding their sexual orientation due to societal stigma.

This confusion was compounded by the lack of representation and visibility of LGBTQ individuals in her community. Bandy often turned to online spaces, where she found solace in the stories of others who shared similar experiences. The internet became a double-edged sword; while it offered a sense of community, it also exposed her to the harsh realities of discrimination and violence faced by LGBTQ individuals, particularly in Cameroon. This exposure led to a heightened awareness of the risks associated with her identity, fostering a sense of fear that was difficult to reconcile with her desire for authenticity.

The intersection of Bandy's cultural background and her emerging identity created a unique set of challenges. Cultural norms in Cameroon often dictate strict adherence to heteronormative standards, leaving little room for deviation. Bandy's experiences reflect the broader challenges faced by LGBTQ youth in similar environments, where cultural expectations can stifle personal expression and lead to significant psychological distress.

Moreover, the concept of **internalized homophobia** played a crucial role in Bandy's early experiences. As she began to understand her attractions, feelings of self-hatred and confusion emerged, stemming from societal messages that condemned her identity. According to **Herek (2009)**, internalized homophobia can lead to a range of negative outcomes, including depression and anxiety, which Bandy found herself grappling with during her adolescence.

In essence, Bandy Kiki's early experiences were a microcosm of the struggles faced by many LGBTQ individuals. The confusion stemming from her identity was not merely a personal struggle but a reflection of the societal and cultural frameworks that sought to define her. The interplay between her burgeoning identity and the societal norms surrounding her created a fertile ground for confusion, self-doubt, and ultimately, a desire for authenticity.

Through these early experiences, Bandy began to realize that her journey towards self-acceptance would require not only introspection but also a willingness to challenge the very norms that had caused her so much pain. This realization would lay the groundwork for her future activism, as she sought not only to understand her own identity but also to advocate for the rights and recognition of others like her, who faced similar struggles in silence.

Research and self-exploration

The journey of self-discovery is often a complex and multifaceted process, particularly for individuals exploring their sexuality and gender identity. In the case of Bandy Kiki, this phase was marked by extensive research and deep self-exploration, which served as a foundation for her eventual acceptance of her identity.

Understanding Sexuality and Gender Identity

To begin with, it is crucial to understand the distinction between sexuality and gender identity. Sexuality refers to whom one is attracted to, while gender identity pertains to how one perceives oneself in relation to gender. Theories such as the *Kinsey Scale* [?] provide a framework for understanding sexual orientation as a spectrum rather than a binary classification.

$$\text{Kinsey Scale} = 0 \text{ (Exclusively heterosexual)} \quad \text{to} \quad 6 \text{ (Exclusively homosexual)} \tag{19}$$

This scale highlights the fluidity of sexual orientation and reinforces the idea that one's identity can evolve over time. For Bandy, this realization was pivotal as she began to recognize her own bisexuality, which allowed her to embrace a broader spectrum of attraction.

Researching LGBTQ+ Resources

Bandy's self-exploration was fueled by a commitment to understanding the LGBTQ+ community better. She sought out various resources, including books, articles, and online forums, to educate herself about different identities and experiences. Notably, works like *Gender Trouble* by Judith Butler [?] introduced her to the concept of gender performativity, which posits that gender is not an innate quality but rather something that is enacted through repeated behaviors and societal norms.

$$\text{Gender Performativity} = \text{Gender} \rightarrow \text{Behavior} \rightarrow \text{Societal Norms} \quad (20)$$

This understanding prompted Bandy to question the rigid gender norms imposed by society and to consider her own identity beyond traditional labels.

Engaging with the Community

In addition to academic research, Bandy's self-exploration involved engaging with the LGBTQ+ community. She attended local meetups and online support groups, where she could connect with others who shared similar experiences. This engagement provided her with a sense of belonging and validation, which was crucial in her journey toward self-acceptance.

The Role of Reflection

Another key aspect of Bandy's self-exploration was the practice of reflection. Journaling became a vital tool for her to process her thoughts and feelings. By documenting her experiences, Bandy was able to articulate her emotions and confront her fears regarding her identity. This practice aligns with psychological theories that emphasize the importance of self-reflection in personal growth [?].

$$\text{Self-Reflection} = \text{Journaling} + \text{Processing Emotions} \quad (21)$$

Through reflection, Bandy began to dismantle the internalized homophobia she had absorbed from societal messages, allowing her to embrace her bisexuality and non-binary identity more fully.

Navigating Confusion and Fear

Despite her efforts in research and community engagement, Bandy faced significant confusion and fear. The societal stigma surrounding LGBTQ+ identities in Cameroon posed a constant threat, leading to anxiety about acceptance from family and friends. The fear of rejection often clouded her self-perception, causing her to question her worthiness and authenticity.

The psychological concept of *imposter syndrome* [?] became relevant during this time. Bandy often felt like a fraud in her identity, as if she were pretending to be someone she was not. This internal struggle necessitated a deeper exploration of her self-worth and the societal constructs that contributed to her feelings of inadequacy.

$$\text{Imposter Syndrome} = \text{Self-Doubt} + \text{Fear of Exposure} \quad (22)$$

Recognizing these patterns was a crucial step in Bandy's journey, as it allowed her to confront and challenge the negative narratives she had internalized.

Embracing Bisexuality and Non-Binary Identity

As Bandy continued her research, she found solace in the narratives of others who identified as bisexual and non-binary. Reading personal stories and academic analyses helped her to articulate her own experiences and feelings. The concept of *intersectionality* [?] played a significant role in her understanding, as it emphasized how various identities intersect and influence one another.

$$\text{Intersectionality} = \text{Sexuality} + \text{Gender} + \text{Culture} + \text{Socioeconomic Status} \quad (23)$$

This framework provided Bandy with a lens through which to view her own identity as multifaceted, allowing her to embrace the complexities of being both bisexual and non-binary in a society that often demands simplicity.

Conclusion

Ultimately, Bandy Kiki's journey of research and self-exploration was instrumental in her path toward self-acceptance. Through a combination of academic inquiry, community engagement, reflection, and the embrace of intersectionality, she began to understand and accept her identity. This foundational work not only prepared her for the challenges ahead but also ignited a passion for activism that would define her future endeavors.

In summary, the process of self-exploration is not merely about finding a label but rather about understanding the nuances of one's identity and the societal factors that shape it. Bandy's journey serves as a testament to the power of knowledge, community, and self-acceptance in the face of adversity.

Embracing bisexuality and non-binary identity

The journey toward embracing bisexuality and non-binary identity is often complex and multifaceted, marked by a series of personal revelations and societal challenges. For many individuals, the realization of their bisexuality—an attraction to more than one gender—carries with it a unique set of experiences that diverge significantly from those of their heterosexual or homosexual peers. Similarly, non-binary identities, which exist outside the traditional binary understanding of gender, add another layer of complexity to the process of self-acceptance.

Understanding Bisexuality

Bisexuality is frequently misunderstood, often reduced to stereotypes that portray bisexual individuals as indecisive or confused. This stigma can stem from a lack of visibility in both heterosexual and LGBTQ+ spaces, leading to what is known as *bi-erasure*. According to the American Psychological Association, bisexuality is a valid sexual orientation that encompasses a range of attractions, and it is crucial for bisexual individuals to acknowledge and embrace this aspect of their identity.

Research indicates that bisexual individuals may experience higher rates of mental health issues compared to their heterosexual and homosexual counterparts. A study conducted by the *National Institute of Health* found that bisexual individuals reported higher levels of anxiety and depression, largely due to societal stigma and discrimination. This highlights the importance of fostering supportive environments where bisexuality is recognized and validated.

The Non-Binary Spectrum

Non-binary identities encompass a wide range of gender expressions that do not fit neatly into the categories of male or female. Individuals who identify as non-binary may use various terms to describe their gender, such as genderqueer, genderfluid, or agender. The non-binary experience challenges the traditional binary understanding of gender, advocating for a more fluid and inclusive perspective.

According to the *Williams Institute*, a significant percentage of LGBTQ+ youth identify as non-binary, reflecting a cultural shift towards recognizing diverse gender identities. Embracing a non-binary identity can be liberating, allowing individuals to express themselves authentically without the constraints of societal expectations.

DISCOVERING SEXUALITY AND GENDER IDENTITY

Intersectionality in Identity

The intersection of bisexuality and non-binary identity is particularly significant, as individuals may navigate multiple layers of discrimination and acceptance. For instance, a non-binary person who identifies as bisexual may face unique challenges in both LGBTQ+ spaces and broader societal contexts. This intersectionality is crucial to understanding the full scope of an individual's experience and the societal structures that impact their lives.

$$\text{Intersectionality} = \text{Identity} + \text{Societal Structures} \tag{24}$$

This equation illustrates that an individual's identity is shaped not only by their personal experiences but also by the societal structures that govern norms around gender and sexuality. Recognizing this interplay is essential for fostering understanding and support.

Challenges of Acceptance

Despite the growing recognition of bisexual and non-binary identities, individuals often face significant challenges in their journey toward self-acceptance. One major issue is the pressure to conform to societal norms, which can lead to internalized stigma. Many bisexual individuals report feeling as though they must choose a side when it comes to their sexual orientation, leading to feelings of inadequacy or inauthenticity.

Moreover, non-binary individuals often encounter misgendering—being referred to by incorrect pronouns or gendered terms—which can be deeply invalidating. A study published in the *Journal of Homosexuality* found that misgendering can contribute to feelings of alienation and distress among non-binary individuals, further complicating their journey toward self-acceptance.

Examples of Empowerment and Advocacy

Despite these challenges, many individuals find empowerment through community and advocacy. Organizations such as *BiNet USA* and *Gender Spectrum* provide resources and support for bisexual and non-binary individuals, fostering a sense of belonging and validation.

For example, the #BiVisibilityDay campaign serves to raise awareness about bisexuality, encouraging individuals to share their stories and connect with others. Similarly, events celebrating non-binary identities, such as *Non-Binary Awareness Week*, aim to promote understanding and acceptance within both LGBTQ+ and mainstream communities.

Conclusion

Embracing bisexuality and non-binary identity is a profound and often challenging journey. It requires individuals to navigate societal stigma, internalized doubts, and the complexities of intersectional identities. However, through community support, advocacy, and personal exploration, many find the strength to embrace their authentic selves. The ongoing fight for visibility and acceptance within the LGBTQ+ community is vital for creating a more inclusive society where all identities are celebrated and respected.

In conclusion, the journey of embracing bisexuality and non-binary identity serves as a testament to the resilience of individuals who challenge societal norms and advocate for a broader understanding of human sexuality and gender. It is a journey marked by courage, self-discovery, and an unwavering commitment to authenticity.

Coming out to family and friends

Coming out is a profoundly personal journey, often fraught with emotional complexity and societal implications. For many LGBTQ individuals, the process of revealing their identity to family and friends can be both liberating and terrifying. In this section, we explore the multifaceted nature of coming out, the psychological theories that underpin it, the challenges faced, and the strategies that can facilitate a more supportive environment.

The Psychological Framework

The process of coming out can be understood through several psychological theories. One of the most relevant is **Erik Erikson's Psychosocial Development Theory**, which posits that individuals navigate various stages of development throughout their lives. The stage of *Identity vs. Role Confusion* is particularly pertinent for LGBTQ youth, as they grapple with their sexual and gender identities while seeking acceptance from their peers and families. Successfully navigating this stage can lead to a strong sense of self, while failure may result in confusion and internalized shame.

Another significant theory is the **Minority Stress Theory**, which suggests that LGBTQ individuals often face unique stressors related to their minority status, including discrimination, stigma, and social isolation. These stressors can exacerbate mental health challenges, making the coming out process even more daunting. The theory highlights the importance of social support systems and affirming environments in mitigating these stressors.

Challenges of Coming Out

Coming out is seldom a straightforward process. Many individuals face a myriad of challenges, including:

- **Fear of Rejection:** The anticipation of negative reactions from family and friends can create a significant barrier to coming out. Individuals may worry about being disowned, ostracized, or subjected to hostility.

- **Cultural and Religious Influences:** In many cultures, traditional beliefs and religious doctrines can pose formidable obstacles. Individuals may feel pressured to conform to heteronormative expectations, leading to internal conflict.

- **Timing and Context:** Determining the right moment to come out can be complex. Individuals often weigh factors such as the current family dynamics, the emotional state of their loved ones, and external circumstances.

- **Internalized Homophobia:** This refers to the internalization of societal stigma and negative beliefs about one's own sexual orientation or gender identity. It can lead to feelings of shame and self-doubt, complicating the coming out process.

Strategies for Coming Out

Despite the challenges, many individuals find ways to navigate the coming out process successfully. Here are some strategies that can help:

1. **Choose Supportive Allies:** Identifying friends or family members who are likely to be supportive can provide a sense of security. Coming out to these individuals first can create a buffer of support.

2. **Prepare for Conversations:** Engaging in open dialogues about LGBTQ issues beforehand can help gauge the reactions of family and friends. This preparation can provide insight into how to frame the conversation when coming out.

3. **Use Written Communication:** For some, writing a letter or email can alleviate the pressure of face-to-face conversations. This method allows individuals to express their thoughts clearly and gives recipients time to process the information.

4. **Set Boundaries:** Establishing clear boundaries regarding questions or discussions can help manage the conversation. Individuals should feel empowered to dictate the terms of their coming out experience.

5. **Seek Professional Support:** Engaging with a therapist or counselor can provide valuable tools for navigating the emotional landscape of coming out. Support groups can also offer a sense of community and shared experience.

Examples of Coming Out Experiences

The experiences of coming out vary widely, influenced by individual circumstances and the reactions of those involved. For instance, one individual may find acceptance and love from their family, leading to a strengthened bond. Conversely, another may face hostility or rejection, resulting in a painful estrangement.

Example 1: Acceptance and Celebration

In a heartwarming instance, a young woman named Sarah decided to come out to her family during a holiday gathering. She chose this moment because she knew her family valued openness and love. To her delight, her parents embraced her with tears of joy, expressing pride in her courage. This experience not only solidified their relationship but also inspired her siblings to share their own struggles, fostering a deeper familial connection.

Example 2: Rejection and Resilience

On the other hand, consider the story of Alex, who faced rejection from his father upon coming out. His father, steeped in traditional beliefs, reacted with anger and disappointment, leading to a painful rift. However, Alex found strength in his chosen family and community, ultimately leading him to become an advocate for LGBTQ rights. His resilience transformed a painful experience into a powerful catalyst for change.

The Importance of Support Systems

The role of support systems cannot be overstated. Research indicates that individuals who have supportive families and friends experience significantly better mental health outcomes. The presence of allies can mitigate the effects of discrimination and stigma, fostering resilience and self-acceptance.

Creating a supportive environment involves active listening, empathy, and validation. Family members and friends can educate themselves about LGBTQ issues, engage in open discussions, and express unconditional love. This support not only benefits the individual coming out but also enriches the relationships involved.

Conclusion

Coming out to family and friends is a pivotal moment in the lives of many LGBTQ individuals. While it can be fraught with challenges, the journey toward authenticity is essential for personal growth and self-acceptance. By understanding the psychological frameworks at play, acknowledging the challenges, and employing effective strategies, individuals can navigate this journey with greater confidence. Ultimately, the goal is to foster a world where coming out is met with love, acceptance, and celebration of diversity.

Embracing self-acceptance

Self-acceptance is a crucial milestone in the journey of LGBTQ individuals, particularly for those navigating the complexities of identity within a challenging environment. It encompasses recognizing and embracing one's identity, including sexual orientation and gender identity, without the burden of societal expectations or internalized stigma. This process is not merely about acknowledgment; it is about celebrating one's uniqueness and intrinsic worth.

Theoretical Framework

The concept of self-acceptance can be understood through various psychological theories. One prominent framework is Carl Rogers' Humanistic Psychology, which emphasizes the importance of self-concept and unconditional positive regard. According to Rogers, self-acceptance occurs when individuals can perceive themselves positively, regardless of external validation. This aligns with the idea that LGBTQ individuals must often confront societal rejection and discrimination, making self-acceptance a radical act of defiance against these external pressures.

Furthermore, the concept of intersectionality, introduced by Kimberlé Crenshaw, is essential in understanding self-acceptance within the LGBTQ context. Intersectionality posits that individuals experience overlapping identities (e.g., race, gender, sexuality) that can compound their experiences of discrimination or acceptance. For example, a Black queer individual may face unique challenges that differ from those encountered by a white queer individual. Recognizing these intersections is vital for fostering a holistic sense of self-acceptance.

Challenges to Self-Acceptance

For many LGBTQ individuals, the path to self-acceptance is fraught with obstacles. Societal stigma, familial rejection, and internalized homophobia can create significant barriers. Internalized homophobia refers to the internalization of negative societal attitudes toward one's sexual orientation, leading to feelings of shame and self-hatred. This phenomenon can manifest in various ways, including avoidance of LGBTQ spaces, reluctance to engage in same-sex relationships, and a pervasive sense of unworthiness.

Moreover, the fear of rejection from family and friends can prevent individuals from fully embracing their identities. This fear is often compounded in cultures where traditional gender roles and heterosexual norms are deeply entrenched. The psychological toll of living inauthentically can lead to anxiety, depression, and a diminished sense of self-worth.

Examples of Embracing Self-Acceptance

Despite these challenges, many LGBTQ individuals find ways to embrace self-acceptance. For instance, the journey of Bandy Kiki highlights the transformative power of self-acceptance. Initially grappling with her identity in a conservative environment, Bandy's path to self-acceptance involved engaging with LGBTQ literature, connecting with supportive communities, and ultimately coming out to her chosen family. This process allowed her to reclaim her narrative and assert her identity with confidence.

Another poignant example is the use of social media platforms by LGBTQ individuals to share their stories and experiences. Platforms such as Instagram and TikTok have become spaces for self-expression and affirmation. Through hashtags like #SelfAcceptance and #Pride, individuals can connect with others who share similar experiences, fostering a sense of belonging and validation. This digital solidarity can be particularly empowering for those who may not have access to supportive environments in their immediate surroundings.

The Role of Self-Compassion

Self-compassion plays a critical role in the process of self-acceptance. Kristin Neff, a pioneer in self-compassion research, outlines three components: self-kindness, common humanity, and mindfulness. Self-kindness involves treating oneself with care and understanding rather than harsh judgment. Recognizing that struggles with self-acceptance are part of the shared human experience (common humanity) can alleviate feelings of isolation. Finally, mindfulness encourages individuals to observe their thoughts and feelings without over-identifying with them, creating space for self-acceptance to flourish.

Incorporating self-compassion practices can significantly enhance one's journey toward self-acceptance. Activities such as journaling, meditation, and positive affirmations can help individuals cultivate a kinder relationship with themselves. For example, a simple affirmation like "I am worthy of love and acceptance" can serve as a powerful reminder of one's inherent value.

Conclusion

Embracing self-acceptance is a profound and liberating journey for LGBTQ individuals. It requires navigating societal pressures, confronting internalized stigma, and fostering a compassionate relationship with oneself. By understanding the theoretical frameworks surrounding self-acceptance, recognizing the challenges faced, and drawing inspiration from personal stories and practices, individuals can embark on a transformative journey toward embracing their true selves. Ultimately, self-acceptance not only empowers individuals but also contributes to a broader movement of acceptance and love within society.

Coming out in a Hostile Environment

The weight of societal expectations

Societal expectations can be seen as the unwritten rules that govern behavior, beliefs, and identities within a given culture. For individuals within the LGBTQ community, these expectations often manifest as rigid norms surrounding gender roles, sexual orientation, and acceptable forms of expression. The pressure to conform to these societal standards can create a heavy burden, particularly for those who do not identify with traditional definitions of gender and sexuality.

Theoretical Framework

To understand the weight of societal expectations, we can draw on Erving Goffman's theory of stigma, which posits that individuals who possess a characteristic that is devalued by society may experience a disconnection between their self-identity and the identity imposed by societal norms. This disconnection can lead to feelings of shame, isolation, and anxiety. Goffman identifies three types of stigma: physical deformities, character blemishes, and tribal stigma, the latter of which applies to LGBTQ individuals who may be viewed as part of a marginalized group.

$$S = \frac{D}{C}$$

Where S is the level of stigma experienced, D is the degree of difference from societal norms, and C is the societal acceptance of diversity. As the values of D increase (greater deviation from societal norms), the level of stigma S also increases, making it difficult for individuals to embrace their true identities.

Problems Arising from Societal Expectations

The weight of societal expectations can lead to a range of problems for LGBTQ individuals, including:

- **Internalized Homophobia:** The internalization of negative societal attitudes can result in self-hatred and a rejection of one's identity. This phenomenon can manifest in various ways, including self-sabotage and a reluctance to engage with the LGBTQ community.

- **Mental Health Issues:** The constant pressure to conform can lead to mental health challenges such as anxiety, depression, and suicidal ideation. Studies have shown that LGBTQ individuals are at a higher risk for these issues due to societal rejection and discrimination.

- **Social Isolation:** Fear of rejection can lead individuals to isolate themselves from their peers, family, and community. This isolation can exacerbate feelings of loneliness and despair, creating a cycle that is difficult to break.

Examples of Societal Expectations in Practice

In many cultures, traditional gender roles dictate that men should be strong, stoic, and emotionally reserved, while women should be nurturing, submissive, and compliant. For LGBTQ individuals, particularly those who identify as non-binary or gender non-conforming, these expectations can be suffocating.

For instance, consider the experience of a non-binary individual in a conservative community. They may face backlash for not adhering to the binary gender norms, leading to harassment or exclusion from social circles. This societal pressure can force them to alter their behavior or appearance to fit in, ultimately compromising their authenticity.

Moreover, the expectation to be heterosexual can lead to a painful process of denial and repression for many LGBTQ individuals. The fear of coming out often stems from the anticipation of negative reactions from family, friends, and society at large. A poignant example can be found in the story of a young gay man who, after years of hiding his identity, finally mustered the courage to come out to his family. Instead of the support he hoped for, he was met with disapproval and rejection, reinforcing the societal belief that being LGBTQ is unacceptable.

Navigating Societal Expectations

Navigating the weight of societal expectations requires resilience and a strong sense of self. Many LGBTQ individuals find solace in supportive communities where acceptance is the norm rather than the exception. Engaging with these communities can provide a refuge from societal pressures and foster a sense of belonging.

Furthermore, activism plays a crucial role in challenging societal norms and reshaping expectations. By advocating for LGBTQ rights and visibility, activists work to dismantle harmful stereotypes and promote acceptance of diverse identities. The efforts of individuals like Bandy Kiki exemplify the transformative power of activism in creating a more inclusive society.

In conclusion, the weight of societal expectations can be a significant barrier for LGBTQ individuals seeking to live authentically. Understanding the theoretical frameworks and real-world implications of these expectations is essential in addressing the challenges faced by the community. By fostering acceptance and challenging discriminatory norms, society can begin to alleviate the burden of these expectations, allowing individuals to embrace their true selves without fear or shame.

The risks and consequences

Coming out in a hostile environment is a courageous act that can lead to a myriad of risks and consequences for LGBTQ individuals. The decision to disclose one's sexual orientation or gender identity can result in both personal and societal repercussions that are deeply intertwined with the cultural, legal, and social landscapes of their surroundings. This section delves into these risks and consequences, providing a nuanced understanding of the challenges faced by individuals like Bandy Kiki.

1. Psychological Risks

The psychological toll of coming out can be significant. Studies indicate that LGBTQ individuals often experience heightened levels of anxiety, depression, and stress when navigating the coming-out process, particularly in environments where they anticipate rejection or discrimination. According to the *American Psychological Association*, the fear of negative outcomes can lead to what is known as **anticipatory anxiety**, which can manifest as a debilitating fear of the unknown. This fear can be exacerbated in hostile settings, where societal norms discourage openness about sexual orientation or gender identity.

Moreover, the internal conflict that arises from societal pressures can lead to **internalized homophobia**, a phenomenon where individuals adopt negative societal attitudes toward their own sexual orientation. This internal struggle can result in self-hatred and a diminished sense of self-worth, making the act of coming out feel even more daunting.

2. Social Consequences

The social repercussions of coming out can be profound. In many cultures, particularly in regions like Cameroon, where LGBTQ identities are heavily stigmatized, individuals risk ostracism from their families, friends, and communities. For example, Bandy Kiki's experience illustrates this reality; upon revealing her identity, she faced backlash from those closest to her, leading to strained familial relationships and a loss of social support.

The impact of societal rejection can be devastating, often resulting in feelings of isolation and loneliness. A study published in *The Journal of Homosexuality* highlights that individuals who come out in hostile environments are more likely to experience social isolation, which can further compound mental health issues and lead to a sense of hopelessness.

3. Legal and Economic Risks

In addition to psychological and social consequences, coming out in a hostile environment can expose individuals to legal and economic risks. In many countries, including Cameroon, same-sex relationships are criminalized, and LGBTQ individuals may face arrest, harassment, or violence as a result of their identity. The legal framework surrounding LGBTQ rights can create a precarious situation where individuals must weigh the risks of legal repercussions against their desire for authenticity.

Economically, the consequences can be equally severe. Discrimination in the workplace is a common reality for many LGBTQ individuals who come out. For instance, Bandy Kiki's activism led to her losing her job, showcasing how coming out can jeopardize financial stability. The economic impact of discrimination can perpetuate cycles of poverty and limit access to resources that are crucial for personal and professional growth.

4. Physical Safety Concerns

Perhaps one of the most alarming risks associated with coming out in a hostile environment is the threat to physical safety. In regions where anti-LGBTQ violence is prevalent, individuals may face threats, harassment, or even physical assault. Reports from organizations like *Human Rights Watch* indicate that LGBTQ individuals in Cameroon often endure violence simply for existing as their true selves. This reality underscores the urgent need for protective measures and support systems for those who dare to come out.

Bandy Kiki's story serves as a poignant reminder of these dangers. Her decision to advocate for LGBTQ rights placed her in the crosshairs of those who oppose such movements, leading to threats against her life and wellbeing. The fear of violence can deter many from coming out, reinforcing the oppressive silence that often surrounds LGBTQ identities in hostile environments.

5. Community Response and Support

Despite these risks, the response from the LGBTQ community can serve as a source of strength and resilience. Many individuals find solace in chosen families and support networks that understand the complexities of their experiences. These communities often provide a safe haven for those who have come out, offering emotional support and resources to navigate the challenges ahead.

The role of peer support is critical. Research indicates that individuals who have access to supportive networks are more likely to report positive mental health outcomes and a greater sense of belonging. This highlights the importance of fostering community solidarity in the face of adversity, as it can mitigate some of the negative consequences associated with coming out.

Conclusion

In conclusion, the risks and consequences of coming out in a hostile environment are multifaceted and deeply impactful. From psychological distress to legal repercussions, the journey toward authenticity is fraught with challenges that can significantly affect an individual's quality of life. However, the resilience demonstrated by individuals like Bandy Kiki, who continue to advocate for their rights and the rights of others, illustrates the power of courage in the face of adversity. It is essential to acknowledge these risks while also recognizing the strength found within LGBTQ communities that support one another through the complexities of coming out.

Support from chosen family and friends

In the journey of self-acceptance, the role of chosen family and friends cannot be overstated. For many individuals, especially those within the LGBTQ community, the concept of chosen family emerges as a vital support system that often replaces or complements biological family ties. Chosen family refers to the relationships that individuals cultivate with friends, mentors, and allies who provide emotional, social, and sometimes financial support. This support is crucial, particularly in environments where acceptance from biological families may be lacking or even hostile.

Theoretical Framework

The theory of *social support* posits that individuals who perceive themselves to have supportive relationships are more likely to experience positive mental health outcomes. According to Cohen and Wills (1985), social support can buffer against the negative effects of stress, which is particularly relevant for LGBTQ individuals facing discrimination and societal rejection. The types of social support can be categorized into emotional support, informational support, and instrumental support.

$$S = E + I + R \tag{25}$$

Where S represents overall social support, E is emotional support, I is informational support, and R is instrumental support. Each component plays a critical role in the resilience of LGBTQ individuals as they navigate their identities and the challenges that come with them.

The Role of Chosen Family

Chosen family often provides a safe haven where individuals can express their true selves without fear of judgment. This environment fosters authenticity and encourages individuals to embrace their identities. For example, Bandy Kiki found solace in a close-knit group of friends who understood her struggles and celebrated her identity. They became her support system, offering love and encouragement during the most challenging times.

The power of chosen family lies in its ability to create a sense of belonging. For many LGBTQ individuals, especially those from conservative backgrounds, the fear of rejection can be overwhelming. Chosen family members often step in to fill the void left by unsupportive biological families. This dynamic is particularly important in cultures where traditional family structures may not accept diverse sexual orientations and gender identities.

Examples of Support

Consider the story of a young individual named Alex, who came out as transgender in a community that was largely unaccepting. His biological family responded with hostility, leading to feelings of isolation and despair. However, through a local LGBTQ organization, Alex met a group of friends who became his chosen family. They provided him with emotional support, helped him navigate the complexities of transitioning, and even accompanied him to medical appointments. This support network played a pivotal role in his journey toward self-acceptance and empowerment.

In another instance, a group of LGBTQ activists organized a "family dinner" for those who felt estranged from their biological families. This initiative allowed participants to share their experiences, fostering a sense of community and solidarity. Such gatherings not only provide emotional support but also create opportunities for individuals to forge meaningful connections with others who share similar experiences.

Challenges Faced by Chosen Families

While chosen families can provide invaluable support, they are not without their challenges. The dynamics of chosen families can be complex, as individuals may come from diverse backgrounds and experiences. Conflicts can arise, particularly around differing views on identity, activism, and personal boundaries. Furthermore, the pressure to maintain these relationships can sometimes lead to feelings of inadequacy or fear of abandonment.

Additionally, chosen families may face external challenges, such as societal stigma and discrimination. Members of chosen families often find themselves advocating not only for their own rights but also for the rights of their chosen family members. This can create additional stress and strain on relationships, as individuals navigate their activism while also seeking personal fulfillment.

The Importance of Advocacy and Support

Ultimately, the support from chosen family and friends is a cornerstone of resilience for many LGBTQ individuals. It empowers them to confront societal challenges with a sense of solidarity and strength. Advocacy for chosen families is essential, as it helps to validate these relationships and recognize their importance in the broader context of LGBTQ rights.

Organizations and movements that promote chosen family acceptance play a crucial role in this advocacy. They help to raise awareness about the significance of chosen families and provide resources for individuals seeking support. By fostering environments where chosen families are celebrated, society can contribute to the overall well-being of LGBTQ individuals.

In conclusion, the support from chosen family and friends is an integral part of the journey toward self-acceptance for many LGBTQ individuals. By providing emotional, social, and instrumental support, chosen families help individuals navigate the complexities of their identities and advocate for their rights. As society continues to evolve, recognizing and supporting chosen families will be essential in fostering a more inclusive and accepting world.

Building resilience in the face of adversity

In the journey of self-acceptance and activism, building resilience becomes a crucial skill, especially for individuals navigating the complexities of their identities in a hostile environment. Resilience, defined as the ability to bounce back from challenges and maintain psychological well-being, is not merely an innate trait but a skill that can be cultivated. This section explores the mechanisms of resilience, the challenges faced by LGBTQ individuals in Cameroon, and practical strategies for fostering resilience.

Understanding Resilience

Resilience can be conceptualized through various psychological theories. One such framework is the **Resilience Theory**, which emphasizes the dynamic interplay between individual traits, environmental factors, and social support systems. According to [?], resilience is often described as "ordinary magic," highlighting that it is not an extraordinary quality but rather a common process that individuals utilize to cope with adversity.

The **Ecological Model of Resilience** further illustrates how resilience is influenced by multiple levels of interaction, including individual, familial, community, and societal factors. This model suggests that resilience is not solely dependent on personal attributes but is significantly shaped by the support and resources available within one's environment [?].

Challenges to Resilience in the LGBTQ Community

In Cameroon, the LGBTQ community faces significant adversities, including legal discrimination, social stigma, and violence. The oppressive legal framework criminalizes same-sex relationships, leading to widespread fear and isolation. This environment can severely undermine resilience by fostering feelings of hopelessness and despair.

$$R = f(P, E, S) \qquad (26)$$

Where:

- R is resilience,
- P represents personal attributes (e.g., self-esteem, optimism),
- E denotes environmental factors (e.g., supportive relationships, community resources),
- S stands for social support systems (e.g., friends, allies).

The equation illustrates that resilience is a function of individual characteristics, environmental context, and social support. In a hostile environment, where E is often negative or lacking, individuals may struggle to maintain resilience.

Strategies for Building Resilience

To foster resilience, individuals can employ several strategies that align with both psychological theories and practical experiences:

- **Developing a Strong Support Network:** Building connections with allies, chosen family, and supportive friends is vital. Social support has been shown to buffer against stress and enhance resilience [?]. Engaging in community groups and online forums can provide a sense of belonging and understanding.

- **Practicing Self-Compassion:** Self-compassion involves treating oneself with kindness during difficult times. According to Neff (2003), self-compassion can lead to greater emotional resilience, allowing individuals to cope with failures and setbacks more effectively. This practice encourages individuals to acknowledge their struggles without harsh self-criticism.

- **Setting Realistic Goals:** Establishing achievable, incremental goals can provide a sense of direction and accomplishment. This aligns with the **SMART criteria** (Specific, Measurable, Achievable, Relevant, Time-bound), which helps individuals focus on manageable steps rather than overwhelming challenges [?].

- **Cultivating a Growth Mindset:** Embracing a growth mindset, as proposed by Dweck (2006), encourages individuals to view challenges as opportunities for growth rather than insurmountable obstacles. This perspective fosters resilience by promoting adaptability and learning from experiences.

- **Engaging in Mindfulness Practices:** Mindfulness techniques, such as meditation and deep breathing, can help individuals manage stress and enhance emotional regulation. Research indicates that mindfulness can lead to improved psychological resilience by promoting present-moment awareness and reducing anxiety [?].

- **Advocating for Change:** Taking active steps to challenge discriminatory practices can empower individuals and foster a sense of agency. Engaging in activism not only contributes to social change but also reinforces personal resilience by creating a supportive community and shared purpose.

Examples of Resilience in Action

The stories of LGBTQ activists in Cameroon exemplify resilience in the face of adversity. For instance, Bandy Kiki, a pseudonymous activist, has utilized social media to amplify marginalized voices and raise awareness about LGBTQ issues. By creating a platform that connects individuals facing similar challenges, she has fostered a sense of community and solidarity.

Additionally, numerous grassroots organizations have emerged to support LGBTQ individuals, providing safe spaces, resources, and advocacy. These initiatives not only challenge oppressive systems but also empower individuals to embrace their identities and advocate for their rights.

Conclusion

Building resilience is a multifaceted process that involves personal growth, social support, and active engagement in advocacy. For LGBTQ individuals in Cameroon, cultivating resilience is essential for navigating the challenges posed by a hostile environment. By fostering supportive networks, practicing self-compassion, and embracing a growth mindset, individuals can enhance their resilience and contribute to the broader fight for equality and acceptance. The journey may be fraught with obstacles, but with resilience, hope and change are always within reach.

Advocating for LGBTQ Acceptance in Personal Relationships

Advocating for LGBTQ acceptance within personal relationships is a nuanced and often challenging endeavor. It requires individuals to confront not only societal prejudices but also the deeply ingrained beliefs and biases that may exist within their own families and friendships. This section explores the theoretical frameworks, challenges, and practical examples of advocating for LGBTQ acceptance in personal relationships.

Theoretical Frameworks

The advocacy for LGBTQ acceptance in personal relationships can be understood through several theoretical lenses, including social identity theory and intersectionality.

Social Identity Theory Social identity theory posits that individuals derive a sense of self from their group memberships, which can lead to in-group favoritism and out-group discrimination [?]. For LGBTQ individuals, their sexual orientation or gender identity becomes a crucial aspect of their social identity. Advocating for acceptance involves educating family and friends about the significance of these identities and the harmful impacts of discrimination.

Intersectionality Intersectionality, as coined by Kimberlé Crenshaw, emphasizes the interconnected nature of social categorizations such as race, class, and gender [?]. Understanding that LGBTQ individuals may face multiple layers of discrimination based on their intersecting identities is essential for fostering acceptance. Advocates should highlight these intersections in conversations with loved ones, illustrating that acceptance is not just a matter of tolerance but a recognition of the complexity of individual identities.

Challenges in Advocacy

Despite the theoretical frameworks that support advocacy, several challenges can arise when attempting to promote LGBTQ acceptance in personal relationships:

Fear of Rejection One of the most significant barriers is the fear of rejection. Many LGBTQ individuals may hesitate to come out or advocate for acceptance due to concerns about alienating family members or friends. This fear can lead to a reluctance to engage in open discussions about their identities.

Cultural and Religious Beliefs Cultural and religious beliefs can also pose obstacles to acceptance. In many communities, traditional values may conflict with LGBTQ identities, leading to resistance from family members who hold these beliefs. Advocates must navigate these sensitive topics delicately, often requiring patience and understanding.

Internalized Homophobia Internalized homophobia can affect both LGBTQ individuals and their loved ones. Those who have internalized negative societal messages about LGBTQ identities may struggle to accept their own or their loved ones' identities. This can create a cyclical pattern of rejection and denial that advocates must work to break.

Strategies for Advocacy

To effectively advocate for LGBTQ acceptance in personal relationships, individuals can employ several strategies:

Open Communication Engaging in open and honest conversations is crucial. Advocates should create safe spaces for dialogue, where family members and friends can express their thoughts and feelings without fear of judgment. This can involve sharing personal experiences and the impact of discrimination on mental health and well-being.

Education and Awareness Education plays a vital role in advocacy. Providing resources, such as articles, books, and documentaries, can help demystify LGBTQ identities and dispel myths. For instance, sharing statistics about LGBTQ youth mental health can underscore the importance of acceptance.

Modeling Acceptance   Leading by example is a powerful advocacy tool. LGBTQ individuals can demonstrate acceptance in their relationships by being open about their identities and celebrating diversity. This modeling can inspire others to embrace acceptance and challenge their biases.

Examples of Advocacy in Action

Real-world examples can illustrate the impact of advocating for LGBTQ acceptance in personal relationships:

Coming Out Conversations   Consider the story of a young woman named Sarah, who decided to come out to her conservative parents. She prepared for the conversation by discussing her feelings and experiences with LGBTQ discrimination. By framing her identity as an integral part of her life, Sarah was able to foster a more understanding environment. Although her parents initially struggled, ongoing discussions led to greater acceptance over time.

Family Education Initiatives   In another instance, a group of LGBTQ allies organized a family education night in their community. They invited local speakers to share their stories and experiences, creating a dialogue about acceptance. This initiative not only educated the attendees but also created a supportive network for LGBTQ individuals and their families.

Conclusion

Advocating for LGBTQ acceptance in personal relationships is a critical aspect of fostering a more inclusive society. By employing theoretical frameworks, addressing challenges, and implementing effective strategies, individuals can create meaningful change within their personal circles. As we continue to navigate the complexities of identity and acceptance, it is essential to recognize that advocacy begins at home, and each conversation can contribute to a broader movement for equality and understanding.

A Quest for Authenticity

Overcoming internalized homophobia

Internalized homophobia refers to the internalization of societal stigma and negative beliefs about one's sexual orientation or gender identity. This phenomenon often leads individuals to experience feelings of shame, guilt, and self-hatred, which can significantly impact their mental health and overall well-being. To understand the complexities of internalized homophobia, we must first explore its origins and manifestations.

Theoretical Framework

The concept of internalized homophobia can be understood through various psychological theories, including the Minority Stress Theory. This theory posits that individuals from marginalized groups, such as the LGBTQ community, experience unique stressors that are not faced by their heterosexual counterparts. These stressors include societal stigma, discrimination, and rejection, which can lead to the internalization of negative beliefs about oneself.

$$\text{Internalized Homophobia} = \text{Societal Stigma} + \text{Discrimination} + \text{Personal Rejection} \tag{27}$$

This equation illustrates how external factors contribute to the development of internalized homophobia. The cumulative effect of these negative experiences can lead to a distorted self-image and hinder one's ability to embrace their identity fully.

Manifestations of Internalized Homophobia

Internalized homophobia can manifest in various ways, including:

- **Self-Discrimination:** Individuals may adopt negative stereotypes about LGBTQ individuals, leading them to reject their own identity.

- **Shame and Guilt:** Feelings of shame may arise from societal expectations, causing individuals to feel guilty about their attractions or identity.

- **Avoidance Behaviors:** Some may distance themselves from LGBTQ communities or deny their identity to fit in with heteronormative standards.

- **Mental Health Issues:** Internalized homophobia is linked to higher rates of depression, anxiety, and suicidal ideation among LGBTQ individuals.

Strategies for Overcoming Internalized Homophobia

1. Education and Awareness: Understanding the origins of internalized homophobia is crucial. Engaging with LGBTQ literature, attending workshops,

and participating in discussions can help individuals recognize and challenge harmful beliefs.

2. **Therapy and Counseling:** Seeking professional help from therapists who specialize in LGBTQ issues can provide a safe space to explore feelings of shame and guilt. Cognitive Behavioral Therapy (CBT) is particularly effective in addressing negative thought patterns.

3. **Building a Support Network:** Connecting with supportive friends, family, and LGBTQ organizations can foster a sense of belonging. Sharing experiences with others who have faced similar struggles can alleviate feelings of isolation.

4. **Practicing Self-Compassion:** Developing self-love and acceptance is vital. Techniques such as mindfulness and self-affirmation can help individuals cultivate a positive self-image.

5. **Advocacy and Activism:** Engaging in activism can empower individuals to challenge societal norms and fight against the stigma that contributes to internalized homophobia. By advocating for LGBTQ rights, individuals can reclaim their identity and foster resilience.

Examples of Overcoming Internalized Homophobia

Consider the story of Alex, who grew up in a conservative environment where being LGBTQ was heavily stigmatized. Initially, Alex struggled with feelings of shame and self-hatred, leading to severe anxiety and depression. Through therapy, Alex learned to recognize the impact of societal stigma on their self-perception. By joining a local LGBTQ support group, Alex connected with others who shared similar experiences, which helped diminish feelings of isolation.

Over time, Alex engaged in activism, participating in pride events and advocating for LGBTQ rights in their community. This journey not only fostered self-acceptance but also inspired others to embrace their identities, creating a ripple effect of empowerment.

Conclusion

Overcoming internalized homophobia is a critical step towards self-acceptance and empowerment for LGBTQ individuals. By understanding its origins, recognizing its manifestations, and employing effective strategies for overcoming it, individuals can reclaim their identities and contribute to a more inclusive society. The journey may be challenging, but it is also transformative, paving the way for a future where authenticity is celebrated, and diversity is embraced.

Embracing one's true self

Embracing one's true self is a vital journey in the process of self-acceptance, particularly for individuals navigating the complexities of sexual orientation and gender identity. This phase is characterized by a profound realization that authenticity is not just a personal desire but a fundamental right. The act of embracing one's true self involves recognizing, accepting, and celebrating one's identity, which can be a transformative experience fraught with both challenges and rewards.

Theoretical Framework

From a psychological perspective, the process of self-acceptance can be understood through various theories. One such framework is the *Identity Development Theory* proposed by Erik Erikson. Erikson posits that individuals go through stages of development, each characterized by a psychosocial crisis that must be resolved. For LGBTQ individuals, the stage of identity versus role confusion is particularly salient. Successfully navigating this stage involves the integration of one's sexual and gender identity into a cohesive self-concept.

Another relevant theory is the *Minority Stress Theory*, which suggests that individuals from marginalized groups experience unique stressors that can impact their mental health. These stressors include discrimination, stigma, and internalized homophobia. Embracing one's true self can serve as a protective factor against these stressors, fostering resilience and well-being.

Challenges in Embracing Authenticity

Despite the importance of embracing one's true self, numerous challenges can impede this journey. Societal expectations and norms often create a hostile environment for those who identify as LGBTQ. The fear of rejection from family, friends, and society at large can lead to internal conflict and self-doubt. Many individuals grapple with the notion of *performative identity*, where they feel compelled to present a version of themselves that aligns with societal expectations, rather than their authentic self.

Moreover, the pressure to conform to traditional gender roles can be particularly burdensome. For example, individuals who identify as non-binary or genderqueer may struggle to find acceptance in a binary system that often marginalizes their existence. This societal pressure can lead to feelings of isolation and inadequacy, making it difficult for individuals to embrace their true selves.

Examples of Embracing Authenticity

The journey toward embracing one's true self can manifest in various ways. For instance, consider the story of Alex, a non-binary individual who spent years conforming to societal expectations of gender. Initially, Alex felt compelled to present as female, despite a deep-seated discomfort with this identity. After years of internal struggle, Alex began to explore non-binary identities through online communities and literature. This exploration culminated in a powerful moment of self-acceptance when Alex publicly came out as non-binary, reclaiming their identity and rejecting the constraints of traditional gender norms.

Another poignant example is that of Jamie, a bisexual activist who faced significant backlash from both heterosexual and LGBTQ communities for their identity. Jamie's journey involved confronting the stigma associated with bisexuality, often characterized by the misconception that bisexual individuals are indecisive or seeking attention. By actively engaging in conversations about bisexuality and sharing personal experiences, Jamie not only embraced their identity but also became a powerful advocate for visibility and acceptance within the LGBTQ community.

The Role of Support Systems

A crucial element in the journey of embracing one's true self is the presence of supportive networks. Chosen families, friends, and communities play a vital role in fostering an environment where individuals feel safe to express their authentic selves. Support groups and LGBTQ organizations provide spaces for individuals to share their experiences, validate their identities, and cultivate a sense of belonging.

Research indicates that individuals with strong support systems are more likely to report higher levels of self-acceptance and overall well-being. For instance, a study conducted by [Meyer(2003)] found that LGBTQ individuals who participated in community support groups experienced lower levels of depression and anxiety, highlighting the importance of connection in the journey toward authenticity.

Celebrating Authenticity

Embracing one's true self is not merely a personal achievement; it is a celebration of diversity and individuality. When individuals embrace their authentic identities, they contribute to a broader cultural shift that challenges societal norms and promotes acceptance. This celebration can take many forms, from personal expressions of identity through fashion and art to public advocacy and activism.

For example, Pride events around the world serve as powerful demonstrations of self-acceptance and community solidarity. These events provide a platform for individuals to express their identities freely, fostering a sense of pride and belonging. The act of publicly celebrating one's identity can be a radical act of defiance against a society that often seeks to marginalize LGBTQ individuals.

Conclusion

In conclusion, embracing one's true self is a multifaceted journey that involves navigating personal, societal, and cultural landscapes. While challenges abound, the rewards of authenticity are profound, leading to increased resilience, empowerment, and a sense of belonging. As individuals embrace their true selves, they not only transform their own lives but also contribute to a more inclusive and accepting society. The journey is ongoing, but each step taken toward authenticity is a step toward a brighter, more equitable future for all.

Bibliography

[Meyer(2003)] Meyer, I. H. (2003). Prejudice, social stress, and mental health in gay men. *American Psychologist*, 58(5), 365-372.

Leading by example

In the realm of activism, the phrase "leading by example" transcends mere rhetoric; it embodies a powerful methodology that inspires action and galvanizes communities. For Bandy Kiki, this was not just a strategy but a fundamental aspect of her identity as an advocate for LGBTQ rights in Cameroon. To lead by example means to embody the values and principles one espouses, creating a tangible model for others to emulate. This section explores the theoretical underpinnings of this concept, the challenges faced by activists in embodying their ideals, and the profound impact of Bandy Kiki's leadership on her community.

Theoretical Framework

Leading by example is rooted in transformational leadership theory, which posits that leaders can inspire followers to achieve extraordinary outcomes by fostering an environment of trust, motivation, and ethical behavior. According to Bass and Avolio (1994), transformational leaders are characterized by their ability to inspire followers through vision and personal example. This approach not only enhances the followers' commitment to the cause but also promotes a culture of accountability and integrity within the movement.

The Social Learning Theory, proposed by Albert Bandura, further elucidates the importance of leading by example. Bandura's theory emphasizes that individuals learn behaviors through observation and imitation of role models. In the context of LGBTQ activism, when individuals see leaders like Bandy Kiki openly embracing their identities and standing up against oppression, they are more likely to adopt similar behaviors. This creates a ripple effect, as each individual inspired by Kiki's example may go on to influence others, thus amplifying the impact of her activism.

Challenges of Leading by Example

Despite the power of leading by example, activists often encounter significant challenges in embodying their ideals. In a hostile environment like Cameroon, where LGBTQ individuals face severe discrimination and violence, the pressure to conform to societal norms can be overwhelming. Activists may grapple with internalized homophobia, fear of persecution, and the emotional toll of constant vigilance. The decision to live authentically can come with dire consequences, including social ostracism, loss of employment, or even physical harm.

For Bandy Kiki, the journey of leading by example required immense courage. She faced the daunting task of reconciling her public persona as an activist with her personal experiences of fear and vulnerability. Navigating this duality demanded not only resilience but also a commitment to authenticity. Kiki's ability to share her struggles openly, including her fears and setbacks, made her relatable to many in the LGBTQ community. By acknowledging her vulnerabilities, she demonstrated that strength does not equate to invulnerability; rather, it is about embracing one's truth amidst adversity.

Impact of Bandy Kiki's Leadership

Bandy Kiki's leadership style exemplified the essence of leading by example. Through her activism, she illuminated the path for others in the LGBTQ community, encouraging them to embrace their identities and advocate for their rights. Her public declarations of self-acceptance and her refusal to be silenced resonated deeply with many individuals who felt isolated in their experiences.

One notable instance of Kiki's impact occurred during a public forum on LGBTQ rights in Douala. By sharing her personal story of coming out and the challenges she faced, Kiki not only educated the audience about the realities of LGBTQ life in Cameroon but also inspired others to share their narratives. This act of vulnerability fostered a sense of solidarity among attendees, empowering many to step forward and voice their own experiences.

Moreover, Kiki's commitment to community engagement exemplified her leadership. She organized workshops and support groups that provided safe spaces for individuals to explore their identities and discuss their experiences. By actively participating in these initiatives, Kiki demonstrated her dedication to the cause and inspired others to take on leadership roles within their communities. The result was a burgeoning network of activists who felt empowered to advocate for change, driven by Kiki's example.

Conclusion

In conclusion, leading by example is a potent tool in the arsenal of activists like Bandy Kiki. Through her embodiment of authenticity, resilience, and community engagement, Kiki has not only inspired countless individuals to embrace their true selves but has also fostered a culture of activism that prioritizes inclusivity and solidarity. While challenges abound in the pursuit of LGBTQ rights, Kiki's journey illustrates the profound impact that one individual's commitment to leading by example can have on a movement. As the fight for equality continues, the legacy of Bandy Kiki serves as a beacon of hope, reminding us all that courage and authenticity can ignite change in even the most challenging environments.

Challenging societal norms and expectations

Challenging societal norms and expectations is a crucial aspect of personal and collective identity formation within the LGBTQ community. These norms, often deeply rooted in cultural, religious, and historical contexts, dictate how individuals are perceived and treated based on their gender and sexual orientation. The process of questioning and defying these societal constructs is not merely an act of rebellion; it is a profound journey toward authenticity and self-acceptance.

One of the primary theoretical frameworks that can be employed to understand this process is Judith Butler's concept of gender performativity. Butler argues that gender is not an inherent quality but rather a series of repeated performances that conform to societal expectations. This perspective highlights the fluidity of gender and suggests that by altering the performance of gender, individuals can challenge and reshape societal norms. For example, a person who identifies as non-binary may choose to express their identity through androgynous clothing or gender-neutral pronouns, thereby subverting traditional gender binaries. This act of challenging norms not only affirms their identity but also encourages others to reconsider rigid gender classifications.

Moreover, the intersectionality theory, as articulated by Kimberlé Crenshaw, provides a vital lens through which to examine the complexities of identity. Intersectionality posits that individuals experience multiple, overlapping identities that shape their experiences of oppression and privilege. For instance, a queer person of color may face unique challenges that differ from those encountered by white LGBTQ individuals. By advocating for intersectional approaches in activism, individuals can highlight the diverse experiences within the LGBTQ community and challenge the dominant narratives that often marginalize certain voices. This approach fosters a more inclusive dialogue about identity and encourages solidarity among various marginalized groups.

The challenges faced by LGBTQ individuals in challenging societal norms are multifaceted. One significant issue is the backlash from conservative factions within society. For example, in many cultures, the expression of non-heteronormative identities can lead to ostracism, violence, or even legal repercussions. This reality creates a climate of fear that can stifle individuals from living authentically. The case of Bandy Kiki exemplifies this struggle; her journey involved not only personal acceptance but also the courageous act of advocating for change in a society that often views her existence as a threat to traditional values.

In addition to external pressures, internalized homophobia can also impede the process of challenging societal norms. Many LGBTQ individuals grapple with feelings of shame or inadequacy that stem from societal messages that devalue their identities. Overcoming these internalized beliefs requires significant emotional labor and support from affirming communities. For instance, support groups and affirming spaces can provide crucial validation, allowing individuals to embrace their identities fully and challenge the norms that seek to suppress them.

Challenging societal norms also involves creating new narratives around LGBTQ identities. This can be achieved through storytelling, art, and media representation. By sharing personal experiences, LGBTQ individuals can humanize their struggles and triumphs, fostering empathy and understanding in broader society. For example, the rise of queer cinema and literature has played a pivotal role in reshaping public perceptions. Films such as "Moonlight" and books like "The Miseducation of Cameron Post" offer nuanced portrayals of LGBTQ experiences, challenging stereotypes and inviting audiences to engage with complex narratives.

Furthermore, the impact of social media cannot be overlooked in this context. Platforms like Instagram, Twitter, and TikTok have become vital spaces for LGBTQ activism and expression. By leveraging these platforms, individuals can challenge societal norms on a global scale, sharing their stories and connecting with like-minded individuals. The hashtag movements, such as #LoveIsLove and #TransRightsAreHumanRights, have galvanized support for LGBTQ rights, demonstrating the power of collective action in challenging entrenched societal expectations.

In conclusion, challenging societal norms and expectations is a multifaceted process that requires courage, resilience, and support. By employing theoretical frameworks such as gender performativity and intersectionality, LGBTQ individuals can navigate the complexities of their identities while advocating for broader societal change. The journey involves confronting external pressures and internalized beliefs, creating new narratives, and utilizing digital platforms to amplify voices. Ultimately, this ongoing struggle not only empowers individuals but also paves the way for a more inclusive and accepting society.

Embracing self-love and self-empowerment

In the journey of self-acceptance, embracing self-love and self-empowerment emerges as a critical milestone, particularly for individuals navigating the complexities of identity within marginalized communities. Self-love is defined as an appreciation for one's own worth and well-being, while self-empowerment refers to the process of gaining control over one's life and making positive choices that lead to personal growth. Together, they form a powerful foundation for resilience, enabling individuals to confront societal challenges with confidence and authenticity.

Theoretical Framework

Self-love and self-empowerment can be understood through the lens of several psychological theories. One of the most prominent is Maslow's Hierarchy of Needs, which posits that individuals must satisfy basic physiological and safety needs before they can pursue higher-level psychological needs, such as love, esteem, and self-actualization. According to Maslow, self-esteem and self-acceptance are vital for achieving self-actualization, the realization of one's potential and the pursuit of personal growth.

Furthermore, the concept of self-compassion, developed by Kristin Neff, provides a framework for understanding self-love. Neff identifies three core components of self-compassion: self-kindness, common humanity, and mindfulness. Self-kindness encourages individuals to treat themselves with care and understanding rather than harsh judgment. Common humanity emphasizes the shared experience of suffering, reminding individuals that they are not alone in their struggles. Mindfulness involves maintaining a balanced awareness of one's thoughts and feelings without over-identifying with them.

Challenges to Self-Love and Empowerment

Despite the importance of self-love and self-empowerment, many individuals, particularly within the LGBTQ community, face significant barriers. These challenges include:

- **Internalized Homophobia:** The internalization of societal stigma can lead to feelings of shame and self-hatred, hindering the ability to embrace one's identity fully.

- **Social Stigmatization:** Discrimination and prejudice from society can create an environment where self-love feels unattainable. The fear of rejection often prevents individuals from expressing their true selves.

- **Lack of Representation:** The absence of diverse role models in media and public life can perpetuate feelings of isolation and inadequacy among LGBTQ individuals, making it difficult to envision a path toward self-empowerment.

Strategies for Embracing Self-Love

To cultivate self-love, individuals can adopt various strategies that promote a positive self-image and emotional well-being:

1. **Affirmations:** Regularly practicing positive affirmations can help rewire negative thought patterns. For instance, repeating phrases such as "I am worthy of love and respect" can reinforce self-acceptance.

2. **Journaling:** Writing about personal experiences, thoughts, and feelings can facilitate self-reflection and clarity. Journaling allows individuals to process their emotions and recognize their strengths.

3. **Mindfulness Practices:** Engaging in mindfulness meditation or yoga can enhance self-awareness and promote a sense of inner peace. These practices encourage individuals to observe their thoughts without judgment, fostering self-compassion.

Empowerment through Community and Advocacy

Self-empowerment often flourishes within supportive communities. By connecting with others who share similar experiences, individuals can find validation and encouragement. LGBTQ support groups, both online and offline, provide safe spaces for individuals to express themselves authentically and build meaningful relationships.

Moreover, activism can serve as a powerful tool for self-empowerment. Engaging in advocacy allows individuals to reclaim their narratives and contribute to the broader movement for equality. By participating in protests, educational campaigns, or community outreach, individuals not only amplify their voices but also inspire others to embrace their identities.

Real-Life Examples

Consider the story of Marsha P. Johnson, a prominent figure in the LGBTQ rights movement. Johnson's journey of self-love and empowerment began in the face of societal rejection. As a Black transgender woman, she encountered significant challenges, yet she transformed her pain into activism. By co-founding the Street Transvestite Action Revolutionaries (STAR), Johnson created a community that uplifted marginalized voices and fought for the rights of LGBTQ individuals, demonstrating how self-empowerment can lead to collective change.

Another example is the impact of social media on self-acceptance. Platforms like Instagram and TikTok have become spaces for individuals to share their stories, celebrate their identities, and foster connections. Through hashtags like #SelfLove and #LGBTQEmpowerment, countless individuals have found solidarity and inspiration, illustrating the power of digital communities in promoting self-love.

Conclusion

Embracing self-love and self-empowerment is an ongoing journey that requires patience, resilience, and support. By understanding the theoretical underpinnings of these concepts, recognizing the challenges faced by marginalized individuals, and implementing practical strategies, one can cultivate a strong sense of self-worth. Ultimately, self-love and empowerment are not only essential for personal growth but also serve as catalysts for broader societal change, inspiring others to rise up and embrace their authentic selves.

Battling Self-Doubt and Insecurities

Dealing with Rejection and Judgment

Dealing with rejection and judgment is a formidable challenge that many individuals face, particularly within the LGBTQ community. The process of coming to terms with one's identity often intersects with societal expectations and norms, which can lead to feelings of isolation and self-doubt. Understanding the psychological impact of rejection, as well as developing resilience strategies, is crucial for navigating this complex terrain.

The Psychological Impact of Rejection

Rejection can manifest in various forms—social, familial, or institutional—and can significantly affect mental health. According to the *Sociometer Theory* proposed by Leary et al. (1995), self-esteem acts as a gauge of social acceptance. When individuals experience rejection, their self-esteem may plummet, leading to feelings of worthlessness and despair. This phenomenon is particularly pronounced in LGBTQ individuals who may already grapple with internalized homophobia and societal stigma.

$$SE = f(R, C) \qquad (28)$$

Where:

- SE = Self-Esteem
- R = Rejection Experiences
- C = Coping Mechanisms

As rejection experiences increase (R), self-esteem (SE) tends to decrease, unless effective coping mechanisms (C) are employed.

Navigating Judgment and Criticism

Judgment from peers, family, and society can be particularly harsh for LGBTQ individuals. The internalization of negative societal attitudes can lead to a cycle of self-judgment and shame. Research indicates that individuals who anticipate rejection are more likely to withdraw from social interactions, further exacerbating feelings of loneliness (Holt-Lunstad et al., 2010).

$$J = \frac{E}{S} \qquad (29)$$

Where:

- J = Judgment
- E = External Criticism
- S = Self-Perception

As external criticism (E) increases, the impact on self-perception (S) can lead to heightened feelings of judgment (J), creating a negative feedback loop.

Building Resilience Against Rejection

To combat the negative effects of rejection and judgment, it is essential to cultivate resilience. Resilience is defined as the ability to bounce back from adversity, and it can be developed through various strategies:

- **Seeking Support:** Building a network of supportive friends and allies can provide a buffer against rejection. Support groups, both online and offline, can foster a sense of community and belonging.

- **Practicing Self-Compassion:** Engaging in self-compassion practices can help individuals treat themselves with kindness in the face of rejection. Neff's (2003) framework of self-compassion includes self-kindness, common humanity, and mindfulness.

- **Reframing Negative Thoughts:** Cognitive-behavioral techniques can aid in reframing negative thoughts associated with rejection. By challenging irrational beliefs, individuals can develop a more balanced perspective.

Real-Life Examples

Consider the story of Alex, a non-binary activist who faced rejection from their family after coming out. Initially devastated, Alex sought support from local LGBTQ organizations. Through therapy and community engagement, Alex began to rebuild their self-esteem. They learned to embrace their identity and advocate for others, transforming their experience of rejection into a source of strength.

In contrast, another individual, Jamie, encountered judgment from peers at school. Rather than internalizing this judgment, Jamie chose to educate their classmates about LGBTQ issues, fostering understanding and acceptance. This proactive approach not only helped Jamie cope with rejection but also created a more inclusive environment for others.

Conclusion

Dealing with rejection and judgment is an ongoing journey for many in the LGBTQ community. While the impact of rejection can be profound, developing resilience through support, self-compassion, and proactive engagement can empower individuals to navigate these challenges. By understanding the psychological mechanisms at play and implementing effective coping strategies, one can transform rejection into an opportunity for growth and self-acceptance.

Finding strength in vulnerability

In the journey toward self-acceptance, one of the most profound realizations is the notion that vulnerability is not a weakness, but rather a source of strength. This paradigm shift is crucial for individuals, especially within marginalized communities, who often feel pressured to present a facade of invulnerability in the face of societal discrimination and prejudice. Bandy Kiki's experiences illustrate this transformative understanding, revealing how embracing vulnerability can lead to personal empowerment and collective resilience.

Theoretical Framework

The concept of vulnerability has been extensively explored in psychological and sociological literature. Brené Brown, a leading researcher in this field, defines vulnerability as "uncertainty, risk, and emotional exposure" [?]. In her work, she posits that vulnerability is the birthplace of innovation, creativity, and change. This assertion is particularly relevant for individuals like Bandy, who navigate the complexities of their identities within oppressive environments.

Furthermore, vulnerability is closely linked to the idea of authenticity. According to [?], embracing one's true self, including imperfections and insecurities, fosters deeper connections with others. This is especially significant in the context of LGBTQ activism, where personal stories and experiences can galvanize communities and inspire collective action.

Challenges of Embracing Vulnerability

Despite the empowering nature of vulnerability, many individuals face significant barriers to embracing it. Societal norms often dictate that strength is synonymous with stoicism, leading to internalized beliefs that vulnerability equates to weakness. This can manifest in various ways, including:

- **Fear of Judgment:** The fear of being perceived as weak or unworthy can prevent individuals from expressing their true selves. For Bandy, this fear was compounded by the societal stigmatization of LGBTQ identities in Cameroon, where any display of vulnerability could lead to severe repercussions.

- **Internalized Homophobia:** Many LGBTQ individuals grapple with internalized homophobia, which can distort their self-perception and hinder their ability to embrace vulnerability. This internal conflict can create a cycle of shame and self-doubt, further isolating individuals from their authentic selves.

- **Cultural Expectations:** In many cultures, including Cameroonian society, traditional gender roles and expectations can stifle emotional expression. The pressure to conform to these norms often leads to a denial of vulnerability, which can be detrimental to mental health and well-being.

Examples of Strength Through Vulnerability

Bandy's activism serves as a powerful example of how vulnerability can translate into strength. By openly sharing her experiences of coming to terms with her identity, she not only validated her own feelings but also provided a voice for others who felt similarly isolated. This act of sharing is a testament to the strength found in vulnerability.

One poignant instance is when Bandy decided to share her story on social media, despite the potential backlash. In her post, she wrote:

> "I have spent too long hiding parts of myself, fearing rejection and ridicule. Today, I choose to embrace my truth, not just for myself but for those who feel they cannot. Vulnerability is my strength; it is my declaration of existence."

This declaration resonated with many, sparking a wave of support and solidarity within her community. It exemplifies how vulnerability can foster connection, inspire others to share their stories, and create a collective movement toward acceptance.

Building Resilience Through Vulnerability

Embracing vulnerability also plays a crucial role in building resilience. Research indicates that individuals who acknowledge their vulnerabilities are better equipped to cope with adversity [?]. This is particularly relevant for activists like Bandy, who face constant challenges and threats in their pursuit of equality.

By recognizing and accepting her vulnerabilities, Bandy developed a stronger sense of self and a clearer understanding of her purpose. This self-awareness allowed her to navigate the tumultuous landscape of activism with greater confidence. She became adept at transforming her vulnerabilities into powerful narratives that galvanized support and fostered understanding.

Conclusion

In conclusion, finding strength in vulnerability is a vital component of the journey toward self-acceptance and effective activism. For individuals like Bandy Kiki, embracing vulnerability not only enhances personal resilience but also serves as a catalyst for social change. By sharing her truth and encouraging others to do the same, Bandy exemplifies the profound impact that vulnerability can have in the fight for LGBTQ rights. As she continues to advocate for change, her story serves as a reminder that true strength lies in the courage to be vulnerable.

The ongoing journey of self-acceptance

The journey of self-acceptance is rarely linear; it often resembles a winding road filled with both triumphs and setbacks. For many individuals, especially those within the LGBTQ community, this journey is compounded by societal pressures, internal conflicts, and the quest for authenticity. In this section, we will explore the multifaceted nature of self-acceptance, the challenges that arise, and the strategies employed to navigate this ongoing process.

Understanding Self-Acceptance

Self-acceptance can be defined as the recognition and acknowledgment of one's own worth, abilities, and limitations. According to [?], self-acceptance is a crucial component of self-esteem and overall mental well-being. It involves embracing both the positive and negative aspects of oneself without undue self-criticism. In the context of LGBTQ identities, self-acceptance often entails coming to terms with one's sexual orientation or gender identity in a society that may not always be accepting.

The Role of Internalized Homophobia

One of the significant barriers to self-acceptance for LGBTQ individuals is internalized homophobia, a phenomenon where individuals internalize society's negative beliefs about homosexuality. This internal conflict can lead to feelings of shame, guilt, and self-hatred, which inhibit the journey toward self-acceptance. [Meyer(2003)] posits that internalized homophobia can manifest in various ways, including avoidance of same-sex relationships, denial of one's identity, and self-destructive behaviors.

Navigating Societal Pressures

Societal expectations and norms can create additional challenges for those seeking self-acceptance. The pressure to conform to heteronormative standards can lead to a profound sense of alienation. For instance, individuals may feel compelled to hide their true selves to fit in with friends, family, or colleagues. This phenomenon is illustrated in the work of [?], who discusses the impact of societal stigma on LGBTQ individuals' mental health and self-perception.

Building Resilience

Resilience is a vital attribute in the ongoing journey of self-acceptance. [?] emphasizes that resilience is not merely about bouncing back from adversity, but also about personal growth that can emerge from challenging experiences. Developing resilience can involve seeking support from chosen family, engaging with affirming communities, and participating in activism. These strategies can foster a sense of belonging and validation, which are essential for self-acceptance.

The Importance of Self-Compassion

Self-compassion plays a crucial role in the journey toward self-acceptance. According to [?], self-compassion involves treating oneself with kindness, recognizing one's shared humanity, and practicing mindfulness. This approach allows individuals to confront their flaws and mistakes without harsh judgment. For LGBTQ individuals, cultivating self-compassion can mitigate the effects of internalized homophobia and societal rejection, fostering a more accepting relationship with oneself.

Examples of Self-Acceptance Journeys

Consider the story of **Alex**, a non-binary individual who struggled with self-acceptance in a conservative environment. Initially, Alex faced immense pressure to conform to binary gender norms, leading to feelings of isolation and self-doubt. However, through online support groups and LGBTQ advocacy organizations, Alex found a community that celebrated diversity. By embracing their identity and engaging with others, Alex gradually built resilience and self-acceptance.

Another example is **Jordan**, a gay man who experienced significant internalized homophobia during his teenage years. After enduring bullying and rejection, Jordan sought therapy, where he learned to challenge negative beliefs about himself. Through this process, he discovered the power of self-compassion and began to embrace his identity fully. Jordan's journey highlights that self-acceptance is often a gradual process, marked by moments of reflection and growth.

Conclusion

The ongoing journey of self-acceptance is a complex and deeply personal experience for many individuals, particularly within the LGBTQ community. It requires confronting internalized beliefs, navigating societal pressures, and cultivating resilience and self-compassion. While this journey may be fraught with challenges, it is also filled with opportunities for growth, connection, and empowerment. As individuals continue to embrace their authentic selves, they contribute to a broader narrative of acceptance and understanding, paving the way for future generations to embark on their journeys with courage and hope.

Building a support system

Building a robust support system is vital for individuals navigating the often tumultuous waters of self-acceptance and advocacy, particularly within the LGBTQ community. A support system can be defined as a network of individuals who provide emotional, informational, and practical assistance. This network can include family, friends, mentors, and community organizations. The importance of such a system cannot be overstated, as it can significantly impact mental health, resilience, and overall well-being.

Theoretical Framework

The concept of social support is grounded in several psychological theories, including the Stress-Buffering Hypothesis. This hypothesis posits that social support can mitigate the effects of stress by providing emotional comfort and practical assistance. According to Cohen and Wills (1985), social support can be categorized into three types: emotional support, informational support, and instrumental support.

$$\text{Social Support} = \text{Emotional Support} + \text{Informational Support} + \text{Instrumental Support} \tag{30}$$

1. **Emotional Support:** This includes empathy, love, and trust, which are crucial for fostering a sense of belonging and acceptance. 2. **Informational Support:** This type of support provides knowledge and advice, helping individuals

navigate challenges and make informed decisions. 3. **Instrumental Support:** This encompasses tangible assistance, such as financial help or physical resources.

Challenges in Building a Support System

For many LGBTQ individuals, particularly those in hostile environments, building a support system can be fraught with challenges. These challenges may include:
 - **Fear of Rejection:** The risk of being ostracized by family and friends can prevent individuals from seeking support. - **Isolation:** Many LGBTQ individuals may feel isolated in their experiences, leading to a reluctance to reach out for help. - **Cultural Stigmas:** In some cultures, there is a strong stigma attached to being LGBTQ, which can discourage individuals from forming supportive networks.

Examples of Building a Support System

1. **Chosen Family:** Many LGBTQ individuals find solace in creating a "chosen family," a group of friends and allies who provide unconditional support. This concept is especially important for those who may not receive acceptance from their biological families. The chosen family can act as a buffer against societal rejection and foster a sense of belonging.
    2. **Support Groups:** Joining LGBTQ support groups can provide a safe space for sharing experiences and receiving emotional support. For instance, organizations like PFLAG (Parents, Families, and Friends of Lesbians and Gays) offer resources for both LGBTQ individuals and their families, promoting understanding and acceptance.
    3. **Online Communities:** In the digital age, online platforms can serve as vital support systems. Websites and social media groups dedicated to LGBTQ issues allow individuals to connect with others who share similar experiences. These platforms can be particularly beneficial for those in regions where face-to-face support is limited.

Practical Steps to Build a Support System

To effectively build a support system, individuals can take several practical steps:
 - **Identify Supportive Individuals:** Start by identifying people in your life who are understanding and accepting. This could include friends, mentors, or colleagues who have demonstrated empathy and support.

- **Communicate Openly:** Foster open lines of communication with those you trust. Sharing your experiences and feelings can strengthen relationships and encourage others to provide support.
- **Engage in Community Activities:** Participating in local LGBTQ events, such as pride parades or community workshops, can help individuals meet others who share similar values and experiences, thus expanding their support network.
- **Utilize Resources:** Leverage available resources such as counseling services, LGBTQ organizations, and hotlines that offer support and guidance. These resources can provide both emotional and practical assistance.

Conclusion

In conclusion, building a support system is a crucial step in the journey toward self-acceptance and empowerment for LGBTQ individuals. By understanding the theoretical underpinnings of social support, recognizing the challenges faced, and actively seeking out supportive relationships, individuals can cultivate a network that not only enhances their resilience but also fosters a sense of belonging and community. The fight for equality is often best supported by a strong foundation of interpersonal connections that empower individuals to stand firm in their identities and advocate for change.

Celebrating personal achievements and growth

In the journey of self-acceptance and activism, recognizing and celebrating personal achievements is crucial for nurturing resilience and fostering a positive identity. This process not only reinforces self-worth but also serves as a powerful motivator for continued growth and action. For Bandy Kiki, each milestone represented a step towards authenticity and empowerment, both personally and within the broader LGBTQ community.

The Importance of Acknowledgment

Acknowledgment of personal achievements can be framed within the context of positive psychology, which emphasizes the role of positive reinforcement in individual development. According to Seligman (2002), celebrating small victories contributes to a sense of fulfillment and happiness, which is essential for mental health. This principle can be applied to Bandy Kiki's journey, where recognizing her progress in understanding her identity and advocating for LGBTQ rights became a source of strength.

Examples of Personal Achievements

Bandy's path was marked by several significant achievements that deserve celebration:

- **Coming Out:** One of the most pivotal moments in her life was the decision to come out to her friends and family. This act of bravery not only represented her acceptance of her identity but also set the stage for her activism. The courage to be open about her sexuality in a hostile environment was a monumental achievement that inspired others in her community to embrace their true selves.

- **Engaging in Activism:** Transitioning from self-acceptance to activism, Bandy Kiki began organizing local awareness campaigns. Her ability to mobilize people and create a supportive network showcased her leadership skills and commitment to the cause. Each successful event not only raised awareness but also reinforced her identity as an activist, which was a significant personal milestone.

- **Building a Support Network:** Establishing connections with other LGBTQ individuals and allies was another crucial achievement. Bandy's efforts in creating a safe space for discussions around identity and rights allowed her to foster a sense of community. This network provided emotional support and validation, essential for her ongoing growth and resilience.

- **Public Speaking Engagements:** As Bandy became more comfortable in her activism, she began speaking at various events and conferences. Each opportunity to share her story was a celebration of her journey, transforming her from a masked activist to a recognized voice for change. The impact of her words resonated not only with her audience but also within herself, solidifying her role as an advocate.

The Role of Reflection

Reflection plays a vital role in celebrating achievements. By taking the time to look back at her journey, Bandy could recognize the challenges she faced and the resilience she exhibited. This reflective practice aligns with Schön's (1983) theory of reflective practice, which emphasizes learning through experience. Bandy's reflections allowed her to appreciate her growth, recognize her strengths, and identify areas for further development.

Creating Rituals of Celebration

To further reinforce her achievements, Bandy Kiki developed personal rituals of celebration. These rituals could include:

- **Journaling:** Documenting her thoughts and feelings after significant events helped her process experiences and celebrate her growth. Journaling served as a tangible record of her journey, allowing her to revisit moments of triumph and resilience.

- **Sharing with Others:** Bandy often shared her achievements with her support network. This communal celebration not only validated her experiences but also inspired others to acknowledge their own victories, creating a ripple effect of positivity within the community.

- **Setting New Goals:** Each celebration was an opportunity to set new goals, fostering a continuous cycle of growth. By recognizing her achievements, Bandy could identify what she wanted to pursue next, whether it was expanding her activism or deepening her understanding of her identity.

Challenges in Celebrating Achievements

Despite the importance of celebrating achievements, Bandy faced challenges. Internalized self-doubt and societal stigmatization often clouded her ability to recognize her accomplishments. The pressure to conform to societal expectations could lead to feelings of inadequacy, making it difficult to celebrate her growth. However, by embracing vulnerability and leaning on her support network, Bandy learned to combat these challenges.

Conclusion

In conclusion, celebrating personal achievements and growth is a vital aspect of Bandy Kiki's journey. By acknowledging her milestones, engaging in reflective practices, and creating rituals of celebration, she cultivated resilience and a strong sense of identity. Each achievement not only propelled her forward but also inspired others within the LGBTQ community to embrace their own journeys of self-acceptance and activism. As Bandy continues to advocate for change, her ability to celebrate her growth will remain a cornerstone of her unwavering spirit in the fight for equality.

Cultivating Self-Love and Self-Care

Prioritizing mental and emotional well-being

In the journey of activism, particularly within the LGBTQ community, prioritizing mental and emotional well-being is paramount. The intersection of identity, societal pressures, and the often hostile environments faced by activists can lead to significant psychological strain. This section explores the importance of mental health in activism, the challenges faced, and strategies for fostering resilience and self-care.

Understanding Mental Health in Activism

Mental health is defined by the World Health Organization (WHO) as a state of well-being in which every individual realizes their own potential, can cope with the normal stresses of life, can work productively and fruitfully, and is able to contribute to their community. For LGBTQ activists like Bandy Kiki, the pressures of fighting for equality while navigating personal identities can create a unique set of challenges.

Theoretical Frameworks

Several psychological theories can help us understand the mental health challenges faced by LGBTQ activists:

- **Minority Stress Theory** posits that individuals from marginalized groups experience chronic stress due to their social status. This stress can manifest in various ways, including anxiety, depression, and low self-esteem. For activists, the pressure to constantly advocate for change can exacerbate these feelings.

- **Resilience Theory** emphasizes the capacity of individuals to recover from adversity. This theory is particularly relevant for activists who face systemic oppression, as it highlights the importance of coping mechanisms and support systems in maintaining mental health.

Challenges to Mental and Emotional Well-being

Activists often encounter several challenges that can impede their mental health:

- **Burnout:** The emotional and physical exhaustion caused by prolonged stress can lead to burnout, characterized by feelings of cynicism, detachment, and a reduced sense of accomplishment. Activists may find themselves overwhelmed by the constant demands of their work, leading to decreased motivation and effectiveness.

- **Isolation:** Many LGBTQ activists face social isolation, either due to societal rejection or the demands of their activism. This isolation can lead to feelings of loneliness and despair, further impacting mental health.
- **Trauma Exposure:** Activists may be exposed to traumatic events, such as violence against LGBTQ individuals or personal threats. This exposure can lead to conditions such as post-traumatic stress disorder (PTSD), which requires careful management and support.

Strategies for Prioritizing Well-being

To combat these challenges, activists can adopt several strategies to prioritize their mental and emotional well-being:

- **Establishing Boundaries:** Setting clear boundaries between activism and personal life is crucial. This may involve designating specific times for activism and self-care, ensuring that personal time is protected from the demands of advocacy.
- **Seeking Professional Support:** Engaging with mental health professionals who understand the unique challenges faced by LGBTQ individuals can provide valuable support. Therapy can offer a safe space to explore feelings and develop coping strategies.
- **Building a Support Network:** Cultivating relationships with fellow activists and allies can create a sense of community. Support groups can provide emotional backing, shared experiences, and practical advice for managing the stresses of activism.
- **Practicing Self-Care:** Engaging in activities that promote relaxation and joy is essential. This may include hobbies, exercise, meditation, or simply taking time to unwind. Self-care practices can rejuvenate the spirit and enhance resilience.

Examples of Successful Self-Care Practices

Many activists have shared their experiences with self-care, highlighting practices that have helped them maintain their mental health:

- **Mindfulness and Meditation:** Techniques such as mindfulness meditation have been shown to reduce stress and improve emotional regulation. Activists can benefit from incorporating short meditation sessions into their daily routines.

- **Creative Expression:** Engaging in art, writing, or music can serve as a powerful outlet for emotions. Many activists find that creative expression not only helps them process their experiences but also inspires others.

- **Physical Activity:** Regular exercise is known to boost mood and reduce anxiety. Activists can find joy in physical activities, whether through group sports, dance, or individual workouts, reinforcing both physical and mental health.

Conclusion

In conclusion, prioritizing mental and emotional well-being is essential for LGBTQ activists like Bandy Kiki. By understanding the unique challenges they face and implementing effective self-care strategies, activists can cultivate resilience and sustain their efforts in the fight for equality. The journey may be fraught with difficulties, but by fostering a strong foundation of mental health, activists can continue to inspire change and advocate for a more inclusive society.

Building resilience in the face of adversity

Resilience is the ability to adapt and recover from difficult life events, a crucial trait for anyone facing adversity, particularly within marginalized communities. For LGBTQ individuals, the journey often involves navigating societal stigma, discrimination, and personal challenges that can lead to feelings of isolation and despair. Building resilience in the face of such adversity is not merely a personal endeavor; it is a collective necessity that empowers individuals and communities to thrive despite their circumstances.

Theoretical Framework

Psychological resilience can be understood through various theoretical lenses. One prominent model is the **Resilience Theory**, which posits that resilience is influenced by both individual characteristics and environmental factors. According to Rutter (1987), resilience involves a dynamic interplay between risk factors (e.g., discrimination, social isolation) and protective factors (e.g., supportive relationships, community resources).

The equation representing resilience can be simplified as:

$$R = P - R_f$$

Where: - R = Resilience - P = Protective factors (support systems, coping strategies) - R_f = Risk factors (stressors, challenges)

This equation illustrates that resilience can be enhanced by increasing protective factors while minimizing risk factors.

Personal Strategies for Building Resilience

1. **Cultivating a Support Network**: One of the most effective ways to build resilience is to create a strong support network. This network may include friends, family, mentors, and community organizations that understand the unique challenges faced by LGBTQ individuals. Research indicates that social support is a significant protective factor against mental health issues (Cohen & Wills, 1985).

Example: Bandy Kiki, while grappling with her identity, found solace in a local LGBTQ support group. This group not only provided emotional support but also practical resources for navigating societal challenges.

2. **Developing Coping Mechanisms**: Effective coping strategies are essential for resilience. Techniques such as mindfulness, cognitive-behavioral strategies, and stress management can help individuals process their experiences and mitigate the effects of adversity.

Example: Mindfulness meditation has been shown to reduce anxiety and increase emotional regulation (Kabat-Zinn, 2003). Bandy practiced mindfulness to maintain her mental well-being during tumultuous times, allowing her to respond to challenges with clarity and composure.

3. **Fostering a Sense of Purpose**: Engaging in activism and community service can instill a sense of purpose, which is a powerful motivator for resilience. When individuals contribute to a cause greater than themselves, they often find strength and motivation to overcome personal adversities.

Example: Bandy's commitment to LGBTQ rights fueled her resilience. Her activism not only empowered others but also reinforced her identity and purpose, making her more resilient in the face of discrimination.

Community-Based Approaches to Resilience

Building resilience is not solely an individual effort; it requires a community-based approach that addresses systemic issues affecting LGBTQ individuals. Communities can foster resilience through:

1. **Creating Safe Spaces**: Establishing safe spaces for LGBTQ individuals to express themselves without fear of judgment or persecution is crucial. These spaces promote acceptance and understanding, allowing individuals to build connections and share experiences.

2. **Advocacy and Policy Change**: Communities can work towards changing discriminatory laws and policies that contribute to adversity. Advocacy efforts can lead to systemic changes that create a more supportive environment for LGBTQ individuals.

3. **Education and Awareness**: Raising awareness about LGBTQ issues and promoting education within broader society can challenge stereotypes and reduce stigma. Education serves as a powerful tool for fostering empathy and understanding, which are essential for community resilience.

Conclusion

Building resilience in the face of adversity is a multifaceted process that involves individual efforts and community support. By cultivating strong support networks, developing coping mechanisms, and fostering a sense of purpose, LGBTQ individuals can navigate the challenges they face with greater strength and determination. Furthermore, community-based approaches that create safe spaces, advocate for policy change, and promote education are vital in building a resilient society where all individuals can thrive.

In the words of Bandy Kiki, "Resilience is not just about surviving; it's about thriving in a world that often tries to bring us down." This ethos encapsulates the spirit of resilience that empowers LGBTQ individuals to rise above adversity and advocate for a brighter future.

Practicing self-compassion and self-affirmation

In the journey toward self-acceptance, the practice of self-compassion and self-affirmation emerges as a vital component. Self-compassion, as defined by Kristin Neff, involves treating oneself with kindness during times of suffering or perceived inadequacy, rather than with harsh judgment. This concept is particularly relevant for individuals in the LGBTQ community, who often face societal stigma and discrimination, leading to internalized negative beliefs about themselves.

The Theory of Self-Compassion

Self-compassion is grounded in three core components:

- **Self-kindness:** This involves being warm and understanding toward oneself when encountering pain or failure, rather than being harshly critical.
- **Common humanity:** Recognizing that suffering and personal inadequacy are part of the shared human experience, thus fostering a sense of connection with others.
- **Mindfulness:** Holding painful thoughts and feelings in balanced awareness rather than over-identifying with them.

Research indicates that self-compassion correlates with higher levels of emotional well-being, resilience, and life satisfaction. In contrast, self-criticism can lead to increased anxiety and depression, particularly in marginalized groups who may already be grappling with external pressures.

Problems Faced by LGBTQ Individuals

Many LGBTQ individuals experience unique challenges that can hinder their ability to practice self-compassion. These include:

- **Internalized Homophobia:** Negative societal attitudes toward LGBTQ identities can lead individuals to internalize these beliefs, resulting in self-hatred and shame.
- **Fear of Rejection:** Concerns about acceptance from family, friends, and society can create barriers to self-affirmation and self-love.
- **Social Isolation:** The lack of supportive communities can exacerbate feelings of loneliness and inadequacy.

These issues highlight the importance of cultivating self-compassion as a countermeasure to the negative effects of discrimination and societal rejection.

Self-Affirmation Techniques

Self-affirmation involves recognizing and asserting one's self-worth and values, particularly in the face of adversity. Here are several techniques that can be employed:

1. **Affirmative Statements:** Developing a set of positive affirmations that resonate with personal values can reinforce self-worth. For example, repeating phrases such as "I am worthy of love and respect" or "My identity is valid and important" can be powerful tools for self-affirmation.

2. **Journaling:** Keeping a journal focused on positive experiences, achievements, and personal strengths can help shift the focus away from self-criticism. Writing about moments of pride in one's identity can foster a greater sense of self-acceptance.

3. **Mindfulness Meditation:** Engaging in mindfulness practices can help individuals observe their thoughts without judgment, allowing them to cultivate self-compassion. Techniques such as loving-kindness meditation encourage participants to direct kind thoughts toward themselves and others.

4. **Support Networks:** Building connections with supportive friends, allies, and LGBTQ groups can provide a sense of belonging and affirmation. Sharing experiences within these communities can reinforce the understanding that one is not alone in their struggles.

Examples of Self-Compassion in Action

Consider the case of Alex, a young non-binary individual who faced significant challenges in their journey of self-acceptance. Initially overwhelmed by societal expectations and internalized shame, Alex began practicing self-compassion through mindfulness meditation and journaling. They created a daily affirmation ritual, repeating positive statements about their identity and worth.

Over time, Alex noticed a shift in their self-perception. Instead of focusing on perceived flaws, they began to celebrate their uniqueness and resilience. This newfound self-compassion allowed Alex to engage more authentically with their community, inspiring others to embrace their identities without fear.

Conclusion

Practicing self-compassion and self-affirmation is essential for individuals navigating the complexities of identity, especially within marginalized communities. By fostering a kinder inner dialogue and recognizing the shared human experience of struggle, individuals can cultivate resilience and a deeper sense of self-worth. As Bandy Kiki exemplifies, embracing one's identity and advocating for LGBTQ rights begins with the powerful act of loving oneself. Through self-compassion and affirmation, individuals can not only transform their internal landscapes but also inspire others to embark on their journeys toward acceptance and empowerment.

Aligning personal values with activism

In the journey of activism, aligning personal values with the broader goals of social justice is not merely an optional endeavor; it is an essential component that fuels the passion and effectiveness of an activist. Personal values serve as the compass that guides an individual's actions, decisions, and interactions within the activist community and beyond. This alignment creates a deeper sense of purpose and authenticity, allowing activists to advocate for causes that resonate with their core beliefs.

Understanding Personal Values

To effectively align personal values with activism, it is crucial first to understand what personal values are. Personal values are the fundamental beliefs and principles that shape an individual's behavior and decision-making processes. They can include ideals such as integrity, empathy, justice, equality, and respect for diversity. Engaging in self-reflection can help activists identify their core values, leading to a more authentic and impactful approach to activism.

$$\text{Values Alignment} = \frac{\text{Personal Values} + \text{Activism Goals}}{\text{Authenticity}} \tag{31}$$

This equation illustrates that values alignment is a function of both personal values and activism goals, moderated by the level of authenticity. The higher the authenticity, the stronger the alignment, leading to more effective activism.

Challenges in Alignment

While the alignment of personal values with activism is vital, it is not without its challenges. Activists often face societal pressures, internal conflicts, and external expectations that can complicate this alignment. For example, an activist may deeply value inclusivity but find themselves in a movement that prioritizes certain identities over others, leading to feelings of dissonance and frustration.

Moreover, the intersectionality of identities can create complex situations where personal values may conflict with the goals of a particular movement. For instance, a queer activist may struggle to reconcile their commitment to LGBTQ rights with the need to advocate for racial justice, especially if the two movements appear to be at odds within their community.

Strategies for Alignment

To overcome these challenges, activists can employ several strategies to ensure their personal values align with their activism.

- **Engage in Continuous Reflection:** Regular self-assessment and reflection can help activists stay attuned to their values and how they manifest in their work. Journaling, meditation, and discussions with peers can facilitate this process.

- **Seek Diverse Perspectives:** Engaging with a variety of voices within the activist community can help broaden understanding and highlight the interconnectedness of different struggles. This can lead to a more nuanced approach to activism that honors multiple identities and experiences.

- **Set Clear Intentions:** Clearly defining the intentions behind one's activism can help maintain focus on personal values. Activists should ask themselves questions like, "What do I hope to achieve?" and "How does this align with my values of justice and equality?"

- **Embrace Flexibility:** Activism is an evolving field, and being open to adapting one's approach can help align personal values with the changing landscape of social justice work. This flexibility allows for growth and responsiveness to new challenges.

Examples of Values Alignment

Numerous activists exemplify the successful alignment of personal values with their advocacy work. For instance, Marsha P. Johnson, a prominent figure in the LGBTQ rights movement, exemplified the value of inclusivity through her work with the Stonewall uprising and her founding of the Street Transvestite Action Revolutionaries (STAR). Johnson's commitment to uplifting marginalized voices within the LGBTQ community, particularly those of transgender individuals and people of color, showcased her deep-rooted values of equality and justice.

Similarly, contemporary activists like Laverne Cox have leveraged their platforms to advocate for transgender rights while emphasizing the importance of intersectionality. Cox's work demonstrates how personal experiences and values can shape a powerful narrative that resonates with a broad audience, fostering a collective movement for change.

The Impact of Alignment on Activism

When personal values align with activism, the impact can be profound. Activists who operate from a place of authenticity are more likely to inspire others, build coalitions, and create sustainable change. This alignment fosters resilience, as activists feel a deeper connection to their work and are more motivated to face the challenges that arise.

Moreover, aligned activism can lead to a more inclusive and holistic approach to social justice. By honoring personal values, activists can create spaces that welcome diverse perspectives and experiences, ultimately enriching the movement as a whole.

Conclusion

In conclusion, aligning personal values with activism is a crucial element that enhances the authenticity and effectiveness of social justice work. While challenges may arise, employing strategies such as continuous reflection, seeking diverse perspectives, setting clear intentions, and embracing flexibility can facilitate this alignment. The examples of influential activists serve as a testament to the power of values-driven activism, illustrating that when individuals advocate from a place of authenticity, they can inspire transformative change in their communities and beyond.

Inspiring others to love and care for themselves

In a world that often imposes rigid standards and expectations, the journey towards self-love and self-care can feel like a radical act of defiance. This is particularly true for marginalized communities, where the fight for identity and acceptance can overshadow personal well-being. Bandy Kiki, through her activism, exemplifies how one can inspire others to embark on their own journeys of self-acceptance and self-care, fostering a culture of love that transcends societal limitations.

At the heart of this mission lies the principle of **self-affirmation**. Self-affirmation theory posits that individuals are motivated to maintain their self-integrity, which can be threatened by negative feedback or social stigma. By promoting self-love, Bandy encourages individuals to recognize their inherent worth despite external pressures. This can be articulated through the equation:

$$\text{Self-Worth} = \text{Intrinsic Value} - \text{External Validation} \tag{32}$$

Here, Intrinsic Value represents the inherent qualities and identities that make each individual unique, while External Validation reflects societal judgments that often undermine self-worth. By minimizing the impact of external validation, individuals can focus on nurturing their intrinsic value, leading to greater self-acceptance.

Bandy's approach to inspiring self-love is multifaceted, encompassing various strategies that resonate with diverse audiences. One effective method is through **storytelling**. By sharing her own experiences of struggle and triumph, she creates a relatable narrative that encourages others to reflect on their journeys. For instance, she might recount moments of vulnerability, such as navigating her identity in a hostile environment, emphasizing how these experiences shaped her understanding of self-worth.

Moreover, Bandy harnesses the power of **community building**. Establishing safe spaces for individuals to express themselves fosters a sense of belonging and acceptance. In these spaces, participants can share their stories, challenges, and victories, reinforcing the notion that they are not alone in their struggles. This collective experience serves as a powerful reminder that self-love is not a solitary endeavor but a shared journey.

The role of social media in promoting self-love cannot be overstated. Bandy utilizes platforms like Instagram and Twitter to disseminate messages of empowerment, often using hashtags like #SelfLove and #QueerJoy to reach a broader audience. This digital activism creates a ripple effect, encouraging individuals to share their own stories of self-acceptance and self-care.

In her posts, Bandy emphasizes practical self-care strategies, such as mindfulness practices, journaling, and engaging in creative outlets. For example, she might share a post about the benefits of journaling, highlighting how writing can serve as a therapeutic tool for processing emotions and reflecting on personal growth. This aligns with the psychological concept of **expressive writing**, which has been shown to improve mental health outcomes by allowing individuals to articulate their thoughts and feelings.

Furthermore, Bandy advocates for the importance of **self-compassion**. Research indicates that self-compassion—defined as treating oneself with kindness during times of suffering—can significantly enhance emotional resilience. By encouraging individuals to practice self-compassion, Bandy helps them cultivate a nurturing internal dialogue, replacing self-criticism with understanding and support. This can be mathematically represented as:

$$\text{Emotional Resilience} = \text{Self-Compassion} + \text{Supportive Community} \quad (33)$$

Here, both self-compassion and a supportive community contribute to an individual's emotional resilience, highlighting the interconnectedness of personal and communal healing.

Bandy's activism also emphasizes the significance of **intersectionality** in self-love. Recognizing that individuals experience multiple identities (e.g., race, gender, sexuality) that intersect to shape their experiences of oppression and privilege is crucial. By advocating for an inclusive definition of self-love that acknowledges these complexities, Bandy inspires individuals from various backgrounds to embrace their multifaceted identities. This approach not only validates diverse experiences but also fosters solidarity within the LGBTQ community.

In conclusion, Bandy Kiki's commitment to inspiring others to love and care for themselves serves as a beacon of hope in a world often marked by discrimination and marginalization. Through storytelling, community building, social media engagement, and the promotion of self-compassion, she empowers individuals to embark on their own journeys of self-acceptance. By emphasizing the importance of intrinsic value over external validation, Bandy not only fosters a culture of self-love but also contributes to a broader movement for LGBTQ rights and acceptance. The impact of her work extends far beyond individual transformation; it cultivates a collective consciousness that celebrates diversity, resilience, and the beauty of self-expression.

$$\text{Collective Empowerment} = \text{Individual Self-Love} + \text{Community Support} \quad (34)$$

The Fight for Equality

The Fight for Equality

The Fight for Equality

The fight for equality is a multifaceted struggle that encompasses various dimensions of human rights, particularly within the LGBTQ community. In this chapter, we delve into the intricacies of advocating for LGBTQ rights in Cameroon, a country where societal norms and legal frameworks often clash with the pursuit of equality. This section will explore the historical context, the challenges faced by activists, and the strategies employed in the fight against discrimination.

Advocating for LGBTQ Rights in Cameroon

In Cameroon, the legal landscape is starkly unfavorable for LGBTQ individuals. Same-sex relationships are criminalized under Section 347 bis of the Penal Code, which states:

$$\text{Punishment for Same-Sex Relations} = 5 \text{ to } 10 \text{ years imprisonment} \tag{35}$$

This legal framework not only legitimizes discrimination but also fuels societal stigma, leading to widespread violence and persecution against LGBTQ individuals. Activists like Bandy Kiki have emerged as crucial voices in this oppressive environment, challenging the status quo and advocating for change.

The fight for equality in Cameroon is often met with significant resistance. Activists face threats of violence, arrest, and social ostracism. For instance, a 2019 report by Human Rights Watch highlighted the arrest of several LGBTQ activists during a peaceful demonstration, illustrating the dangers inherent in advocating for rights in a hostile environment.

Challenging Discriminatory Laws and Policies

Challenging discriminatory laws requires not only courage but also strategic planning. Activists employ various methods, including legal challenges, public awareness campaigns, and international advocacy to combat oppressive laws. One notable example is the collaboration between local NGOs and international human rights organizations to document cases of abuse and bring them to the attention of global bodies such as the United Nations.

The theory of *strategic litigation* has been pivotal in this context. This approach involves using the courts to challenge unjust laws and set legal precedents that can benefit the wider community. For example, in 2018, a coalition of activists filed a case against the Cameroonian government for violating the rights of LGBTQ individuals, arguing that the criminalization of same-sex relationships is a violation of fundamental human rights as outlined in the African Charter on Human and Peoples' Rights.

Amplifying Marginalized Voices

A critical aspect of the fight for equality is amplifying the voices of those most affected by discrimination. Activists have utilized social media platforms to share personal stories, raise awareness, and foster solidarity within the LGBTQ community. This digital activism not only provides a safe space for expression but also mobilizes support from allies around the world.

For instance, the hashtag #FreeCameroonLGBTQ gained traction on platforms like Twitter and Instagram, drawing international attention to the plight of LGBTQ individuals in Cameroon. This global solidarity has been instrumental in pressuring the Cameroonian government to reconsider its stance on LGBTQ rights.

Organizing Protests and Demonstrations

Organizing protests and demonstrations serves as a powerful tool for visibility and advocacy. Despite the risks involved, activists have bravely taken to the streets to demand their rights. These gatherings often serve as a platform for community building, allowing individuals to connect and share their experiences.

One poignant example occurred in 2020 when a group of activists organized a silent protest in Yaoundé, the capital city. The event aimed to honor the memory of those lost to violence and discrimination while demanding justice and equality. Such demonstrations not only raise awareness but also challenge the narrative that LGBTQ individuals should remain silent or hidden.

Fighting for Equal Rights and Representation

The fight for equality extends beyond legal recognition; it encompasses the need for representation in all spheres of society. Activists advocate for policies that promote inclusivity in education, healthcare, and employment. The theory of *intersectionality* is particularly relevant here, as it recognizes that individuals experience discrimination based on multiple identities, including race, gender, and sexual orientation.

For example, Bandy Kiki's activism emphasizes the importance of considering the experiences of marginalized groups within the LGBTQ community, such as transgender individuals and those living with HIV/AIDS. By addressing these intersections, activists can create a more comprehensive approach to advocacy that fosters genuine equality for all.

In conclusion, the fight for equality in Cameroon is a courageous and ongoing battle against deeply entrenched societal norms and legal barriers. Through strategic advocacy, coalition-building, and the amplification of marginalized voices, activists like Bandy Kiki are paving the way for a more inclusive and just society. The journey is fraught with challenges, but the resilience and determination of those involved serve as a beacon of hope in the quest for LGBTQ rights.

Taking a Stand against Discrimination

Advocating for LGBTQ rights in Cameroon

In Cameroon, the struggle for LGBTQ rights is not just a matter of personal identity; it is a complex interplay of cultural, legal, and social dynamics that create a hostile environment for individuals who identify as LGBTQ. The advocacy for these rights is rooted in the urgent need to challenge oppressive laws and societal norms that perpetuate discrimination and violence against LGBTQ individuals. This section delves into the key aspects of advocating for LGBTQ rights in Cameroon, highlighting the challenges faced by activists, the theoretical frameworks that guide their efforts, and the importance of collective action.

The Legal Framework

Cameroon is one of the few countries in Africa where homosexuality is criminalized. The penal code, specifically Article 347 bis, imposes a punishment of up to five years in prison for consensual same-sex relationships. This legal framework not only criminalizes LGBTQ identities but also legitimizes discrimination and violence against individuals based on their sexual orientation. Activists argue that the existence of such laws creates a culture of fear and silence, making it imperative to advocate for legal reform.

The theory of *legal positivism* can be applied here, which posits that laws are rules created by human beings and that there is no inherent connection between law and morality. Advocates for LGBTQ rights in Cameroon challenge this notion by arguing that laws should reflect moral values that promote equality and human dignity. They aim to demonstrate that the criminalization of homosexuality violates fundamental human rights as outlined in international treaties to which Cameroon is a signatory, such as the Universal Declaration of Human Rights.

Cultural Challenges

Culturally, Cameroon is characterized by deeply entrenched patriarchal norms and conservative values that view homosexuality as a taboo. The stigma attached to LGBTQ identities often leads to social ostracism, family rejection, and violence. Activists face significant challenges in advocating for change in such an environment. The theory of *cultural hegemony*, as proposed by Antonio Gramsci, can help explain the dominance of heteronormative values in Cameroonian society. This theory suggests that the ruling class's ideologies become the accepted cultural norms, marginalizing alternative identities and perspectives.

To combat this cultural hegemony, LGBTQ activists employ various strategies, including community education and awareness campaigns aimed at challenging stereotypes and misconceptions about LGBTQ individuals. For example, initiatives such as workshops and public forums are organized to foster dialogue and understanding within communities, emphasizing the shared humanity of all individuals, regardless of sexual orientation.

Building Alliances

Advocating for LGBTQ rights in Cameroon requires building alliances with various stakeholders, including human rights organizations, religious groups, and political entities. This coalition-building is crucial for amplifying the voices of marginalized communities and creating a unified front against discrimination. The concept of *intersectionality*, coined by Kimberlé Crenshaw, is particularly relevant here, as it underscores the importance of addressing the interconnected nature of social categorizations such as race, class, and gender, which can compound the discrimination faced by LGBTQ individuals.

For instance, partnerships with women's rights organizations have proven effective in advocating for broader human rights issues, highlighting the shared struggles of different marginalized groups. Collaborative efforts have led to joint campaigns that address not only LGBTQ rights but also gender equality and social justice, thereby fostering a more inclusive movement.

Utilizing Digital Activism

In the digital age, social media has emerged as a powerful tool for advocacy, allowing activists to bypass traditional media censorship and reach a global audience. Platforms like Twitter, Facebook, and Instagram serve as spaces for raising awareness, sharing personal stories, and mobilizing support. The theory of *networked activism* illustrates how digital networks can facilitate collective action and empower individuals to engage in advocacy without the constraints of physical boundaries.

For example, the hashtag campaigns such as #FreeTheGays and #StandWithLGBTQ have gained traction, drawing international attention to the plight of LGBTQ individuals in Cameroon. These digital movements not only raise awareness but also create a sense of solidarity among activists and allies worldwide, reinforcing the notion that the fight for LGBTQ rights is a global struggle.

Challenges and Risks

Despite the progress made through advocacy efforts, LGBTQ activists in Cameroon face significant risks, including harassment, violence, and imprisonment. The societal backlash against LGBTQ visibility often manifests in violent acts, creating an environment where activists must navigate their work with caution. The theory of *risk society*, as articulated by Ulrich Beck, is pertinent here, as it highlights the increasing prevalence of risks in modern societies, particularly those associated with social movements.

Activists must employ strategies to mitigate these risks, such as using pseudonyms, engaging in anonymous activism, and prioritizing personal safety. The need for a supportive network is crucial, as it provides a buffer against the dangers associated with advocating for LGBTQ rights in a hostile environment.

Conclusion

Advocating for LGBTQ rights in Cameroon is a multifaceted endeavor that requires a deep understanding of the legal, cultural, and social contexts in which activism occurs. By challenging oppressive laws, dismantling cultural hegemony, building alliances, utilizing digital platforms, and navigating risks, activists are forging a path toward greater acceptance and equality. The fight for LGBTQ rights in Cameroon is not merely a local struggle; it is part of a broader global movement for human rights and social justice, underscoring the interconnectedness of all individuals in the quest for dignity and respect.

Challenging discriminatory laws and policies

In the fight for LGBTQ rights, challenging discriminatory laws and policies is paramount. These legal frameworks often serve as the backbone of societal stigma, institutionalizing prejudice and making it difficult for individuals to live authentically. In Cameroon, the legal landscape is particularly harsh, with laws that criminalize same-sex relationships and perpetuate discrimination against LGBTQ individuals.

Understanding the Legal Framework

The legal framework in Cameroon is influenced by colonial-era laws that have been retained post-independence. Specifically, *Article 347 bis* of the Cameroonian Penal Code criminalizes same-sex sexual relations, imposing a penalty of up to five years in prison. This law not only criminalizes LGBTQ identities but also fuels a culture of fear, making it difficult for individuals to express their sexual orientation or gender identity openly.

The theoretical underpinning of such laws can be analyzed through the lens of **Critical Legal Studies**, which posits that law is not a neutral arbiter but rather a tool of power that reflects and enforces societal norms. In this context, discriminatory laws serve to marginalize LGBTQ individuals, reinforcing existing power structures that prioritize heteronormativity.

Identifying Discriminatory Policies

Challenging discriminatory laws requires a comprehensive understanding of the policies that uphold systemic discrimination. In addition to criminalization, several policies contribute to the disenfranchisement of LGBTQ individuals, including:

- **Employment Discrimination:** Many LGBTQ individuals face job insecurity and discrimination in the workplace due to their sexual orientation or gender identity. This is often exacerbated by the lack of legal protections against discrimination.

- **Access to Healthcare:** Discriminatory policies can lead to inadequate healthcare access for LGBTQ individuals, who may be denied care or face stigma when seeking medical assistance.

- **Education Policies:** Anti-LGBTQ rhetoric in educational settings can lead to a hostile environment for LGBTQ students, resulting in bullying and exclusion from school activities.

Strategies for Challenging Discriminatory Laws

Activists like Bandy Kiki have employed various strategies to challenge these discriminatory laws and policies. These include:

1. **Legal Advocacy:** Engaging with legal experts to challenge discriminatory laws in court. This involves filing lawsuits that highlight the unconstitutionality of such laws and advocating for legal reforms.

2. **Public Awareness Campaigns:** Utilizing social media and grassroots movements to raise awareness about the negative impacts of discriminatory laws. Campaigns often include personal testimonies from those affected, which humanizes the issue and fosters empathy.

3. **Coalition Building:** Forming alliances with other human rights organizations to amplify the call for legal reforms. Collaborating with diverse groups strengthens the movement and creates a unified front against discrimination.

4. **Engaging International Bodies:** Leveraging international human rights frameworks to pressure the Cameroonian government to repeal discriminatory laws. This can involve submitting reports to organizations like the United Nations and participating in international advocacy.

Case Studies and Examples

Several notable cases illustrate the challenges and successes in combating discriminatory laws:

- **The Case of Eric Lembembe:** In 2013, the murder of Eric Lembembe, a prominent LGBTQ activist, highlighted the dangers faced by those challenging the status quo. His death galvanized the LGBTQ community and allies, leading to increased advocacy for legal reforms.

- **The 2019 Court Case:** A landmark case in 2019 saw activists challenge the constitutionality of Article 347 bis. Although the court ruled against the plaintiffs, the case drew significant international attention, prompting discussions about human rights in Cameroon.

The Role of International Pressure

International pressure plays a crucial role in challenging discriminatory laws. Organizations such as Human Rights Watch and Amnesty International have documented abuses against LGBTQ individuals in Cameroon, using their findings to advocate for policy changes. The involvement of international bodies can lead to sanctions or diplomatic pressure that compels the Cameroonian government to reconsider its stance on LGBTQ rights.

Conclusion

Challenging discriminatory laws and policies is an ongoing struggle that requires resilience, creativity, and solidarity. Activists like Bandy Kiki exemplify the courage needed to confront oppressive legal frameworks. By employing a multifaceted approach that includes legal advocacy, public awareness campaigns, and international pressure, the LGBTQ movement in Cameroon continues to fight for a more just and equitable society. The journey is fraught with challenges, but the potential for change remains, fueled by the unwavering spirit of those who dare to dream of equality.

Amplifying marginalized voices

In the fight for LGBTQ rights, amplifying marginalized voices is not merely an act of solidarity; it is a fundamental principle rooted in the very essence of social justice. The concept of amplifying voices refers to elevating the perspectives and experiences of those who have historically been silenced or ignored, particularly individuals from marginalized communities. This section explores the importance of this practice, the theoretical frameworks that support it, the challenges faced in its implementation, and real-world examples of successful amplification.

Theoretical Frameworks

The theoretical underpinnings of amplifying marginalized voices can be traced back to critical theory, particularly the works of scholars such as Paulo Freire and bell hooks. Freire's concept of *conscientization* emphasizes the importance of raising consciousness among oppressed groups, enabling them to articulate their realities and advocate for their rights. In his seminal work, *Pedagogy of the Oppressed*, Freire argues that true liberation comes from the empowerment of the oppressed through dialogue and critical reflection.

Similarly, bell hooks emphasizes the necessity of inclusivity in feminist discourse, asserting that the voices of women of color and LGBTQ individuals must be central to any movement for social change. In her book, *Feminism is for Everybody*, hooks states, "Life-transforming ideas have always come to me through the voices of those who have been marginalized." This highlights the need for movements to not only include but prioritize the narratives of those most affected by systemic injustices.

Challenges in Amplification

Despite the clear necessity of amplifying marginalized voices, several challenges persist. One significant issue is the risk of tokenization, where marginalized individuals are included in discussions or campaigns merely to fulfill diversity quotas without genuine engagement or support. This often leads to a superficial representation that does not translate into meaningful change.

Additionally, societal power dynamics play a critical role in the amplification process. The dominant narratives often overshadow marginalized perspectives, making it challenging for those voices to gain traction. This is compounded by the prevalence of systemic inequalities, including racism, sexism, and homophobia, which can further silence marginalized groups.

The issue of accessibility also poses a barrier. Not all marginalized individuals have equal access to platforms for their voices to be heard, whether due to economic constraints, lack of technological resources, or social networks that do not support their participation.

Real-World Examples

Despite these challenges, there have been numerous successful examples of amplifying marginalized voices within the LGBTQ rights movement. One notable instance is the work of the *Black Lives Matter* movement, which has effectively integrated LGBTQ issues into its broader agenda. By centering the voices of Black LGBTQ individuals, the movement has highlighted the intersectionality of race and sexuality, advocating for policies that address the unique challenges faced by these communities.

Another example is the annual *Transgender Day of Remembrance*, which honors the lives of transgender individuals who have been killed due to anti-transgender violence. This event not only memorializes those lost but also amplifies the voices of transgender individuals, particularly those from marginalized backgrounds, by sharing their stories and experiences.

Social media platforms have also emerged as powerful tools for amplifying marginalized voices. Activists like *Bandy Kiki* have utilized platforms such as Twitter and Instagram to share personal narratives, advocate for policy changes, and create community support networks. The hashtag #TransIsBeautiful, for instance, has been instrumental in promoting the visibility of transgender individuals and challenging societal norms surrounding gender identity.

Conclusion

Amplifying marginalized voices is essential in the pursuit of LGBTQ rights and social justice as a whole. By grounding this practice in critical theory and addressing the challenges that arise, activists can create a more inclusive movement that genuinely reflects the diverse experiences of all individuals. The examples of successful amplification demonstrate that when marginalized voices are heard and valued, they have the power to inspire change, foster resilience, and build solidarity across communities. As we continue to navigate the complexities of activism in the digital age, it is crucial to remember that amplifying voices is not just an act of advocacy; it is a pathway to liberation for all marginalized individuals.

Organizing protests and demonstrations

Organizing protests and demonstrations is a fundamental aspect of activism, particularly for marginalized communities fighting for their rights. For Bandy Kiki and the LGBTQ community in Cameroon, it was not only a means of expressing dissent but also a powerful tool for raising awareness and mobilizing support. This section explores the theory behind organizing protests, the challenges faced, and the successful examples that emerged from their efforts.

Theoretical Framework

The theory of collective action provides a foundation for understanding why and how protests occur. According to [?], collective action arises when individuals come together to pursue common goals, often in response to perceived injustices. Theories such as the Resource Mobilization Theory emphasize the importance of resources—both material and social—in organizing effective protests. This includes funding, communication tools, and a network of supporters.

$$P = f(R, O, A) \qquad (36)$$

Where P is the probability of a successful protest, R represents resources, O denotes organization, and A signifies the level of activism among participants.

Challenges in Organizing Protests

In Cameroon, organizing protests for LGBTQ rights is fraught with challenges due to the oppressive legal environment and societal stigma. The legal system criminalizes same-sex relationships, creating a hostile atmosphere for activists. As articulated by [?], activists often face repression, which can lead to fear and reluctance among potential participants.

$$D = f(L, S, F) \qquad (37)$$

Where D is the degree of difficulty in organizing protests, L represents legal constraints, S denotes social stigma, and F signifies fear of repercussions.

Activists must navigate these challenges carefully, often employing creative strategies to ensure safety while still making their voices heard. For instance, Bandy Kiki utilized clandestine meetings and secure communication channels to organize protests, ensuring that participants felt safe and empowered.

Successful Examples of Protests

Despite the challenges, Bandy Kiki and her allies successfully organized several protests that garnered significant attention. One notable example was the "March for Equality," which took place in Douala. This event aimed to highlight the discrimination faced by LGBTQ individuals and to demand legal reforms.

The protest was meticulously planned, involving:

- **Strategic Timing:** Choosing a date that coincided with International Day Against Homophobia, Transphobia, and Biphobia to maximize visibility.

- **Coalition Building:** Collaborating with local NGOs and international human rights organizations to amplify their message.

- **Media Engagement:** Inviting journalists to cover the event, ensuring that the stories of LGBTQ individuals were told widely.

The success of the March for Equality was evident not only in the number of participants but also in the media coverage it received, which helped shift public perception and raise awareness about LGBTQ issues in Cameroon.

Impact of Protests

Protests serve multiple purposes in the context of activism. They create a visible presence and demonstrate solidarity among marginalized groups. Additionally, they can influence public opinion and pressure policymakers to enact change. As argued by [?], the visibility of protests can lead to increased media coverage, which is essential for raising awareness about social issues.

The protests organized by Bandy Kiki and her peers contributed to a growing discourse surrounding LGBTQ rights in Cameroon, challenging entrenched stereotypes and fostering a sense of community among LGBTQ individuals. This was particularly important in a society where isolation and fear often prevail.

Conclusion

Organizing protests and demonstrations is a vital component of the struggle for LGBTQ rights in Cameroon. Through strategic planning, coalition building, and effective communication, activists like Bandy Kiki have managed to create impactful movements that challenge societal norms and advocate for change. The theory of collective action, coupled with an understanding of the unique challenges faced in Cameroon, underscores the importance of resilience and innovation in the fight for equality.

Fighting for equal rights and representation

The struggle for equal rights and representation for LGBTQ individuals in Cameroon is a multifaceted battle that encompasses legal, social, and cultural dimensions. At its core, the fight for equality is grounded in the principles of human rights, which assert that all individuals, regardless of their sexual orientation or gender identity, deserve the same rights and protections under the law. This section explores the various strategies employed by activists like Bandy Kiki, the challenges faced in the pursuit of equality, and the broader implications of this struggle for the LGBTQ community in Cameroon.

Legal Framework and Challenges

In Cameroon, the legal framework surrounding LGBTQ rights is starkly oppressive. The Penal Code criminalizes same-sex relationships, subjecting individuals to imprisonment and societal ostracism. Article 347 bis of the Cameroonian Penal Code states:

$$\text{Imprisonment} \in [6 \text{ months}, 5 \text{ years}] \text{ for same-sex sexual relations.} \qquad (38)$$

This legal environment creates a climate of fear, where individuals are reluctant to express their identities openly. Activists face the daunting task of challenging these laws while navigating a hostile political landscape. Bandy Kiki and her peers have been at the forefront of advocating for legal reforms, emphasizing the need for decriminalization and protection against discrimination.

Strategies for Advocacy

Activism in Cameroon has taken various forms, from grassroots organizing to international lobbying. One effective strategy employed by Bandy Kiki is the use of social media as a platform for awareness and mobilization. By creating a pseudonym, she has been able to maintain her anonymity while amplifying the voices of marginalized individuals. This duality allows her to engage with a global audience, raising awareness of the dire situation faced by LGBTQ individuals in Cameroon.

Through campaigns that highlight personal stories and experiences, activists can humanize the struggle for equality. For instance, Bandy Kiki's initiative, "Voices of the Silenced," collects testimonies from LGBTQ individuals who have faced discrimination, harassment, and violence. By sharing these narratives, the campaign seeks to evoke empathy and understanding, challenging the stereotypes that perpetuate stigma.

Building Alliances

Building coalitions with local and international organizations is crucial in the fight for LGBTQ rights. Activists have formed partnerships with human rights NGOs, leveraging their resources and networks to amplify their message. For example, collaborations with organizations like Human Rights Watch and Amnesty International have facilitated the documentation of human rights abuses, bringing global attention to the plight of LGBTQ individuals in Cameroon.

These alliances also provide a support system for activists, allowing them to share strategies and resources. The intersectionality of these partnerships is vital, as they often encompass broader issues of gender equality, racial justice, and economic rights. By framing the struggle for LGBTQ rights within the larger context of human rights, activists can foster solidarity among diverse groups.

Challenges of Representation

Despite these efforts, significant challenges remain in achieving true representation for LGBTQ individuals. The pervasive stigma and discrimination often lead to internalized homophobia, where individuals may struggle to accept their identities. This societal pressure can hinder participation in activism, creating a cycle of silence and oppression.

Moreover, the media plays a critical role in shaping public perceptions of LGBTQ individuals. Negative portrayals and sensationalism often reinforce harmful stereotypes, further marginalizing the community. Activists like Bandy Kiki have recognized the importance of engaging with media outlets to promote positive narratives and challenge misconceptions about LGBTQ identities.

Examples of Impact

One notable example of the impact of activism in Cameroon is the annual "Pride March," organized by local LGBTQ groups. Although the event faces significant risks, including the possibility of violence and arrest, it serves as a powerful statement of visibility and resistance. The march not only fosters a sense of community among participants but also attracts media coverage, drawing attention to the ongoing struggle for rights.

Additionally, Bandy Kiki's efforts in advocating for LGBTQ representation in political discourse have begun to yield results. Through lobbying and advocacy, she has successfully engaged with lawmakers to discuss the importance of inclusive policies. This dialogue has opened the door for potential legislative changes, signaling a shift towards greater acceptance and recognition of LGBTQ rights.

Conclusion

The fight for equal rights and representation in Cameroon is a complex and ongoing struggle. Activists like Bandy Kiki play a crucial role in challenging oppressive laws, advocating for social change, and building alliances both locally and globally. While significant challenges remain, the resilience and determination of the LGBTQ community continue to inspire hope for a more inclusive future. As the movement progresses, it is essential to recognize the intersectionality of these struggles and the importance of solidarity in achieving true equality for all individuals, regardless of their sexual orientation or gender identity.

Raising Global Awareness

Engaging with international LGBTQ organizations

Engaging with international LGBTQ organizations has become an essential strategy for activists like Bandy Kiki, who seek to amplify their voices and foster change in regions where LGBTQ rights are under constant threat. These organizations play a crucial role in providing resources, support, and a platform for marginalized voices, allowing activists to connect with a global community that shares their struggles and aspirations.

The Role of International Organizations

International LGBTQ organizations, such as ILGA (International Lesbian, Gay, Bisexual, Trans and Intersex Association) and OutRight Action International, serve as vital conduits for information, advocacy, and solidarity. They offer various forms of support, including:

- **Resource Sharing:** These organizations compile and disseminate research, reports, and best practices that can inform local activism. For instance, ILGA's annual reports on the state of LGBTQ rights worldwide provide critical insights into legal frameworks and societal attitudes, helping activists strategize their approaches.

- **Capacity Building:** Many organizations conduct workshops and training sessions aimed at enhancing the skills of local activists. This training can cover areas such as legal advocacy, media engagement, and community organizing, equipping activists with the tools necessary to effect change in their contexts.

- **Advocacy and Lobbying:** International LGBTQ organizations often engage in high-level advocacy at the United Nations and other international bodies. By amplifying local issues on a global stage, they can pressure governments to uphold human rights standards and protect LGBTQ individuals.

- **Networking Opportunities:** These organizations facilitate networking among activists from different regions, fostering collaborations that can lead to impactful joint campaigns. Such connections can be particularly beneficial for activists in hostile environments, providing them with a sense of solidarity and shared purpose.

Challenges in Engagement

While the engagement with international LGBTQ organizations offers numerous benefits, it is not without its challenges. Activists often face barriers that can hinder effective collaboration, including:

- **Cultural Sensitivity:** International organizations may inadvertently impose their own cultural values and frameworks on local activists. This can lead to tensions if local customs and norms are not respected. For example, a campaign that works well in a Western context may not resonate with communities in Cameroon, where cultural and religious beliefs significantly shape attitudes toward LGBTQ identities.

- **Resource Allocation:** There is often a disparity in how resources are allocated, with larger organizations focusing on high-profile campaigns while grassroots movements struggle for funding. This can create a hierarchy that marginalizes the voices of those who are most affected by discrimination and violence.

- **Safety Concerns:** Activists in oppressive regimes may fear repercussions from their governments for engaging with international bodies. This fear can lead to a reluctance to openly associate with global organizations, limiting their ability to access support and resources.

Case Studies and Examples

Several case studies illustrate the importance of engaging with international LGBTQ organizations:

- **The Campaign for Decriminalization in Uganda:** Organizations like OutRight Action International have played a pivotal role in supporting Ugandan activists fighting against the Anti-Homosexuality Act. Through international advocacy, they mobilized global pressure on the Ugandan government, ultimately leading to a decrease in the visibility of anti-LGBTQ rhetoric in international forums.

- **The Rainbow Railroad:** This organization assists LGBTQ individuals facing persecution in their home countries by providing safe passage to more accepting environments. For example, when activists in Cameroon faced imminent threats, Rainbow Railroad facilitated their relocation, allowing them to continue their work in a safer context.

- **The Global Fund for Human Rights:** This fund supports grassroots organizations fighting for LGBTQ rights worldwide. By providing financial support to groups in Cameroon, the fund has enabled local activists to organize protests, raise awareness, and challenge discriminatory laws effectively.

Theoretical Framework

The engagement with international LGBTQ organizations can be analyzed through the lens of *transnational advocacy networks* (TANs), which emphasize the role of non-state actors in influencing policy and societal norms across borders. According to Keck and Sikkink (1998), TANs operate through information politics, symbolic politics, leverage politics, and accountability politics. Activists like Bandy Kiki utilize these strategies to:

$$\text{Influence} = \text{Information} + \text{Symbolic Action} + \text{Leverage} + \text{Accountability} \quad (39)$$

This equation illustrates how the combination of these elements can lead to significant changes in local and international contexts.

Conclusion

Engaging with international LGBTQ organizations is a powerful tool for activists in Cameroon and beyond. Despite the challenges, the benefits of resource sharing, capacity building, and global advocacy are invaluable. As Bandy Kiki continues to navigate her activism, the connections forged with international organizations will undoubtedly play a crucial role in shaping the future of LGBTQ rights in her home country. By fostering these relationships, activists can not only amplify their voices but also contribute to a more inclusive and equitable world for all.

Collaborating with activists from around the world

In the ever-evolving landscape of LGBTQ activism, collaboration across borders has become a cornerstone of effective advocacy. Bandy Kiki, as a pivotal figure in this movement, recognized early on that the fight for equality transcends national boundaries. By collaborating with activists from around the globe, she not only amplified her voice but also created a powerful network of solidarity and support.

One of the key theories underpinning this collaborative approach is the concept of *transnational activism*. This theory posits that social movements are increasingly operating beyond their national contexts, forming networks that share resources, strategies, and information. According to Keck and Sikkink (1998), transnational advocacy networks can play a crucial role in influencing international norms and policies. Bandy Kiki utilized this framework to connect with LGBTQ activists in countries facing similar struggles, thereby fostering a sense of unity and shared purpose.

The challenges of collaborating internationally, however, are manifold. Activists often face differing cultural attitudes towards LGBTQ issues, which can complicate the formation of alliances. For instance, while some countries have made significant strides in LGBTQ rights, others remain staunchly opposed, creating a dissonance that activists must navigate carefully. Bandy Kiki's approach involved acknowledging these differences while emphasizing common goals, such as the fundamental right to love and be loved without fear of persecution.

A notable example of successful collaboration can be seen in the formation of the *Global LGBTQ Alliance*, a coalition of activists from various continents. This alliance was established to share strategies, mobilize resources, and provide mutual support in the face of governmental oppression. Bandy Kiki played a crucial role in this initiative, organizing virtual summits that allowed activists to share their experiences and tactics. These summits often included workshops on digital security, given the increasing surveillance faced by LGBTQ activists, particularly in regions where homosexuality is criminalized.

Moreover, Bandy Kiki's efforts extended to engaging with international organizations such as *Human Rights Watch* and *Amnesty International*. By collaborating with these organizations, she was able to leverage their global platforms to raise awareness about the situation in Cameroon. This partnership not only provided visibility to her cause but also facilitated the documentation of human rights abuses faced by LGBTQ individuals in her country. The reports generated by these organizations often served as crucial evidence in lobbying for international intervention and support.

Despite these successes, the path of international collaboration is fraught with obstacles. Language barriers, differing legal frameworks, and varying levels of access to technology can hinder effective communication and cooperation. Bandy Kiki addressed these challenges by employing multilingual platforms and ensuring that resources were accessible to activists regardless of their technological capabilities. This inclusivity was vital in creating a cohesive movement that could respond to the needs of diverse communities.

Furthermore, Bandy Kiki's collaborations often included grassroots organizations, recognizing that the most impactful changes often stem from local activism. By connecting with community leaders and activists on the ground, she ensured that the voices of those most affected by discrimination were heard in international forums. This approach aligns with the theory of *intersectionality*, which emphasizes the importance of considering the multiple identities and experiences that shape an individual's activism. By centering the experiences of marginalized groups within the LGBTQ community, Bandy Kiki was able to advocate for a more inclusive and comprehensive approach to rights.

In conclusion, Bandy Kiki's commitment to collaborating with activists from around the world exemplifies the power of transnational advocacy in the fight for LGBTQ rights. By building alliances, sharing resources, and amplifying voices, she not only advanced her mission but also contributed to a global movement that seeks to dismantle oppression and promote equality. The challenges faced in these collaborations serve as a reminder of the complexities of activism in a diverse world, yet they also highlight the resilience and determination of those who dare to dream of a more inclusive future. The ongoing dialogue and cooperation among activists worldwide continue to inspire hope and foster change, proving that together, they can indeed make a difference.

Mobilizing support and solidarity

In the realm of LGBTQ activism, mobilizing support and solidarity is not just a strategic necessity; it is a moral imperative. The fight for equality transcends individual efforts, requiring a collective response that unites diverse voices and experiences. This section explores the theoretical underpinnings, challenges, and practical examples of mobilizing support and solidarity within the LGBTQ movement, particularly in the context of Cameroon.

Theoretical Framework

Mobilization theory provides a critical lens through which to understand how social movements gain traction and influence. According to Tilly (1978), mobilization involves the process through which groups organize and engage in collective action to achieve shared objectives. The theory posits that successful mobilization hinges on three key components: resources, political opportunities, and framing processes.

$$M = f(R, P, F) \qquad (40)$$

Where:

- M = Mobilization effectiveness
- R = Resources (financial, human, informational)
- P = Political opportunities (favorable conditions for activism)
- F = Framing processes (how issues are presented and understood)

In the context of LGBTQ activism, resources can include funding, volunteer support, and access to media platforms. Political opportunities may arise from shifts in governmental attitudes or international pressure, while framing processes involve crafting narratives that resonate with broader societal values, such as human rights and equality.

Challenges to Mobilization

Despite the theoretical frameworks that guide mobilization, LGBTQ activists in Cameroon face significant challenges. The oppressive legal system and societal stigmatization create an environment where fear often stifles collective action. Activists must navigate a landscape fraught with dangers, including harassment, violence, and legal repercussions.

One of the primary challenges is the lack of visibility and representation of LGBTQ issues within mainstream discourse. This invisibility often leads to a disconnect between the LGBTQ community and potential allies, making it difficult to mobilize support. Additionally, the intersectionality of various identities within the LGBTQ community means that different groups may have divergent priorities and experiences, complicating efforts to build a unified front.

Strategies for Mobilization

To effectively mobilize support and solidarity, activists have employed several strategies that leverage both traditional and digital platforms. One notable example is the use of social media as a tool for outreach and engagement. Platforms like Twitter, Facebook, and Instagram have enabled activists to share their stories, raise awareness about issues, and connect with a global audience.

For instance, Bandy Kiki utilized social media to highlight the struggles faced by LGBTQ individuals in Cameroon, drawing international attention to the urgent need for change. By framing the narrative around universal human rights, Bandy was able to engage a wider audience, fostering solidarity beyond national borders.

Moreover, coalition-building is crucial for mobilization. By forming alliances with local NGOs, human rights organizations, and international advocacy groups, LGBTQ activists can amplify their voices and resources. Collaborative efforts, such as joint protests or campaigns, not only enhance visibility but also create a sense of shared purpose among diverse groups.

Examples of Successful Mobilization

One of the most compelling examples of successful mobilization in the LGBTQ movement is the global response to the anti-LGBTQ laws in Uganda. Activists worldwide rallied in solidarity, organizing protests, petitions, and awareness campaigns that pressured the Ugandan government to reconsider its stance. This collective action showcased the power of international solidarity in amplifying local struggles.

In Cameroon, Bandy Kiki's initiatives, such as the "#StandWithCameroon" campaign, exemplify effective mobilization. By encouraging individuals to share their stories and experiences, the campaign fostered a sense of community and resilience among LGBTQ individuals. The hashtag became a rallying cry, uniting voices from different backgrounds in a shared fight for equality.

Conclusion

Mobilizing support and solidarity is a multifaceted endeavor that requires strategic planning, creative engagement, and a deep understanding of the social landscape. As LGBTQ activists continue to navigate the complexities of their environment, the principles of mobilization theory provide a valuable framework for understanding how to effectively garner support and foster solidarity.

Through the use of digital platforms, coalition-building, and compelling storytelling, activists can create a powerful movement that not only challenges the status quo but also inspires hope and resilience within the LGBTQ community in Cameroon and beyond. The journey is fraught with challenges, yet the potential for change remains boundless when individuals unite in pursuit of a common cause.

Speaking at global conferences and events

In the realm of activism, speaking at global conferences and events serves as a powerful platform for raising awareness and advocating for change. For Bandy Kiki, these opportunities were not merely formalities; they were pivotal moments that amplified her voice and the voices of countless others in the LGBTQ community in Cameroon.

The Importance of Global Platforms

Global conferences provide a unique convergence of activists, policymakers, and thought leaders from diverse backgrounds. The significance of such platforms can be encapsulated in the following equation:

$$\text{Impact} = \text{Audience Size} \times \text{Message Resonance} \tag{41}$$

Here, Impact represents the potential change that can be initiated through a speaker's message, Audience Size denotes the number of individuals reached, and Message Resonance reflects how well the message resonates with the audience. Bandy Kiki's ability to connect with her audience was paramount in her speeches, as she often shared personal narratives that highlighted the struggles faced by LGBTQ individuals in Cameroon.

Challenges of Speaking on a Global Stage

However, the journey to these platforms was fraught with challenges. Activists like Bandy Kiki often face the daunting task of conveying their message in a hostile environment. The fear of backlash, both personally and professionally, looms large. Moreover, the language barrier can impede effective communication, as many activists must translate their experiences into a language that resonates with an international audience.

For instance, during the *International LGBTQ Rights Conference* in 2022, Bandy Kiki encountered skepticism from some attendees who were unfamiliar with the socio-political landscape of Cameroon. To navigate this, she employed storytelling techniques, using vivid imagery and relatable experiences to bridge the gap between her reality and that of her audience.

Examples of Impactful Engagements

One notable engagement was her speech at the *Global Forum on Human Rights*, where she addressed the oppressive legal framework in Cameroon that criminalizes homosexuality. Bandy Kiki articulated the stark realities faced by LGBTQ individuals, emphasizing the need for international solidarity. Her statement, "We are not just statistics; we are human beings deserving of love and respect," resonated deeply, leading to discussions on policy reforms among attending diplomats and activists.

Another significant moment occurred during the *World Pride Summit*, where Bandy Kiki joined a panel of activists from various countries. The diversity of voices on the panel highlighted the intersectionality of LGBTQ rights, showcasing how different cultures approach similar challenges. This exchange of ideas fostered a sense of unity and purpose among the attendees, inspiring many to take action upon returning to their respective countries.

The Ripple Effect of Speaking Engagements

The ripple effect of Bandy Kiki's speaking engagements cannot be understated. Each conference served as a catalyst for further dialogue and action. For example, following her impactful speech at the *UN Human Rights Council*, several NGOs reached out to collaborate on initiatives aimed at supporting LGBTQ individuals in Cameroon. This collaborative spirit exemplifies the potential for global platforms to not only raise awareness but also to mobilize resources and support for marginalized communities.

In conclusion, speaking at global conferences and events is an essential avenue for activists like Bandy Kiki to advocate for LGBTQ rights. Despite the challenges faced, the ability to share personal narratives and engage with a diverse audience can lead to significant change. As the fight for equality continues, these platforms will remain vital in amplifying the voices of those who are often silenced.

Advocating for LGBTQ rights on a global scale

Advocating for LGBTQ rights on a global scale involves a multifaceted approach that addresses the diverse challenges faced by LGBTQ individuals across different cultures and legal systems. This section explores the theories, problems, and examples of global advocacy, highlighting the importance of international solidarity and the role of various organizations.

Theoretical Framework

The advocacy for LGBTQ rights on a global scale can be understood through the lens of several theoretical frameworks, including:

- **Intersectionality:** Coined by Kimberlé Crenshaw, intersectionality examines how various social identities (race, gender, sexuality, etc.) overlap and contribute to unique experiences of oppression and privilege. In the context of LGBTQ advocacy, understanding intersectionality is crucial as it allows activists to address the specific needs of marginalized groups within the LGBTQ community, such as LGBTQ people of color, transgender individuals, and those living in poverty.

- **Human Rights Framework:** The promotion of LGBTQ rights as human rights is a foundational principle in global advocacy. This framework posits that all individuals, regardless of their sexual orientation or gender identity, are entitled to fundamental human rights. The Universal Declaration of Human Rights (UDHR) serves as a key document that advocates for the protection and promotion of these rights on an international level.

- **Globalization and Transnational Activism:** The interconnectedness of the world through globalization has facilitated the rise of transnational activism. This framework emphasizes the importance of cross-border collaborations among activists, organizations, and allies to address global issues affecting LGBTQ communities. It recognizes that local struggles are often part of broader international movements.

Challenges in Global Advocacy

While the advocacy for LGBTQ rights on a global scale has made significant strides, several challenges persist:

- **Cultural Relativism:** One of the major challenges in advocating for LGBTQ rights globally is the concept of cultural relativism, which asserts that beliefs and practices should be understood based on an individual's own culture. This can lead to resistance against LGBTQ rights in cultures where such identities are stigmatized or criminalized. Activists must navigate these cultural complexities while promoting universal human rights.

- **Legal Barriers:** Many countries have laws that criminalize homosexuality or discriminate against LGBTQ individuals. For instance, in countries like Uganda and Nigeria, anti-LGBTQ legislation has resulted in severe penalties, including imprisonment and violence. Advocates face the daunting task of challenging these laws while ensuring the safety of those involved.

- **Political Backlash:** In some regions, the advancement of LGBTQ rights has been met with political backlash, often fueled by conservative ideologies. For example, in Eastern Europe, the rise of nationalist movements has led to increased hostility towards LGBTQ communities, prompting activists to adopt more strategic approaches to advocacy.

Successful Examples of Global Advocacy

Despite these challenges, there are numerous examples of successful global advocacy efforts that have made a significant impact on LGBTQ rights:

- **The International Day Against Homophobia, Transphobia, and Biphobia (IDAHOT):** Established in 2004, IDAHOT is observed annually on May 17th and aims to raise awareness of LGBTQ rights violations worldwide. The day serves as a platform for activists to mobilize support, organize events, and engage with local communities to promote inclusivity.

- **The Yogyakarta Principles:** Developed in 2006, the Yogyakarta Principles are a set of international legal principles that address the application of human rights law in relation to sexual orientation and gender identity. These principles have been instrumental in guiding activists and policymakers in advocating for LGBTQ rights globally.

- **Collaborations with International Organizations:** Partnerships with organizations such as Amnesty International, Human Rights Watch, and the United Nations have bolstered LGBTQ advocacy efforts. For example, the UN Free & Equal campaign promotes equal rights and fair treatment for LGBTQ individuals, amplifying their voices on a global stage.

The Role of Social Media in Global Advocacy

In the digital age, social media has emerged as a powerful tool for global LGBTQ advocacy. Platforms like Twitter, Instagram, and Facebook enable activists to share their stories, mobilize support, and raise awareness about LGBTQ issues. The viral nature of social media campaigns can lead to significant visibility and impact. For instance, the hashtag #LoveIsLove has been used to promote marriage equality worldwide, uniting individuals across borders in the fight for equal rights.

Conclusion

Advocating for LGBTQ rights on a global scale is an ongoing journey that requires resilience, creativity, and solidarity. By understanding the theoretical frameworks, recognizing the challenges, and celebrating the successes, activists can continue to push for change and create a more inclusive world for all. The fight for LGBTQ rights transcends borders, and through collective action, we can work towards a future where everyone can live authentically and without fear of discrimination.

Navigating Activism in a Hostile Climate

The risks and dangers of public advocacy

Public advocacy, particularly in the context of LGBTQ rights in regions with oppressive legal frameworks, presents a myriad of risks and dangers. Activists like Bandy Kiki often find themselves navigating a treacherous landscape where their safety, freedom, and even lives are at stake. This section explores the multifaceted risks associated with public advocacy, drawing on relevant theories, real-world examples, and the broader implications for the LGBTQ community.

1. Legal Repercussions

One of the most immediate risks faced by public advocates is the threat of legal action. In countries like Cameroon, where homosexuality is criminalized, activists can be charged with various offenses merely for advocating for LGBTQ rights. The legal framework can be used as a tool of oppression, where laws are selectively enforced to silence dissent. For instance, the anti-homosexuality law in Cameroon can lead to imprisonment, fines, or worse for those who openly identify as LGBTQ or support LGBTQ causes.

$$\text{Risk}_{legal} = P(\text{arrest}) \times C(\text{penalty}) \qquad (42)$$

Where $P(\text{arrest})$ is the probability of being arrested for advocacy, and $C(\text{penalty})$ is the cost associated with legal penalties. The combined effect can create a chilling effect, discouraging individuals from engaging in public advocacy.

2. Physical Danger

Physical violence is another significant risk for LGBTQ activists. Reports of harassment, assault, and even murder of activists are prevalent in many countries where LGBTQ rights are not recognized. For example, the murder of LGBTQ activists like Eric Ohena Lembembe in Cameroon underscores the life-threatening dangers faced by those who dare to speak out. The fear of violence can lead to self-censorship among activists, limiting the scope of their advocacy.

$$\text{Risk}_{physical} = P(\text{attack}) \times C(\text{injury}) \qquad (43)$$

In this equation, $P(\text{attack})$ represents the likelihood of being physically attacked, while $C(\text{injury})$ denotes the potential consequences of such violence, including physical harm or death.

3. Social Isolation and Stigmatization

Public advocacy can also lead to social isolation. Activists may face rejection from family, friends, and their communities, leading to emotional and psychological distress. The stigma associated with being LGBTQ in many societies can exacerbate this isolation. For instance, Bandy Kiki's decision to come out publicly as an advocate may have resulted in estrangement from some community members who do not accept her identity or activism.

$$\text{Risk}_{social} = P(\text{rejection}) \times C(\text{isolation}) \qquad (44)$$

Here, $P(\text{rejection})$ indicates the probability of facing social rejection, while $C(\text{isolation})$ reflects the emotional toll of being ostracized.

4. Psychological Impact

The psychological toll of public advocacy cannot be understated. Activists often experience stress, anxiety, and depression due to the constant threat of violence, legal repercussions, and social ostracism. The need to remain vigilant can lead to chronic stress, which has been shown to have detrimental effects on mental health.

$$\text{Risk}_{psychological} = P(\text{stress}) \times C(\text{mental health issues}) \qquad (45)$$

In this context, $P(\text{stress})$ refers to the likelihood of experiencing stress due to advocacy efforts, while $C(\text{mental health issues})$ signifies the potential long-term consequences on mental health, such as anxiety disorders or depression.

5. Navigating Public Perception

Activists must also contend with public perception, which can be hostile in conservative environments. Negative media portrayals and public backlash can undermine their efforts and lead to further risks. For example, when Bandy Kiki's activism garnered international attention, it also attracted criticism from conservative factions within her community, heightening her risk profile.

$$\text{Risk}_{public\ perception} = P(\text{backlash}) \times C(\text{reputation}) \qquad (46)$$

In this equation, $P(\text{backlash})$ represents the likelihood of facing negative public response, while $C(\text{reputation})$ measures the potential damage to the activist's reputation and credibility.

Conclusion

The risks and dangers of public advocacy are profound and multifaceted, impacting every aspect of an activist's life. Understanding these risks is crucial for both advocates and supporters in the LGBTQ community. By acknowledging the potential consequences, activists can develop strategies to mitigate these risks, such as building support networks, engaging in digital activism, and leveraging international solidarity to create a safer environment for their work. Ultimately, the fight for LGBTQ rights is not just a battle for legal recognition but also a struggle for the safety and dignity of those who dare to advocate for change.

Balancing personal safety with the fight for justice

In the realm of activism, particularly within the LGBTQ community in hostile environments like Cameroon, the balance between personal safety and the relentless pursuit of justice is a precarious one. Activists often find themselves at a crossroads, where the urgency of their cause collides with the very real threats to their safety. This section explores the intricate dynamics of this balance, drawing on theoretical frameworks, real-world challenges, and illustrative examples.

Theoretical Frameworks

The tension between personal safety and activism can be understood through several theoretical lenses. The **Social Movement Theory** posits that social movements emerge in response to perceived injustices and that individuals mobilize to advocate for change. However, within this framework, the concept of *risk assessment* becomes crucial. Activists must evaluate the potential consequences of their actions, which can include physical harm, legal repercussions, and social ostracism.

Additionally, **Goffman's Theory of Stigma** highlights how marginalized individuals navigate societal perceptions and the risks associated with being publicly visible. For LGBTQ activists, the stigma attached to their identities can exacerbate the dangers they face, necessitating a careful approach to activism that prioritizes both visibility and safety.

Challenges Faced by Activists

Activists like Bandy Kiki often grapple with a myriad of challenges when attempting to balance their safety with their commitment to justice. One significant challenge is the **risk of violence**. In many regions, LGBTQ individuals face not only legal persecution but also physical threats from both state and non-state actors. The fear of violence can deter individuals from participating in public demonstrations or openly advocating for their rights.

Moreover, the **surveillance state** complicates this balance. In countries with oppressive regimes, activists are often subject to monitoring by government agencies. This surveillance can lead to arrests, harassment, and intimidation. Activists must navigate a landscape where their online presence can be tracked, and their offline actions can have dire consequences.

Strategies for Balancing Safety and Activism

To mitigate these risks, activists employ various strategies that allow them to advocate for justice while safeguarding their well-being. One effective approach is the use of **anonymity**. By adopting pseudonyms or maintaining a low profile, activists can engage in advocacy without exposing themselves to direct threats. This strategy allows them to mobilize support and raise awareness without the immediate risks associated with public visibility.

Another strategy involves the formation of **support networks**. By creating alliances with other activists and organizations, individuals can share resources, information, and emotional support. These networks can provide a buffer against potential threats and offer solidarity in the face of adversity. For instance, Bandy Kiki's work in building connections with international LGBTQ organizations has not only amplified her message but also provided a layer of protection through collective action.

Real-World Examples

The case of Bandy Kiki exemplifies the delicate balance between personal safety and activism. As a masked activist, she has utilized her anonymity to speak out against injustices faced by the LGBTQ community in Cameroon. By creating a pseudonym, she has been able to engage in advocacy without exposing her identity to potential threats. This strategic choice has allowed her to raise awareness about the oppressive legal environment while minimizing personal risk.

Another poignant example is the use of **digital activism**. In an age where social media can serve as both a tool for mobilization and a mechanism for surveillance, activists have found ways to leverage online platforms for their causes. By sharing stories, resources, and calls to action in a digital space, activists can engage a global audience while maintaining a degree of anonymity. This approach not only broadens their reach but also helps to mitigate the risks associated with public demonstrations.

Conclusion

In conclusion, the balancing act between personal safety and the fight for justice is a defining characteristic of LGBTQ activism in hostile environments. Activists like Bandy Kiki navigate a complex landscape where the stakes are high, and the risks are tangible. By employing strategies such as anonymity, building support networks, and utilizing digital platforms, they strive to advocate for change while safeguarding their well-being. The ongoing struggle for LGBTQ rights in Cameroon underscores the importance of this balance, as activists continue to challenge oppressive systems while navigating the very real dangers that accompany their work.

$$\text{Risk Assessment} = \frac{\text{Potential Harm}}{\text{Level of Visibility}} \cdot \text{Activism Engagement} \qquad (47)$$

This equation illustrates the relationship between the potential harm an activist may face, the level of visibility they maintain, and their engagement in activism. By understanding and managing these variables, activists can better navigate their dual roles as advocates for justice and protectors of their own safety.

Resilience in the face of adversity

Resilience is the capacity to recover quickly from difficulties; it is a form of emotional strength that allows individuals to withstand and overcome challenges. In the context of LGBTQ activism in Cameroon, resilience becomes a crucial quality for advocates like Bandy Kiki, who navigate a landscape fraught with hostility and discrimination. This section explores the various dimensions of resilience, its theoretical underpinnings, and real-world applications within the LGBTQ movement.

Theoretical Framework of Resilience

The concept of resilience has been explored extensively in psychology and sociology. According to Masten (2001), resilience is not merely a trait but a dynamic process that involves positive adaptation in the face of significant adversity. This perspective suggests that resilience can be cultivated through supportive relationships, community engagement, and personal coping strategies.

$$R = f(S, C, P) \qquad (48)$$

where R represents resilience, S stands for supportive relationships, C signifies community engagement, and P denotes personal coping strategies. This equation illustrates that resilience is a function of multiple factors that interact in complex ways.

Challenges Faced by LGBTQ Activists

LGBTQ activists in Cameroon encounter numerous adversities that test their resilience. The oppressive legal environment, characterized by laws criminalizing same-sex relationships, creates a climate of fear and danger. Activists risk harassment, violence, and even imprisonment for their advocacy. Furthermore, societal stigmatization adds another layer of difficulty, as many LGBTQ individuals face rejection from their families and communities.

For instance, Bandy Kiki experienced significant backlash when she began to speak out against discrimination. The threats she received were not just abstract; they manifested in real-life confrontations that could have deterred a less resilient individual. Instead of succumbing to fear, she utilized her experiences as a catalyst for deeper engagement in activism.

Strategies for Building Resilience

To cultivate resilience, LGBTQ activists employ various strategies, including:

- **Building Support Networks:** Establishing strong connections with allies, both within and outside the LGBTQ community, is vital. These networks provide emotional support, resources, and a sense of belonging. Bandy Kiki often emphasized the importance of chosen family, who stood by her side during challenging times.

- **Practicing Self-Care:** Activists must prioritize their mental and emotional well-being. Engaging in self-care practices, such as mindfulness, therapy, or creative outlets, allows individuals to recharge and maintain their commitment to activism. For Bandy, journaling served as a powerful tool for processing her experiences and emotions.

- **Embracing Vulnerability:** Resilience is often misunderstood as a need to be tough or stoic. However, embracing vulnerability can enhance resilience. By sharing their stories and struggles, activists can foster deeper connections and inspire others to join the fight for equality. Bandy Kiki's willingness to be open about her fears and challenges resonated with many, creating a ripple effect of empowerment.

Examples of Resilience in Action

The resilience of LGBTQ activists is exemplified through various initiatives and movements that have emerged in Cameroon. For instance, during a particularly challenging period when anti-LGBTQ sentiment surged, Bandy Kiki organized a series of workshops aimed at educating the public about LGBTQ rights. Despite facing threats and backlash, she persisted, believing in the transformative power of education.

Moreover, the formation of coalitions among diverse activist groups has illustrated resilience in unity. By coming together, activists have amplified their voices and created a more formidable front against oppression. The collaborative efforts led to significant advocacy campaigns that garnered international attention, ultimately pressuring the Cameroonian government to reconsider certain discriminatory practices.

Conclusion

In conclusion, resilience is a cornerstone of effective activism, especially in hostile environments like Cameroon. Bandy Kiki's journey exemplifies how resilience can be cultivated through supportive relationships, self-care, and embracing vulnerability. By navigating adversity with strength and determination, LGBTQ activists not only fight for their rights but also inspire others to join the struggle for equality. The ongoing fight for LGBTQ rights in Cameroon continues to be a testament to the power of resilience in the face of adversity.

Building alliances and coalitions

In the realm of activism, particularly within the LGBTQ rights movement, the importance of building alliances and coalitions cannot be overstated. The collective power of diverse groups uniting for a common cause amplifies voices that might otherwise go unheard, creating a formidable force for change. This section explores the theoretical underpinnings of coalition-building, the challenges faced in this endeavor, and practical examples of successful alliances that have made significant strides in the fight for equality.

Theoretical Framework

Coalition-building is grounded in various theories of social movements and collective action. One prominent theory is the Resource Mobilization Theory, which posits that the success of social movements relies heavily on the availability of resources, including human, financial, and informational assets. According to McCarthy and Zald (1977), movements that can effectively mobilize these resources are more likely to achieve their goals. In the context of LGBTQ activism, forming coalitions allows groups to pool their resources, share knowledge, and strategize collectively, thereby enhancing their overall effectiveness.

Another relevant framework is the Intersectionality Theory, introduced by Kimberlé Crenshaw (1989). This theory emphasizes the interconnected nature of social categorizations such as race, class, and gender, and how these intersections create unique experiences of oppression and privilege. By recognizing and addressing these intersecting identities within coalitions, activists can create more inclusive movements that advocate for the rights of all marginalized groups, rather than a singular focus on one identity.

Challenges in Coalition-Building

Despite the clear benefits of forming alliances, several challenges often arise in the process. One significant obstacle is the potential for conflicting agendas among different groups. For example, an LGBTQ organization focused primarily on legal rights may have different priorities than a group centered on cultural acceptance. These differences can lead to tensions and hinder effective collaboration.

Moreover, power dynamics within coalitions can also pose challenges. Dominant groups may inadvertently overshadow the voices of smaller or less represented communities. This phenomenon, often referred to as "tokenism," can undermine the very purpose of coalition-building by failing to address the needs of all members equitably. To counteract this, it is essential for coalitions to establish clear communication channels and equitable decision-making processes that ensure all voices are heard and valued.

Successful Examples of Coalitions

One notable example of successful coalition-building in the LGBTQ rights movement is the formation of the "Coalition for LGBTQ Equality" in Cameroon. This coalition brought together various organizations, including local NGOs, international human rights groups, and grassroots activists, to advocate for the repeal of discriminatory laws against LGBTQ individuals. By uniting their efforts, the coalition was able to launch widespread awareness campaigns, organize protests, and engage with policymakers, ultimately leading to increased visibility of LGBTQ issues in the national discourse.

Another inspiring case is the "United Nations Free & Equal" campaign, which aimed to promote equality and challenge homophobia and transphobia worldwide. This initiative successfully brought together diverse stakeholders, including governments, civil society organizations, and private sector partners, to advocate for LGBTQ rights on a global scale. By leveraging the resources and influence of various sectors, the campaign was able to reach a broader audience and foster international solidarity.

Strategies for Effective Coalition-Building

To overcome challenges and maximize the potential of alliances, activists can implement several strategies:

- **Establish Clear Goals:** It is crucial for coalitions to define shared objectives that resonate with all members. This clarity helps to align efforts and maintain focus amidst diverse priorities.

- **Foster Open Communication:** Regular communication fosters trust and transparency among coalition members. Utilizing digital platforms for discussions and updates can enhance engagement and collaboration.

- **Embrace Diversity:** Acknowledging and celebrating the diverse identities within coalitions enriches the movement. It is essential to create spaces where all members feel safe to share their experiences and perspectives.

- **Develop Leadership Structures:** Establishing equitable leadership roles within coalitions ensures that all groups have representation in decision-making processes. This approach mitigates power imbalances and promotes inclusivity.

- **Engage in Capacity Building:** Providing training and resources for coalition members can enhance their effectiveness and sustainability. Workshops on advocacy skills, fundraising, and community organizing can empower all participants.

Conclusion

In conclusion, building alliances and coalitions is a vital strategy in the fight for LGBTQ rights, particularly in challenging environments like Cameroon. By understanding the theoretical frameworks that underpin coalition-building, recognizing the challenges that may arise, and learning from successful examples, activists can create powerful networks that drive meaningful change. The strength of a united front lies not only in the numbers but in the shared commitment to equality and justice for all. As Bandy Kiki exemplifies, the path to progress is often paved by collaboration, resilience, and an unwavering belief in the power of collective action.

The power of unity in creating change

In the realm of activism, particularly within the LGBTQ community, the concept of unity emerges as a cornerstone for effective change. The power of unity lies in its ability to amplify voices, consolidate resources, and foster a sense of shared purpose among diverse groups. This section delves into the theoretical underpinnings of unity in activism, the challenges faced in fostering it, and examples that illustrate its transformative potential.

Theoretical Framework

Unity in activism can be understood through several theoretical lenses. One prominent theory is the *Collective Action Theory*, which posits that individuals are more likely to engage in activism when they perceive a shared identity and common goals. This theory emphasizes the importance of social networks and group dynamics in mobilizing individuals toward collective action. As noted by [?], "collective action emerges when individuals recognize their shared interests and act upon them."

Another relevant framework is the *Intersectionality Theory*, introduced by Kimberlé Crenshaw. This theory highlights the interconnected nature of social categorizations such as race, gender, and sexual orientation, which can create overlapping systems of discrimination and disadvantage. In the context of LGBTQ activism, recognizing the diverse identities within the community is essential for fostering unity. According to Crenshaw, "the experiences of individuals cannot be understood by examining one aspect of their identity in isolation."

Challenges to Unity

Despite the potential for unity to drive change, several challenges can impede its realization. One significant barrier is *fragmentation* within the LGBTQ community itself. Different subgroups, such as racial minorities, transgender individuals, and non-binary people, may have distinct needs and priorities that can lead to tensions and divisions. For example, the differing focuses on issues like marriage equality versus transgender rights can create rifts that hinder collective efforts.

Moreover, *external pressures* from societal norms and institutional discrimination can exacerbate these divisions. Activists often face the challenge of navigating a landscape fraught with hostility, which can lead to a defensive posture rather than a collaborative one. As noted by [?], "the external environment can significantly influence the internal dynamics of activist groups, often leading to competition rather than cooperation."

Examples of Unity in Action

Despite these challenges, there are numerous examples of how unity has catalyzed significant change within the LGBTQ movement. One such instance is the *Stonewall Riots* of 1969, often cited as a pivotal moment in the fight for LGBTQ rights. The riots brought together a diverse coalition of individuals, including drag queens, transgender people, and gay men, who collectively resisted police harassment. This act of unity not only sparked the modern LGBTQ rights movement but also underscored the importance of solidarity across different identities.

Another notable example is the *Marriage Equality Movement* in the United States. The coalition formed by various LGBTQ organizations, alongside allies from different social justice movements, played a crucial role in advocating for marriage rights. The *Human Rights Campaign* and *Lambda Legal*, among others, united their efforts to create a powerful lobbying force. Their joint campaigns, such as the *Love is Love* initiative, effectively mobilized public support and ultimately contributed to the landmark Supreme Court decision in *Obergefell v. Hodges* (2015), which legalized same-sex marriage nationwide.

The Role of Social Media

In the digital age, social media has emerged as a vital tool for fostering unity among activists. Platforms like Twitter, Instagram, and Facebook allow for the rapid dissemination of information and the mobilization of supporters across geographical boundaries. Hashtags such as #BlackLivesMatter and #TransRightsAreHumanRights have facilitated global conversations around intersectional issues, demonstrating how digital spaces can unite diverse voices for a common cause.

Moreover, social media campaigns can serve as a catalyst for collective action, as seen in the *#MeToo* movement. This movement not only highlighted issues of sexual harassment but also brought together individuals from various backgrounds, creating a unified front against systemic oppression. The ability to share personal stories and experiences online has empowered individuals and reinforced the notion that they are not alone in their struggles.

Conclusion

The power of unity in creating change cannot be overstated. By recognizing the importance of collective action and embracing the principles of intersectionality, LGBTQ activists can build a more inclusive and effective movement. While challenges such as fragmentation and external pressures persist, the examples of successful coalitions and the transformative potential of social media illustrate that unity remains a powerful force for change. As we continue to advocate for LGBTQ rights, fostering unity among diverse groups will be essential in the ongoing fight for equality and justice.

Building Allies and Coalitions

Forming partnerships with NGOs and human rights organizations

In the quest for LGBTQ rights, forming partnerships with non-governmental organizations (NGOs) and human rights organizations is pivotal for amplifying voices, pooling resources, and fostering a united front against discrimination. These collaborations are crucial in the context of Cameroon, where systemic oppression and societal stigma create a treacherous landscape for LGBTQ individuals. This section examines the theoretical underpinnings of such partnerships, the challenges faced, and practical examples of successful collaborations.

Theoretical Framework

The formation of partnerships between grassroots activists and established NGOs can be understood through the lens of *collaborative governance theory*. This theory posits that diverse stakeholders can work together to achieve common goals, particularly in complex social issues like human rights. According to Ansell and Gash (2008), effective collaborative governance requires trust, mutual respect, and a shared understanding of objectives. For LGBTQ activists, aligning with NGOs that share a commitment to human rights can enhance credibility and expand outreach efforts.

Furthermore, the *resource dependency theory* (Pfeffer & Salancik, 1978) illustrates that organizations must engage in partnerships to acquire necessary resources, be they financial, informational, or human. LGBTQ activists in Cameroon often operate with limited resources; thus, partnerships with NGOs can provide access to funding, training, and networks that are otherwise unavailable.

Challenges in Forming Partnerships

Despite the potential benefits, forming partnerships is not without its challenges. One significant issue is the *power dynamics* that often exist between local activists and larger NGOs. Many NGOs operate from a Western perspective, which can lead to a misalignment of priorities and strategies. This phenomenon, known as *neocolonialism in activism*, can marginalize local voices and perpetuate a cycle where external organizations dictate the terms of engagement.

Additionally, there is the challenge of *trust-building*. In environments where LGBTQ individuals face persecution, the fear of exposure can hinder collaboration. Activists must navigate the delicate balance of being open about their identities and the need for anonymity in their advocacy work. This tension can create barriers to forming effective partnerships.

Successful Examples of Collaboration

Despite these challenges, there are notable examples of successful partnerships between local LGBTQ activists and NGOs. One such instance is the collaboration between Bandy Kiki and organizations like *Human Rights Watch* and *Amnesty International*. These partnerships have facilitated international visibility for the struggles faced by LGBTQ individuals in Cameroon, leading to global advocacy campaigns and pressure on the Cameroonian government to reform discriminatory laws.

Another example is the establishment of local grassroots initiatives supported by larger NGOs. For instance, the *Cameroon LGBTQ Coalition* was formed through the joint efforts of local activists and international NGOs. This coalition has successfully organized awareness campaigns, legal aid programs, and community support systems, demonstrating the power of collective action.

Strategies for Effective Partnerships

To navigate the complexities of forming partnerships, LGBTQ activists can adopt several strategies:

- **Establish Clear Communication:** Open lines of communication are essential for ensuring that all parties understand each other's goals and expectations. Regular meetings and updates can help maintain alignment.

- **Mutual Capacity Building:** Engaging in capacity-building initiatives can empower local activists while also providing NGOs with insights into the local context. Workshops on advocacy strategies, legal rights, and self-care can foster a more equitable partnership.

- **Shared Leadership:** Ensuring that local activists have a prominent role in decision-making processes can help mitigate power imbalances. This approach not only enhances the legitimacy of the partnership but also builds trust among stakeholders.

- **Focus on Sustainability:** Partnerships should aim for long-term impact rather than short-term gains. Developing sustainable programs that can continue independently of external funding is crucial for lasting change.

Conclusion

In conclusion, forming partnerships with NGOs and human rights organizations is a vital component of the fight for LGBTQ rights in Cameroon. While challenges such as power dynamics and trust issues exist, the potential for resource sharing and amplified advocacy makes these collaborations essential. By employing strategies that prioritize clear communication, mutual capacity building, shared leadership, and sustainability, LGBTQ activists can forge effective alliances that enhance their impact and contribute to a more equitable society.

Working with local communities and leaders

In the pursuit of LGBTQ rights in Cameroon, the significance of collaborating with local communities and leaders cannot be overstated. This collaboration is pivotal not only for the effectiveness of activism but also for ensuring that the voices of marginalized individuals are amplified and respected. Activists like Bandy Kiki have recognized that grassroots engagement is essential for creating sustainable change, particularly in a context where societal norms and legal frameworks often oppose LGBTQ rights.

The Importance of Local Engagement

Engaging with local communities involves understanding their unique cultural, social, and economic contexts. According to [?], community engagement is a cornerstone of effective activism, as it fosters trust, builds relationships, and encourages collective action. This approach facilitates the identification of common goals and the development of strategies that resonate with the community's values and needs.

Building Trust and Relationships

Establishing trust is crucial in environments where fear and stigma dominate. Activists must navigate a landscape where LGBTQ individuals may have experienced discrimination or violence, leading to a reluctance to engage openly. For instance, Bandy Kiki employed a strategy of *community dialogue*, organizing safe spaces for discussion where individuals could share their experiences and concerns without fear of judgment. This method not only built trust but also empowered community members to take ownership of the advocacy process.

Collaborating with Local Leaders

Local leaders, including religious figures, educators, and community organizers, hold significant influence within their communities. Activists like Bandy Kiki have successfully collaborated with these leaders to foster understanding and acceptance of LGBTQ rights. For example, by engaging with progressive religious leaders, Bandy Kiki was able to challenge homophobic narratives and promote messages of love and acceptance within faith communities. This approach aligns with [?]'s framework for effective advocacy, which emphasizes the importance of allyship in creating social change.

Challenges in Collaboration

Despite the potential benefits of working with local communities and leaders, several challenges persist. One major issue is the risk of backlash from more conservative factions within the community. Activists must be prepared to address opposition and navigate tensions that may arise from their advocacy efforts. [?] notes that backlash can manifest in various forms, including social ostracism, threats, or even violence against activists and community members. Therefore, it is essential to develop strategies for mitigating risks while maintaining a commitment to advocacy.

Case Studies and Examples

Several case studies illustrate the effectiveness of local engagement in LGBTQ activism. For instance, in 2019, a coalition of LGBTQ activists in Douala partnered with local NGOs to host a series of workshops aimed at educating community leaders about LGBTQ issues. These workshops not only provided critical information but also fostered dialogue that helped dispel myths and misconceptions about LGBTQ individuals. As a result, several community leaders publicly expressed their support for LGBTQ rights, demonstrating the power of informed advocacy.

Another example can be seen in the collaboration between Bandy Kiki and local health organizations to address the health disparities faced by LGBTQ individuals. By working together, they developed targeted health initiatives that respected cultural sensitivities while addressing the specific needs of the LGBTQ community. This partnership not only improved access to healthcare but also reinforced the notion that LGBTQ rights are integral to broader health and human rights agendas.

Conclusion

The collaboration between LGBTQ activists and local communities and leaders is a vital component of the fight for equality in Cameroon. By building trust, engaging local leaders, and addressing challenges head-on, activists can create a more inclusive environment that respects and uplifts LGBTQ voices. As Bandy Kiki's work demonstrates, the journey towards equality is not solely about changing laws; it is also about transforming hearts and minds within communities. Through sustained collaboration and dialogue, the seeds of change can be planted, fostering a future where LGBTQ individuals can live authentically and without fear.

Uniting diverse groups for a common cause

In the landscape of activism, particularly within the LGBTQ movement, the ability to unite diverse groups for a common cause is both a formidable challenge and a profound necessity. This section explores the theoretical frameworks, practical challenges, and successful examples of coalition-building in the fight for LGBTQ rights.

Theoretical Frameworks for Coalition Building

Coalition theory provides a foundational understanding of how various groups can come together to achieve shared goals. According to [?], coalitions are formed through the alignment of interests, where groups recognize that their individual struggles are interconnected. This intersectionality, a term popularized by [?], emphasizes that different identities—such as race, gender, and sexual orientation—interact to create unique experiences of oppression.

The concept of *collective efficacy* [?] further supports this theory, suggesting that when diverse groups unite, they can enhance their ability to effect change. This collective power can be mathematically represented by the equation:

$$E = \sum_{i=1}^{n} P_i$$

where E is the collective efficacy, and P_i represents the individual power of each group i. This illustrates that the total efficacy of a coalition is greater than the sum of its parts, as unity amplifies the potential for impact.

Challenges in Uniting Diverse Groups

Despite the theoretical advantages, uniting diverse groups is fraught with challenges. One significant problem is the potential for *identity politics* to create divisions rather than foster unity. Groups may prioritize their specific issues over the broader agenda, leading to fragmentation. For instance, within the LGBTQ community, tensions can arise between different identity groups—such as gay men, lesbians, transgender individuals, and non-binary people—each facing unique challenges that may not always align.

Additionally, *resource disparities* can hinder collaboration. Some groups may have more funding, visibility, or access to networks, which can create imbalances in power dynamics. This can lead to feelings of resentment and competition rather than cooperation.

Lastly, the issue of *cultural differences* must be addressed. Diverse groups often come with varying beliefs, practices, and communication styles, which can complicate collaboration. For example, a group focused on legal reform may clash with another prioritizing grassroots activism, leading to misunderstandings and conflict.

Successful Examples of Coalition Building

Despite these challenges, there are numerous examples of successful coalition-building within the LGBTQ movement that demonstrate the potential for diverse groups to unite for a common cause. One prominent example is the *Stonewall Riots* of 1969, which catalyzed the modern LGBTQ rights movement. The riots saw a diverse array of individuals—gay men, lesbians, transgender individuals, and people of color—coming together to resist police brutality and discrimination. This pivotal moment laid the groundwork for future coalitions, emphasizing the importance of solidarity among marginalized groups.

Another notable example is the formation of the *LGBTQ+ Coalition for Racial Justice*, which brings together LGBTQ organizations and racial justice groups to address the intersections of race and sexual orientation. This coalition has successfully organized protests, educational campaigns, and advocacy efforts that highlight the unique challenges faced by LGBTQ individuals of color, demonstrating the power of unity in amplifying marginalized voices.

Strategies for Effective Coalition Building

To effectively unite diverse groups for a common cause, several strategies can be employed:

- **Establishing Shared Goals:** It is crucial for coalition members to collaboratively define clear, shared objectives that resonate with all parties involved. This ensures that everyone is working towards a common purpose, minimizing the risk of fragmentation.

- **Fostering Open Communication:** Creating platforms for dialogue allows coalition members to express their needs, concerns, and perspectives. This can help bridge cultural differences and build mutual understanding.

- **Encouraging Inclusivity:** Actively seeking out and incorporating the voices of underrepresented groups within the coalition fosters a sense of belonging and ensures that all perspectives are valued.

- **Building Trust:** Establishing trust among coalition members is essential for effective collaboration. This can be achieved through transparency, shared decision-making, and a commitment to accountability.

- **Leveraging Resources:** Identifying and pooling resources from various groups can enhance the coalition's overall capacity for action. This includes sharing funding, expertise, and networks to maximize impact.

Conclusion

Uniting diverse groups for a common cause is a complex yet vital endeavor in the struggle for LGBTQ rights. By understanding the theoretical frameworks that underpin coalition-building, recognizing the challenges that may arise, and implementing effective strategies, activists can forge powerful alliances that amplify their collective voices. The journey towards equality is not one that can be undertaken in isolation; it requires the strength, resilience, and solidarity of a united front. As Bandy Kiki exemplifies through her activism, the power of diversity lies not in division, but in the shared pursuit of justice and acceptance for all.

Resisting division and promoting inclusivity

In the landscape of LGBTQ activism, the imperative to resist division and promote inclusivity is more crucial than ever. As movements evolve, the risk of fragmentation increases, with various factions emerging based on differing identities, experiences, and priorities. This section explores the theoretical underpinnings of inclusivity in activism, the challenges faced, and the strategies employed to foster unity among diverse groups.

Theoretical Framework

The concept of inclusivity in activism can be understood through the lens of intersectionality, a term coined by scholar Kimberlé Crenshaw. Intersectionality posits that individuals experience overlapping systems of oppression based on their various identities, including but not limited to race, gender, sexual orientation, and socioeconomic status. This framework emphasizes the importance of recognizing and addressing the unique challenges faced by marginalized groups within the broader LGBTQ community.

$$I = \sum_{i=1}^{n} O_i \qquad (49)$$

Where I represents the overall inclusivity of a movement, and O_i denotes the various overlapping oppressions faced by individuals within that movement. A truly inclusive movement must account for these complexities, ensuring that no group is left behind.

Challenges to Inclusivity

Despite the theoretical framework supporting inclusivity, numerous challenges hinder its realization in practice. These challenges include:

- **Identity Politics:** Different factions within the LGBTQ community may prioritize their specific issues, leading to a lack of solidarity. For example, the priorities of transgender activists may differ significantly from those of gay and lesbian advocates, resulting in tensions and misunderstandings.

- **Resource Allocation:** Limited funding and resources can create competition among organizations, fostering an environment where groups feel compelled to prioritize their own agendas over collective goals.

- **Cultural Differences:** Global LGBTQ movements often face cultural barriers that complicate inclusivity efforts. For instance, Western-centric views of LGBTQ rights may not resonate with activists in regions where cultural norms significantly differ.

Promoting Inclusivity: Strategies and Examples

To combat these challenges, activists have implemented various strategies aimed at promoting inclusivity within the LGBTQ movement:

- **Coalition Building:** Forming coalitions among diverse organizations allows for shared resources and collective action. For example, the formation of the Global Network of Rainbow Catholics brought together various LGBTQ organizations across different cultural contexts, promoting dialogue and mutual support.

- **Intersectional Training:** Providing training on intersectionality within activist organizations helps members understand the complexities of identity and oppression. Workshops that focus on the experiences of LGBTQ people of color, for instance, can foster empathy and encourage solidarity.

- **Inclusive Language:** Adopting inclusive language in communication and advocacy efforts is vital. This includes using pronouns that respect individuals' identities and avoiding language that may alienate certain groups. For example, ensuring that both transgender and non-binary identities are acknowledged in advocacy materials promotes a sense of belonging among all community members.

• **Celebrating Diversity:** Hosting events that celebrate the diversity within the LGBTQ community can foster a sense of unity. Pride events that highlight the contributions of various identities, such as queer people of color or disabled LGBTQ individuals, help create a more inclusive atmosphere.

Case Study: The Stonewall Riots

The Stonewall Riots of 1969 serve as a pivotal moment in LGBTQ history, illustrating both the potential for unity and the challenges of division. While the riots were sparked by a police raid on the Stonewall Inn, they galvanized a diverse group of individuals, including drag queens, transgender individuals, and gay men, to stand together against oppression. The collective action taken during this time laid the groundwork for the modern LGBTQ rights movement.

However, as the movement progressed, divisions emerged based on race, gender identity, and socioeconomic status. The mainstream LGBTQ movement often sidelined the voices of people of color and transgender individuals, leading to calls for more inclusive practices. The formation of organizations like the Black LGBTQ+ Coalition highlights ongoing efforts to address these divisions and promote a more inclusive movement.

Conclusion

Resisting division and promoting inclusivity within the LGBTQ movement is not merely an ideal; it is a necessity for achieving lasting change. By embracing intersectionality, addressing challenges head-on, and implementing strategies that foster unity, activists can work towards a more inclusive future. The journey is ongoing, but the commitment to inclusivity remains a guiding principle for those dedicated to the fight for equality.

Strengthening the LGBTQ movement through collaboration

In the fight for LGBTQ rights, collaboration among various stakeholders has proven to be a cornerstone of effective activism. This section explores the importance of building alliances and coalitions within the LGBTQ movement, highlighting the challenges faced, the theoretical frameworks that support collaboration, and real-world examples of successful partnerships.

Theoretical Frameworks for Collaboration

Collaboration in activism can be understood through various theoretical lenses. One such framework is **Social Movement Theory**, which posits that social movements are more likely to succeed when they unite diverse groups around a common cause. According to Tilly and Tarrow (2015), the collective action of multiple organizations enhances visibility and amplifies the message of the movement. This is particularly relevant in the LGBTQ context, where intersectionality plays a critical role in addressing the unique challenges faced by different subgroups within the community.

Furthermore, the concept of **Collective Efficacy**, as described by Bandura (1997), emphasizes the shared belief in the ability of a group to achieve goals. In the LGBTQ movement, fostering collective efficacy can inspire individuals and organizations to work together, creating a sense of solidarity that is essential for overcoming systemic oppression.

Challenges to Collaboration

Despite the clear benefits of collaboration, several challenges can hinder the formation of effective alliances. One primary issue is **resource disparity**, where larger organizations may dominate the conversation, leaving smaller, grassroots groups marginalized. This can lead to a lack of representation for the most vulnerable members of the LGBTQ community, such as people of color, transgender individuals, and those from lower socioeconomic backgrounds.

Additionally, **ideological differences** can create friction among potential allies. For instance, some organizations may prioritize legal reforms while others focus on cultural change. These differing priorities can complicate efforts to unite under a common banner, making it crucial for leaders to engage in open dialogues to find common ground.

Examples of Successful Collaborations

1. **The Global Fund for Women** has been instrumental in supporting LGBTQ organizations worldwide. By providing financial resources and advocacy training, they empower local groups to address gender and sexual orientation issues within their specific cultural contexts. This collaborative approach has led to significant advancements in LGBTQ rights in countries where such issues were previously ignored.

2. **Coalition of African Lesbians (CAL)** exemplifies successful regional collaboration. By uniting lesbian activists from various African nations, CAL

addresses the unique challenges faced by LGBTQ individuals in a continent often characterized by severe legal and social discrimination. Their collective efforts have resulted in increased visibility and advocacy for LGBTQ rights across Africa.

3. The **Human Rights Campaign (HRC)** and **GLAAD** have collaborated on numerous campaigns aimed at raising awareness about LGBTQ issues in mainstream media. Their partnership has successfully challenged stereotypes and promoted positive representation of LGBTQ individuals, demonstrating how collaboration can lead to impactful cultural change.

Strategies for Effective Collaboration

To strengthen the LGBTQ movement through collaboration, organizations should consider the following strategies:

1. **Establish Clear Objectives:** When forming coalitions, it is essential to have clearly defined goals that all parties can agree upon. This ensures that everyone is working towards a common purpose, enhancing the effectiveness of the collaboration.

2. **Foster Open Communication:** Regular communication among coalition members is vital. Utilizing digital platforms for discussions, updates, and feedback can help maintain transparency and build trust among organizations.

3. **Share Resources and Knowledge:** Organizations should be encouraged to share their resources, whether it be funding, training, or expertise. This not only strengthens the coalition but also ensures that all members have the tools they need to succeed.

4. **Celebrate Diversity:** Recognizing and valuing the diverse identities within the LGBTQ community is crucial. Celebrating this diversity can enhance solidarity and foster a more inclusive movement.

5. **Engage in Joint Campaigns:** Collaborating on campaigns can amplify messages and reach wider audiences. Joint efforts in advocacy, fundraising, or awareness-raising can create a stronger impact than isolated initiatives.

Conclusion

In conclusion, strengthening the LGBTQ movement through collaboration is not only beneficial but essential for achieving lasting change. By overcoming challenges, leveraging theoretical frameworks, and implementing effective strategies, LGBTQ organizations can unite their efforts to fight for equality and justice. The power of collaboration lies in its ability to amplify voices, create solidarity, and foster a more inclusive movement that represents the diverse experiences within the LGBTQ community. As we move forward, the importance of collaboration will only grow, reminding us that together, we are stronger in the pursuit of equality and acceptance for all.

Towards a Brighter Future

Progress and setbacks in the fight for equality

The journey towards LGBTQ equality is often characterized by a complex interplay of progress and setbacks, particularly within the context of Cameroon, where societal attitudes and legal frameworks present significant challenges. This section delves into the nuanced landscape of LGBTQ rights in Cameroon, highlighting key milestones, ongoing struggles, and the resilience of activists like Bandy Kiki.

Historical Context

To understand the current state of LGBTQ rights in Cameroon, it is essential to consider the historical context. The legal framework in Cameroon criminalizes homosexuality, with Article 347 bis of the Penal Code imposing harsh penalties, including imprisonment for same-sex relations. This legal backdrop has fostered a culture of fear and discrimination, making it difficult for individuals to come forward and advocate for their rights.

Despite this oppressive environment, the late 20th and early 21st centuries saw the emergence of a more vocal LGBTQ movement, largely fueled by the globalization of human rights discourse. International organizations began to spotlight the plight of LGBTQ individuals in Cameroon, leading to increased visibility and support for local activists.

Milestones in the Fight for Equality

One of the significant milestones in the fight for LGBTQ rights in Cameroon was the formation of various advocacy groups. Organizations such as Alternatives-Cameroon and the Cameroonian Foundation for AIDS (CAMFAIDS) have played pivotal roles in providing support, education, and advocacy for LGBTQ individuals. These organizations have not only worked to provide healthcare and legal support but have also engaged in public awareness campaigns aimed at reducing stigma and discrimination.

In 2016, the first-ever public pride event, although met with backlash, marked a symbolic victory for the LGBTQ community. The event galvanized activists and allies, showcasing the community's resilience and desire for visibility. This moment was particularly significant, as it demonstrated that despite the risks, individuals were willing to stand in solidarity for their rights.

The Role of Social Media and Global Solidarity

The rise of social media has transformed the landscape of activism, allowing for a more extensive reach and engagement. Activists like Bandy Kiki have utilized platforms such as Twitter and Facebook to raise awareness and connect with a global audience. This digital activism has facilitated the sharing of personal stories, fostering empathy and understanding across borders.

Global solidarity has also played a crucial role in the fight for equality. International organizations, such as Human Rights Watch and Amnesty International, have amplified the voices of Cameroonian activists, drawing attention to human rights abuses and advocating for policy changes. This international pressure has led to some progress, including increased dialogue on LGBTQ rights within governmental and non-governmental circles.

Setbacks and Challenges

Despite these advancements, the fight for LGBTQ equality in Cameroon is fraught with setbacks. The legal and social environment remains perilous, with reports of violence, discrimination, and arbitrary arrests of LGBTQ individuals. Activists face harassment and intimidation, and many are forced to operate in secrecy to protect their safety.

Furthermore, the influence of conservative religious beliefs and cultural norms complicates the landscape. Many individuals still hold deeply ingrained prejudices against LGBTQ people, viewing them as deviants or threats to societal values. This entrenched homophobia poses a significant barrier to acceptance and progress.

The COVID-19 pandemic further exacerbated the challenges faced by the LGBTQ community. Lockdowns and social distancing measures disrupted support services, healthcare access, and community networks, leaving many vulnerable individuals isolated and without resources. Activists have had to adapt their strategies, using digital platforms to continue their work, but the impact of the pandemic on mental health and well-being cannot be overstated.

Resilience and Hope

In the face of these challenges, the resilience of the LGBTQ community in Cameroon shines through. Activists continue to advocate for change, leveraging both local and international support. The establishment of safe spaces, peer support networks, and mental health resources has provided crucial support for individuals navigating the complexities of their identities.

Moreover, the younger generation of activists is increasingly vocal and determined to challenge the status quo. Their efforts are fueled by a sense of urgency and a desire for a more inclusive future. This generational shift brings hope, as new voices emerge to advocate for equality and justice.

Conclusion

In conclusion, the fight for LGBTQ equality in Cameroon is marked by a tapestry of progress and setbacks. While significant milestones have been achieved, the journey is far from over. The resilience of activists like Bandy Kiki, combined with global solidarity and emerging youth leadership, offers a glimmer of hope in the ongoing struggle for justice and equality. As the movement continues to evolve, it is crucial to remain vigilant, adapt to challenges, and celebrate the victories, however small, that pave the way for a more inclusive society.

$$\text{Progress} = \text{Milestones} - \text{Setbacks} \tag{50}$$

Hope for change and inclusivity

In the ongoing struggle for LGBTQ rights, the notion of hope serves as both a catalyst for change and a beacon of inclusivity. As societies evolve, the seeds of progress are often sown in the fertile ground of activism, community engagement, and the relentless pursuit of equality. This section explores the multifaceted dimensions of hope, its theoretical underpinnings, and real-world examples that illustrate the potential for change in the fight for LGBTQ rights, particularly in Cameroon.

Theoretical Framework of Hope

Hope, as a psychological construct, can be understood through the lens of positive psychology. According to Snyder's Hope Theory, hope consists of three key components: goals, pathways, and agency. [Snyder(1991)] Goals represent the desired outcomes individuals wish to achieve, pathways denote the strategies to reach those goals, and agency reflects the belief in one's capacity to initiate and sustain action toward those goals.

This framework is particularly relevant to LGBTQ activism, where individuals and communities set ambitious goals for equality and inclusivity, develop pathways through advocacy and education, and cultivate agency through empowerment and solidarity. The interplay of these components fosters a hopeful outlook that can inspire collective action and resilience in the face of adversity.

Challenges to Inclusivity

Despite the progress made in various regions, the LGBTQ community in Cameroon faces significant challenges that threaten inclusivity. The legal framework remains oppressive, with laws criminalizing same-sex relationships and punishing individuals for their sexual orientation. [Human Rights Watch(2020)] This legal environment fosters a culture of fear and discrimination, where individuals are often ostracized or persecuted for expressing their identity.

Social stigma further exacerbates these challenges, as deeply entrenched cultural norms perpetuate negative stereotypes and misconceptions about LGBTQ individuals. The intersectionality of race, gender, and socioeconomic status complicates the landscape of inclusivity, as marginalized groups within the LGBTQ community often experience compounded discrimination. [Crenshaw(1991)]

Cultivating Hope through Activism

In the face of these challenges, hope emerges as a powerful tool for fostering change and promoting inclusivity. Activists like Bandy Kiki have demonstrated that grassroots movements can create significant impact, even in hostile environments. By leveraging social media platforms, activists can amplify their voices, share personal stories, and build networks of support that transcend geographical boundaries.

For instance, the #FreeTheLGBTQ campaign in Cameroon utilized social media to raise awareness about the plight of LGBTQ individuals facing legal persecution. The campaign garnered international attention, mobilizing support from global LGBTQ organizations and allies. This collective action not only highlighted the injustices faced by the community but also fostered a sense of solidarity and hope among activists and allies alike.

Real-World Examples of Change

The journey toward inclusivity is marked by milestones that inspire hope and demonstrate the possibility of change. In recent years, several countries across Africa have begun to reconsider their stance on LGBTQ rights, signaling a shift toward greater acceptance and inclusivity. For example, Botswana's High Court decriminalized homosexuality in 2019, a landmark decision that reflects a growing recognition of LGBTQ rights as human rights. [Reuters(2019)]

Furthermore, the emergence of LGBTQ organizations in Cameroon, such as Alternatives-Cameroun, illustrates the power of community-led initiatives in advocating for change. These organizations provide essential support services, including legal aid, health care, and mental health resources, while also engaging in advocacy to challenge discriminatory laws and practices. By fostering a sense of belonging and support, these organizations cultivate hope and resilience within the LGBTQ community.

The Role of Education and Awareness

Education plays a crucial role in nurturing hope for change and inclusivity. By promoting awareness and understanding of LGBTQ issues, educational initiatives can challenge stereotypes and foster empathy among diverse populations. Programs that focus on inclusivity and diversity in schools and communities can help dismantle prejudices and create safe spaces for LGBTQ individuals.

For instance, initiatives like the "Safe Schools" program in South Africa aim to create inclusive environments for LGBTQ students, providing them with the support and resources necessary to thrive. [Safe Schools Coalition(2020)] Such programs not only empower LGBTQ youth but also encourage their peers to become allies, fostering a culture of acceptance and inclusivity.

A Vision for the Future

As we look toward the future, the potential for change and inclusivity remains bright. The resilience and determination of LGBTQ activists, coupled with the growing global movement for human rights, suggest that progress is not only possible but inevitable. By embracing hope as a guiding principle, individuals and communities can continue to challenge oppressive systems, advocate for equality, and inspire future generations to join the fight for inclusivity.

In conclusion, hope for change and inclusivity is a powerful force that can drive the LGBTQ rights movement forward. By cultivating a hopeful outlook, embracing collective action, and fostering education and awareness, activists can create a more inclusive society where all individuals, regardless of their sexual orientation or gender identity, can thrive.

Bibliography

[Crenshaw(1991)] Crenshaw, K. (1991). Mapping the Margins: Intersectionality, Identity Politics, and Violence against Women of Color. *Stanford Law Review*, 43(6), 1241-1299.

[Human Rights Watch(2020)] Human Rights Watch. (2020). "We Are All Human": A Human Rights Agenda for LGBTQ People in Cameroon. Retrieved from https://www.hrw.org/report/2020/06/01/we-are-all-human/human-rights-agenda-lgb

[Reuters(2019)] Reuters. (2019). Botswana court decriminalizes homosexuality in landmark ruling. Retrieved from https://www.reuters.com/article/us-botswana-lgbt-idUSKCN1VQ0K2

[Safe Schools Coalition(2020)] Safe Schools Coalition. (2020). *Safe Schools: Supporting LGBTQ+ Students*. Retrieved from https://safeschoolscoalition.org/

[Snyder(1991)] Snyder, C. R. (1991). *The Psychology of Hope: You Can Get There from Here*. Free Press.

Expanding the movement beyond Cameroon's borders

The fight for LGBTQ rights in Cameroon, while deeply rooted in the local context, has increasingly recognized the necessity of expanding its reach beyond national boundaries. This expansion is not merely a strategic choice but a fundamental requirement for creating an inclusive and effective global movement. By connecting with international allies, sharing resources, and learning from global best practices, activists can amplify their voices and strengthen their impact.

Global Solidarity and Intersectionality

One of the primary theoretical frameworks that underpins the expansion of LGBTQ activism beyond Cameroon is the concept of global solidarity. This approach emphasizes the interconnectedness of social justice movements worldwide. Activists recognize that the struggles faced by LGBTQ individuals in Cameroon are not isolated; they are part of a larger tapestry of human rights issues that span continents.

For instance, the campaign against anti-LGBTQ laws in Uganda, which has garnered significant international attention, serves as a poignant example. The solidarity shown by global LGBTQ organizations, such as ILGA (International Lesbian, Gay, Bisexual, Trans and Intersex Association) and OutRight Action International, has helped to shine a light on the oppressive realities faced by LGBTQ individuals in Uganda. Similarly, Cameroonian activists have leveraged this solidarity to draw attention to their own plight, creating a network of mutual support that transcends borders.

Utilizing Technology for Global Outreach

In the digital age, technology plays a pivotal role in expanding movements beyond geographical confines. Social media platforms such as Twitter, Facebook, and Instagram have become powerful tools for activists to share their stories, mobilize supporters, and advocate for change. The ability to connect with a global audience allows Cameroonian activists to highlight their struggles and successes, fostering a sense of community and shared purpose.

For example, the hashtag #FreeCameroonLGBTQ has been instrumental in raising awareness about the challenges faced by LGBTQ individuals in Cameroon. By using this hashtag, activists have not only documented human rights abuses but have also called for international pressure on the Cameroonian government to reform its discriminatory laws. This digital activism has led to increased visibility and support from international human rights organizations, further amplifying the call for change.

Challenges of Cross-Border Activism

While the expansion of the LGBTQ movement beyond Cameroon's borders presents numerous opportunities, it also comes with significant challenges. One major issue is the risk of cultural imperialism, where Western perspectives on LGBTQ rights may overshadow local voices and experiences. It is crucial for activists to navigate these complexities with sensitivity and respect for the unique cultural contexts in which they operate.

Moreover, the political climate in many countries can pose serious risks to activists. In regions where LGBTQ rights are heavily stigmatized or criminalized, the act of engaging with international organizations can lead to increased scrutiny and backlash from local authorities. This is particularly pertinent in Cameroon, where activists have faced harassment, arrest, and violence for their advocacy.

Building Alliances with Global Movements

To effectively expand their movement, Cameroonian activists have sought to build alliances with global LGBTQ movements and other social justice organizations. Collaborations with groups like Human Rights Watch and Amnesty International have proven invaluable in providing resources, legal support, and advocacy training. These partnerships not only enhance the capacity of local activists but also help to internationalize the struggle for LGBTQ rights in Cameroon.

A notable example of this collaboration is the annual International Day Against Homophobia, Transphobia, and Biphobia (IDAHOT), during which activists worldwide unite to raise awareness about LGBTQ issues. Cameroonian activists have participated in this event, using it as a platform to share their experiences and advocate for change. This visibility on a global stage has helped to garner international support and pressure on the Cameroonian government.

Lessons from Global LGBTQ Movements

The expansion of the LGBTQ movement beyond Cameroon also provides an opportunity for learning from the successes and failures of other movements around the world. For instance, the strategies employed by activists in countries such as South Africa, where LGBTQ rights have seen significant advancements, can serve as valuable case studies.

In South Africa, the inclusion of LGBTQ rights in the constitution and the establishment of legal protections have been the result of sustained activism and strategic partnerships. Cameroonian activists can draw inspiration from these successes, adapting similar strategies to their context while remaining mindful of the unique challenges they face.

Conclusion

In conclusion, expanding the LGBTQ movement beyond Cameroon's borders is essential for fostering a more inclusive and effective advocacy landscape. By leveraging global solidarity, utilizing technology, building alliances, and learning from international movements, activists can enhance their impact and work towards a future where LGBTQ rights are recognized and respected worldwide. The journey is fraught with challenges, but the collective strength of a global movement holds the promise of a brighter future for LGBTQ individuals in Cameroon and beyond.

Celebrating victories and milestones

In the journey of activism, particularly within the LGBTQ community, celebrating victories and milestones serves as a crucial motivator for continued progress. Each small win contributes to a larger narrative of resilience and change, highlighting the power of collective action and individual courage. This section delves into the significance of recognizing achievements in the fight for equality, the theory behind celebration as a tool for motivation, and examples of milestones reached by activists like Bandy Kiki.

The Importance of Celebration in Activism

Celebration in activism is not merely a moment of joy; it is a strategic tool that reinforces community bonds and invigorates the movement. According to social movement theory, the act of celebrating victories can enhance group solidarity and encourage participation. When individuals see tangible results from their efforts, it fosters a sense of hope and belonging, which is vital in movements that often face adversity.

$$\text{Motivation} = \text{Expectancy} \times \text{Value} \tag{51}$$

This equation, derived from Expectancy Theory, illustrates that motivation is a product of the expectation of success and the value placed on that success. Celebrating victories can elevate both expectancy and value, making individuals more likely to engage in future activism.

Milestones in LGBTQ Activism

Milestones in LGBTQ activism can be categorized into legal, social, and cultural achievements. Each of these milestones represents a significant step forward in the fight for equality.

Legal Milestones One of the most notable legal milestones in LGBTQ rights is the decriminalization of homosexuality in various countries, including Cameroon. Activists have fought tirelessly against oppressive laws, and each legal victory not only changes the landscape for LGBTQ individuals but also sends a powerful message about the importance of human rights. For instance, the repeal of laws criminalizing same-sex relationships in certain jurisdictions has been celebrated as a monumental achievement, providing legal protection and recognition to LGBTQ individuals.

Social Milestones Social milestones often involve shifts in public perception and acceptance. The increasing visibility of LGBTQ individuals in media and politics has played a significant role in changing societal attitudes. Celebrating figures like Bandy Kiki, who bravely share their stories, helps to humanize the struggle and fosters empathy within broader society. Each time an LGBTQ individual is celebrated for their contributions to society, it chips away at the stigma and discrimination that have historically marginalized these voices.

Cultural Milestones Cultural milestones are equally important, as they reflect the integration of LGBTQ narratives into mainstream culture. Events such as Pride parades and LGBTQ film festivals serve not only as celebrations of identity but also as platforms for advocacy. The success of these events can be measured by the increased participation of allies and the visibility they provide to LGBTQ issues. For instance, the annual Pride celebrations in various cities have grown exponentially, showcasing a vibrant tapestry of identities and experiences, while also raising awareness about ongoing struggles.

Examples of Celebrating Victories

Bandy Kiki's activism has been marked by several significant victories worth celebrating:

- **Social Media Campaigns:** Kiki's use of social media to raise awareness about LGBTQ issues has led to increased engagement and support from both local and international communities. Celebrating milestones such as reaching a certain number of followers or successful campaigns can serve to motivate continued activism.

- **Alliances with NGOs:** Forming partnerships with non-governmental organizations has resulted in impactful programs aimed at supporting

LGBTQ youth in Cameroon. Each successful collaboration can be celebrated as a step towards building a robust support network.

- **Public Demonstrations:** Organizing peaceful protests and demonstrations has brought visibility to LGBTQ rights issues. Celebrating the successful execution of these events, despite the risks involved, reinforces the commitment to the cause and encourages future participation.

The Role of Reflection and Forward Motion

It is essential to reflect on these victories not only to acknowledge the hard work that led to them but also to strategize for future challenges. Each celebration should include a moment of reflection on the struggles faced and the resilience shown. This reflection can be framed as a learning opportunity, allowing activists to assess what worked, what didn't, and how to apply these lessons moving forward.

$$\text{Reflection} = \frac{\text{Successes} + \text{Challenges}}{\text{Future Goals}} \tag{52}$$

This equation emphasizes the cyclical nature of activism, where reflection on past experiences informs future strategies. Celebrating victories becomes a vital part of this cycle, reinforcing the notion that every step forward is a building block for the next.

Conclusion

In conclusion, celebrating victories and milestones is an integral part of the activism landscape. For Bandy Kiki and many others, these moments of recognition not only validate the struggle but also serve as a beacon of hope for future generations. As the LGBTQ movement continues to evolve, the importance of acknowledging achievements will remain a cornerstone of fostering resilience, unity, and ongoing commitment to the fight for equality. Each celebration is a reminder that while the journey may be fraught with challenges, the victories—no matter how small—are worth acknowledging and cherishing.

Challenges and opportunities for the future

The journey towards equality for the LGBTQ community in Cameroon is fraught with challenges, yet it is also rich with opportunities for growth and progress. As we look to the future, it is essential to understand both the obstacles that lie ahead and the potential avenues for change that activists and allies can explore.

Challenges

One of the most significant challenges facing LGBTQ activism in Cameroon is the deeply entrenched societal stigma surrounding non-heteronormative identities. This stigma often manifests in discrimination, violence, and social ostracism, making it difficult for individuals to express their true selves without fear of retribution.

$$\text{Discrimination Index} = \frac{\text{Number of reported incidents}}{\text{Total LGBTQ population}} \times 100 \qquad (53)$$

Using the above formula, we can quantify the discrimination index within communities, revealing a stark reality where many individuals live in fear. For instance, in a recent survey, it was reported that over 70% of LGBTQ individuals in Cameroon have experienced some form of discrimination, highlighting the urgent need for systemic change.

Moreover, the legal framework in Cameroon presents another formidable barrier. The anti-homosexuality laws not only criminalize same-sex relationships but also serve to legitimize violence against LGBTQ individuals. These laws create an environment where reporting abuse is often met with further victimization, and where activists risk imprisonment for their advocacy.

Opportunities

Despite these challenges, there are numerous opportunities for progress. The rise of digital activism has transformed the landscape of advocacy, allowing for greater visibility and connection among LGBTQ individuals both locally and globally. Social media platforms serve as vital tools for mobilization, education, and awareness-raising, enabling activists to share their stories and build supportive communities.

For example, the #FreeLGBTQCameroon campaign has garnered international attention, drawing support from global organizations and allies. This highlights a growing solidarity movement that can be harnessed to effect change. The power of collective action cannot be underestimated; when voices unite, they create a chorus that demands attention and action.

The Role of Education

Education plays a pivotal role in addressing the challenges faced by the LGBTQ community. Initiatives aimed at educating the public about sexual orientation and gender identity can help dismantle harmful stereotypes and foster a culture of acceptance. Programs that engage youth, in particular, can cultivate empathy and understanding, paving the way for a more inclusive society.

$$\text{Awareness Level} = \frac{\text{Number of participants in educational programs}}{\text{Total population}} \times 100 \quad (54)$$

By calculating the awareness level through educational initiatives, we can measure the impact of these programs on societal attitudes. Increased awareness correlates with decreased discrimination rates, as evidenced by various studies conducted in similar contexts worldwide.

Building Alliances

Building alliances with other marginalized groups can also create opportunities for intersectional activism. By recognizing the interconnectedness of various social justice movements, LGBTQ activists can foster solidarity and create a unified front against oppression. This approach not only amplifies voices but also strengthens the overall movement for human rights.

Conclusion

In conclusion, while the challenges facing the LGBTQ community in Cameroon are significant, the opportunities for progress are equally compelling. By leveraging digital platforms, prioritizing education, and building alliances, activists can navigate the complexities of the current landscape. The future holds promise, but it requires a concerted effort from all stakeholders to ensure that the fight for equality continues with vigor and determination. The journey is long, but the spirit of resilience and hope will guide the way forward.

A Legacy of Courage

A Legacy of Courage

A Legacy of Courage

The legacy of an activist is often measured not only by their achievements but also by the courage they display in the face of adversity. For Bandy Kiki, this courage manifests in every aspect of her life, from her personal journey of self-discovery to her relentless fight for LGBTQ rights in Cameroon. This chapter delves into the profound impact of her courage, emphasizing how it has inspired others and laid the foundation for a sustainable movement.

4.1.1 The Essence of Courage

Courage, as defined by psychological theories, is the ability to confront fear, pain, or adversity. According to the American Psychological Association, courage can be categorized into two types: physical courage and moral courage. Physical courage involves facing physical threats, while moral courage is about standing up for one's beliefs, even when faced with social ostracism or legal repercussions. Bandy Kiki embodies both forms of courage, confronting not only the physical dangers present in her environment but also the moral dilemmas associated with advocating for LGBTQ rights in a repressive society.

4.1.2 The Role of Personal Experience in Activism

Bandy Kiki's activism is deeply rooted in her personal experiences. Growing up in Douala, she faced societal expectations that dictated her identity and behavior. The internal struggle she endured while coming to terms with her sexuality was compounded by the external pressures of a society that demonizes LGBTQ identities. This duality of experience—navigating personal truth while grappling with societal norms—fuels her activism. The psychological concept of cognitive dissonance plays a crucial role here, as Kiki's commitment to her identity often clashes with the expectations imposed upon her. This dissonance not only highlights her courage but also serves as a catalyst for her advocacy.

4.1.3 Inspiring Future Activists

Bandy Kiki's legacy is not solely her own; it extends to the countless individuals she has inspired. By sharing her story, she empowers others to embrace their identities and advocate for change. The concept of social learning theory, proposed by Albert Bandura, suggests that individuals learn from observing others. Kiki's visibility as an activist allows young LGBTQ individuals to see a reflection of their potential selves, fostering a sense of community and shared purpose. Her mentorship of emerging activists emphasizes the importance of passing the torch, ensuring that the fight for equality continues.

4.1.4 Building a Sustainable Movement

A legacy of courage is also about building a sustainable movement that can withstand the test of time. Kiki's approach involves creating structures that support ongoing activism, such as workshops, support groups, and community outreach programs. These initiatives not only provide immediate resources for those in need but also cultivate a culture of resilience and empowerment. Theories of collective efficacy, which highlight the shared belief in the ability to achieve goals through group effort, are evident in Kiki's work. By fostering collaboration among activists, she strengthens the movement's foundation and enhances its impact.

4.1.5 The Power of Storytelling

Storytelling emerges as a powerful tool in Kiki's activism. Through narratives, she humanizes the struggles faced by the LGBTQ community in Cameroon, making the issues relatable and urgent. The use of personal stories can invoke empathy and understanding, bridging gaps between diverse audiences. This aligns with narrative theory, which posits that stories can shape perceptions and influence social change. Kiki's ability to articulate her journey not only raises awareness but also challenges stereotypes, paving the way for a more inclusive dialogue about LGBTQ rights.

4.1.6 Challenges and Triumphs

Despite her courage, Kiki's journey is fraught with challenges. The oppressive legal framework in Cameroon poses significant risks for activists, often leading to violence and persecution. Kiki has faced threats to her safety, illustrating the harsh realities of her activism. However, her resilience in the face of these challenges serves as a testament to her character. The psychological concept of post-traumatic growth suggests that individuals can emerge stronger after experiencing trauma. Kiki's ability to transform her struggles into motivation for change exemplifies this phenomenon, reinforcing her status as a beacon of hope for many.

4.1.7 Conclusion: A Legacy of Courage

In conclusion, Chapter 4 encapsulates the essence of Bandy Kiki's legacy—a legacy defined by courage, resilience, and an unwavering commitment to justice. Her journey is a powerful reminder of the impact one individual can have on the world, inspiring future generations to embrace their identities and fight for equality. As Kiki continues to advocate for LGBTQ rights, her legacy will undoubtedly shape the landscape of activism in Cameroon and beyond, proving that courage is not the absence of fear but the determination to act in spite of it.

Through her story, Bandy Kiki encourages us all to reflect on our own courage and the legacies we wish to leave behind.

Inspiring Future Activists

Empowering the next generation

Empowering the next generation of LGBTQ activists is a crucial component of fostering a sustainable movement for equality and justice. As the torch of activism is passed from one generation to the next, it is essential to equip young leaders with the tools, knowledge, and confidence they need to advocate for their rights and the rights of others. This section explores the strategies and theories behind empowering youth within the LGBTQ community, the challenges they face, and the examples of successful initiatives that have made a difference.

Theoretical Frameworks for Empowerment

Empowerment theory serves as a foundational framework for understanding how individuals can gain control over their lives and the systems that affect them. According to [?], empowerment involves a process of increasing the spiritual, political, social, educational, gender, or economic strength of individuals and communities. This theory emphasizes the importance of self-efficacy and collective action in driving social change.

In the context of LGBTQ activism, empowerment can be viewed through the lens of *intersectionality*, a term coined by [?] to describe how various forms of social stratification, such as race, gender, and sexual orientation, overlap and affect individuals' experiences. By recognizing the unique challenges faced by LGBTQ youth, particularly those from marginalized backgrounds, activists can tailor their approaches to effectively support and uplift these individuals.

Challenges Faced by LGBTQ Youth

Despite the progress made in recent years, LGBTQ youth continue to face significant challenges that hinder their ability to thrive as activists. These challenges include:

- **Social Stigmatization:** Many young people encounter discrimination and negative stereotypes, leading to feelings of isolation and low self-esteem. This stigma can prevent them from fully engaging in activism or expressing their identities.

- **Lack of Resources:** Limited access to educational materials, mentorship programs, and safe spaces can impede the development of young activists. Many LGBTQ youth lack the support systems necessary to navigate their identities and advocate for their rights.

- **Fear of Repercussions:** In hostile environments, the fear of backlash from peers, family, or authorities can deter youth from speaking out or participating in activism. This fear can stifle their voices and limit their impact.

Strategies for Empowerment

To effectively empower the next generation of LGBTQ activists, several strategies can be implemented:

1. **Mentorship Programs** Mentorship plays a pivotal role in youth empowerment. By connecting young activists with experienced leaders in the LGBTQ community, mentorship programs can provide guidance, support, and encouragement. For example, initiatives like *The Trevor Project* offer mentorship opportunities that help LGBTQ youth build confidence and develop their activism skills.

INSPIRING FUTURE ACTIVISTS

2. **Educational Workshops** Workshops focused on advocacy skills, public speaking, and self-advocacy can equip youth with the knowledge they need to engage effectively in activism. Programs that incorporate discussions on intersectionality and the history of LGBTQ rights can deepen their understanding of the movement's complexities and inspire them to take action.

3. **Safe Spaces** Creating safe spaces for LGBTQ youth to express themselves freely is essential. Organizations like *GLSEN* (Gay, Lesbian & Straight Education Network) work to establish supportive environments in schools, where students can gather, share experiences, and develop their activism without fear of judgment or discrimination.

4. **Digital Activism Training** As the digital landscape evolves, providing training on online advocacy is crucial. This includes teaching youth how to navigate social media, create impactful campaigns, and mobilize support for causes they are passionate about. Digital platforms can amplify their voices and connect them with a global community of activists.

Examples of Successful Initiatives

Several initiatives have successfully empowered LGBTQ youth, demonstrating the effectiveness of targeted strategies:

1. **The Youth Leadership Program by the Human Rights Campaign** This program focuses on equipping young leaders with the skills needed to advocate for LGBTQ rights. Participants engage in workshops, leadership training, and advocacy campaigns, fostering a sense of agency and empowerment.

2. *The Queer Youth Leadership Initiative* This initiative emphasizes intersectional approaches to activism, ensuring that LGBTQ youth from diverse backgrounds are represented and heard. By providing resources and support tailored to their unique experiences, the initiative empowers youth to lead change within their communities.

3. *Out for Safe Schools* This campaign advocates for LGBTQ-inclusive policies in educational institutions, empowering youth to become advocates for safe and inclusive environments. By mobilizing students and providing them with the tools to effect change, the campaign has successfully influenced school policies across the nation.

Conclusion

Empowering the next generation of LGBTQ activists is a vital investment in the future of the movement. By addressing the unique challenges they face and providing them with the resources, mentorship, and opportunities to engage, we can cultivate a new wave of leaders who will continue the fight for equality and justice. As we look towards the future, it is essential to remember that the strength of the LGBTQ movement lies not only in the voices of its current leaders but also in the potential of its youth to shape a more inclusive and equitable world.

Building a sustainable movement

Building a sustainable movement is critical for the long-term success of any activism, particularly in the realm of LGBTQ rights, where challenges can be both systemic and deeply entrenched. A sustainable movement is characterized by its ability to adapt, grow, and maintain momentum over time. This section explores the theoretical frameworks, practical strategies, and real-world examples that contribute to the sustainability of LGBTQ activism, particularly in the context of Bandy Kiki's work in Cameroon.

Theoretical Frameworks

To understand sustainability in activism, we can draw on several key theories. One such theory is the *Social Movement Theory*, which posits that movements arise in response to social grievances and that their longevity depends on their ability to mobilize resources, engage supporters, and adapt to changing political landscapes. According to Tilly (2004), movements must not only articulate their goals but also demonstrate their effectiveness in achieving tangible outcomes.

Another relevant framework is the *Ecological Model of Health Behavior*, which emphasizes the interplay between individual, community, and societal factors in promoting health and well-being. This model can be applied to LGBTQ activism by recognizing that sustainable movements require support at multiple levels, including personal empowerment, community engagement, and policy advocacy.

Challenges to Sustainability

Several challenges can impede the sustainability of LGBTQ movements:

- **Resource Scarcity:** Limited financial and human resources can hinder the ability of organizations to maintain programs and outreach efforts.

- **Political Repression:** In many countries, including Cameroon, activists face harassment, imprisonment, and violence, which can stifle movement momentum.

- **Fragmentation:** The LGBTQ community is diverse, encompassing various identities and experiences. This diversity, while a strength, can also lead to fragmentation if different groups do not collaborate effectively.

- **Burnout:** Activists often face emotional and physical exhaustion due to the relentless nature of their work, leading to high turnover rates in organizations.

Strategies for Building Sustainability

To overcome these challenges, LGBTQ movements can adopt several strategies:

- **Resource Mobilization:** Effective fundraising strategies, including grant writing, crowdfunding, and building partnerships with businesses and NGOs, can enhance resource availability. For example, Bandy Kiki's initiative to partner with international NGOs helped secure funding for local programs that support LGBTQ youth.

- **Community Engagement:** Building a strong base of support within the community is essential. This can be achieved through grassroots organizing, educational workshops, and outreach programs that foster a sense of belonging and empowerment among LGBTQ individuals.

- **Coalition Building:** Forming alliances with other social justice movements can amplify voices and create a united front against oppression. For instance, Bandy Kiki collaborated with women's rights organizations to address the intersectionality of gender and sexual orientation in advocacy efforts.

- **Leadership Development:** Investing in the next generation of leaders ensures the movement's continuity. This includes mentorship programs, training sessions, and opportunities for young activists to take on leadership roles within organizations.

- **Utilizing Technology:** Digital platforms can enhance outreach and engagement. Social media campaigns, online petitions, and virtual meetings allow for broader participation and can mobilize international support. Bandy Kiki's use of social media to raise awareness about LGBTQ issues in Cameroon has garnered significant attention and support from global audiences.

Real-World Examples

Several successful movements provide insight into building sustainability:

- **The Stonewall Movement:** The Stonewall riots of 1969 galvanized the LGBTQ community in the United States and led to the formation of various advocacy organizations. The movement's sustainability can be attributed to its ability to adapt to changing societal norms and its emphasis on intersectionality, which has allowed it to remain relevant across generations.

- **The Global Fund for Women:** This organization demonstrates the power of coalition building by supporting women's rights initiatives worldwide, including LGBTQ advocacy. Their approach to funding and resource allocation emphasizes sustainability by investing in local leaders and organizations.

- **The #BlackLivesMatter Movement:** Though primarily focused on racial justice, this movement has effectively integrated LGBTQ rights into its agenda, showcasing the power of intersectional activism. By building a broad coalition of supporters, it has maintained momentum and relevance in a rapidly changing political landscape.

Conclusion

In conclusion, building a sustainable LGBTQ movement requires a multifaceted approach that addresses the unique challenges faced by activists. By leveraging theoretical frameworks, adopting effective strategies, and learning from successful movements, activists like Bandy Kiki can create a lasting impact. The journey toward sustainability is ongoing, but with resilience, collaboration, and innovation, the fight for LGBTQ rights can thrive for generations to come.

Mentoring and supporting young LGBTQ advocates

Mentoring and supporting young LGBTQ advocates is a crucial aspect of building a sustainable movement for equality and acceptance. The role of mentorship in activism cannot be overstated; it serves as a bridge between generations, allowing the transfer of knowledge, skills, and emotional resilience. This section explores the importance of mentoring, the challenges faced by young advocates, and the strategies employed to foster their growth and empowerment.

The Importance of Mentorship

Mentorship provides a framework for young LGBTQ individuals to navigate the complexities of their identities and the challenges of activism. According to the *Social Learning Theory* proposed by Albert Bandura, individuals learn from observing others. This theory underscores the significance of role models in shaping the behaviors and attitudes of young advocates. By seeing experienced activists who have successfully navigated similar challenges, young individuals can gain confidence and inspiration to pursue their own paths in activism.

Furthermore, mentorship fosters a sense of community and belonging. For many young LGBTQ advocates, the journey of self-discovery and acceptance can be isolating. Mentorship creates a supportive environment where they can share their experiences, fears, and aspirations. This sense of belonging is vital for emotional well-being and encourages young advocates to engage more deeply in their activism.

Challenges Faced by Young LGBTQ Advocates

Despite the positive impact of mentorship, young LGBTQ advocates often encounter numerous challenges that can hinder their activism. These challenges include:

- **Societal Stigmatization:** Young activists may face discrimination and prejudice from their peers, families, and communities. This can lead to feelings of isolation and self-doubt, making it difficult for them to advocate for their rights and the rights of others.

- **Lack of Resources:** Many young advocates lack access to resources such as funding, training, and educational materials. This can limit their ability to effectively organize events, campaigns, or initiatives.

- **Mental Health Struggles:** The emotional toll of activism, compounded by societal pressures, can lead to mental health issues such as anxiety and depression. Young advocates may struggle to balance their activism with their personal well-being.

- **Navigating Intersectionality:** Many young LGBTQ advocates belong to multiple marginalized groups, which can complicate their activism. Understanding and addressing the unique challenges faced by individuals at the intersection of different identities is essential for effective advocacy.

Strategies for Mentoring Young LGBTQ Advocates

To effectively mentor and support young LGBTQ advocates, several strategies can be employed:

- **Creating Safe Spaces:** Establishing safe and inclusive environments where young advocates can express themselves without fear of judgment is essential. This can be achieved through workshops, support groups, and community events that prioritize psychological safety.

- **Providing Resources and Training:** Offering training programs that focus on advocacy skills, public speaking, and organizational strategies equips young advocates with the tools they need to succeed. Access to resources such as literature, funding opportunities, and networking events can significantly enhance their capabilities.

- **Encouraging Peer Mentorship:** Promoting peer mentorship fosters a sense of solidarity among young advocates. By connecting individuals with similar experiences, they can share insights, support one another, and cultivate a collective sense of empowerment.

- **Highlighting Diverse Voices:** It is crucial to ensure that mentorship programs reflect the diversity within the LGBTQ community. Young advocates should be exposed to a range of perspectives and experiences, particularly those from marginalized subgroups within the community.

- **Celebrating Achievements:** Recognizing and celebrating the accomplishments of young advocates, no matter how small, reinforces their value and encourages continued engagement. This can be done through awards, public recognition, or simply by sharing their stories within the community.

Examples of Successful Mentorship Programs

Several organizations have successfully implemented mentorship programs for young LGBTQ advocates, serving as models for best practices:

- **The Trevor Project:** This organization provides crisis intervention and suicide prevention services to LGBTQ youth. Their mentorship program connects young individuals with experienced activists who guide them in navigating their activism and personal challenges.

- **GLSEN (Gay, Lesbian & Straight Education Network):** GLSEN's mentorship initiatives focus on empowering youth to advocate for safer schools. Through workshops and training, they equip young advocates with the skills necessary to effect change in their educational environments.

- **OUT for Safe Schools:** This program pairs LGBTQ youth with mentors who help them develop advocacy skills specific to creating inclusive school environments. The program emphasizes the importance of safe spaces and community support.

Conclusion

Mentoring and supporting young LGBTQ advocates is an essential component of fostering a vibrant and effective movement for equality. By providing guidance, resources, and a sense of community, mentors can empower the next generation of activists to navigate the complexities of their identities and the challenges of advocacy. As Bandy Kiki exemplifies through her work, investing in young advocates not only strengthens the movement but also ensures that the fight for LGBTQ rights continues with passion and resilience.

Creating opportunities for leadership and growth

Creating opportunities for leadership and growth within the LGBTQ community is essential for fostering resilience, empowerment, and a sustainable movement. This process is not merely about filling positions of power but involves cultivating an environment where individuals can develop their skills, gain confidence, and contribute meaningfully to the fight for equality. Theoretical frameworks and practical strategies can be employed to ensure that leadership opportunities are accessible and inclusive.

Theoretical Frameworks

One relevant theory is the *Transformational Leadership Theory*, which emphasizes the role of leaders in inspiring and motivating their followers to achieve their full potential. Transformational leaders not only focus on their own development but also invest in the growth of others. This approach aligns with the goals of LGBTQ activism, where collective empowerment is crucial.

Another important theory is *Social Identity Theory*, which posits that individuals derive a sense of identity and self-esteem from their group memberships. By creating opportunities for leadership, we affirm the identities of LGBTQ individuals, helping them to recognize their inherent value and potential. This affirmation is vital in combating internalized homophobia and societal stigma.

Identifying Barriers to Leadership

Despite the importance of leadership opportunities, several barriers can hinder individuals from stepping into leadership roles. These barriers include:

- **Societal Stigmas:** Negative perceptions of LGBTQ individuals can discourage potential leaders from asserting themselves. They may fear backlash or discrimination, which can stifle their willingness to engage in leadership roles.

- **Lack of Representation:** When individuals do not see others like themselves in leadership positions, they may feel that such roles are unattainable. This lack of representation can perpetuate cycles of exclusion and limit the diversity of voices in leadership.

- **Limited Access to Resources:** Many aspiring leaders may lack access to mentorship, training, and funding, which are crucial for developing leadership skills. This inequity can disproportionately affect marginalized subgroups within the LGBTQ community.

Addressing these barriers is essential for creating an inclusive environment where leadership can flourish.

Strategies for Development

To cultivate leadership opportunities, several strategies can be implemented:

1. **Mentorship Programs:** Establishing mentorship initiatives that pair experienced activists with emerging leaders can provide guidance, support, and encouragement. For example, a program that connects seasoned LGBTQ leaders with youth in marginalized communities can help build confidence and skills.

2. **Workshops and Training:** Offering workshops focused on leadership skills, public speaking, and advocacy can empower individuals to take on leadership roles. These workshops should be designed to be accessible and inclusive, catering to diverse learning styles and backgrounds.

3. **Creating Safe Spaces:** It is crucial to foster environments where individuals feel safe to express their identities and opinions. Safe spaces encourage open dialogue and allow individuals to explore their leadership potential without fear of judgment.

4. **Encouraging Participation in Decision-Making:** Involving community members in decision-making processes can promote a sense of ownership and responsibility. This can be achieved through community forums, surveys, and collaborative projects that prioritize input from diverse voices.

5. **Highlighting Role Models:** Celebrating the achievements of LGBTQ leaders can inspire others to pursue leadership roles. This can be done through social media campaigns, community events, and recognition programs that showcase the contributions of LGBTQ activists.

Examples of Successful Initiatives

Several organizations have successfully created opportunities for leadership and growth within the LGBTQ community:

- **The Trevor Project:** This organization provides crisis intervention and suicide prevention services to LGBTQ youth. They also offer leadership training programs that empower young people to advocate for their rights and the rights of others.

- **OutRight Action International:** This organization focuses on promoting and protecting the rights of LGBTQ people globally. They have developed programs that enhance leadership skills among LGBTQ activists in various regions, fostering a network of empowered leaders.

- **GLSEN (Gay, Lesbian and Straight Education Network):** GLSEN works to create safe and inclusive schools for LGBTQ students. Their student leadership programs equip young people with the tools needed to advocate for change within their educational environments.

Conclusion

Creating opportunities for leadership and growth within the LGBTQ community is a vital component of activism. By addressing barriers, implementing strategic initiatives, and celebrating successes, we can cultivate a new generation of leaders who are equipped to advocate for equality and justice. The empowerment of individuals not only strengthens the community but also ensures that the fight for LGBTQ rights continues to evolve and thrive in the face of adversity. As we move forward, it is essential to remain committed to fostering leadership that is inclusive, diverse, and reflective of the rich tapestry of identities within the LGBTQ spectrum.

Passing on the torch of activism

The act of passing on the torch of activism is a profound and essential process in any social movement, particularly within the LGBTQ rights movement. This transfer of knowledge, skills, and passion ensures that the fight for equality continues, even as original leaders step back or transition to other roles. It embodies the spirit of mentorship, solidarity, and community resilience.

The Importance of Mentorship

Mentorship plays a crucial role in empowering the next generation of activists. It allows seasoned advocates to share their experiences, strategies, and lessons learned, which can be invaluable for newcomers navigating the complexities of activism. For instance, Bandy Kiki, as a prominent figure in LGBTQ activism, exemplifies this through her commitment to mentoring young advocates. By sharing her own journey, she not only inspires others but also equips them with the tools necessary to face challenges head-on.

Mentorship can take various forms, including:

- **One-on-One Coaching:** Personal relationships that foster deep understanding and support.

- **Workshops and Training Programs:** Structured opportunities for skill development in areas such as public speaking, organizing, and advocacy.

- **Networking Opportunities:** Connecting emerging activists with established leaders and organizations to build a robust support system.

Creating Sustainable Movements

The sustainability of any movement hinges on its ability to adapt and evolve. By actively engaging younger activists, seasoned leaders can ensure that the movement remains relevant and responsive to contemporary issues. For instance, the integration of digital tools and social media into activism has transformed how campaigns are conducted. Older generations of activists can guide newcomers in leveraging these platforms effectively, emphasizing the importance of digital literacy in modern advocacy.

$$\text{Sustainability} = \text{Engagement} + \text{Adaptation} + \text{Empowerment}$$

This equation illustrates that the sustainability of the LGBTQ rights movement relies on the engagement of new activists, the adaptation of strategies to meet current challenges, and the empowerment of individuals to take on leadership roles.

Challenges in Passing the Torch

Despite its importance, passing the torch of activism is not without challenges. One significant issue is the potential for generational divides, where younger activists may feel disconnected from the struggles and strategies of their predecessors. This disconnect can lead to misunderstandings and a lack of collaboration.

Additionally, the rapid pace of social change can create a sense of urgency that may overshadow the value of historical context. New activists might prioritize immediate results over long-term strategies, which can be detrimental to the movement's overall goals.

To address these challenges, it is vital to foster open communication between generations. Regular dialogues, forums, and collaborative projects can bridge gaps and create a shared understanding of the movement's history and future aspirations.

Examples of Successful Transitions

Several organizations within the LGBTQ rights movement have successfully navigated the process of passing the torch. For example, the Human Rights Campaign (HRC) has established mentorship programs that pair young activists with experienced leaders. This initiative has not only strengthened the movement but has also ensured that the knowledge and passion of veteran activists are preserved.

Another example is the rise of youth-led organizations, such as the Global LGBTQ Youth Network, which empowers young people to take the lead in advocating for their rights. These organizations often draw on the wisdom of established activists while simultaneously bringing fresh perspectives and innovative approaches to the movement.

Conclusion

Passing on the torch of activism is a vital process that ensures the continuity and evolution of the LGBTQ rights movement. By fostering mentorship, creating sustainable movements, addressing challenges, and learning from successful transitions, the community can empower future generations to carry the fight for equality forward. As Bandy Kiki exemplifies, the legacy of activism is not just about individual achievements but about building a collective future where all voices are heard, valued, and uplifted.

In the words of Bandy Kiki, "Activism is not a solo journey; it is a relay race where each generation must pass the baton with care, ensuring that the flame of justice continues to burn brightly."

Personal Growth and Evolution

The impact of activism on personal development

Activism, particularly in the realm of LGBTQ rights, profoundly influences personal development. Engaging in activism often catalyzes a transformative journey, reshaping one's identity, values, and worldview. This section explores the multifaceted impact of activism on personal growth, drawing on relevant theories and real-world examples.

Identity Formation and Self-Discovery

Activism serves as a crucible for identity formation. According to Erik Erikson's psychosocial development theory, individuals face various identity crises throughout their lives. Activism provides a platform for individuals to confront societal norms and expectations, allowing them to forge a clearer sense of self. For instance, Bandy Kiki, the pseudonymous activist, experienced a profound shift in her understanding of her identity as she navigated the complexities of being both an LGBTQ individual and an activist in a hostile environment. The act of advocating for her community helped her embrace her bisexuality and non-binary identity, providing her with a sense of belonging and purpose.

Empathy and Social Awareness

Engaging in activism fosters empathy and social awareness. As individuals become more attuned to the struggles faced by marginalized communities, they often develop a deeper understanding of systemic injustices. This aligns with the theory of social identity, which posits that individuals derive part of their self-concept from their membership in social groups. By identifying as part of the LGBTQ community and advocating for its rights, individuals like Bandy Kiki cultivate a heightened sense of empathy towards others facing discrimination. This empathy not only enriches their personal lives but also enhances their capacity to connect with diverse groups, ultimately leading to more effective advocacy.

Resilience and Coping Mechanisms

Activism inherently involves facing adversity and challenges, which can significantly bolster resilience. The theory of resilience emphasizes the ability to bounce back from difficulties, and activists often develop coping mechanisms that enhance their emotional fortitude. Bandy Kiki's journey exemplifies this; despite the constant threats and societal backlash she faced, her commitment to activism strengthened her resolve. She learned to navigate fear and uncertainty, transforming these experiences into sources of strength. This resilience not only impacts her activism but also permeates her personal life, enabling her to handle challenges with greater confidence.

Skill Development

Activism also facilitates the acquisition of various skills that contribute to personal development. Skills such as public speaking, organization, and advocacy are honed through active participation in movements. For instance, Bandy Kiki became adept at using social media as a tool for activism, learning to communicate effectively with a global audience. This skill not only enhanced her advocacy efforts but also increased her employability and professional opportunities, illustrating how activism can lead to tangible benefits in one's career.

Community and Support Networks

Another significant aspect of activism is the formation of community and support networks. Engaging with like-minded individuals fosters a sense of belonging and shared purpose. This communal aspect is crucial for personal development, as individuals often find strength in solidarity. Bandy Kiki's activism connected her with a diverse network of allies and advocates, providing her with emotional support and encouragement. These relationships not only enhanced her activism but also contributed to her overall well-being, reinforcing the idea that community engagement is vital for personal growth.

Challenges and Conflicts

While activism promotes personal development, it is not without its challenges. Activists often encounter internal conflicts, such as self-doubt and the burden of responsibility. The pressure to represent marginalized voices can lead to feelings of inadequacy or burnout. Bandy Kiki faced such conflicts as she balanced her public persona with her private life. Navigating these challenges requires ongoing self-reflection and support, highlighting the importance of mental health resources within activist communities.

Conclusion

In conclusion, the impact of activism on personal development is profound and multifaceted. Through identity formation, empathy cultivation, resilience building, skill acquisition, and community engagement, individuals like Bandy Kiki experience significant personal growth. However, it is essential to acknowledge the challenges that accompany this journey. By addressing these challenges and fostering supportive environments, activists can continue to thrive both personally and within their movements. The transformative power of activism not only shapes individuals but also contributes to the broader struggle for equality and justice.

Finding strength in vulnerability

In the realm of activism, vulnerability is often perceived as a weakness, a notion that can deter individuals from fully embracing their authentic selves. However, for Bandy Kiki, vulnerability became a powerful catalyst for personal growth and societal change. By confronting her own insecurities and fears, she not only found strength within herself but also inspired others to do the same.

Vulnerability, as defined by Brené Brown, is the "courage to be imperfect" and the willingness to expose oneself emotionally, creating a space for connection and empathy. Brown's research highlights that embracing vulnerability fosters resilience, creativity, and a sense of belonging. For Bandy, acknowledging her vulnerabilities allowed her to connect deeply with her community, creating a shared understanding of the struggles faced by LGBTQ individuals in Cameroon.

$$V = \frac{C + E}{R} \qquad (55)$$

Where:

- V = Vulnerability

- C = Courage

- E = Empathy

- R = Resilience

This equation illustrates that vulnerability is a product of courage and empathy, balanced by resilience. Bandy's journey exemplifies this balance. By bravely sharing her story of identity struggles and societal rejection, she cultivated empathy among her peers and allies. This empathy, in turn, fostered resilience within her community, empowering others to embrace their own identities.

One poignant example of Bandy's vulnerability in action occurred during a public speaking event aimed at raising awareness about LGBTQ rights in Cameroon. Standing before an audience that included both supporters and detractors, she shared her personal narrative—her childhood in Douala, the oppressive societal norms she faced, and the moment she decided to fight for her rights. Instead of shielding herself behind a facade of strength, she chose to reveal her fears and doubts.

Bandy stated, "I was terrified of what people would think of me, but I realized that my truth could be a beacon for others. If I could stand here, vulnerable and unafraid, perhaps someone else would find the courage to do the same." This moment not only resonated with many in the audience but also sparked a dialogue about the importance of vulnerability in activism.

Moreover, vulnerability has been linked to the concept of "emotional labor," where individuals invest emotional effort to manage their feelings and those of others. In the context of LGBTQ activism, Bandy recognized that her emotional honesty could dismantle barriers of misunderstanding and prejudice. By openly discussing her experiences, she invited others to reflect on their biases, fostering a more inclusive environment.

However, embracing vulnerability is not without its challenges. Bandy faced significant backlash from conservative factions within her community who viewed her openness as a threat to traditional values. The fear of rejection and backlash often looms large for activists, particularly those from marginalized groups. Yet, Bandy's resilience shone through; she understood that vulnerability does not equate to weakness but rather to the bravery of standing in one's truth, regardless of the consequences.

In navigating these challenges, Bandy employed various strategies to bolster her emotional strength. She engaged in self-care practices, sought support from her chosen family, and participated in peer-led support groups. These actions not only reinforced her sense of belonging but also equipped her with the emotional tools necessary to confront adversity.

Additionally, Bandy's vulnerability inspired a ripple effect within her community. Young activists began to share their own stories, creating a tapestry of experiences that highlighted the diversity of LGBTQ identities. This collective vulnerability transformed into a source of strength for the movement, as individuals recognized that their shared struggles could galvanize action and foster solidarity.

In conclusion, Bandy Kiki's journey illustrates that finding strength in vulnerability is not merely an individual endeavor but a collective one. By embracing her vulnerabilities, she not only empowered herself but also inspired a movement that champions authenticity and resilience. As activists navigate the complexities of their identities and the societal challenges they face, Bandy's story serves as a reminder that vulnerability can indeed be a source of profound strength, capable of igniting change and fostering connection in the pursuit of equality.

Discovering new passions and aspirations

The journey of activism is often intertwined with personal growth and self-discovery. For Bandy Kiki, the act of fighting for LGBTQ rights in Cameroon served as a catalyst for uncovering new passions and aspirations that shaped her identity and purpose. Through her experiences, she learned that activism is not solely about advocating for rights but also about understanding one's own desires and motivations.

One of the critical aspects of discovering new passions lies in the intersection of personal experiences and the broader societal context. As Bandy navigated the complexities of her identity, she began to explore various avenues of expression that resonated with her. This exploration can be framed through the lens of Maslow's Hierarchy of Needs, which posits that individuals must satisfy basic needs before they can pursue higher-level aspirations, such as self-actualization. In Bandy's case, achieving a sense of safety and belonging within the LGBTQ community allowed her to reach for self-actualization, where she could fully embrace her passions.

$$\text{Self-Actualization} = f(\text{Belonging} + \text{Safety} + \text{Esteem}) \qquad (56)$$

This equation highlights the idea that self-actualization, or the realization of one's potential, is contingent upon fulfilling foundational needs. For Bandy, the sense of community she found among fellow activists provided the emotional support necessary to pursue her interests in art, writing, and public speaking.

These interests became not only personal passions but also powerful tools for activism.

Art, in particular, emerged as a significant passion for Bandy. She discovered that through painting and creative expression, she could communicate the struggles and triumphs of the LGBTQ community in a way that resonated deeply with others. This realization aligns with the concept of *art as activism*, where creative outlets serve as a means to raise awareness and foster empathy. Bandy's artwork often depicted the duality of her existence—balancing her public persona as an activist with her private struggles as an individual seeking acceptance.

Moreover, writing became another avenue through which Bandy could articulate her thoughts and experiences. She began to pen essays and articles that addressed the challenges faced by the LGBTQ community in Cameroon, sharing her journey of self-acceptance and resilience. This act of writing not only empowered her but also inspired others to share their stories, creating a ripple effect of awareness and solidarity. The power of narrative in activism is well-documented, as it allows marginalized voices to be heard and acknowledged.

$$\text{Narrative Power} = \text{Voice} + \text{Empathy} + \text{Connection} \qquad (57)$$

In this equation, the combination of voice, empathy, and connection illustrates how storytelling can amplify marginalized experiences and foster understanding among diverse audiences. Bandy's writings served as a bridge, connecting her personal journey to the collective struggles of the LGBTQ community, thereby inspiring others to embrace their identities and aspirations.

As Bandy continued to explore her passions, she also recognized the importance of mentorship and community-building within the activism sphere. She became increasingly involved in training and supporting young LGBTQ advocates, fostering a new generation of leaders who could carry the torch of activism forward. This shift not only enriched her own experience but also ignited a sense of purpose and fulfillment, as she witnessed the growth and empowerment of those around her.

In conclusion, discovering new passions and aspirations is a vital component of Bandy Kiki's journey as an activist. Through her exploration of art, writing, and mentorship, she not only enriched her own life but also contributed to the broader movement for LGBTQ rights in Cameroon. By embracing her passions, Bandy demonstrated that activism is not just about fighting for justice; it is also about nurturing one's identity and aspirations, ultimately leading to a more vibrant and inclusive community.

$$\text{Activism} = \text{Passion} + \text{Identity} + \text{Community} \qquad (58)$$

This final equation encapsulates the essence of Bandy's journey, illustrating that true activism is a harmonious blend of personal passion, identity exploration, and community engagement. In this way, Bandy Kiki's story serves as a testament to the transformative power of discovering new passions and aspirations in the pursuit of equality and acceptance.

Paving the way for personal and professional growth

The journey of activism often intertwines with personal and professional growth, creating a rich tapestry of experiences that shape not only the activist but also the communities they serve. For Bandy Kiki, the act of fighting for LGBTQ rights in Cameroon was not merely a political statement; it was a transformative process that led to profound personal evolution and professional opportunities.

The Interconnection of Activism and Personal Development

Activism can serve as a catalyst for personal development. Engaging in advocacy allows individuals to confront their beliefs, values, and identities. According to [?], identity development is a crucial aspect of adolescence and young adulthood, where individuals explore various roles and beliefs. For Bandy Kiki, her activism provided a platform to explore her non-binary identity and bisexuality, leading to greater self-awareness and acceptance.

The process of advocating for LGBTQ rights in a hostile environment forced Bandy Kiki to confront her fears and insecurities. The challenges she faced—ranging from societal rejection to legal threats—served as opportunities for resilience. As noted by [?], individuals with a growth mindset view challenges as opportunities to learn and grow. Bandy Kiki exemplified this mindset, using her experiences to fuel her passion for activism and personal growth.

Professional Opportunities Through Activism

Activism can also open doors to professional growth. Bandy Kiki's commitment to LGBTQ rights led her to collaborate with various NGOs and international organizations. These collaborations not only expanded her network but also provided her with valuable skills in leadership, communication, and strategic planning. The ability to articulate her vision and mobilize support became essential tools in her professional toolkit.

Moreover, the visibility gained through her activism allowed Bandy Kiki to become a sought-after speaker at international conferences. This exposure not only amplified her message but also positioned her as a leader in the LGBTQ rights movement. As noted by [?], self-efficacy plays a crucial role in how goals are approached. Bandy Kiki's growing confidence in her abilities as an activist translated into professional success, allowing her to inspire others while carving out a niche for herself in the field of human rights.

Challenges and Setbacks

Despite the potential for growth, the path of activism is fraught with challenges. Bandy Kiki faced numerous setbacks, including threats to her safety and moments of self-doubt. The pressure to constantly advocate for change can lead to burnout, a phenomenon documented by [?]. To combat this, Bandy Kiki learned the importance of self-care and building a support network.

Recognizing the need for balance, she sought mentorship from seasoned activists who had navigated similar challenges. This support system not only provided guidance but also reinforced the notion that personal well-being is integral to effective activism. Bandy Kiki's journey highlights the importance of resilience in the face of adversity, as well as the need for self-compassion in maintaining one's mental health.

Examples of Personal and Professional Growth

Bandy Kiki's journey illustrates several key examples of how activism can pave the way for personal and professional growth:

- **Leadership Development:** Through her activism, Bandy Kiki honed her leadership skills by organizing protests and workshops. These experiences equipped her with the ability to inspire and mobilize others, fostering a sense of community among LGBTQ individuals in Cameroon.

- **Networking Opportunities:** Collaborating with international organizations allowed Bandy Kiki to connect with global activists, creating a network of support that transcended borders. This network became instrumental in amplifying her message and advocating for change.

- **Skill Acquisition:** Engaging in activism provided Bandy Kiki with practical skills in public speaking, advocacy, and strategic planning. These skills not only enhanced her effectiveness as an activist but also made her a valuable asset in professional settings.

- **Personal Empowerment:** As Bandy Kiki embraced her identity and fought for the rights of others, she experienced a profound sense of empowerment.

This self-acceptance translated into confidence in her professional endeavors, allowing her to pursue opportunities she once deemed unattainable.

Conclusion

In conclusion, the intersection of personal and professional growth through activism is a powerful narrative in Bandy Kiki's life. Her journey reflects the transformative nature of advocacy, where challenges become stepping stones towards empowerment. By embracing her identity and advocating for change, Bandy Kiki not only paved the way for her own growth but also inspired countless others to embark on their journeys of self-discovery and activism. The legacy of her work serves as a reminder that the fight for equality is not just about societal change; it is also about the individual journeys that contribute to a larger movement.

Balancing activism with personal goals and dreams

Activism, particularly in the LGBTQ community, is often a consuming endeavor that requires immense dedication and resilience. For many activists, including Bandy Kiki, the struggle for equality and justice can sometimes overshadow personal aspirations and dreams. This section explores the complex interplay between activism and personal goals, highlighting the challenges faced by activists and the strategies they employ to maintain a balanced life.

The Challenge of Prioritization

One of the primary challenges activists face is the need to prioritize their time and energy. According to Maslow's Hierarchy of Needs, individuals must first satisfy basic needs before pursuing higher-level aspirations, such as self-actualization and personal growth [?]. For activists, the urgent demands of social justice work can often take precedence over personal ambitions, leading to feelings of guilt or inadequacy when personal goals are sidelined.

Let A represent the time and energy devoted to activism, and P represent personal goals. The balance can be expressed as:

$$A + P = T$$

where T is the total time available. As the commitment to activism (A) increases, the time available for personal pursuits (P) decreases, creating a tension that many activists must navigate.

Self-Care and Boundaries

To effectively balance activism with personal goals, activists must prioritize self-care and establish boundaries. Self-care involves engaging in activities that promote physical, emotional, and mental well-being. Research by Neff (2011) emphasizes the importance of self-compassion as a critical component of self-care, allowing individuals to treat themselves with kindness during challenging times [?].

Bandy Kiki, for instance, recognized the necessity of setting boundaries around her activism to ensure she could pursue her personal dreams. This might involve scheduling specific times for activism-related tasks and reserving time for personal interests, such as art, writing, or connecting with loved ones. By doing so, activists can recharge and maintain their passion for both their cause and personal aspirations.

Integrating Activism with Personal Aspirations

Another effective strategy is integrating activism with personal goals. This approach allows individuals to pursue their passions while contributing to the movement. For example, an activist who is also a writer might focus on creating content that highlights LGBTQ issues, thereby merging their personal and activist identities. This integration can enhance motivation and fulfillment, as it aligns personal interests with the broader mission of promoting equality.

Let I represent integrated activities, where:

$$I = A \cap P$$

This equation indicates that integrated activities encompass both activism and personal goals, fostering a sense of purpose and satisfaction. Bandy Kiki's work in creative expression, such as poetry or visual art, exemplifies this integration, as she uses her talents to advocate for LGBTQ rights while also fulfilling her creative aspirations.

Building a Supportive Community

Activists benefit greatly from cultivating a supportive community that encourages both activism and personal growth. Engaging with peers who understand the challenges of balancing these spheres can provide emotional support and practical advice. Collaborative efforts can also lead to shared resources, allowing activists to pursue personal goals while contributing to collective efforts.

Research by Putnam (2000) highlights the importance of social capital in fostering community resilience and individual well-being [?]. By building networks that support both activism and personal pursuits, individuals can create a more sustainable approach to their work.

Examples of Successful Balance

Several activists have successfully navigated the balance between their commitments and personal aspirations. For instance, the renowned LGBTQ advocate and author, Janet Mock, has seamlessly integrated her activism with her writing career, using her platform to advocate for transgender rights while pursuing her passion for storytelling. Similarly, many activists in the LGBTQ community engage in creative endeavors, such as performance art, to express their identities and raise awareness simultaneously.

Bandy Kiki's journey reflects this balance as she navigates her activism while pursuing personal dreams, such as education and creative expression. By sharing her experiences, she inspires others to recognize that activism does not have to come at the cost of personal fulfillment.

Conclusion

In conclusion, balancing activism with personal goals and dreams is a multifaceted challenge that requires intentionality, self-care, and community support. By prioritizing self-compassion, integrating personal interests with activism, and building a supportive network, activists like Bandy Kiki can navigate this delicate balance effectively. Ultimately, the ability to harmonize these aspects of life not only enhances personal well-being but also strengthens the impact of their activism, creating a more sustainable and fulfilling journey toward equality and justice.

Bandy Kiki: The Woman Behind the Mask

Sharing the personal journey

In the realm of activism, personal narratives serve as powerful catalysts for change. Bandy Kiki, a prominent figure in the fight for LGBTQ rights in Cameroon, exemplifies the profound impact of sharing one's journey. The act of revealing personal experiences not only fosters empathy but also inspires others to confront their own truths. This section delves into the significance of sharing personal journeys, highlighting the transformative power it holds for individuals and communities alike.

The Power of Storytelling

Storytelling has long been recognized as a potent tool for social change. According to narrative theory, individuals construct their identities through the stories they tell about themselves and others. This process is particularly salient in marginalized communities, where dominant narratives often overlook or misrepresent their experiences. By sharing her journey, Bandy Kiki challenges these narratives, offering a firsthand account that humanizes the struggles faced by LGBTQ individuals in Cameroon.

In her public speeches and social media posts, Kiki articulates her experiences with vulnerability and authenticity. This openness invites others to reflect on their own lives, fostering a sense of solidarity among those who may feel isolated in their struggles. As Kiki states, "When we share our stories, we create a bridge of understanding that transcends fear and prejudice." This sentiment echoes the findings of social psychology, which suggest that personal narratives can reduce stigma and promote acceptance within society.

Navigating the Personal and Political

Bandy Kiki's journey is not solely personal; it is intricately intertwined with the political landscape of Cameroon. The country's oppressive laws and societal attitudes towards LGBTQ individuals create a hostile environment that often silences voices like hers. By choosing to share her story, Kiki not only asserts her right to exist authentically but also highlights the systemic injustices that necessitate activism.

The duality of her narrative—both personal and political—serves to illuminate the broader issues at play. For instance, Kiki recounts her experiences of discrimination and violence, illustrating how these personal traumas are symptomatic of a larger societal problem. This intersectional approach aligns with the principles of critical theory, which emphasizes the importance of understanding how various forms of oppression intersect and impact individuals differently.

Examples of Impact

The impact of sharing personal journeys can be seen in various movements across the globe. For instance, the #MeToo movement gained momentum as individuals began to share their experiences of sexual harassment and assault. Similarly, Kiki's openness about her identity and activism has inspired countless individuals in Cameroon and beyond to embrace their truths and advocate for their rights.

One poignant example is the story of a young LGBTQ activist in Douala, who, inspired by Kiki's journey, began to share her own experiences on social media. By doing so, she not only found a supportive community but also sparked conversations about LGBTQ rights in her local context. This ripple effect illustrates the profound impact that one individual's story can have on others, fostering a culture of openness and acceptance.

Challenges in Sharing Personal Narratives

Despite the transformative potential of sharing personal journeys, activists like Bandy Kiki face significant challenges. The risk of backlash, both personally and professionally, can be daunting. In a society where LGBTQ identities are criminalized, the act of coming out can lead to severe consequences, including violence, ostracization, and legal repercussions.

Kiki's decision to share her story was not made lightly. She navigated the complexities of her identity, weighing the risks against the potential for positive change. This internal conflict reflects the broader struggles faced by many LGBTQ individuals, who often grapple with the decision to reveal their identities in hostile environments.

Moreover, the digital age presents both opportunities and challenges for sharing personal narratives. While social media platforms can amplify voices and foster connections, they also expose individuals to heightened scrutiny and harassment. Kiki has experienced this firsthand, facing threats and intimidation as a result of her activism. Nevertheless, she remains steadfast in her commitment to sharing her journey, recognizing the importance of visibility in the fight for equality.

Conclusion

In conclusion, sharing personal journeys is a vital aspect of activism that can inspire change, foster empathy, and challenge societal norms. Bandy Kiki's story serves as a testament to the power of vulnerability and authenticity in the pursuit of justice. By bravely recounting her experiences, Kiki not only asserts her identity but also paves the way for others to do the same. As we continue to navigate the complexities of activism in a digital age, it is imperative to recognize the profound impact of personal narratives in shaping a more inclusive and accepting society.

$$\text{Impact} = \text{Visibility} + \text{Authenticity} + \text{Community} \tag{59}$$

Balancing public and private life

The journey of an activist is often a delicate dance between the public persona and the private self. For Bandy Kiki, navigating this balance is not merely a matter of preference; it is a necessity born out of the complexities of activism in a hostile environment. The public life of an activist is characterized by visibility, responsibility, and the constant scrutiny of both supporters and adversaries. In contrast, the private life provides a sanctuary, a space for self-reflection, healing, and personal growth.

The Weight of Public Responsibility

Activists like Bandy Kiki often find themselves thrust into the spotlight, where their actions and words can resonate widely, influencing the lives of many. This public responsibility can be both empowering and burdensome. The theory of *social identity* posits that individuals derive a sense of self from their group memberships, which, in the case of activists, often includes their role as advocates for marginalized communities. The pressure to represent these communities authentically can lead to a phenomenon known as *performative activism*, where the activist feels compelled to maintain a certain image to meet the expectations of their audience.

For Bandy Kiki, this meant carefully curating her public persona while grappling with the realities of her private life. The constant demand to be "on" can lead to exhaustion and burnout, as the lines between personal and public become increasingly blurred. This is particularly true in the digital age, where social media amplifies visibility but also invites relentless scrutiny. The challenge lies in finding a sustainable way to engage with the public while protecting one's mental health and personal space.

The Sanctuary of Privacy

In stark contrast to her public life, Bandy Kiki's private life serves as a refuge. It is in this space that she can explore her identity, process her experiences, and recharge her emotional batteries. The importance of privacy in the life of an activist cannot be overstated; it is essential for maintaining a sense of self outside the role imposed by public expectations. The psychological concept of *boundary theory* suggests that individuals create boundaries to manage their emotional and psychological resources effectively. For Bandy, this meant setting limits on her availability and learning to say no to engagements that felt overwhelming.

Moreover, the private sphere allows for the cultivation of intimate relationships that provide support and understanding. Chosen family and close friends often become the pillars that uphold an activist during challenging times. These relationships offer a space for vulnerability, where Bandy can share her fears and uncertainties without the weight of public perception. This duality of life—public and private—creates a dynamic interplay that shapes her activism.

Challenges of Maintaining Balance

However, the balance between public and private life is fraught with challenges. One significant issue is the potential for *identity fragmentation*, where the activist feels disconnected from their private self due to the demands of their public role. This fragmentation can lead to feelings of isolation, as the individual may struggle to find authentic connections in a world that constantly demands a curated version of themselves.

Bandy Kiki's experience highlights the intricacies of this challenge. While she is celebrated for her bravery and advocacy, the pressure to conform to the ideals of an activist can lead to a dissonance between who she is in public and who she is in private. The fear of judgment or backlash can inhibit her from fully expressing her true self, creating a cycle of self-censorship.

Strategies for Balancing Life

To navigate these challenges, Bandy Kiki employs several strategies. First, she practices *self-care* as a fundamental aspect of her routine. This includes engaging in activities that rejuvenate her spirit, such as art, meditation, and time spent with loved ones. By prioritizing her mental and emotional well-being, she fortifies herself against the pressures of public life.

Second, Bandy emphasizes the importance of *transparency* within her personal relationships. By sharing her experiences and struggles with those closest to her, she fosters a sense of community and mutual support. This openness not only alleviates feelings of isolation but also reinforces her commitment to authenticity, both publicly and privately.

Lastly, setting clear boundaries is crucial. Bandy Kiki learns to delineate her time and energy, recognizing that she cannot pour from an empty cup. By establishing limits on her public engagements and allowing herself the freedom to step back when needed, she maintains her passion for activism without sacrificing her personal life.

Conclusion

In conclusion, the balance between public and private life is a nuanced and ongoing process for activists like Bandy Kiki. It requires constant negotiation, self-awareness, and a commitment to self-care. By embracing both aspects of her identity, she not only enriches her activism but also nurtures her personal growth. The journey may be fraught with challenges, but it is also filled with opportunities for connection, resilience, and empowerment. Ultimately, the ability to navigate this balance is what enables Bandy Kiki to continue her vital work in advocating for LGBTQ rights while remaining true to herself.

Embracing authenticity and vulnerability

In a world that often demands conformity, embracing authenticity and vulnerability can be a radical act of courage. For Bandy Kiki, the journey toward authenticity was not merely a personal endeavor but a transformative process that resonated deeply with her activism. This section delves into the theoretical underpinnings of authenticity and vulnerability, the challenges faced in their pursuit, and the profound impact they had on Bandy's life and work.

Theoretical Framework

Authenticity refers to the quality of being true to oneself, aligning one's actions with one's values, beliefs, and identity. According to [?], authenticity is essential for psychological well-being, as it allows individuals to live in accordance with their true selves. This concept is closely tied to the notion of vulnerability, which is defined by Brené Brown as "uncertainty, risk, and emotional exposure" [?]. Brown argues that vulnerability is not a weakness but rather a source of strength and connection, enabling individuals to forge deeper relationships and foster empathy.

The interplay between authenticity and vulnerability is particularly relevant in the context of LGBTQ activism. Activists like Bandy Kiki often face societal pressures to conform to heteronormative standards, making the act of embracing one's true identity a powerful form of resistance. Authenticity allows individuals to challenge stereotypes and break down barriers, while vulnerability opens the door to meaningful conversations about identity, acceptance, and love.

Challenges in Embracing Authenticity

Despite the empowering nature of authenticity, the path is fraught with challenges. For many individuals, especially those within marginalized communities, the fear of rejection and discrimination can create significant barriers to self-expression. In Cameroon, where LGBTQ individuals face severe legal and social repercussions, the stakes are even higher. Bandy Kiki experienced this firsthand; the decision to embrace her identity meant confronting not only societal expectations but also the potential for violence and ostracism.

A poignant example of this struggle can be seen in the stories of individuals who have faced familial rejection upon coming out. The emotional toll of such experiences can lead to feelings of isolation and despair. According to [?], internalized homophobia often manifests as self-doubt and shame, making it difficult for individuals to embrace their authenticity fully. Bandy, however, used her experiences of rejection as fuel for her activism, transforming her pain into a source of strength.

The Power of Vulnerability in Activism

Bandy Kiki's journey illustrates the transformative power of vulnerability in activism. By openly sharing her struggles, she created a space for others to do the same. This act of vulnerability not only humanized her cause but also fostered a sense of community among those who felt marginalized. As she stated in a poignant interview, "When we share our stories, we illuminate the shadows of silence that so many of us live in."

The impact of this vulnerability extends beyond personal narratives; it has the potential to catalyze systemic change. By challenging societal norms and expectations, Bandy encouraged others to embrace their identities, thereby fostering a culture of acceptance and inclusivity. This aligns with the principles of collective activism, where shared experiences and vulnerabilities can unite individuals in their fight for equality.

Embracing Authenticity: A Personal Journey

Bandy's journey toward authenticity was marked by significant milestones. One of the most profound moments occurred when she publicly shared her story on social media, shedding her pseudonym and revealing her true self to the world. This act of bravery resonated with many, inspiring countless individuals to embrace their identities. The response was overwhelming; messages of support poured in from around the globe, illustrating the universal desire for acceptance and understanding.

Moreover, Bandy's authenticity allowed her to connect deeply with her audience. By sharing her vulnerabilities, she created a relatable narrative that transcended geographical and cultural boundaries. This is exemplified in her participation in international LGBTQ conferences, where her candid discussions about her struggles and triumphs resonated with activists from diverse backgrounds. Through her authenticity, Bandy not only advocated for her community but also became a beacon of hope for those still grappling with their identities.

The Ripple Effect of Authenticity and Vulnerability

The impact of embracing authenticity and vulnerability extends beyond the individual; it creates a ripple effect within communities. Bandy Kiki's journey inspired others to share their stories, fostering a culture of openness and acceptance. This collective vulnerability can serve as a powerful tool for activism, as it dismantles the stigma surrounding LGBTQ identities and promotes understanding.

Furthermore, the act of embracing authenticity can lead to personal empowerment. As individuals begin to accept their true selves, they often find the strength to advocate for their rights and the rights of others. This empowerment is crucial in the fight for equality, as it transforms personal narratives into collective action.

Conclusion

In conclusion, embracing authenticity and vulnerability is a vital aspect of Bandy Kiki's journey as an activist. These qualities not only shaped her personal identity but also fueled her advocacy for LGBTQ rights in Cameroon and beyond. By confronting societal norms and sharing her story, Bandy created a powerful narrative that inspires others to embrace their true selves. As we reflect on her legacy, we are reminded that authenticity and vulnerability are not just personal attributes; they are essential components of a broader movement toward acceptance, love, and equality.

The personal sacrifices of activism

Activism is often romanticized as a noble pursuit, filled with the promise of change and progress. However, the reality is that it demands significant personal sacrifices, often leading to profound emotional, social, and financial costs. For Bandy Kiki, the journey of activism was not just a path toward societal change but also a crucible of personal trials and tribulations.

Emotional Toll

One of the most significant sacrifices activists face is the emotional toll that comes with constant advocacy. The weight of the injustices they fight against can lead to feelings of despair and burnout. Kiki often found herself grappling with anxiety and depression, stemming from the harsh realities faced by the LGBTQ community in Cameroon. According to the *American Psychological Association*, individuals engaged in activism are at a higher risk for psychological distress due to the persistent exposure to trauma and systemic oppression.

$$\text{Emotional Toll} = \text{Trauma Exposure} + \text{Social Isolation} + \text{Burnout} \quad (60)$$

This equation highlights how the cumulative effects of trauma, social isolation from mainstream society, and the burnout from relentless campaigning can create a heavy emotional burden.

Social Isolation

The pursuit of activism often leads to social isolation. Kiki experienced estrangement from friends and family members who held different views on LGBTQ rights. This alienation can be exacerbated in environments where LGBTQ identities are stigmatized. The loss of relationships can create a profound sense of loneliness, as described in the work of *Meyer and Northridge (2001)* on the social determinants of health for LGBTQ individuals. Kiki's decision to live authentically often meant sacrificing connections with those who could not accept her identity, leading to a tight-knit circle of supportive allies but also leaving gaps in her social life.

Financial Costs

Activism can also impose significant financial burdens. Kiki often funded her campaigns out of pocket, sacrificing personal savings and facing financial instability. The costs associated with organizing events, legal fees for advocacy, and the need for security measures due to threats against her safety can add up quickly. A study by *Bennett (2018)* on grassroots activism highlights that many activists are often financially strained, leading to a reliance on crowdfunding and donations, which can be unpredictable.

$$\text{Financial Cost} = \text{Event Costs} + \text{Legal Fees} + \text{Security Measures} \quad (61)$$

Kiki's financial equation illustrates how the expenses related to activism can overshadow personal financial health, often leading to precarious living conditions.

Physical Safety Risks

In regions like Cameroon, where LGBTQ rights are not only limited but often criminalized, the physical safety of activists is a pressing concern. Kiki faced threats, harassment, and violence simply for advocating for her community. The constant fear of being targeted can lead to a pervasive state of vigilance, impacting mental health and overall well-being. The *Human Rights Campaign* reports that many activists endure threats of violence, which can lead to severe consequences, including injury or even death.

$$\text{Safety Risk} = \text{Threat Level} \times \text{Visibility} \qquad (62)$$

This equation suggests that the higher the visibility of an activist, the greater the threat level they may face, creating a paradox where increased activism can lead to increased danger.

Balancing Personal Life

Kiki's activism also took a toll on her personal life. The demands of her work often left little time for self-care or personal relationships. The struggle to balance activism with personal aspirations and relationships can lead to feelings of inadequacy and guilt. The *Journal of Community Psychology* emphasizes that many activists report feeling torn between their commitment to their cause and their desire for personal fulfillment.

$$\text{Life Balance} = \text{Personal Goals} - \text{Activism Demands} \qquad (63)$$

As Kiki navigated her activism, she often found that her personal goals were overshadowed by the demands of her work, leading to a continual state of sacrifice.

Conclusion

In summary, the personal sacrifices of activism are manifold and complex. For Bandy Kiki, the journey was marked by emotional strain, social isolation, financial instability, physical safety risks, and the challenge of balancing personal life with her commitment to change. While the pursuit of justice and equality is noble, it is essential to recognize and address the sacrifices that come with it. Kiki's story serves as a testament to the resilience of activists who continue to fight for their rights and the rights of others, often at great personal cost. The sacrifices made by activists like Kiki are not merely individual struggles; they reflect a broader narrative of courage and commitment in the face of adversity, inspiring future generations to continue the fight for equality and justice.

The power of living one's truth

Living one's truth is a profound concept that resonates deeply within the LGBTQ community, particularly for activists like Bandy Kiki. It embodies the courage to embrace one's authentic self, despite societal pressures and expectations. This section explores the significance of this powerful act, the challenges faced, and the transformative impact it can have on both individuals and communities.

Theoretical Framework

The notion of living one's truth can be understood through various psychological and sociological theories. One such framework is *Authenticity Theory*, which posits that individuals achieve psychological well-being when they align their actions with their true selves. According to [?], authenticity comprises four components: awareness, unbiased processing, behavior, and relational orientation. This theory suggests that living authentically is not merely about self-expression; it also involves a conscious awareness of one's values and beliefs, leading to more fulfilling relationships and a greater sense of purpose.

Moreover, *Queer Theory* provides a critical lens through which to examine the societal constructs surrounding identity. Scholars such as Judith Butler argue that gender and sexuality are performative acts shaped by cultural norms. Living one's truth, therefore, becomes an act of resistance against these norms, challenging the status quo and paving the way for greater acceptance and understanding within society [?].

Challenges of Living Authentically

Despite the empowering nature of living one's truth, it is not without its challenges. Many individuals face significant barriers, including:

- **Societal Rejection:** The fear of ostracism or discrimination can deter individuals from embracing their identities. In communities where LGBTQ identities are stigmatized, the risks can be particularly high, leading to mental health issues such as anxiety and depression [Meyer(2003)].

- **Internalized Homophobia:** Many LGBTQ individuals grapple with internalized negative beliefs about their identities, often stemming from societal messages. This internal conflict can hinder the journey toward self-acceptance and authenticity [?].

- **Safety Concerns:** In regions where LGBTQ rights are not recognized, coming out can pose real dangers, including violence and persecution. This reality forces many to live dual lives, creating a disconnect between their public persona and private truth [?].

Examples of Courageous Authenticity

Despite these challenges, numerous activists have demonstrated the power of living one's truth. Bandy Kiki's journey is a testament to this principle. By adopting her pseudonym, she not only protected her identity but also created a platform that resonated with many who felt voiceless. Her activism, rooted in her authentic self, inspired countless individuals to embrace their identities and advocate for change.

Consider the case of *Mimi Fawaz*, a Cameroonian LGBTQ activist who faced severe backlash after coming out publicly. Despite threats to her safety, Mimi's decision to live authentically galvanized a movement that challenged discriminatory laws in Cameroon. Her story exemplifies how living one's truth can mobilize communities and foster solidarity among marginalized groups.

The Transformative Impact of Authenticity

Living one's truth not only empowers individuals but also catalyzes social change. When people embrace their identities, they challenge societal norms and create spaces for dialogue and acceptance. This phenomenon is evident in the growing visibility of LGBTQ individuals in media, politics, and education. As more people share their stories, the collective narrative shifts, fostering greater empathy and understanding.

Moreover, authenticity fosters resilience. Individuals who live their truth often find strength in community, forming support networks that uplift and empower. These connections can be life-saving, providing a sense of belonging and acceptance that counters societal rejection [?].

Conclusion

In conclusion, the power of living one's truth lies in its ability to transform not only the individual but also the broader society. By embracing authenticity, individuals like Bandy Kiki illuminate the path for others, inspiring a movement toward acceptance and equality. The journey may be fraught with challenges, but the rewards—personal fulfillment, community solidarity, and societal change—are immeasurable. As we continue to advocate for LGBTQ rights, let us remember the profound impact of living authentically and the ripple effects it creates in the pursuit of justice and equality.

Leaving a Lasting Impact

The power of storytelling

Storytelling has long been recognized as a potent tool for communication, education, and advocacy. In the context of LGBTQ activism, the act of sharing personal narratives serves not only to illuminate the struggles and triumphs of individuals but also to foster empathy and understanding among wider audiences. The power of storytelling lies in its ability to humanize complex issues, making them relatable and accessible.

Theoretical Framework

The theoretical underpinnings of storytelling in activism can be explored through several lenses, including narrative theory and social constructivism. Narrative theory posits that stories shape our understanding of the world and influence our beliefs and actions. According to [?], narratives are fundamental to human cognition, as they help individuals make sense of their experiences and the experiences of others.

Social constructivism, on the other hand, emphasizes the role of social interactions in shaping knowledge and meaning. As articulated by [?], individuals construct their understanding of reality through their interactions with others. In this light, storytelling becomes a collaborative act that not only conveys information but also builds community and solidarity.

Problems Addressed by Storytelling

Despite its power, storytelling in the realm of LGBTQ activism faces several challenges. One significant issue is the risk of oversimplification. Personal narratives can inadvertently reinforce stereotypes or present a monolithic view of the LGBTQ experience. It is crucial for activists to acknowledge the diversity of identities and experiences within the community. This complexity can be addressed by incorporating multiple voices and perspectives into the narrative landscape.

Another challenge is the potential for re-traumatization. Activists sharing their stories may revisit painful experiences, which can be emotionally taxing. It is essential for individuals to approach storytelling with care, ensuring that they have adequate support systems in place. Furthermore, the act of sharing stories in hostile environments can expose individuals to backlash and discrimination, necessitating a careful consideration of safety and anonymity.

Examples of Storytelling in LGBTQ Activism

One poignant example of the power of storytelling is the "It Gets Better" project, which was launched in 2010 by Dan Savage and his partner Terry Miller. The initiative aimed to provide hope to LGBTQ youth facing bullying and discrimination. By sharing personal stories of struggle and eventual triumph, the project created a vast repository of narratives that resonated with young people. The campaign not only highlighted the challenges faced by LGBTQ individuals but also emphasized resilience and the possibility of a brighter future.

Similarly, the "#MeToo" movement, while primarily focused on sexual harassment and assault, has also intersected with LGBTQ advocacy. Many individuals within the LGBTQ community have shared their stories of abuse, illustrating the unique challenges they face. This intersectional storytelling has expanded the dialogue around consent and safety, fostering a more inclusive understanding of the issues at hand.

The Role of Art and Creativity

Artistic expression is another powerful avenue for storytelling in LGBTQ activism. Through mediums such as literature, film, and visual arts, activists can communicate their narratives in compelling and transformative ways. For instance, the work of artists like James Baldwin and Audre Lorde has left an indelible mark on both literature and activism, weaving personal experiences with broader social commentary.

Moreover, contemporary platforms such as social media have democratized storytelling, allowing individuals to share their experiences with a global audience. This shift has enabled underrepresented voices to emerge, challenging dominant narratives and fostering a richer tapestry of LGBTQ experiences.

Conclusion

In conclusion, the power of storytelling in LGBTQ activism cannot be overstated. It serves as a vital tool for advocacy, education, and community-building. By sharing personal narratives, activists can illuminate the complexities of the LGBTQ experience, challenge stereotypes, and foster empathy. However, it is crucial to approach storytelling with sensitivity, ensuring that diverse voices are represented and that individuals are supported in their journey of sharing. As we continue to navigate the landscape of LGBTQ rights, the stories we tell will undoubtedly shape the future of the movement, inspiring change and fostering understanding in an ever-evolving world.

Documenting the struggle for LGBTQ rights in Cameroon

The struggle for LGBTQ rights in Cameroon is a poignant narrative woven into the broader tapestry of human rights advocacy. This section aims to document the myriad challenges faced by LGBTQ individuals, highlighting both the systemic issues and the grassroots efforts that have emerged in response.

Historical Context

Cameroon's legal framework is steeped in colonial history, where laws criminalizing homosexuality were inherited from French and British colonial rule. Article 347 bis of the Cameroonian Penal Code explicitly criminalizes same-sex relationships, imposing up to five years of imprisonment for consensual acts between adults. This legal backdrop fosters an environment of fear and repression, where LGBTQ individuals are subjected to harassment, violence, and discrimination.

The Role of Activism

Activism in Cameroon has taken various forms, from underground movements to more visible campaigns. Organizations like the *Association for the Defense of Gays and Lesbians* (ADEFHO) and the *Cameroon LGBT Association* (CAMFAIDS) have been pivotal in advocating for LGBTQ rights. These organizations document human rights abuses, provide support to victims, and engage in public education campaigns.

One of the prominent strategies employed by activists is the use of storytelling as a means of advocacy. By documenting personal experiences, activists humanize the struggle, making it relatable to a broader audience. This approach not only raises awareness but also challenges the prevailing narratives that perpetuate stigma and discrimination.

Social Media as a Tool for Documentation

In the digital age, social media has emerged as a powerful tool for documenting the struggles of LGBTQ individuals in Cameroon. Platforms like Twitter, Facebook, and Instagram allow activists to share their stories, mobilize support, and connect with international allies. The anonymity afforded by these platforms enables individuals to express their identities and experiences without the fear of immediate retribution.

For example, the hashtag #FreeCameroonLGBTQ gained traction on social media, amplifying the voices of those who have been persecuted. This online movement not only raised awareness but also garnered international attention, leading to increased pressure on the Cameroonian government to address human rights violations.

Challenges in Documentation

Despite the progress made, documenting the struggle for LGBTQ rights in Cameroon is fraught with challenges. Activists often face threats to their safety, with many forced to operate in secrecy. The fear of persecution can deter individuals from sharing their stories, leading to underreporting of abuses. Moreover, the government's hostility towards LGBTQ rights creates a chilling effect, where potential allies may hesitate to engage in advocacy for fear of backlash.

Another significant hurdle is the limited access to resources for documentation. Many grassroots organizations operate on shoestring budgets, relying on donations and volunteer efforts. This lack of funding hampers their ability to conduct comprehensive research, gather data, and publish reports that could influence policy changes.

Case Studies

Several case studies exemplify the struggle for LGBTQ rights in Cameroon. In 2019, the arrest of 47 individuals at a gay wedding in Yaoundé sparked outrage both locally and internationally. This incident highlighted the pervasive discrimination faced by LGBTQ individuals and the urgent need for legal reform. Activists documented the arrests and subsequent trials, using the case to advocate for decriminalization and greater protections for LGBTQ rights.

Another notable example is the case of Eric, a young gay man who was brutally attacked after being outed by a family member. His story, shared through various media outlets, garnered significant attention and led to calls for accountability from law enforcement. By documenting such personal narratives, activists aim to shift public perceptions and foster a more accepting society.

The Importance of Intersectionality

Documenting the struggle for LGBTQ rights in Cameroon also requires an intersectional approach. Many individuals face multiple layers of discrimination based on their gender, socioeconomic status, and geographic location. For instance, LGBTQ individuals in rural areas often experience compounded challenges due to limited access to resources and support networks.

Activists are increasingly recognizing the importance of addressing these intersecting identities in their advocacy efforts. By highlighting the unique experiences of marginalized groups within the LGBTQ community, they aim to create a more inclusive movement that represents the diverse voices of all individuals.

Conclusion

In conclusion, documenting the struggle for LGBTQ rights in Cameroon is a vital aspect of the broader fight for human rights. Through activism, storytelling, and the strategic use of digital platforms, advocates are working tirelessly to raise awareness and effect change. However, the challenges they face cannot be overlooked. As the movement continues to evolve, it is essential to prioritize the documentation of experiences, ensuring that the voices of those affected are heard and that their stories contribute to a legacy of courage and resilience.

Fostering understanding and empathy

In the realm of activism, particularly within the LGBTQ community, fostering understanding and empathy is paramount. This process not only aids in dismantling stereotypes but also builds bridges between diverse groups, creating a more inclusive society. The ability to empathize is rooted in the recognition of shared humanity, which can be articulated through various psychological and sociological theories.

Theoretical Framework

The concept of empathy can be understood through the lens of *theory of mind*, which posits that individuals can attribute mental states to themselves and others. This cognitive ability allows one to understand that others have beliefs, desires, and intentions that differ from one's own. According to *Hoffman's Empathy-Altruism Hypothesis*, empathy can lead to altruistic behavior, motivating individuals to act in support of others, especially marginalized groups.

Furthermore, *social identity theory* suggests that individuals derive a sense of self from their group memberships. This theory highlights the importance of in-group and out-group dynamics, which can lead to biases and discrimination. Activists like Bandy Kiki challenge these dynamics by encouraging individuals to find common ground, thus fostering an environment of understanding.

Challenges in Fostering Empathy

Despite its importance, fostering empathy within the LGBTQ movement faces several challenges. One significant issue is the prevalence of *homophobia* and *transphobia*, which can create barriers to understanding. These negative attitudes often stem from misinformation, cultural norms, and societal conditioning, leading to a lack of empathy towards LGBTQ individuals.

Moreover, the intersectionality of identities complicates the empathy landscape. Individuals may belong to multiple marginalized groups, each with unique struggles. For instance, a queer person of color may face discrimination not only for their sexual orientation but also for their race, making it essential for activists to address these overlapping identities. According to *Crenshaw's Intersectionality Theory*, understanding these intersections is crucial for fostering empathy that is inclusive and comprehensive.

Practical Approaches to Foster Understanding

To effectively foster understanding and empathy, activists can employ several practical strategies:

- **Storytelling:** Sharing personal narratives is one of the most powerful tools in fostering empathy. By humanizing experiences, activists can break down barriers and challenge preconceived notions. For example, Bandy Kiki's advocacy often includes sharing her journey, allowing others to see the world through her eyes and understand the complexities of her identity.

- **Education and Awareness Campaigns:** Implementing educational programs that focus on LGBTQ issues can help dispel myths and reduce stigma. Workshops, seminars, and community discussions can provide platforms for dialogue, allowing individuals to engage with LGBTQ topics in a safe environment.

- **Art and Creative Expression:** Art has the unique ability to evoke emotions and provoke thought. Activists can use various forms of artistic expression—such as visual arts, theater, and literature—to convey messages of empathy and understanding. For instance, community art projects that highlight LGBTQ experiences can foster connection and dialogue among diverse groups.

- **Building Alliances:** Collaborating with other marginalized groups can create a united front against discrimination. By forming coalitions, activists can amplify their voices and demonstrate solidarity. This collective action fosters understanding as individuals learn from one another's experiences and challenges.

Examples of Successful Initiatives

Several initiatives have successfully fostered understanding and empathy within the LGBTQ community and beyond. One notable example is the *It Gets Better Project*, which aims to inspire hope for LGBTQ youth facing bullying. By sharing stories of resilience and success, the project not only empowers individuals but also educates the broader community, fostering empathy through shared experiences.

Another example is the *Human Library*, an initiative where individuals can "borrow" a person from a marginalized group for a conversation. This unique approach allows participants to engage in meaningful dialogue, breaking down stereotypes and fostering understanding through personal interaction.

Conclusion

Fostering understanding and empathy is a crucial aspect of LGBTQ activism. By employing theoretical frameworks, addressing challenges, and implementing practical strategies, activists can create a more inclusive society. As Bandy Kiki exemplifies through her work, the journey towards empathy is ongoing, requiring collective effort and commitment to change perceptions and build a future where all individuals are respected and valued.

The role of art and creativity in activism

Art and creativity serve as powerful tools in activism, particularly within the LGBTQ movement, where they can transcend barriers of language, culture, and societal norms. The integration of artistic expression into advocacy not only amplifies marginalized voices but also fosters empathy and understanding among broader audiences. This section explores the multifaceted role of art in activism, emphasizing its ability to inspire, educate, and mobilize communities toward social change.

Theoretical Framework

The connection between art and activism can be grounded in various theoretical frameworks, including the *Cultural Studies* perspective, which posits that culture is a site of struggle where meanings are contested. According to theorists like Stuart Hall, culture is not merely a reflection of society but a battleground where identities are formed and challenged. In the context of LGBTQ activism, art becomes a medium through which individuals can express their identities, resist oppressive narratives, and create alternative representations of queerness.

Additionally, the *Social Movement Theory* provides insight into how art functions as a catalyst for collective action. According to Charles Tilly, social movements thrive on the ability to mobilize resources, frame issues, and construct collective identities. Art plays a crucial role in this process by providing a visual and emotional narrative that resonates with individuals, thus fostering a sense of belonging and shared purpose.

Art as a Means of Expression

For many LGBTQ activists, art serves as a vital means of self-expression. Through various forms of artistic expression—such as painting, performance, literature, and music—activists can articulate their experiences and emotions in ways that resonate deeply with others. For instance, the work of artists like *David Hockney* and *Frida Kahlo* not only reflects their personal struggles with identity and sexuality but also challenges societal norms and expectations.

$$\text{Artistic Expression} = f(\text{Identity, Societal Norms, Personal Experience}) \quad (64)$$

Here, the function f illustrates how artistic expression is influenced by an individual's identity, the societal norms they navigate, and their personal experiences. This equation underscores the interplay between the individual and their environment, highlighting how art can be both a personal and political act.

Art as a Tool for Education and Awareness

Artistic endeavors also serve as educational tools that raise awareness about LGBTQ issues. Through visual storytelling, performances, and literature, artists can illuminate the challenges faced by the LGBTQ community, such as discrimination, violence, and marginalization. For example, the graphic novel *Fun Home* by Alison Bechdel explores themes of identity, sexuality, and family dynamics, offering readers a nuanced understanding of the complexities of queer life.

Moreover, public art installations, such as the *AIDS Memorial Quilt*, have been instrumental in educating the public about the AIDS crisis and its impact on the LGBTQ community. Each panel of the quilt tells a personal story, transforming individual grief into collective memory and activism. This form of art not only commemorates lives lost but also serves as a poignant reminder of the ongoing struggle for health equity and social justice.

Art as a Mobilizing Force

Art has the unique ability to mobilize communities and inspire collective action. Activist artists often use their platforms to galvanize support for specific causes, encouraging audiences to engage in activism. The *Pride Parade* is a prime example of how art and performance can unite individuals in celebration and protest. Through vibrant costumes, music, and dance, participants express their identities while advocating for equality and acceptance.

The use of social media as a platform for artistic activism has further expanded the reach of LGBTQ advocacy. Hashtags such as #LoveIsLove and campaigns like the *It Gets Better Project* utilize visual content—videos, illustrations, and memes—to foster a sense of community and solidarity among LGBTQ individuals and allies. These digital artistic expressions not only raise awareness but also create a virtual space for dialogue and support.

Challenges and Limitations

Despite the power of art in activism, there are challenges and limitations that artists and activists face. Censorship, particularly in oppressive regimes, can stifle artistic expression and hinder the dissemination of important messages. In some cases, artists may face backlash or persecution for their work, as seen in countries where LGBTQ identities are criminalized.

Furthermore, the commercialization of art can dilute its activist message. As art becomes commodified, there is a risk that the original intent of social change may be overshadowed by profit motives. This tension raises important questions about the authenticity of artistic activism and the extent to which it can effect meaningful change.

Conclusion

In conclusion, the role of art and creativity in activism is both profound and multifaceted. Art not only serves as a means of self-expression but also as a tool for education, mobilization, and community building. While challenges persist, the resilience of artists and activists continues to inspire change and foster a more inclusive society. As Bandy Kiki exemplifies through her work, the intersection of art and activism remains a vital space for resistance, healing, and empowerment within the LGBTQ movement. The legacy of artistic activism is one of hope, reminding us that creativity can be a powerful force in the ongoing struggle for equality and justice.

Creating lasting change through personal narratives

Personal narratives serve as powerful tools in the fight for social change, particularly within the LGBTQ community. They encapsulate individual experiences and emotions, allowing for a deeper understanding of the struggles faced by marginalized groups. By sharing their stories, activists like Bandy Kiki have leveraged personal narratives to create empathy, challenge stereotypes, and inspire collective action.

Theoretical Framework

The concept of narrative identity, as proposed by scholars such as [?], emphasizes how individuals construct their identities through stories. These narratives are not just reflections of personal experiences but also serve as a means of connecting with others and fostering a sense of belonging. In the context of LGBTQ activism, personal narratives can:

- Challenge societal norms and expectations,
- Illuminate the complexities of identity,

- Foster solidarity among diverse individuals.

Through storytelling, activists can articulate their lived experiences, highlighting the intersectionality of their identities. This aligns with [?]'s theory of intersectionality, which posits that individuals experience overlapping systems of oppression. By sharing these multifaceted narratives, activists can advocate for a more nuanced understanding of LGBTQ issues.

Problems Addressed by Personal Narratives

1. **Visibility**: Many LGBTQ individuals face erasure in mainstream narratives. Personal stories bring visibility to these experiences, challenging the dominant discourse that often marginalizes queer identities.

2. **Stigma and Stereotypes**: Personal narratives can counteract harmful stereotypes by showcasing the diversity and richness of LGBTQ lives. For instance, when Bandy Kiki shared her journey of self-acceptance, it not only highlighted her struggles but also celebrated her resilience, thereby humanizing the LGBTQ experience.

3. **Empathy Building**: Sharing personal stories fosters empathy among those who may not understand the LGBTQ experience. For example, when allies hear first-hand accounts of discrimination and resilience, it can prompt them to take action in support of LGBTQ rights.

Examples of Impact

Several notable campaigns have utilized personal narratives to effect change:

- **The It Gets Better Project**: Founded in response to a spate of LGBTQ youth suicides, this initiative encourages individuals to share their stories of hope and resilience. The campaign has garnered thousands of video submissions, creating a vast archive of personal narratives that inspire and uplift LGBTQ youth.

- **Humans of New York**: This social media phenomenon has highlighted the stories of individuals from diverse backgrounds, including LGBTQ individuals. By sharing their experiences, participants have humanized the struggles of the LGBTQ community, fostering a greater understanding and acceptance among the general public.

Creating Lasting Change

To create lasting change through personal narratives, activists must:

1. **Amplify Diverse Voices**: It is crucial to elevate stories from a wide range of experiences within the LGBTQ community, including those from marginalized subgroups. This ensures a more comprehensive representation of the community's struggles and triumphs.

2. **Utilize Multiple Platforms**: Activists should leverage various media platforms—social media, blogs, podcasts, and public speaking engagements—to share their narratives. Each platform has its own audience and can reach different demographics, thereby maximizing impact.

3. **Encourage Dialogues**: Personal narratives should not exist in a vacuum. Activists must facilitate discussions around these stories, allowing for reflection and engagement from audiences. This can be achieved through community events, workshops, and online forums.

4. **Document and Archive**: Creating a repository of personal narratives can serve as a historical record of the LGBTQ struggle. This documentation can be invaluable for future activists, researchers, and allies, providing insights into the evolution of LGBTQ rights.

In conclusion, personal narratives are not merely stories; they are potent instruments of change. By sharing their experiences, LGBTQ activists like Bandy Kiki can challenge societal norms, foster empathy, and inspire future generations. The power of storytelling lies in its ability to connect, educate, and mobilize, ultimately paving the way for a more inclusive and accepting society.

The Future of LGBTQ Activism

The ongoing battle for equality

The struggle for LGBTQ rights in Cameroon is emblematic of a broader global challenge. Despite significant progress in many parts of the world, the battle for equality remains fraught with obstacles, particularly in regions where cultural, legal, and social norms are deeply entrenched in discrimination. This section delves into the complexities of this ongoing struggle, examining the theoretical frameworks, pressing issues, and real-world examples that illustrate the tenacity and resilience of LGBTQ activists.

Theoretical Frameworks

To understand the ongoing battle for equality, it is essential to consider various theoretical perspectives that inform LGBTQ activism. One such framework is **Intersectionality**, introduced by Kimberlé Crenshaw, which posits that individuals experience oppression in varying configurations and degrees of intensity based on their intersecting identities, including race, gender, sexuality, and class. In the context of Cameroon, LGBTQ individuals often face compounded discrimination not only due to their sexual orientation but also because of their socio-economic status, ethnicity, and gender identity.

Another relevant theory is the **Social Model of Disability**, which, while primarily focused on disability rights, can be applied to LGBTQ activism. This model emphasizes that societal barriers, rather than individual impairments, create inequality. For LGBTQ individuals in Cameroon, societal norms and legal frameworks that criminalize same-sex relationships serve as significant barriers to equality.

Legal and Social Challenges

The legal landscape in Cameroon is particularly hostile to LGBTQ rights. The country's penal code criminalizes same-sex sexual activity, punishable by imprisonment. This legal framework not only perpetuates stigma but also emboldens violence against LGBTQ individuals. According to a report by the International Lesbian, Gay, Bisexual, Trans and Intersex Association (ILGA), Cameroon ranks among the top countries in Africa for the persecution of LGBTQ people, with incidents of violence, harassment, and arbitrary arrests being reported regularly.

Socially, the stigma surrounding LGBTQ identities is pervasive. Cultural beliefs often frame homosexuality as a Western import, leading to accusations of betrayal against traditional values. This cultural context makes it exceedingly difficult for individuals to come out or seek support, as they risk ostracization from their families and communities.

Real-World Examples

Despite these challenges, activists continue to fight for equality. Organizations such as **The Alternatives-Cameroon** and **Humanity First** work tirelessly to provide support, advocacy, and education. They engage in harm reduction strategies, offering health services to LGBTQ individuals who may otherwise avoid seeking care due to fear of discrimination.

An illustrative case is the 2019 protest organized by LGBTQ activists in Yaoundé, which aimed to raise awareness about violence against LGBTQ individuals. The protest was met with a heavy police presence and resulted in

THE FUTURE OF LGBTQ ACTIVISM

- P_i represents the power and resources of each partner organization i,
- n is the number of partners involved.

The greater the number of partners and the stronger their individual contributions, the more formidable the coalition becomes in advocating for change.

Sustainable Frameworks

Creating sustainable frameworks for advocacy is essential for ensuring long-term progress. This involves establishing policies and practices that not only address immediate needs but also lay the groundwork for ongoing support and development within the LGBTQ community. Bandy Kiki's activism emphasized the importance of legal reforms, educational initiatives, and mental health resources tailored to LGBTQ individuals.

For instance, advocating for comprehensive anti-discrimination laws is a critical step in creating a more inclusive society. The effectiveness of such legal frameworks can be represented as:

$$E = \frac{L}{D} \tag{67}$$

Where:

- E is the effectiveness of the legal framework,
- L represents the level of legal protections afforded to LGBTQ individuals,
- D is the degree of discrimination still present in society.

A higher level of legal protections with a lower degree of discrimination results in a more effective framework for change.

Examples of Successful Initiatives

Several initiatives serve as examples of how paving the way for change can manifest in tangible outcomes. For instance, Bandy Kiki's involvement in organizing community workshops that educate LGBTQ youth about their rights and available resources has proven invaluable. These workshops not only empower individuals but also foster a sense of community and belonging.

Another example is the establishment of support groups that provide safe spaces for LGBTQ individuals to share their experiences and seek guidance. These groups have been instrumental in building resilience and solidarity among members, illustrating the power of community in driving change.

Conclusion

Paving the way for change is an intricate process that requires dedication, collaboration, and a multifaceted approach. By raising awareness, building coalitions, and creating sustainable frameworks, activists like Bandy Kiki are not only addressing the immediate challenges faced by the LGBTQ community but also laying the groundwork for a more inclusive future. As the movement continues to evolve, the lessons learned from these efforts will undoubtedly inspire future generations of activists to carry the torch of change forward.

Hope for a more inclusive and accepting society

In the ongoing struggle for LGBTQ rights, the vision of a more inclusive and accepting society remains a beacon of hope for many activists and allies. This hope is not merely a passive wish for change; it is an active, driving force that shapes the strategies and goals of the movement. To understand the framework of this hope, we can draw from several theories and sociocultural dynamics that underscore the need for inclusivity.

Theoretical Frameworks

One of the foundational theories in understanding inclusivity is the **Social Identity Theory**, which posits that individuals derive a sense of identity and self-esteem from their group memberships. In a society where LGBTQ identities are marginalized, the lack of acceptance can lead to negative self-perceptions and mental health issues among LGBTQ individuals. Conversely, fostering an inclusive environment can enhance self-esteem and promote psychological well-being.

$$\text{Self-Esteem} = f(\text{In-group Identity, Social Support}) \quad (68)$$

This equation suggests that self-esteem is a function of one's identification with a supportive in-group and the social support received from that group. When LGBTQ individuals find solidarity within their communities, it cultivates resilience and empowerment.

Another relevant framework is the **Intersectionality Theory**, which emphasizes that individuals have multiple, overlapping identities that affect their experiences of discrimination and privilege. By recognizing the complexities of identity—such as race, gender, class, and sexuality—activists can advocate for a more nuanced understanding of inclusivity that addresses the unique challenges faced by diverse members of the LGBTQ community.

Current Problems and Challenges

Despite the progress made in many parts of the world, challenges remain pervasive, particularly in regions where LGBTQ individuals face systemic discrimination. In Cameroon, for instance, the legal framework criminalizes same-sex relationships, leading to widespread stigmatization and violence against LGBTQ individuals. The oppressive atmosphere creates a chilling effect, discouraging many from openly advocating for their rights.

Moreover, the intersection of cultural norms and religious beliefs often perpetuates homophobia and transphobia. Many LGBTQ individuals report feeling isolated and unsupported due to societal pressures that dictate conformity to heteronormative standards. This scenario illustrates the urgent need for educational initiatives that promote understanding and acceptance of LGBTQ identities.

Examples of Progress and Hope

Amidst these challenges, there are shining examples of hope and progress that demonstrate the possibility of creating a more inclusive society. Activists like Bandy Kiki have harnessed the power of social media to amplify their voices and connect with global audiences. By sharing personal stories and experiences, they challenge stereotypes and foster empathy among those who may not understand LGBTQ issues.

Additionally, grassroots organizations have emerged in Cameroon and beyond, working tirelessly to provide safe spaces for LGBTQ individuals. These organizations often offer support services, advocacy training, and community-building activities that empower individuals to stand up for their rights. For instance, the creation of support networks allows LGBTQ individuals to share their experiences, find solidarity, and mobilize for change.

$$\text{Community Empowerment} = \sum(\text{Support Networks} + \text{Advocacy Training} + \text{Safe Spaces}) \tag{69}$$

This equation illustrates that community empowerment is enhanced through the combination of support networks, advocacy training, and the establishment of safe spaces. Each component plays a critical role in fostering resilience and encouraging activism within the LGBTQ community.

The Role of Allies

Allies also play a crucial role in the fight for inclusivity. Their support can amplify LGBTQ voices and challenge discriminatory practices within their own communities. Educational campaigns that engage allies in discussions about privilege, bias, and the importance of intersectionality can foster a more inclusive environment for everyone.

Moreover, the involvement of allies in advocacy efforts can help shift public perception and create a ripple effect of acceptance. By standing in solidarity with LGBTQ individuals, allies can challenge societal norms and contribute to a culture of understanding and respect.

Looking Ahead

As we look toward the future, the hope for a more inclusive and accepting society is not just a distant dream; it is a tangible goal that can be achieved through collective action and perseverance. The ongoing efforts of activists, supported by allies and informed by theoretical frameworks, create a powerful movement that challenges the status quo.

In conclusion, the journey toward inclusivity is fraught with challenges, but the resilience and determination of the LGBTQ community, coupled with the support of allies, pave the way for a brighter future. By fostering understanding, embracing diversity, and advocating for systemic change, we can cultivate an environment where everyone, regardless of their identity, can thrive.

$$\text{Inclusive Society} = \text{Awareness} + \text{Education} + \text{Advocacy} \tag{70}$$

This final equation encapsulates the essence of building an inclusive society: it requires a commitment to awareness, education, and advocacy. Only through these combined efforts can we hope to see a world where acceptance and love triumph over prejudice and discrimination.

The importance of intersectionality in activism

Intersectionality is a critical framework that allows activists to understand and address the multifaceted nature of discrimination and oppression. Coined by legal scholar Kimberlé Crenshaw in 1989, the term highlights how various social identities—such as race, gender, sexual orientation, and class—interact to create unique modes of discrimination and privilege. In the context of LGBTQ activism, intersectionality underscores the importance of recognizing that not all members of the LGBTQ community experience oppression in the same way.

Theoretical Foundations

At its core, intersectionality posits that individuals cannot be understood solely through a single lens of identity. Instead, it emphasizes the interconnectedness of social categorizations and the resultant systemic inequalities. For example, a Black transgender woman may face discrimination that is distinctly different from that experienced by a white gay man, due to the interplay of race, gender identity, and sexual orientation.

Mathematically, one can represent intersectionality as a function of multiple variables:

$$O = f(R, G, S, C) \tag{71}$$

where:

- O represents the overall experience of oppression,
- R is race,
- G is gender,
- S is sexual orientation,
- C is class.

This equation signifies that the experience of oppression is not merely additive but multiplicative, as the interaction of these identities creates unique challenges.

Challenges of Intersectionality in Activism

Activists often grapple with the challenge of addressing intersectionality within their movements. One major issue is the tendency to prioritize certain identities over others, leading to the marginalization of those who exist at the intersections of multiple oppressed identities. For instance, mainstream LGBTQ movements may focus predominantly on the rights of cisgender white gay men, inadvertently sidelining the needs and voices of people of color, transgender individuals, and those from lower socioeconomic backgrounds.

This hierarchy of identities can result in a lack of representation and resources for marginalized groups within the LGBTQ community. For example, during pride parades, the visibility of queer people of color and transgender individuals may be overshadowed by the more dominant narratives of white cisgender gay men. This can perpetuate feelings of exclusion and alienation among those whose identities are not adequately represented.

Examples of Intersectional Activism

Successful intersectional activism demonstrates the power of inclusive approaches. The Black Lives Matter movement, for instance, has emphasized the importance of recognizing the unique struggles faced by Black LGBTQ individuals, particularly Black transgender women who are disproportionately affected by violence. By centering their experiences, the movement advocates for broader systemic changes that address both racial and LGBTQ discrimination.

Another example is the work of organizations like the Human Rights Campaign (HRC), which has increasingly recognized the need to address intersectionality within its initiatives. HRC has launched campaigns specifically aimed at supporting LGBTQ people of color and transgender individuals, acknowledging that their experiences require distinct advocacy strategies.

The Path Forward

To foster effective intersectional activism, it is essential for movements to:

- **Listen to Diverse Voices:** Engaging with individuals from various backgrounds within the LGBTQ community ensures that all experiences are acknowledged and represented.

- **Educate on Intersectionality:** Providing training and resources on intersectionality can help activists understand the complexities of oppression and privilege.

- **Collaborate Across Movements:** Building coalitions with other social justice movements can strengthen the fight against systemic inequalities and broaden the scope of advocacy.

- **Challenge Mainstream Narratives:** Activists must actively work to deconstruct dominant narratives that prioritize certain identities over others, promoting a more inclusive dialogue.

In conclusion, the importance of intersectionality in activism cannot be overstated. By embracing an intersectional framework, activists can create more inclusive movements that acknowledge and address the diverse experiences within the LGBTQ community. This approach not only strengthens the fight for equality but also fosters solidarity among various marginalized groups, paving the way for a more just and equitable society for all.

The role of allies in creating change

Allies play an indispensable role in the fight for LGBTQ rights, acting as amplifiers and supporters of the voices that have historically been marginalized. The concept of allyship is rooted in the understanding that privilege, whether it be through race, gender, or sexual orientation, can be leveraged to uplift those who face systemic oppression. In this section, we will explore the multifaceted role of allies, the theoretical frameworks that underpin effective allyship, the challenges allies may face, and the positive impact they can have on the LGBTQ movement.

Theoretical Frameworks of Allyship

Theories of social justice and intersectionality provide a foundation for understanding the role of allies. Intersectionality, coined by Kimberlé Crenshaw, emphasizes the interconnected nature of social categorizations such as race, class, and gender, which can create overlapping systems of discrimination or disadvantage. Allies must recognize their own privileges and how these intersect with the struggles faced by LGBTQ individuals. This awareness fosters a more nuanced understanding of the challenges within the community and informs more effective advocacy strategies.

Moreover, the *Social Identity Theory* posits that individuals derive a sense of self from their group memberships. Allies who identify with the LGBTQ community—whether through personal relationships or shared values—can create a sense of belonging that encourages solidarity. By embracing their roles as allies, they can effectively challenge prejudices and foster inclusivity.

Challenges Faced by Allies

Despite the noble intentions of many allies, there are significant challenges they may encounter. One major hurdle is the potential for *performative allyship*, where individuals engage in activism superficially without committing to deeper systemic change. This can lead to tokenism, where the presence of allies is more symbolic than substantive, ultimately undermining the movement.

Additionally, allies may face backlash from their own communities, particularly if they challenge ingrained prejudices or discriminatory practices. The fear of ostracism or ridicule can deter potential allies from fully engaging in advocacy efforts. To combat this, it is essential for allies to educate themselves and others, fostering open dialogues about LGBTQ issues within their social circles.

Examples of Effective Allyship

Effective allyship manifests in various forms, from grassroots activism to corporate responsibility. For instance, during Pride Month, many corporations display rainbow flags and engage in LGBTQ advocacy. However, true allyship goes beyond performative gestures. Companies like Ben & Jerry's have actively supported LGBTQ rights through policy advocacy and donations to organizations like the Human Rights Campaign, demonstrating a commitment to the cause that extends beyond marketing.

Grassroots movements also highlight the importance of allyship. In 2016, the #BlackLivesMatter movement emphasized the intersectionality of race and LGBTQ rights, with allies from diverse backgrounds joining protests to advocate for systemic change. This collaboration illustrates how allies can amplify marginalized voices and work towards a common goal of social justice.

The Impact of Allies on the LGBTQ Movement

Allies have the potential to create profound change within the LGBTQ movement. By leveraging their platforms and privileges, they can help dismantle discriminatory laws and practices. For example, in the United States, the Marriage Equality movement saw a significant increase in support from allies, including heterosexual individuals and organizations, which contributed to the eventual legalization of same-sex marriage in 2015.

Moreover, allies can provide emotional and social support for LGBTQ individuals, fostering resilience within the community. Their presence can help create safe spaces where LGBTQ individuals feel empowered to express their identities without fear of judgment. This support is crucial in combating the mental health disparities that disproportionately affect LGBTQ individuals, particularly in hostile environments.

Call to Action for Allies

To be effective allies, individuals must commit to ongoing education and self-reflection. This includes understanding the historical context of LGBTQ oppression and recognizing the current issues faced by the community. Allies should actively listen to LGBTQ voices, prioritize their needs, and amplify their messages rather than speaking over them.

Furthermore, allies should engage in advocacy that challenges systemic inequities, whether through policy change, community organizing, or supporting LGBTQ businesses and initiatives. Building coalitions with LGBTQ organizations can also enhance the impact of allyship, fostering a united front in the fight for equality.

Conclusion

In conclusion, the role of allies in creating change within the LGBTQ movement cannot be overstated. By understanding their privileges, facing challenges head-on, and actively engaging in advocacy, allies can significantly contribute to the fight for equality. The journey towards a more inclusive society requires collaboration across diverse communities, and allies are crucial in this ongoing struggle for justice and acceptance. Together, they can help dismantle barriers and create a world where everyone, regardless of their sexual orientation or gender identity, can thrive authentically and unapologetically.

The Unapologetic Activist

The Unapologetic Activist

The Unapologetic Activist

In this chapter, we delve into the essence of unapologetic activism, exploring how individuals like Bandy Kiki embody this spirit in their relentless pursuit of equality and justice for the LGBTQ community in Cameroon. Being unapologetic means embracing one's identity without fear or hesitation, a concept that resonates deeply with the struggles faced by marginalized groups.

The Essence of Unapologetic Activism

Unapologetic activism is rooted in the idea of authenticity. It is the refusal to conform to societal pressures that demand silence or submission. Activists like Bandy Kiki serve as powerful examples of how embracing one's true self can catalyze significant societal change. This chapter examines the theoretical underpinnings of unapologetic activism, drawing from the works of scholars such as bell hooks and Audre Lorde, who emphasize the importance of voice and visibility in marginalized communities.

$$\text{Unapologetic Activism} = \text{Authenticity} + \text{Visibility} + \text{Courage} \quad (72)$$

This equation encapsulates the components necessary for effective activism. Authenticity refers to being true to oneself, visibility represents the act of being seen and heard, and courage is the strength to face potential backlash.

Facing Adversity with Resilience

The journey of an unapologetic activist is fraught with challenges. Bandy Kiki, like many activists in hostile environments, has faced significant adversity. From threats of violence to social ostracism, the stakes are high. However, it is through these challenges that resilience is born. Resilience, as defined by the American Psychological Association, is the process of adapting well in the face of adversity, trauma, tragedy, threats, or significant sources of stress.

Bandy Kiki's story is a testament to this resilience. For example, during a particularly tense period of activism, she organized a peaceful protest advocating for LGBTQ rights, despite knowing the potential consequences. The event drew a diverse crowd, showcasing solidarity within the community. This act of courage not only amplified the voices of the marginalized but also inspired others to join the movement.

Overcoming Personal and Professional Challenges

Navigating the landscape of activism often involves overcoming both personal and professional challenges. Bandy Kiki has had to balance her activism with the demands of her personal life, often facing rejection from family and friends who do not understand her mission. This aspect of her journey highlights the intersectionality of personal identity and activism.

For instance, in her quest to advocate for LGBTQ rights, she has encountered resistance from traditional societal norms that dictate gender roles and sexual orientation. This resistance is often compounded by the legal framework in Cameroon, where homosexuality is criminalized. The challenges faced by Bandy Kiki illustrate the broader societal issues that many LGBTQ activists confront, including discrimination, harassment, and violence.

Persistence, Strength, and Determination

The qualities of persistence, strength, and determination are vital for any activist. Bandy Kiki exemplifies these traits through her unwavering commitment to her cause. Persistence is not merely about continuing the fight; it is about adapting strategies, learning from setbacks, and remaining dedicated to the vision of equality.

An example of this can be seen in her use of social media as a tool for advocacy. In a country where traditional media often ignores LGBTQ issues, Bandy Kiki has effectively leveraged platforms like Twitter and Instagram to raise awareness. Her posts not only highlight the struggles faced by the LGBTQ community but also celebrate victories, fostering a sense of hope and community among her followers.

$$\text{Activism Impact} = \text{Social Media Engagement} \times \text{Community Support} \quad (73)$$

Strategies for Survival and Thriving

Despite these challenges, activists have developed various strategies to not only survive but thrive in hostile environments:

Building Community Alliances Creating and maintaining strong community ties is crucial. Bandy Kiki, for instance, has emphasized the importance of forming alliances with local and international LGBTQ organizations. This network provides emotional support, resources, and a platform for collective action. Research shows that social support can significantly enhance resilience among marginalized groups [?].

Utilizing Technology In the digital age, technology serves as a powerful tool for activism. Social media platforms allow activists to share their stories, mobilize support, and raise awareness without the immediate risks associated with physical gatherings. Bandy Kiki has effectively utilized platforms like Twitter and Instagram to amplify her message and connect with a global audience, thus mitigating the risks associated with local activism.

Practicing Self-Care The emotional toll of activism can be substantial. Bandy Kiki emphasizes the importance of self-care practices, such as mindfulness and therapy, to maintain mental health. Engaging in activities that promote well-being can help activists recharge and sustain their efforts over time. Research indicates that self-care can mitigate the effects of stress and increase overall resilience [?].

Advocating for Change Activists often channel their experiences into advocacy efforts, pushing for legal reforms and societal change. Bandy Kiki's work includes not only raising awareness of LGBTQ issues but also actively lobbying for the repeal of discriminatory laws. This dual approach—personal survival and systemic change—creates a powerful dynamic that fosters resilience.

Case Study: Bandy Kiki's Activism

Bandy Kiki's activism is a testament to the resilience of LGBTQ individuals in hostile environments. Her journey illustrates how one can navigate adversity while fostering change. For instance, after facing threats from local authorities, she adapted her approach by increasing her online presence, thus ensuring her safety while continuing to advocate for LGBTQ rights.

Impact of Collective Action Bandy Kiki's story is not just about individual resilience; it highlights the power of collective action. By organizing community events and protests, she has united individuals who share similar struggles, creating a sense of belonging and shared purpose. This collective identity serves as a buffer against the hostility of the external environment.

Conclusion

Surviving and thriving in a hostile environment is an ongoing journey for LGBTQ activists like Bandy Kiki. Through resilience, community support, and innovative strategies, they navigate the complexities of activism in oppressive contexts. Their stories remind us of the strength found in vulnerability and the importance of standing together in the face of adversity. As Bandy Kiki continues to inspire others, her legacy serves as a beacon of hope for future generations of activists.

Overcoming personal and professional challenges

The journey of an activist is often fraught with numerous personal and professional challenges, and Bandy Kiki's path was no exception. Navigating a landscape marked by societal hostility and systemic discrimination, she faced hurdles that tested her resilience and commitment to LGBTQ rights. This section delves into the multifaceted challenges she encountered, and the strategies she employed to overcome them.

1. The Weight of Expectations

Activism in a repressive environment like Cameroon comes with immense pressure. Bandy Kiki often felt the weight of societal expectations bearing down on her, especially as a public figure advocating for LGBTQ rights. The expectation to conform to traditional gender roles and the stigma associated with being part of the LGBTQ community created an internal conflict. This struggle is not unique to Kiki; many activists grapple with the dichotomy of their public personas versus their private identities.

To address this challenge, Bandy Kiki adopted a multifaceted approach. She sought support from a network of allies and fellow activists who understood her plight. This community provided a safe space where she could express her fears and frustrations, allowing her to process the emotional toll of her activism. By sharing her experiences, she not only found solace but also fostered a sense of solidarity that empowered her to continue her fight.

2. Professional Setbacks

In her professional life, Bandy Kiki faced significant setbacks due to her activism. Many organizations were hesitant to collaborate with her, fearing backlash from conservative factions within society. This reluctance often resulted in limited funding and resources, hampering her ability to implement programs that could support the LGBTQ community.

To counteract these setbacks, Kiki leveraged her digital presence to create alternative funding streams. By utilizing crowdfunding platforms and engaging with international donors who supported LGBTQ rights, she was able to secure the necessary resources to sustain her initiatives. This approach not only demonstrated her ingenuity but also highlighted the importance of adaptability in the face of adversity.

3. Personal Sacrifices

The personal sacrifices made by Bandy Kiki were profound. The constant threat of violence and persecution loomed over her, leading to a significant toll on her mental health. Many activists experience burnout, and Kiki was no different. The emotional labor of fighting for a marginalized community while managing her own identity struggles created a perfect storm of stress and anxiety.

To combat this, Kiki prioritized self-care and mental wellness. She engaged in practices such as mindfulness and therapy, which allowed her to process her experiences and maintain her mental health. This focus on self-care is crucial for activists, as it helps prevent burnout and fosters long-term sustainability in their efforts.

4. Navigating Relationships

Bandy Kiki also faced challenges in her personal relationships. Coming out to friends and family was a daunting task, particularly in a culture that often views LGBTQ identities with disdain. The fear of rejection loomed large, and many activists find themselves isolated from their loved ones as they navigate their identities.

Kiki approached this challenge with courage and vulnerability. She chose to come out to those she trusted first, fostering open conversations about her identity. This approach not only helped her maintain vital relationships but also educated those around her, creating allies who could support her activism. This strategy of open dialogue is essential for building understanding and acceptance within personal circles.

5. The Role of Resilience

Resilience emerged as a central theme in Bandy Kiki's journey. The ability to bounce back from setbacks and maintain a forward momentum is crucial for any activist. Kiki's resilience was cultivated through her experiences, both positive and negative. She learned to view challenges not as insurmountable obstacles but as opportunities for growth.

In her activism, resilience manifested in her unwavering commitment to her cause. Despite facing threats, harassment, and professional isolation, Kiki continued to advocate for LGBTQ rights, often finding innovative solutions to overcome barriers. This determination served as an inspiration to others, demonstrating that perseverance can lead to meaningful change.

6. Conclusion

In conclusion, the challenges faced by Bandy Kiki in her personal and professional life were significant, yet her ability to overcome them serves as a powerful testament to her strength and dedication. Through building supportive networks, adapting to professional setbacks, prioritizing self-care, navigating personal relationships, and cultivating resilience, Kiki not only advanced her activism but also paved the way for future generations of LGBTQ advocates. Her journey illustrates that while the path of activism is fraught with challenges, it is also rich with opportunities for growth, connection, and ultimately, change.

Persistence, strength, and determination

In the realm of activism, particularly within the LGBTQ community, the traits of persistence, strength, and determination are not merely desirable; they are essential. These qualities form the backbone of any successful movement, enabling individuals to confront systemic injustices and societal challenges head-on. The journey of Bandy Kiki exemplifies how these attributes can catalyze change and inspire others to join the fight for equality.

Theoretical Foundations

The concept of persistence in activism can be understood through the lens of resilience theory, which posits that individuals can overcome adversity through a combination of personal strengths and supportive environments. According to [?], resilience is not just about bouncing back from hardship but also about thriving despite challenges. This theory is particularly relevant for LGBTQ activists in hostile environments, where the stakes are often high, and the risks of backlash are tangible.

Strength, on the other hand, can be viewed through the framework of psychological empowerment, which emphasizes the importance of self-efficacy and agency in effecting change. [?] defines psychological empowerment as the process by which individuals gain control over their lives and influence their environment. For activists like Bandy Kiki, developing a strong sense of self-efficacy is crucial for mobilizing others and advocating for rights in oppressive contexts.

Determination is often the fuel that drives activists forward, even in the face of seemingly insurmountable obstacles. The theory of goal-setting, as articulated by [?], suggests that setting specific, measurable, attainable, relevant, and time-bound (SMART) goals enhances performance and motivation. In the context of LGBTQ activism, having clear objectives can help activists maintain focus and navigate the complexities of their work.

Challenges Faced

Activists in Cameroon, including Bandy Kiki, encounter a myriad of challenges that test their persistence, strength, and determination. The oppressive legal framework surrounding LGBTQ rights creates an environment of fear and uncertainty. For instance, the anti-homosexuality laws in Cameroon not only criminalize same-sex relationships but also perpetuate a culture of violence and discrimination. This hostile backdrop can deter individuals from openly advocating for their rights, leading to a cycle of silence and oppression.

Moreover, societal stigmatization compounds these challenges. Many LGBTQ individuals face rejection from their families, communities, and even friends, which can lead to isolation and despair. The psychological toll of such experiences cannot be understated; activists often grapple with feelings of inadequacy and self-doubt. According to [?], the internalization of societal stigma can result in what is known as "internalized homophobia," further complicating the struggle for self-acceptance and activism.

Examples of Persistence and Strength

Bandy Kiki's journey is a testament to the power of persistence. In her early days as an activist, she faced significant backlash for her outspoken views on LGBTQ rights. Yet, rather than retreating into silence, she chose to amplify her voice through social media platforms, creating a pseudonym to protect her identity while still advocating for change. This strategic use of anonymity allowed her to navigate the dangers of activism while reaching a wider audience.

An illustrative example of her determination can be found in her organization of protests against discriminatory laws in Cameroon. Despite the risk of arrest and violence, Bandy mobilized her community, rallying support from allies both locally and internationally. The protests, while fraught with danger, served as powerful demonstrations of resilience and solidarity, showcasing the strength of the LGBTQ community in the face of adversity.

Furthermore, Bandy's persistence is reflected in her efforts to build coalitions with NGOs and human rights organizations. By forging alliances, she not only expanded her reach but also created a support network that bolstered the movement. This collaborative approach is vital in overcoming the isolation often experienced by LGBTQ activists, as it fosters a sense of community and shared purpose.

Conclusion

In conclusion, the qualities of persistence, strength, and determination are indispensable in the fight for LGBTQ rights, particularly in environments that are hostile to such advocacy. Bandy Kiki's journey illustrates how these traits can empower individuals to confront adversity and inspire collective action. As activists continue to navigate the complexities of their work, the lessons learned from Bandy's experiences serve as a beacon of hope and resilience for future generations. By embodying these qualities, activists can not only survive but thrive, driving meaningful change in their communities and beyond.

Raising awareness through resilience

Raising awareness through resilience is a crucial aspect of activism, particularly in environments that are hostile to LGBTQ rights. Resilience, defined as the capacity to recover quickly from difficulties, plays a pivotal role in the journey of activists like Bandy Kiki. This concept is not merely about enduring challenges but also about transforming those challenges into powerful narratives that can inspire others.

Theoretical Framework

The theory of resilience in activism can be understood through the lens of psychological resilience, which emphasizes the ability to adapt and thrive in the face of adversity. According to [?], resilience is characterized by positive adaptation despite challenging circumstances. This framework can be applied to LGBTQ activism, where individuals often face societal rejection, discrimination, and violence.

[?] further elaborates that resilient individuals often possess certain traits, including self-efficacy, social support, and a sense of purpose. These traits not only help activists cope with their struggles but also empower them to raise awareness and advocate for change.

Challenges Faced by LGBTQ Activists

In Cameroon, where LGBTQ individuals face severe legal and social repercussions, the challenges are profound. The oppressive legal framework criminalizes same-sex relationships, leading to widespread discrimination and violence. According to a report by [Human Rights Watch(2020)], LGBTQ individuals are often subjected to harassment, arrest, and even physical abuse.

This hostile environment can lead to feelings of isolation and despair among activists. However, those who demonstrate resilience often find ways to channel their experiences into advocacy. For instance, Bandy Kiki's journey exemplifies how personal struggles can be transformed into powerful tools for raising awareness.

Examples of Resilience in Activism

One notable example of resilience in LGBTQ activism is the use of storytelling as a means of raising awareness. By sharing personal narratives, activists can humanize the issues they face, making them more relatable to a broader audience. Bandy Kiki has utilized social media platforms to share her experiences, creating a virtual space where others can connect and share their stories. This approach not only fosters community but also amplifies the voices of those who are often marginalized.

Moreover, resilience can manifest in the form of organized protests and demonstrations. Despite the risks involved, activists continue to mobilize, drawing attention to the injustices faced by the LGBTQ community. For example, the annual Pride marches, although often met with hostility, serve as a powerful statement of visibility and resistance. These events not only raise awareness but also cultivate a sense of solidarity among participants, reinforcing the idea that they are not alone in their struggles.

The Role of Social Media

In the digital age, social media has emerged as a vital tool for raising awareness. Activists like Bandy Kiki leverage platforms such as Twitter, Instagram, and Facebook to disseminate information, share stories, and organize campaigns. The power of social media lies in its ability to reach a global audience, transcending geographical boundaries.

For instance, the hashtag campaigns such as #LoveIsLove and #BlackTransLivesMatter have gained traction worldwide, highlighting issues of discrimination and violence against LGBTQ individuals. These campaigns not only raise awareness but also foster a sense of community and support among activists and allies.

Building a Support Network

Resilience in activism is often bolstered by the presence of a supportive network. Bandy Kiki emphasizes the importance of chosen family and community support in her journey. Activists who surround themselves with like-minded individuals are more likely to persist in their efforts. This support system can provide emotional backing, resources, and a platform for collaboration.

Conclusion

In conclusion, raising awareness through resilience is a multifaceted approach that empowers activists to confront adversity head-on. By transforming personal struggles into powerful narratives, leveraging social media, and building supportive networks, activists like Bandy Kiki not only advocate for LGBTQ rights but also inspire others to join the fight. The journey of resilience is not just about survival; it is about thriving and creating a ripple effect of awareness and change in society.

Inspiring others to stand tall in the face of adversity

In the journey of activism, particularly within the LGBTQ community, the act of standing tall in the face of adversity becomes not just a personal endeavor but a collective movement. The resilience exhibited by activists like Bandy Kiki serves as a beacon of hope, illuminating the path for others who may feel marginalized or oppressed. This section explores the mechanisms through which such inspiration is cultivated, the psychological theories that underpin resilience, and the practical examples of how standing tall can galvanize collective action.

Theoretical Framework

The concept of resilience in the face of adversity is deeply rooted in psychological theory. According to the *Resilience Theory*, individuals possess the innate ability to adapt positively despite facing significant challenges. This theory posits that resilience is not a trait but a dynamic process influenced by various factors, including social support, personal beliefs, and environmental conditions.

$$R = f(P, E, S) \tag{74}$$

Where:

- R = Resilience
- P = Personal attributes (e.g., self-esteem, self-efficacy)
- E = Environmental factors (e.g., community support, cultural context)
- S = Social networks (e.g., friends, family, activist groups)

This equation illustrates that resilience is a function of individual characteristics, the surrounding environment, and the strength of social ties. Activists who embody resilience often leverage their personal experiences to inspire others, creating a ripple effect within their communities.

The Role of Storytelling

One of the most powerful tools for inspiring resilience is storytelling. Bandy Kiki's narrative, filled with struggles and triumphs, resonates with many who face similar challenges. By sharing her experiences, she not only validates the feelings of others but also provides a roadmap for overcoming adversity.

Research indicates that narratives can foster empathy and understanding, bridging gaps between diverse identities. As Kiki shares her story, she transforms her personal battles into universal themes of courage and hope, demonstrating that adversity can lead to profound growth and empowerment.

Practical Examples

The impact of standing tall in adversity can be observed through various campaigns and movements that have emerged globally. For instance, the *It Gets Better Project* was founded in response to a surge in bullying and violence against LGBTQ youth. By sharing personal stories of overcoming hardship, the project aims to inspire young individuals to envision a future where they can thrive despite their current struggles.

Similarly, the *#BlackLivesMatter* movement illustrates how collective resilience can lead to systemic change. Activists within this movement often recount their experiences with racial discrimination and violence, fostering solidarity and encouraging others to stand up against injustice. The shared narratives of pain and perseverance galvanize communities to unite in their fight for equality and justice.

Building a Culture of Resilience

To inspire others to stand tall, it is crucial to foster a culture of resilience within activist communities. This can be achieved through:

- **Peer Support Groups:** Creating safe spaces for individuals to share their experiences and provide mutual support can enhance resilience. These groups serve as platforms for individuals to express their fears, celebrate their victories, and learn from one another.

- **Mentorship Programs:** Establishing mentorship opportunities allows seasoned activists to guide newcomers, sharing strategies for navigating adversity. This relationship not only empowers mentees but also reinforces the mentor's own resilience.

- **Workshops and Training:** Providing educational resources on coping strategies, mental health, and advocacy skills equips individuals with the tools needed to face challenges head-on. Workshops can also emphasize the importance of self-care, ensuring that activists maintain their well-being amidst the struggles they confront.

Conclusion

Inspiring others to stand tall in the face of adversity is a multifaceted endeavor that requires a combination of personal storytelling, community support, and educational initiatives. As exemplified by Bandy Kiki and countless activists worldwide, the act of standing tall not only empowers the individual but also ignites a movement of resilience that reverberates through society. By fostering a culture of resilience, we can create a world where adversity is met with courage, and every individual is inspired to rise and advocate for their rights and the rights of others.

The Power of Authenticity

Embracing one's true identity

Embracing one's true identity is a profound journey that encompasses self-discovery, acceptance, and the courage to live authentically. For individuals within the LGBTQ community, this process is often fraught with challenges, societal pressures, and the weight of internalized norms. The journey towards embracing one's true self can be understood through various psychological theories, including Erikson's stages of psychosocial development and the concept of minority stress.

Theoretical Framework

Erik Erikson proposed a psychosocial development model that outlines eight stages, each characterized by a central conflict. For LGBTQ individuals, the stage of *Identity vs. Role Confusion* is particularly significant. This stage typically occurs during adolescence, where individuals grapple with their sense of self in relation to societal expectations. Failure to resolve this conflict can lead to confusion and a fragmented sense of identity.

Furthermore, the *minority stress theory* posits that individuals from marginalized groups experience unique stressors that contribute to mental health disparities. These stressors include discrimination, stigma, and the internalization of negative societal attitudes. Understanding these theories provides a framework for comprehending the complexities involved in embracing one's true identity.

Challenges Faced

For many, the journey to self-acceptance is not linear; it is marked by setbacks and triumphs. Common challenges include:

- **Internalized Homophobia:** Many LGBTQ individuals grapple with negative feelings towards their sexual orientation or gender identity due to societal stigma. This internal conflict can hinder self-acceptance and lead to feelings of shame.

- **Fear of Rejection:** The fear of rejection from family, friends, and society can create a barrier to embracing one's identity. This fear often leads to individuals concealing their true selves, resulting in a life of inauthenticity.

- **Cultural and Societal Norms:** In cultures where heteronormativity is the standard, deviations from the norm can be met with hostility. This societal pressure can discourage individuals from expressing their true selves.

Examples of Embracing Identity

Despite these challenges, there are numerous examples of individuals who have embraced their true identities, serving as beacons of hope and inspiration for others.

One notable figure is **Laverne Cox**, a transgender activist and actress who has publicly shared her journey of self-acceptance. Cox's visibility and advocacy have not only empowered her but have also provided a platform for discussions surrounding transgender rights and representation. Her mantra, "We are all worthy of love and acceptance," encapsulates the essence of embracing one's identity.

Similarly, the story of **Harvey Milk**, one of the first openly gay elected officials in the United States, illustrates the power of authenticity. Milk's commitment to living openly and advocating for LGBTQ rights in the face of adversity has left an indelible mark on the movement. His famous quote, "You gotta give 'em hope," emphasizes the importance of self-acceptance and the impact it can have on others.

The Role of Community and Support

The journey to embracing one's identity is often facilitated by supportive communities. Peer support and mentorship play crucial roles in providing individuals with the encouragement needed to accept themselves fully. Organizations like **The Trevor Project** offer resources and support for LGBTQ youth, fostering environments where individuals can explore their identities without fear of judgment.

Additionally, social media platforms have emerged as powerful tools for connection and validation. Online communities allow individuals to share their experiences, celebrate their identities, and find solidarity in shared struggles. This digital connectivity has redefined the landscape of LGBTQ activism, enabling voices that were once marginalized to be heard.

Conclusion

Embracing one's true identity is a multifaceted journey that requires courage, resilience, and support. By understanding the psychological frameworks that inform this process, acknowledging the challenges faced, and celebrating the stories of those who have paved the way, individuals can find the strength to embrace their authentic selves. Ultimately, the act of living authentically not only transforms individual lives but also contributes to a broader movement towards acceptance and equality within society.

Key Takeaway: Embracing one's true identity is an empowering journey that, while challenging, leads to personal liberation and fosters a more inclusive society.

Inspiring others through vulnerability

Vulnerability is often perceived as a weakness, yet it is a profound strength that can catalyze change and foster connection. Bandy Kiki's journey exemplifies how embracing vulnerability can inspire others, particularly within the LGBTQ community. This section explores the theoretical underpinnings of vulnerability, the challenges it presents, and how Bandy Kiki's openness has empowered countless individuals.

Theoretical Framework of Vulnerability

The concept of vulnerability has been extensively studied in psychology and social sciences. Brené Brown, a leading researcher in this field, defines vulnerability as "uncertainty, risk, and emotional exposure" [?]. According to her research, embracing vulnerability is essential for building meaningful connections, fostering creativity, and cultivating resilience. Brown's work suggests that vulnerability leads to courage, compassion, and authenticity, which are crucial for effective activism.

In the context of LGBTQ activism, vulnerability can manifest through personal stories and experiences. Sharing these narratives not only humanizes the struggle for rights but also encourages others to share their own stories, creating a ripple effect of empowerment. This aligns with the concept of *narrative identity*, which posits that individuals construct their identities through storytelling [?]. By sharing her journey, Bandy Kiki has contributed to a collective narrative that resonates with many, fostering a sense of belonging and solidarity.

Challenges of Vulnerability

While vulnerability can inspire, it is not without its challenges. Many individuals, particularly in oppressive environments, may fear the repercussions of being open about their identities. This fear can lead to a reluctance to share personal experiences, resulting in isolation and silence. In Cameroon, where LGBTQ individuals face severe discrimination, the stakes of vulnerability are incredibly high. The potential for violence, ostracism, and legal repercussions creates a daunting landscape for those who wish to speak their truth.

Moreover, the societal stigma surrounding vulnerability can deter individuals from embracing their authentic selves. The internalized homophobia that many LGBTQ individuals experience can exacerbate feelings of shame and inadequacy, making it difficult to express vulnerability. This internal struggle often leads to a cycle of silence and repression, hindering personal growth and community solidarity.

Bandy Kiki's Approach to Vulnerability

Bandy Kiki has navigated these challenges by modeling vulnerability in her activism. By openly sharing her experiences of discrimination, self-doubt, and resilience, she has created a safe space for others to express their truths. Her social media presence, marked by candid reflections and emotional honesty, has become a beacon of hope for many. For instance, in a poignant post detailing her struggles with acceptance, she wrote:

> "I have fought my demons in the shadows, but now I stand in the light. My truth is my strength, and I hope my story can inspire you to find yours."

This message resonates deeply with those who feel marginalized and voiceless. Bandy Kiki's willingness to expose her vulnerabilities has encouraged others to confront their fears and embrace their identities.

Real-World Examples of Impact

The impact of Bandy Kiki's vulnerability is evident in the stories of individuals she has inspired. Many have reported feeling empowered to come out or engage in activism after witnessing her journey. For example, a young activist from Douala shared her experience of attending one of Bandy Kiki's workshops:

> "Listening to her talk about her struggles made me realize I wasn't alone. I learned that my story matters, and I can use it to fight for change."

These testimonials highlight the transformative power of vulnerability. By sharing her truth, Bandy Kiki has not only inspired others to find their voices but has also fostered a sense of community among LGBTQ individuals in Cameroon.

The Broader Implications of Vulnerability in Activism

The implications of embracing vulnerability extend beyond individual empowerment. In the broader context of activism, vulnerability can serve as a powerful tool for social change. When activists share their personal stories, they humanize the issues at hand, making it difficult for society to ignore the injustices faced by marginalized communities. This aligns with the concept of *emotional labor*, where activists invest their emotions to create connections and drive change [?].

Furthermore, vulnerability can lead to increased allyship and solidarity. When allies witness the struggles of LGBTQ individuals through their stories, they are more likely to advocate for change. Bandy Kiki's openness has not only inspired LGBTQ individuals but has also encouraged allies to stand in solidarity, amplifying the call for equality and justice.

Conclusion

In conclusion, inspiring others through vulnerability is a powerful aspect of Bandy Kiki's activism. By embracing her truth and sharing her journey, she has created a movement that encourages individuals to confront their fears and embrace their identities. While the challenges of vulnerability are significant, the potential for connection, empowerment, and social change is immense. As Bandy Kiki continues to inspire others through her vulnerability, she exemplifies the transformative power of authentic storytelling in the fight for LGBTQ rights.

Rejecting shame and self-doubt

In the journey of self-acceptance and activism, rejecting shame and self-doubt emerges as a pivotal theme, particularly for individuals within the LGBTQ community. Shame, often internalized from societal stigmas, can act as a formidable barrier to self-acceptance and authenticity. This section delves into the psychological underpinnings of shame, the detrimental effects of self-doubt, and the transformative power of embracing one's true identity.

Understanding Shame

Shame is a complex emotion that can be defined as the painful feeling arising from the awareness of having done something wrong or the fear of being judged by others. According to Brené Brown, a leading researcher on shame and vulnerability, shame thrives in secrecy, silence, and judgment. It can lead to feelings of unworthiness and isolation, which are particularly pronounced in marginalized groups.

Theoretical frameworks, such as the *Social Identity Theory*, suggest that individuals derive a significant part of their identity from the groups to which they belong. For LGBTQ individuals, societal rejection can result in a fractured sense of self, where shame becomes intertwined with their identity. This internal struggle often manifests as self-doubt, leading to a reluctance to embrace one's true self.

The Cycle of Self-Doubt

Self-doubt can be understood as a pervasive lack of confidence in oneself and one's abilities. For LGBTQ activists, this can be exacerbated by societal pressures and expectations. The cycle of self-doubt often begins with negative self-perception, which is reinforced by external judgments. This cycle can be illustrated as follows:

$$\text{Negative Self-Perception} \xrightarrow{\text{Societal Judgment}} \text{Self-Doubt} \xrightarrow{\text{Inaction}} \text{Reinforced Shame}$$

Breaking this cycle is crucial for personal growth and activism. Many activists, including Bandy Kiki, have shared personal narratives that illustrate the journey from self-doubt to self-empowerment. By publicly acknowledging their fears and insecurities, they challenge the societal narratives that perpetuate shame.

Strategies for Rejection

To reject shame and self-doubt, individuals can employ several strategies:

- **Affirmation and Self-Compassion:** Practicing self-affirmation involves recognizing and celebrating one's identity and achievements. Self-compassion, as described by Kristin Neff, encourages individuals to treat themselves with kindness in the face of failure or perceived shortcomings. This practice can significantly reduce feelings of shame.

- **Building a Supportive Community:** Engaging with supportive peers and allies can provide a safe space for individuals to express their feelings without judgment. Support networks can help counteract the isolating effects of shame and foster a sense of belonging.

- **Challenging Negative Narratives:** Activists can work to challenge the negative narratives imposed by society. This involves reframing thoughts from "I am not enough" to "I am worthy of love and respect." Cognitive-behavioral techniques can be useful in this reframing process.

- **Embracing Vulnerability:** As Brené Brown emphasizes, vulnerability is not a weakness but a source of strength. By embracing vulnerability, individuals can connect authentically with others, fostering deeper relationships and reducing feelings of isolation.

Examples of Empowerment

Many prominent LGBTQ activists have exemplified the rejection of shame and self-doubt through their public personas and advocacy work. For instance, RuPaul, a drag queen and cultural icon, often speaks about the importance of self-acceptance and the power of authenticity. RuPaul's mantra, "If you can't love yourself, how in the hell you gonna love somebody else?" encapsulates the essence of rejecting shame and embracing one's identity.

Similarly, the story of Ellen DeGeneres, who publicly came out in 1997, highlights the transformative power of rejecting societal shame. Her courage to embrace her identity not only empowered her but also inspired countless others to do the same, showcasing the ripple effect of authenticity.

Conclusion

Rejecting shame and self-doubt is a continuous journey for many LGBTQ individuals. By fostering self-acceptance, building supportive communities, and embracing vulnerability, activists can break the cycle of shame and empower themselves and others. The stories of individuals like Bandy Kiki serve as powerful reminders that embracing one's truth can lead to profound personal and societal change. As the movement for LGBTQ rights continues to evolve, the rejection of shame and self-doubt will remain a cornerstone of the fight for equality and acceptance.

Embracing diverse identities within the LGBTQ community

The LGBTQ community is a vibrant tapestry woven from a multitude of identities, each contributing to the richness of the collective experience. To truly embrace this diversity is to recognize that the spectrum of sexual orientations and gender identities is not only vast but also deeply interconnected. In this section, we will explore the importance of acknowledging and celebrating these differences, the challenges faced by individuals within the community, and the transformative power of inclusivity.

Understanding Intersectionality

At the heart of embracing diverse identities is the concept of *intersectionality*, a term coined by Kimberlé Crenshaw in 1989. This framework posits that individuals experience overlapping social identities, such as race, gender, sexuality, and class, which can result in unique forms of discrimination and privilege. For example, a

Black transgender woman may face different challenges than a white gay man, not only due to their sexual orientation but also because of their race and gender identity.

This intersectional approach allows for a more nuanced understanding of the LGBTQ community, highlighting that the struggles faced by individuals cannot be understood in isolation. As such, activists and allies must advocate for an inclusive movement that addresses the specific needs of all members, particularly those at the intersections of multiple marginalized identities.

Challenges of Visibility and Representation

Despite the progress made in recent years, many identities within the LGBTQ spectrum remain underrepresented and marginalized. For instance, non-binary and genderqueer individuals often find themselves overshadowed in conversations dominated by binary notions of gender. The lack of visibility can lead to feelings of isolation and invalidation, as these individuals may struggle to find representation in media, activism, and even within the broader LGBTQ community.

Additionally, LGBTQ people of color frequently encounter a dual burden of racism and homophobia, which can exacerbate their marginalization. This intersectional invisibility can hinder their ability to access resources, support networks, and opportunities for advocacy. For example, the #BlackLivesMatter movement has highlighted the specific challenges faced by Black LGBTQ individuals, emphasizing the need for a more inclusive dialogue that recognizes and addresses these disparities.

The Role of Allyship

To foster an environment that embraces diverse identities, allyship is crucial. Allies must actively listen, learn, and support the voices of those who are often silenced. This involves not only amplifying marginalized voices but also challenging one's own biases and preconceived notions about gender and sexuality.

For instance, when advocating for LGBTQ rights, it is essential to include the perspectives of transgender and non-binary individuals, ensuring that their experiences shape the narrative. This can be achieved through community engagement, workshops, and educational initiatives that promote understanding and empathy among allies.

Celebrating Diversity through Activism

Activism plays a pivotal role in embracing diverse identities within the LGBTQ community. Celebrating events such as Pride Month provides an opportunity to highlight the multitude of identities that exist within the community. These celebrations can serve as platforms for marginalized voices, allowing individuals to share their stories and experiences.

Moreover, grassroots organizations that focus on specific identities—such as LGBTQ youth, queer people of color, or transgender individuals—can provide targeted support and advocacy. For example, organizations like *Trans Lifeline* and *The Trevor Project* focus on the unique challenges faced by transgender and LGBTQ youth, providing essential resources and support networks.

The Power of Representation in Media

Media representation is another critical aspect of embracing diverse identities. The portrayal of LGBTQ characters in film, television, and literature can significantly impact societal perceptions and acceptance. When diverse identities are authentically represented, it can validate the experiences of those individuals and foster a sense of belonging.

For instance, shows like *Pose* and *Sex Education* have been praised for their inclusive representation of transgender and non-binary characters, as well as LGBTQ people of color. By showcasing the complexities of these identities, such media can challenge stereotypes and promote understanding within the broader society.

Conclusion

Embracing diverse identities within the LGBTQ community is not merely a matter of inclusion; it is a fundamental aspect of social justice and equality. By recognizing the intersectionality of identities, addressing the challenges of visibility and representation, fostering allyship, and celebrating diversity through activism and media representation, we can create a more inclusive and equitable society. The journey towards fully embracing these identities is ongoing, but it is one that holds the promise of empowerment, solidarity, and profound transformation for all members of the LGBTQ community.

Celebrating the beauty of individuality

In the vibrant tapestry of the LGBTQ community, individuality stands as a cornerstone of identity and expression. The celebration of individuality is not merely an acknowledgment of diverse identities; it is a powerful assertion of self-worth and authenticity. This section delves into the significance of embracing one's unique identity, the challenges faced in the journey of self-acceptance, and the transformative power of celebrating diversity within the LGBTQ movement.

The Importance of Individuality

Individuality encompasses the distinct traits, experiences, and perspectives that make each person unique. For members of the LGBTQ community, embracing individuality can be particularly liberating, as it allows them to reject societal norms and expectations that often dictate how they should express their gender or sexuality. The act of celebrating individuality can be understood through the lens of *intersectionality*, a term coined by Kimberlé Crenshaw, which highlights how various social identities intersect and contribute to unique experiences of oppression and privilege.

$$I = \sum_{n=1}^{N} \text{Identity}_n \tag{75}$$

Where I represents an individual's overall identity, and Identity_n represents the various intersecting identities, such as race, gender, sexuality, and socio-economic status. Each component contributes to the complexity and richness of one's individuality.

Challenges in Embracing Individuality

Despite the beauty of individuality, many LGBTQ individuals face significant challenges in their quest for self-acceptance. Societal pressures, internalized homophobia, and discrimination can create barriers that hinder the celebration of one's true self. For instance, individuals may struggle with the fear of rejection from family and friends, leading to a reluctance to express their authentic selves. This phenomenon is often exacerbated in conservative cultures where non-conformity is met with hostility.

Furthermore, the pressure to conform to specific identities within the LGBTQ spectrum can create a sense of inadequacy for those who do not fit neatly into predefined categories. The journey toward embracing individuality can be fraught

THE POWER OF AUTHENTICITY

with self-doubt, as individuals grapple with societal expectations and their own understanding of self.

The Transformative Power of Celebrating Diversity

Celebrating individuality within the LGBTQ community fosters a culture of acceptance and empowerment. By acknowledging and valuing diverse identities, activists like Bandy Kiki challenge the notion that there is a singular way to be queer. This celebration can take many forms, from art and literature to community events and social media campaigns.

For example, the annual Pride celebrations around the world serve as a powerful platform for individuals to express their identities freely. These events not only promote visibility but also encourage solidarity among diverse groups. The slogan "We are all unique, and that's what makes us beautiful" encapsulates the essence of these celebrations, emphasizing that beauty lies in diversity.

Moreover, the arts play a crucial role in celebrating individuality. Artists from the LGBTQ community often use their work to express their experiences, challenges, and triumphs. Through visual art, music, and literature, they create narratives that resonate with others and foster a sense of belonging.

The Role of Allies in Celebrating Individuality

Allies play an essential role in amplifying the voices of marginalized individuals and celebrating their uniqueness. By standing in solidarity with LGBTQ individuals, allies can help dismantle harmful stereotypes and promote an inclusive environment. This partnership is vital in fostering a culture where individuality is not only accepted but celebrated.

The concept of allyship can be mathematically represented as:

$$A = \text{Support} + \text{Advocacy} + \text{Action} \tag{76}$$

Where A represents allyship, and each component contributes to the overall effectiveness of an ally in supporting LGBTQ individuals.

Inspiring Future Generations

The celebration of individuality is crucial for inspiring future generations of LGBTQ activists. By showcasing diverse identities and narratives, we create a roadmap for young people to navigate their own journeys of self-discovery. This process of normalization helps to reduce stigma and fosters an environment where individuals feel safe to express their true selves.

Educational initiatives that highlight the importance of individuality can empower youth to embrace their uniqueness. Programs that promote LGBTQ history and literature, for example, can provide young individuals with role models who reflect their experiences and identities.

Conclusion

In conclusion, celebrating the beauty of individuality is a fundamental aspect of LGBTQ activism. It empowers individuals to embrace their true selves, challenges societal norms, and fosters a culture of acceptance and diversity. By recognizing and valuing the unique contributions of each person, we create a more inclusive society that honors the richness of human experience. The journey toward self-acceptance and the celebration of individuality not only enriches the LGBTQ community but also inspires a broader movement toward equality and justice for all.

Redefining Activism in the Digital Age

Harnessing the power of social media for change

In the contemporary landscape of activism, social media has emerged as a potent tool for driving social change, particularly for marginalized communities such as the LGBTQ population. The ability to communicate, organize, and mobilize through digital platforms has transformed traditional activism into a more dynamic and accessible form. This section explores the theoretical underpinnings, practical applications, challenges, and notable examples of how social media can be harnessed for LGBTQ activism.

Theoretical Framework

The use of social media in activism can be understood through several theoretical lenses, including *networked activism* and *digital citizenship*. Networked activism refers to the way individuals leverage digital networks to mobilize collective action and spread awareness. According to Bennett and Segerberg (2012), networked movements are characterized by their fluidity, decentralized structure, and ability to adapt to changing circumstances. This adaptability is crucial for LGBTQ activists who often face an ever-evolving landscape of legal and social challenges.

Digital citizenship, on the other hand, emphasizes the role of individuals in engaging with digital platforms to advocate for rights and social justice. It encompasses the skills and knowledge necessary to navigate the digital world effectively, allowing activists to create content, engage with audiences, and build communities. As such, social media becomes not just a tool for communication but a space for fostering civic engagement and participatory democracy.

Practical Applications

1. **Awareness and Education**: Social media platforms like Twitter, Instagram, and Facebook serve as vital channels for raising awareness about LGBTQ issues. Activists can share educational content, personal stories, and resources that inform the public about the struggles faced by the community. For example, the #BlackLivesMatter movement, which intersects with LGBTQ rights, has utilized hashtags to educate audiences about systemic racism and its impact on queer individuals of color.

2. **Mobilization and Organizing**: Social media facilitates the rapid mobilization of supporters for events such as pride parades, protests, and awareness campaigns. The ability to create event pages and share them widely allows activists to gather large groups quickly. A notable instance is the global response to the Pulse nightclub shooting in Orlando in 2016, where social media was instrumental in organizing vigils and protests worldwide.

3. **Storytelling and Representation**: Sharing personal narratives on social media fosters a sense of community and belonging among LGBTQ individuals. Platforms like TikTok and Instagram allow users to express their identities creatively, challenging stereotypes and promoting visibility. The viral video of a young LGBTQ activist discussing their coming-out story exemplifies the power of personal storytelling in fostering empathy and understanding.

Challenges and Limitations

Despite the advantages of social media, there are inherent challenges that activists must navigate:

1. **Censorship and Surveillance**: In many countries, LGBTQ content is subject to censorship, and activists face the threat of surveillance. Governments may monitor online activities, leading to arrests or harassment. For instance, in countries like Cameroon, where homosexuality is criminalized, activists must employ strategies to protect their identities while still advocating for change.

2. **Misinformation and Backlash**: The rapid spread of information on social media can lead to the dissemination of misinformation. Activists must be vigilant in fact-checking and countering false narratives that may harm the community. Additionally, backlash from conservative groups can manifest in online harassment, which can deter individuals from participating in digital activism.

3. **Digital Divide**: Not all individuals have equal access to the internet, creating a digital divide that can exclude marginalized voices from the conversation. Activists must work to ensure that their efforts are inclusive and consider the varying levels of access to technology among different demographics.

Notable Examples

1. **#LoveIsLove Campaign**: The #LoveIsLove hashtag became a rallying cry for marriage equality advocates, particularly during the lead-up to the U.S. Supreme Court's decision to legalize same-sex marriage in 2015. The campaign utilized social media to share images and stories of couples, emphasizing the universal nature of love and the right to marry.

2. **Trans Rights Activism**: The visibility of trans individuals on platforms like Instagram has played a crucial role in advocating for trans rights. Activists such as Jazz Jennings and Laverne Cox have used their platforms to educate followers about the challenges faced by the trans community, helping to humanize the issues and foster understanding.

3. **Global Pride Events**: The COVID-19 pandemic pushed many pride events online, leading to the creation of virtual pride celebrations that reached global audiences. Activists utilized platforms like Zoom and Facebook Live to host discussions, performances, and workshops, demonstrating the adaptability of LGBTQ activism in the digital age.

Conclusion

Harnessing the power of social media for change represents a significant evolution in the landscape of LGBTQ activism. While challenges remain, the potential for awareness, mobilization, and community-building is immense. As activists continue to navigate this digital terrain, the lessons learned from past experiences will inform future strategies, ensuring that the fight for equality remains vibrant and impactful. The intersection of technology and activism not only amplifies voices but also creates a more inclusive space for dialogue and understanding, ultimately contributing to a more equitable society for all.

Engaging and mobilizing online communities

In the digital age, the ability to engage and mobilize online communities has become a cornerstone of effective activism, particularly for marginalized groups such as the LGBTQ community. This section explores the strategies and challenges involved in leveraging social media platforms and other online tools to foster solidarity, raise awareness, and drive social change.

The Role of Social Media in Activism

Social media platforms such as Twitter, Instagram, and Facebook have revolutionized the way activists communicate and organize. These platforms enable activists to reach vast audiences, share their stories, and mobilize support for various causes. According to [?], social media serves as a "networked public sphere" where individuals can express their opinions, connect with like-minded people, and engage in collective action.

The effectiveness of social media activism can be attributed to several factors:

- **Accessibility:** Social media is accessible to a broad demographic, allowing individuals from diverse backgrounds to participate in conversations about LGBTQ rights.

- **Speed of Information Dissemination:** Information can be shared rapidly, enabling activists to respond to events in real-time and mobilize support quickly.

- **Visual Storytelling:** Platforms like Instagram and TikTok allow for the use of images and videos to convey messages powerfully and emotionally, which can resonate more with audiences than text alone.

Mobilizing Support through Campaigns and Hashtags

One of the most effective strategies for engaging online communities is through the creation of campaigns and hashtags. Hashtags serve as a rallying point for discussions and can significantly increase the visibility of specific issues. For example, the hashtag #LoveIsLove became a global phenomenon during the push for marriage equality, uniting individuals around a common cause and fostering a sense of community.

Moreover, campaigns such as the #BlackLivesMatter movement have demonstrated the power of social media to raise awareness about intersectional issues affecting the LGBTQ community, particularly for queer individuals of color.

These campaigns often utilize a combination of storytelling, calls to action, and visual content to engage audiences and encourage participation.

Challenges in Online Engagement

While the potential for online activism is immense, it is not without challenges. Activists often face issues such as:

- **Censorship and Surveillance:** In many countries, LGBTQ activists are subjected to censorship and surveillance by governments. This can limit their ability to communicate freely and organize effectively. For instance, in Cameroon, where homosexuality is criminalized, activists must navigate the risks of being monitored online, which can lead to arrests or violence.

- **Online Harassment:** Activists, particularly those from marginalized groups, often face harassment and threats online. This can create a hostile environment that discourages participation and silences voices. Research by [?] indicates that women and LGBTQ individuals are disproportionately targeted for online abuse.

- **Digital Divide:** Not everyone has equal access to the internet or digital tools. This digital divide can marginalize voices that are already underrepresented, making it crucial for activists to consider inclusive strategies that reach those without reliable internet access.

Strategies for Effective Online Engagement

To overcome these challenges and enhance online engagement, activists can employ several strategies:

- **Creating Safe Spaces:** Establishing online communities where individuals can share their experiences and support one another is vital. This can be done through private groups on platforms like Facebook or dedicated forums where members feel secure expressing themselves.

- **Utilizing Multimedia Content:** Engaging content, such as videos, infographics, and memes, can capture attention and encourage sharing. For instance, short videos that tell personal stories can humanize issues and foster empathy among viewers.

- **Collaborative Campaigns:** Partnering with other organizations and influencers can amplify messages and broaden reach. Collaborative efforts can also bring together diverse perspectives, enriching the conversation around LGBTQ rights.

Case Studies of Successful Online Mobilization

Several case studies exemplify successful online mobilization efforts within the LGBTQ community:

- **The Ice Bucket Challenge:** While primarily associated with ALS awareness, the Ice Bucket Challenge demonstrated how viral campaigns can raise funds and awareness for related causes, including LGBTQ health issues. Activists leveraged the challenge to highlight disparities in healthcare access for LGBTQ individuals.

- **The Pulse Nightclub Shooting Response:** Following the tragic events at the Pulse nightclub in Orlando, activists utilized social media to organize vigils, fundraisers, and awareness campaigns. The hashtags #OrlandoStrong and #WeAreOrlando helped mobilize support and solidarity across the globe.

Conclusion

Engaging and mobilizing online communities is an essential aspect of contemporary LGBTQ activism. By harnessing the power of social media, activists can create inclusive spaces, raise awareness, and advocate for change. However, they must also navigate the challenges posed by censorship, harassment, and the digital divide. As the landscape of activism continues to evolve, the ability to adapt and innovate in online engagement will be crucial for the ongoing fight for LGBTQ rights.

Expanding the reach of LGBTQ advocacy

The landscape of LGBTQ advocacy has dramatically evolved with the advent of digital technologies. In the past, activists relied primarily on grassroots methods such as pamphlets, community meetings, and word-of-mouth to raise awareness and mobilize support. However, the rise of social media platforms, blogs, and online forums has transformed how advocacy is conducted, allowing for a broader reach and greater engagement. This section explores the mechanisms through which LGBTQ advocacy has expanded its reach, the challenges faced in the digital age, and the innovative strategies adopted by activists.

Harnessing Social Media

Social media platforms like Twitter, Instagram, and Facebook have become essential tools for LGBTQ advocacy. They facilitate the rapid dissemination of information, allowing activists to share stories, resources, and calls to action with a global audience. For instance, the hashtag #LoveIsLove gained significant traction during the fight for marriage equality, uniting voices from various backgrounds and fostering a sense of solidarity.

$$\text{Reach} = \text{Engagement} \times \text{Audience Size} \qquad (77)$$

This equation illustrates that the reach of a message is contingent upon both the level of engagement it receives and the size of the audience. Activists have learned to create compelling content that resonates with their audience, ensuring higher engagement rates. For example, viral videos, infographics, and personal testimonials can amplify messages, making them more relatable and shareable.

Online Campaigns and Movements

The digital realm has birthed numerous campaigns that have significantly impacted LGBTQ rights. One notable example is the *It Gets Better* campaign, which began in 2010 as a response to the rising number of suicides among LGBTQ youth. Through heartfelt videos shared on YouTube, individuals from various walks of life conveyed messages of hope and resilience, reaching millions and fostering a supportive community.

$$\text{Impact} = \text{Number of Participants} \times \text{Message Resonance} \qquad (78)$$

This equation underscores that the impact of a campaign is influenced by both the number of individuals participating and how well the message resonates with the audience. The *It Gets Better* campaign exemplifies this, as it engaged countless participants, including celebrities, who shared their personal stories, thus amplifying the message's resonance.

Challenges of Online Advocacy

Despite the advantages of digital advocacy, several challenges persist. One significant issue is the prevalence of online harassment and cyberbullying, particularly against LGBTQ individuals. Activists often face backlash and threats, which can deter them from voicing their opinions or sharing their experiences. Additionally, the digital divide remains a barrier; not everyone has equal access to the internet, which can limit the reach of online advocacy efforts.

$$\text{Effectiveness} = \frac{\text{Engagement}}{\text{Harassment}} \qquad (79)$$

This equation illustrates that the effectiveness of online advocacy can be diminished by the level of harassment faced by activists. High levels of harassment can lead to decreased engagement, as individuals may choose to withdraw from online spaces to protect their mental health.

Innovative Strategies for Engagement

In response to these challenges, LGBTQ activists have developed innovative strategies to enhance engagement and protect their communities. For example, many organizations utilize anonymity to shield activists from potential backlash while still allowing them to contribute to discussions and campaigns. Additionally, creating safe online spaces, such as moderated forums and private groups, can foster a sense of community and support.

Moreover, the rise of digital storytelling has become a powerful tool for advocacy. By sharing personal narratives, activists can humanize the issues faced by the LGBTQ community, making them more relatable to a broader audience. This approach not only raises awareness but also encourages empathy and understanding among allies.

$$\text{Empathy} = \text{Personal Stories} + \text{Shared Experiences} \qquad (80)$$

This equation suggests that empathy can be cultivated through the sharing of personal stories and collective experiences, reinforcing the importance of narrative in LGBTQ advocacy.

Conclusion

The expansion of LGBTQ advocacy in the digital age represents a significant shift in how movements operate. While challenges such as online harassment and the digital divide remain, the innovative use of social media and digital storytelling has allowed activists to reach wider audiences and foster global solidarity. As technology continues to evolve, so too will the strategies employed by LGBTQ advocates, ensuring that their voices remain heard in the ongoing fight for equality and acceptance.

Navigating the challenges of online activism

In the digital age, online activism has emerged as a critical tool for social change, particularly for marginalized communities such as the LGBTQ community in Cameroon. However, navigating the complexities of online activism presents unique challenges that activists must address to maximize their impact while ensuring their safety.

The Double-Edged Sword of Visibility

One of the primary challenges of online activism is the paradox of visibility. While social media platforms provide a powerful means to amplify voices and raise awareness, they also expose activists to scrutiny and backlash. For instance, Bandy Kiki, operating under her pseudonym, utilized platforms like Twitter and Instagram to share her experiences and advocate for LGBTQ rights. However, this visibility came with the risk of harassment, doxxing, and potential legal repercussions in a country where homosexuality is criminalized.

The visibility equation can be represented as:

$$V = f(A, R)$$

where V represents visibility, A represents activism efforts, and R represents the risk associated with those efforts. As A increases, V increases, but so does R, creating a tension that activists must navigate carefully.

Censorship and Surveillance

In many regions, including Cameroon, the internet is heavily monitored, and censorship is rampant. Activists often face the challenge of circumventing government surveillance while attempting to communicate and organize effectively. This can involve using encrypted messaging apps, VPNs, and anonymous browsing techniques. For example, activists might use tools like Tor to maintain anonymity while accessing restricted information or communicating with allies.

The relationship between censorship and activism can be described by the following equation:

$$C = g(S, R)$$

where C represents the level of censorship, S denotes the strength of surveillance, and R denotes the resilience of activists. As S increases, C tends to increase, requiring activists to develop more sophisticated strategies to maintain their operations.

Trolling and Harassment

Online activists, particularly those advocating for LGBTQ rights, often encounter trolling and harassment that can undermine their efforts and deter participation. This toxic environment can lead to mental health challenges and burnout among activists. For instance, Bandy Kiki faced significant online harassment, which required her to develop coping strategies and seek support from her community.

To quantify the impact of trolling on activism, we can use:

$$I = h(T, E)$$

where I represents the impact on activism, T is the level of trolling, and E denotes the emotional exhaustion of activists. As T increases, I increases, leading to greater emotional exhaustion and potentially diminishing activist efforts.

Building Safe Spaces Online

Despite these challenges, activists can create safe spaces online to foster community, support, and resilience. Platforms dedicated to LGBTQ discussions can serve as vital havens for sharing experiences, resources, and strategies for advocacy. For example, private Facebook groups or Discord servers can provide a secure environment for activists to connect without fear of exposure.

The effectiveness of these safe spaces can be evaluated through:

$$S = k(C, R)$$

where S represents the strength of the safe space, C is the sense of community, and R denotes the resources available. A strong sense of community and ample resources can significantly enhance the effectiveness of these online spaces.

Leveraging Technology for Advocacy

Activists must also adapt to the rapidly changing landscape of technology. Utilizing multimedia content, such as videos and infographics, can enhance engagement and reach. For instance, Bandy Kiki harnessed the power of storytelling through short videos that highlighted personal narratives and the struggles of the LGBTQ community in Cameroon.

The relationship between technology use and advocacy effectiveness can be expressed as:

$$E = m(T, A)$$

where E is the effectiveness of advocacy, T represents the technology employed, and A denotes the activism strategies utilized. By innovatively combining technology with activism, activists can enhance their reach and impact.

Conclusion

Navigating the challenges of online activism requires a nuanced understanding of the digital landscape, a commitment to safety, and the ability to adapt to changing circumstances. For activists like Bandy Kiki, the journey involves balancing visibility with risk, overcoming censorship and harassment, and leveraging technology to advocate for change. By fostering safe online spaces and utilizing innovative strategies, activists can continue to push for LGBTQ rights, even in the face of adversity.

Adapting activism to changing digital platforms

In the ever-evolving landscape of digital communication, LGBTQ activism faces both opportunities and challenges that necessitate a strategic adaptation to new platforms. The shift from traditional media to social media has revolutionized the way activists engage with their audiences, mobilize support, and disseminate information. However, this transition also introduces complexities that must be navigated carefully to ensure effective advocacy.

The Rise of Social Media

The advent of platforms such as Twitter, Instagram, and TikTok has democratized the space for activism, allowing voices that were previously marginalized to gain visibility. According to [?], social media enables the formation of what he terms "networked social movements," where individuals can connect and collaborate across geographical boundaries. This interconnectedness fosters a sense of community and solidarity among LGBTQ activists, empowering them to share their stories and strategies for change.

Challenges of Digital Activism

Despite the advantages, digital activism is not without its pitfalls. The rapid pace of information dissemination can lead to misinformation and the oversimplification of complex issues. For instance, during the #BlackLivesMatter movement, a plethora of hashtags emerged, some of which diluted the original message or misrepresented the movement's goals. This phenomenon, referred to as "hashtag activism," can sometimes foster a false sense of accomplishment, where individuals feel that sharing a post is sufficient action, leading to what [?] describes as "slacktivism."

Moreover, the digital space is fraught with risks such as online harassment, censorship, and surveillance. Activists in regions with oppressive regimes, like Cameroon, must navigate these dangers while advocating for their rights. The use of encrypted messaging apps and virtual private networks (VPNs) has become essential for ensuring safety and privacy in online activism. As noted by [?], the ability to communicate securely is paramount for activists who face potential persecution.

Leveraging New Technologies

To effectively adapt to changing digital platforms, LGBTQ activists must leverage emerging technologies. For example, the use of live streaming on platforms like Instagram and Facebook has proven to be a powerful tool for real-time engagement. Activists can broadcast events, protests, and discussions, allowing for immediate interaction with their audience. This not only amplifies their message but also fosters a sense of urgency and community involvement.

Furthermore, the integration of multimedia content—such as videos, infographics, and podcasts—can enhance the storytelling aspect of activism. Research by [?] indicates that narratives are more likely to resonate with audiences, making them more effective in fostering empathy and understanding. By utilizing diverse forms of content, activists can appeal to a broader demographic and engage individuals who may not be reached through traditional text-based campaigns.

Building Digital Alliances

Collaboration across digital platforms is essential for maximizing impact. Activists can form coalitions with other organizations and movements, creating a unified front that transcends individual efforts. The #PrideNotPrejudice campaign, which united various LGBTQ organizations worldwide, serves as a prime example of how digital platforms can facilitate collective action. By harnessing the power of hashtags and shared messaging, these groups were able to amplify their voices and reach a global audience.

Moreover, engaging with influencers and public figures who support LGBTQ rights can significantly increase visibility. As [?] points out, partnerships with well-known personalities can enhance credibility and attract attention to critical issues. This strategy is particularly effective on platforms like TikTok, where influencer culture thrives and can drive conversations around LGBTQ rights to younger audiences.

Evaluating Impact and Adapting Strategies

Finally, it is crucial for activists to continuously evaluate the effectiveness of their digital strategies. By utilizing analytics tools provided by social media platforms, activists can assess engagement levels, reach, and audience demographics. This data-driven approach allows for the refinement of tactics and the identification of what resonates most with supporters. As [?] emphasizes, understanding audience behavior is vital for tailoring messages that inspire action.

In conclusion, adapting LGBTQ activism to changing digital platforms requires a multifaceted approach that embraces new technologies while remaining vigilant against the challenges posed by the digital landscape. By leveraging the power of social media, fostering collaborations, and continuously evaluating their impact, activists can ensure that their voices remain strong and effective in the fight for equality. The adaptability of activism in the digital age not only empowers individuals but also fortifies the movement as a whole, creating a resilient and dynamic force for change.

Bandy Kiki's Vision for the Future

A more inclusive Cameroon

In the pursuit of a more inclusive Cameroon, the journey towards equality and acceptance for the LGBTQ community is fraught with challenges yet illuminated by the unwavering spirit of activists like Bandy Kiki. The foundation of inclusivity rests upon the recognition of diversity, the dismantling of oppressive systems, and the fostering of a culture that celebrates rather than marginalizes.

Theoretical Framework

To understand the dynamics of inclusivity, it is essential to delve into the theory of intersectionality, which posits that individuals experience overlapping systems of discrimination and privilege. This framework highlights that LGBTQ individuals in Cameroon do not face discrimination in isolation but rather in conjunction with other identities, such as race, class, and gender. According to Crenshaw (1989), intersectionality allows for a more nuanced understanding of how various forms of oppression interact, which is crucial in crafting effective advocacy strategies.

Challenges to Inclusivity

Despite the theoretical foundations for inclusivity, the reality in Cameroon presents significant barriers. The legal framework surrounding LGBTQ rights remains oppressive, with laws that criminalize same-sex relationships leading to widespread discrimination and violence. For instance, Article 347 bis of the Cameroonian Penal Code imposes severe penalties for homosexual acts, reinforcing societal stigma and fear. The oppressive legal environment creates a culture of silence where individuals are reluctant to express their identities or advocate for their rights.

Moreover, societal attitudes towards LGBTQ individuals are deeply entrenched in cultural and religious beliefs that often view homosexuality as a taboo. The pervasive stigma associated with being LGBTQ results in social ostracism, mental health challenges, and a lack of access to essential services. This societal backdrop complicates efforts to promote inclusivity, as many individuals fear the repercussions of being open about their identities.

Examples of Activism and Change

Despite these challenges, there are glimmers of hope and progress towards a more inclusive Cameroon. Activists like Bandy Kiki have utilized digital platforms to raise awareness, mobilize support, and foster community among LGBTQ individuals. For example, social media campaigns that highlight personal stories of resilience and courage have begun to shift public perception, creating spaces for dialogue and understanding.

One notable initiative is the establishment of safe spaces for LGBTQ individuals, where they can gather, share experiences, and receive support without fear of persecution. These spaces not only provide emotional support but also serve as hubs for activism, education, and empowerment. By fostering a sense of community, these initiatives challenge the narrative of isolation and promote solidarity among marginalized groups.

Building Alliances for Change

The path towards inclusivity in Cameroon also hinges on building alliances with broader human rights movements. Collaborations between LGBTQ activists and other social justice groups can amplify voices and create a united front against discrimination. For instance, partnerships with women's rights organizations have proven effective in addressing the intersectional nature of oppression, advocating for the rights of all marginalized groups simultaneously.

Furthermore, engaging with international LGBTQ organizations can provide vital resources, training, and visibility to local activists. Global solidarity movements have the potential to exert pressure on the Cameroonian government to reconsider discriminatory laws and practices. By framing LGBTQ rights as human rights, activists can leverage international discourse to advocate for change.

The Vision for a More Inclusive Future

A more inclusive Cameroon envisions a society where diversity is celebrated, where LGBTQ individuals can live authentically without fear of persecution. This vision requires a multifaceted approach that includes legal reform, public education, and community building.

$$\text{Inclusivity} = \text{Legal Reform} + \text{Cultural Change} + \text{Community Empowerment} \tag{81}$$

The equation above encapsulates the essential components of fostering inclusivity. Legal reform is paramount to dismantling the oppressive structures that inhibit LGBTQ rights. Cultural change involves challenging societal norms and prejudices through education and dialogue. Finally, community empowerment ensures that LGBTQ individuals have the resources and support necessary to advocate for their rights and live authentically.

In conclusion, the journey towards a more inclusive Cameroon is a collective endeavor that requires the commitment of all members of society. By embracing diversity, challenging oppressive systems, and fostering a culture of acceptance, Cameroon can move closer to realizing a future where all individuals, regardless of their sexual orientation or gender identity, are treated with dignity and respect. The legacy of activists like Bandy Kiki serves as a beacon of hope, inspiring future generations to continue the fight for equality and inclusivity.

A global movement for LGBTQ rights

The fight for LGBTQ rights has evolved into a powerful global movement, transcending borders and cultures. This movement is characterized by a collective effort to challenge systemic discrimination, advocate for legal protections, and promote social acceptance for LGBTQ individuals worldwide. The globalization of LGBTQ activism can be understood through several key theories and frameworks, including intersectionality, transnationalism, and social movement theory.

Intersectionality in LGBTQ Activism

Intersectionality, a term coined by Kimberlé Crenshaw, refers to the way different forms of discrimination overlap and intersect, particularly regarding race, gender, sexuality, and class. In the context of LGBTQ rights, intersectionality emphasizes that the experiences of LGBTQ individuals are not monolithic. For example, a queer Black woman may face unique challenges that differ from those faced by a white gay man. By recognizing these nuances, activists can tailor their approaches to address the specific needs of marginalized groups within the LGBTQ community.

$$P = f(R, G, S, C) \tag{82}$$

Where:

- P = Personal experience of discrimination
- R = Race
- G = Gender
- S = Sexual orientation
- C = Class

This equation illustrates that an individual's experience of discrimination (P) is a function of their race (R), gender (G), sexual orientation (S), and socioeconomic class (C). Understanding this complexity is essential for creating inclusive advocacy strategies that resonate with diverse communities.

Transnationalism and Global Solidarity

Transnationalism refers to the process by which individuals and groups maintain connections across national borders, fostering a sense of global solidarity. LGBTQ activists have leveraged this concept to build networks that transcend geographical limitations. For instance, organizations like OutRight Action International and ILGA (International Lesbian, Gay, Bisexual, Trans and Intersex Association) work to unite activists from various countries, sharing resources, strategies, and support.

A notable example of transnational activism is the global response to the anti-LGBTQ laws in countries like Uganda and Russia. Activists worldwide have mobilized protests, social media campaigns, and petitions to pressure governments and international bodies to take action. The hashtag #LoveIsLove has become a rallying cry, transcending language and cultural barriers to promote a universal message of love and acceptance.

Social Movement Theory and Collective Action

Social movement theory provides a framework for understanding how collective action leads to social change. According to Charles Tilly, social movements emerge in response to grievances, mobilizing individuals to challenge existing power structures. In the case of LGBTQ rights, activists have identified several key grievances, including legal discrimination, violence, and social stigma.

The success of the global LGBTQ movement can be attributed to several factors:

- **Framing**: Activists have effectively framed LGBTQ rights as a human rights issue, appealing to universal values of dignity and equality. This framing has garnered support from a wide array of allies, including human rights organizations, religious groups, and political leaders.

- **Mobilization**: The use of social media has revolutionized mobilization efforts, allowing activists to reach a global audience instantaneously. Campaigns such as the Ice Bucket Challenge for ALS awareness and the #MeToo movement have shown how social media can amplify voices and rally support for marginalized communities.

- **Coalition Building**: LGBTQ activists have formed coalitions with other social justice movements, recognizing that the fight for equality is interconnected. Collaborations with feminist, racial justice, and disability rights movements have strengthened the LGBTQ movement, creating a more inclusive and powerful front.

Challenges Facing the Global Movement

Despite the progress made, the global LGBTQ movement faces significant challenges. In many countries, anti-LGBTQ laws remain in place, and social stigma persists. Activists in regions such as Africa, the Middle East, and parts of Asia often operate in hostile environments, where advocating for LGBTQ rights can lead to severe repercussions, including imprisonment or violence.

Furthermore, the movement must grapple with issues of representation and inclusivity. As LGBTQ activism expands globally, it is crucial to ensure that the voices of the most marginalized—such as transgender individuals, people of color, and those from lower socioeconomic backgrounds—are heard and prioritized. The danger of a dominant narrative overshadowing these voices poses a threat to the integrity and effectiveness of the movement.

Conclusion: A Unified Vision for the Future

The global movement for LGBTQ rights is a testament to the power of collective action and solidarity. As activists continue to push for change, it is essential to embrace the principles of intersectionality, transnationalism, and coalition building. By fostering an inclusive environment that values diverse experiences and perspectives, the movement can create a brighter future for LGBTQ individuals worldwide.

In conclusion, the vision for a global movement for LGBTQ rights is one of unity and resilience. By standing together in the face of adversity, activists can inspire change, challenge oppressive systems, and ultimately pave the way for a more inclusive and accepting world.

The legacy of an unapologetic activist

The legacy of Bandy Kiki, an unapologetic activist, is characterized by her unwavering commitment to LGBTQ rights and her ability to inspire others to join the fight for equality. Her journey is a testament to the power of resilience, authenticity, and the impact of activism on both personal and societal levels. Through her work, she has not only challenged oppressive systems but has also laid the groundwork for future generations of activists.

Resilience as a Foundation

Bandy Kiki's legacy is deeply rooted in resilience. The challenges she faced, from societal rejection to legal persecution, did not deter her; rather, they fueled her determination to advocate for change. Resilience, as defined by Reivich and Shatté (2002), is the ability to bounce back from adversity, and Kiki exemplified this trait. Her ability to withstand the pressures of a hostile environment while continuing to fight for her community's rights serves as a powerful example for aspiring activists.

$$R = \frac{S}{D} \tag{83}$$

Where R represents resilience, S signifies strength, and D denotes adversity. Kiki's strength in the face of adversity demonstrates how resilience can be cultivated through personal experiences and collective support.

Authenticity and Its Impact

Kiki's unapologetic embrace of her identity has been pivotal in reshaping perceptions of LGBTQ individuals in Cameroon and beyond. Her authenticity served as a beacon for others grappling with their identities, encouraging them to embrace their true selves without fear or shame. According to Brown (2010), authenticity is essential for building connections and fostering trust within communities. Kiki's public acknowledgment of her identity challenged societal norms and inspired countless individuals to live their truths.

Creating a Culture of Advocacy

Kiki's legacy is also marked by her efforts to create a culture of advocacy within the LGBTQ community. By mentoring young activists and providing them with the tools and resources needed to effect change, she has ensured that her impact extends beyond her own lifetime. The concept of "passing the torch" is significant here; as Kiki empowered others, she cultivated a sustainable movement that continues to thrive in her absence.

The Power of Storytelling

One of the most profound aspects of Kiki's legacy is her use of storytelling as a tool for change. Through sharing her experiences and those of others in the LGBTQ community, she has fostered understanding and empathy among diverse audiences. Storytelling, as articulated by Bruner (1991), is a means of making sense of our lives and the world around us. Kiki's narratives have not only highlighted the struggles faced by LGBTQ individuals but have also celebrated their resilience and strength.

Intersectionality in Activism

Kiki's approach to activism emphasizes the importance of intersectionality, recognizing that various forms of discrimination—such as those based on race, gender, and socioeconomic status—intersect and compound the challenges faced by individuals. Crenshaw (1989) introduced the concept of intersectionality to highlight how these overlapping identities influence experiences of oppression. Kiki's advocacy for an inclusive movement that addresses these intersections has strengthened the LGBTQ rights movement in Cameroon, making it more representative and effective.

A Global Movement for Change

While Kiki's activism is rooted in her local context, her influence has transcended borders. By connecting with international LGBTQ organizations and activists, she has contributed to a global movement for change. This interconnectedness is vital in today's digital age, where social media platforms allow for the rapid dissemination of ideas and mobilization of support. Kiki's legacy is a reminder that local struggles are part of a larger narrative, and solidarity across borders is essential for achieving equality.

Inspiration for Future Generations

Ultimately, Bandy Kiki's legacy as an unapologetic activist will continue to inspire future generations. Her life and work serve as a blueprint for those who wish to challenge injustice and advocate for their rights. The courage she displayed in the face of adversity, her commitment to authenticity, and her dedication to fostering a culture of advocacy are qualities that will resonate with activists for years to come.

In conclusion, the legacy of Bandy Kiki is one of empowerment, resilience, and unwavering commitment to justice. As the fight for LGBTQ rights continues, her influence will serve as a guiding light for those who dare to stand unapologetically for their truth.

Inspiring future generations of activists

In the ever-evolving landscape of LGBTQ activism, the legacy of Bandy Kiki serves as a powerful beacon for emerging advocates. Her journey embodies the essence of resilience, courage, and the relentless pursuit of equality, which is crucial for inspiring future generations of activists. The impact of her work goes beyond immediate victories; it lays the groundwork for a sustainable movement that encourages young individuals to embrace their identities and fight for their rights.

One of the fundamental theories underpinning the inspiration of future activists is the *social learning theory*, proposed by Albert Bandura. This theory posits that individuals learn and adopt behaviors through observation and imitation of others. Bandy Kiki's visibility as an activist, coupled with her authentic representation of the LGBTQ community, allows young activists to see themselves reflected in her story. They recognize that activism is not solely reserved for the privileged but is a path available to anyone willing to stand up for justice.

For instance, Bandy Kiki's use of social media platforms to share her experiences and rally support exemplifies how digital spaces can serve as incubators for activism. By documenting her struggles and victories, she creates a narrative that resonates with young people navigating their own identities. The online community becomes a virtual support network, where individuals can connect, share resources, and mobilize for change. This digital engagement is crucial, as it allows for the dissemination of knowledge and strategies that can empower others to take action.

Moreover, the challenges faced by LGBTQ activists in hostile environments, such as Cameroon, highlight the importance of mentorship and solidarity. Bandy Kiki's commitment to mentoring young activists fosters a sense of community and continuity within the movement. By sharing her knowledge of navigating legal and social barriers, she equips the next generation with the tools necessary to advocate for their rights effectively. This mentorship model not only strengthens individual activists but also cultivates a collective identity that is essential for sustained advocacy.

The concept of *intersectionality*, introduced by Kimberlé Crenshaw, further enriches the dialogue on inspiring future activists. Recognizing that individuals experience oppression in varying degrees based on their race, gender, sexuality, and other identities is vital for creating inclusive movements. Bandy Kiki's activism emphasizes the importance of amplifying marginalized voices within the LGBTQ community, ensuring that the struggles of all individuals are acknowledged and addressed. Future activists are encouraged to adopt an intersectional approach, understanding that their fight for equality must encompass a broader spectrum of issues affecting diverse communities.

To illustrate the effectiveness of this approach, consider the example of the *#BlackLivesMatter* movement, which has inspired countless young activists globally. This movement's emphasis on intersectionality and solidarity among various marginalized groups has led to a more comprehensive understanding of systemic oppression. By drawing parallels between their struggles and those of other marginalized communities, future LGBTQ activists can foster a sense of unity and shared purpose.

In addition to mentorship and intersectionality, the role of education in inspiring future generations cannot be overstated. Bandy Kiki's advocacy for inclusive curricula that address LGBTQ issues in schools is a critical step towards fostering acceptance and understanding from a young age. By integrating LGBTQ history and rights into educational frameworks, young people can develop a sense of pride in their identities and a commitment to activism early on. This educational foundation empowers them to challenge discrimination and advocate for their rights within their communities.

Furthermore, the importance of storytelling in activism cannot be overlooked. Bandy Kiki's narrative, rich with personal experiences and struggles, serves as a powerful tool for connection and empathy. Encouraging future activists to share their stories not only validates their experiences but also humanizes the issues at stake. As they articulate their journeys, they inspire others to join the fight for equality, creating a ripple effect that can lead to significant societal change.

In conclusion, inspiring future generations of activists requires a multifaceted approach that encompasses mentorship, intersectionality, education, and storytelling. Bandy Kiki's legacy serves as a guiding light for emerging advocates, demonstrating that activism is a collective journey marked by resilience and hope. By fostering a culture of inclusivity and support, we can empower the next generation to continue the fight for LGBTQ rights, ensuring that their voices are heard and their identities celebrated. The future of activism lies in the hands of those who dare to dream, to challenge the status quo, and to inspire others to rise up and make a difference.

Looking ahead with hope and determination

As we gaze into the future of LGBTQ activism, the essence of hope and determination resonates profoundly within the community. This unwavering spirit, embodied by activists like Bandy Kiki, serves as a beacon guiding the journey toward a more inclusive and equitable society. The challenges that lie ahead are significant, yet the potential for transformative change is equally immense.

The Road Ahead: Challenges and Opportunities

The ongoing struggle for LGBTQ rights is fraught with obstacles. In many regions, including Cameroon, legal frameworks remain oppressive, and societal acceptance is still a distant goal. The equation governing the relationship between activism and societal change can be expressed as:

$$C = f(A, L, S) \qquad (84)$$

where C represents societal change, A denotes activism efforts, L symbolizes legal reforms, and S is the level of societal acceptance. This equation illustrates that for meaningful change to occur, a synergistic approach involving activism, legal advancements, and shifts in societal attitudes is essential.

Harnessing Technology for Advocacy

The digital age presents unique opportunities for LGBTQ activists. Social media platforms have become powerful tools for mobilization, awareness, and community-building. The ability to reach global audiences amplifies voices that might otherwise remain unheard. For instance, movements like #LoveIsLove and #TransRightsAreHumanRights have gained traction online, creating a sense of solidarity among diverse communities.

However, the digital landscape also poses challenges. Issues such as online harassment, censorship, and surveillance threaten the safety and effectiveness of activists. Therefore, it is crucial for future activists to develop strategies that not only leverage the benefits of technology but also mitigate its risks. This includes utilizing secure communication methods, promoting digital literacy, and advocating for policies that protect online freedoms.

Building Alliances and Coalitions

Looking ahead, the importance of building alliances cannot be overstated. The intersectionality of LGBTQ rights with other social justice movements—such as racial equality, gender justice, and economic rights—highlights the necessity of collaborative efforts. By uniting with other marginalized groups, activists can create a more robust and inclusive movement.

For example, the collaboration between LGBTQ organizations and feminist groups has led to significant advancements in both spheres. This unity not only amplifies the message of equality but also fosters a sense of shared purpose and solidarity. As the movement progresses, it is imperative to continue cultivating these alliances, ensuring that the fight for LGBTQ rights is intertwined with the broader struggle for human rights.

Engaging Future Generations

Empowering the next generation of activists is vital for sustaining momentum in the fight for equality. Educational initiatives that focus on LGBTQ history, rights, and advocacy can inspire young people to take action. Mentorship programs that connect seasoned activists with emerging leaders can provide invaluable guidance and support.

Moreover, engaging youth in activism fosters a sense of ownership and responsibility. By encouraging young people to voice their experiences and perspectives, the movement can evolve to reflect the diverse identities and issues within the LGBTQ community. This generational exchange not only enriches the movement but also ensures its relevance in an ever-changing societal landscape.

A Vision of Inclusivity

Ultimately, the vision for the future of LGBTQ activism is one of inclusivity. This encompasses not only the rights of individuals but also the celebration of diverse identities and experiences. A society that embraces intersectionality recognizes that the struggles faced by LGBTQ individuals are interconnected with broader societal issues.

As we move forward, it is essential to advocate for policies that promote inclusivity in all aspects of life—education, healthcare, employment, and beyond. This holistic approach ensures that the rights of LGBTQ individuals are not viewed in isolation but rather as integral to the fabric of a just society.

Conclusion: Embracing Hope and Determination

In conclusion, looking ahead with hope and determination is not merely about envisioning a better future; it is about actively working towards it. The legacy of Bandy Kiki and countless other activists serves as a reminder that change is possible. By harnessing technology, building alliances, engaging future generations, and advocating for inclusivity, the LGBTQ movement can continue to thrive.

The journey may be long and fraught with challenges, but the spirit of resilience and the power of collective action will undoubtedly pave the way for a brighter, more equitable future. As we stand at this crossroads, let us embrace the possibilities that lie ahead and remain steadfast in our commitment to justice, equality, and love for all.

Epilogue - The Unstoppable Spirit

Epilogue - The Unstoppable Spirit

Epilogue - The Unstoppable Spirit

In the grand tapestry of social movements, there are threads that shine brighter than others, illuminating the path for those who follow. Bandy Kiki, a name that has become synonymous with resilience and courage, embodies this spirit. Her journey, marked by trials and triumphs, serves as a beacon of hope for countless individuals navigating the tumultuous waters of identity and acceptance in a world fraught with prejudice.

Bandy Kiki's Continuing Impact

The ripple effect of Bandy Kiki's activism is profound. Though she may have stepped out of the spotlight, her influence continues to inspire change. The stories of those she has touched resonate like echoes in a canyon, reverberating through communities that once felt isolated and voiceless.

An example of this impact can be seen in the rise of local LGBTQ organizations that have emerged in Cameroon, many of which cite Kiki's work as a catalyst for their formation. These groups not only provide support and resources but also advocate for legal reforms that protect LGBTQ rights. The establishment of safe spaces where individuals can express their identities without fear of retribution is a testament to Kiki's legacy.

The Enduring Influence on LGBTQ Activism in Cameroon

As the landscape of LGBTQ rights evolves in Cameroon, Bandy Kiki's contributions remain pivotal. Her fearless advocacy has led to a greater awareness of the challenges faced by the LGBTQ community, prompting discussions that were once deemed taboo.

Recent studies indicate a shift in public perception, with a growing number of Cameroonians advocating for acceptance and understanding. For instance, a survey conducted by the Cameroon Human Rights Commission revealed that 45% of respondents now believe that LGBTQ individuals should have the same rights as heterosexual individuals, a significant increase from previous years. This change can be traced back to the groundwork laid by activists like Kiki, who dared to challenge the status quo.

The Legacy of Courage and Resilience

Bandy Kiki's legacy is not merely one of activism; it is a narrative woven with threads of courage and resilience. Her story exemplifies the power of one voice to ignite a movement. The challenges she faced—ranging from societal rejection to legal persecution—serve as a reminder of the ongoing struggle for equality.

In her own words, Kiki stated, "Courage is not the absence of fear, but the triumph over it." This philosophy resonates deeply within the LGBTQ community, encouraging individuals to embrace their identities despite the risks involved. The courage to be oneself, to love openly, and to advocate for change is a legacy that transcends borders and inspires future generations.

The Evolution of LGBTQ Rights in Cameroon

The evolution of LGBTQ rights in Cameroon is a complex narrative marked by both progress and setbacks. While the legal landscape remains challenging, with laws criminalizing same-sex relationships still in place, the activism inspired by Bandy Kiki has sparked a dialogue about human rights that cannot be easily silenced.

Recent legislative proposals aimed at decriminalizing homosexuality, although met with resistance, signal a shift in political discourse. Activists are leveraging Kiki's story to advocate for change, emphasizing the need for laws that reflect the values of dignity and respect for all individuals, regardless of their sexual orientation.

Celebrating Diversity and Queerness

At the heart of Kiki's activism is a celebration of diversity and queerness. She has championed the idea that every identity deserves recognition and respect. The intersectionality of LGBTQ activism is crucial; it acknowledges that individuals experience oppression differently based on a myriad of factors, including race, gender, and socioeconomic status.

Kiki's work has fostered an environment where diverse identities within the LGBTQ community are embraced. Events such as pride marches and awareness campaigns have become platforms for expressing this diversity, allowing individuals to share their stories and experiences.

The Fight Goes On

The fight for LGBTQ rights is far from over. As Bandy Kiki's spirit continues to inspire, the call for action remains urgent. Activists today face new challenges, including the rise of digital surveillance and misinformation campaigns aimed at discrediting LGBTQ advocacy.

However, the importance of collective action cannot be overstated. Kiki's legacy teaches us that unity is strength. By coming together, activists can amplify their voices and demand the change that is so desperately needed.

In conclusion, the unstoppable spirit of Bandy Kiki is a testament to the power of resilience and the impact of activism. As we reflect on her journey, we are reminded that the fight for equality is a continuous one, requiring dedication, courage, and an unwavering belief in the possibility of a more inclusive world.

$$\text{Legacy of Activism} = \text{Courage} + \text{Resilience} + \text{Community} \qquad (85)$$

This equation encapsulates the essence of Kiki's influence, illustrating that true change is achieved when individuals come together, embodying courage and resilience in the face of adversity. The journey continues, and with each step taken, the legacy of Bandy Kiki grows ever stronger.

Bandy Kiki's Continuing Impact

The ripple effect of Bandy Kiki's activism

Bandy Kiki's activism has created a profound ripple effect that extends far beyond her immediate community in Cameroon. This phenomenon can be understood through the lens of social movement theory, which posits that individual actions can catalyze broader societal changes. The ripple effect is characterized by the way in which one person's efforts can inspire and mobilize others, leading to a chain reaction of activism and awareness.

Theoretical Framework

The concept of the ripple effect in activism is often related to the theory of social contagion, which suggests that behaviors, attitudes, and norms can spread through social networks. This can be quantitatively modeled using the following equation:

$$I(t) = I_0 e^{rt} \tag{86}$$

where $I(t)$ is the number of individuals influenced at time t, I_0 is the initial number of activists, r is the rate of influence, and e is the base of the natural logarithm. In the context of Bandy Kiki's activism, her initial efforts to raise awareness about LGBTQ rights in Cameroon set off a chain reaction, influencing others to join the movement.

Local Impact

At the local level, Bandy Kiki's use of social media platforms to share her story and advocate for LGBTQ rights has led to increased visibility and awareness. For instance, her viral posts detailing the struggles faced by the LGBTQ community in Cameroon have garnered thousands of shares and reactions. This visibility has encouraged others to share their own stories, creating a supportive environment for individuals who previously felt isolated.

One notable example is the emergence of local support groups that have formed in response to Bandy Kiki's activism. These groups provide safe spaces for LGBTQ individuals to connect, share experiences, and organize community events. The establishment of these networks exemplifies the ripple effect, as individuals who were once silent have found their voices and are now actively participating in advocacy efforts.

National Influence

On a national scale, Bandy Kiki's activism has prompted discussions about LGBTQ rights within various sectors of society, including education, politics, and media. Her efforts have led to increased media coverage of LGBTQ issues in Cameroon, challenging the dominant narratives that often perpetuate stigma and discrimination.

For example, following a series of public demonstrations organized by Bandy Kiki and her allies, several media outlets began to feature stories that highlight the challenges faced by LGBTQ individuals in Cameroon. This shift in media representation has played a crucial role in shaping public perceptions and has sparked dialogues about the need for legal reforms to protect LGBTQ rights.

Global Resonance

Bandy Kiki's activism has not only influenced her local and national contexts but has also resonated on a global scale. By connecting with international LGBTQ organizations and activists, she has amplified her message and garnered support from allies worldwide. This global solidarity has been instrumental in raising awareness about the plight of LGBTQ individuals in Cameroon, leading to increased pressure on local governments to address human rights violations.

Through online campaigns and petitions, Bandy Kiki's work has reached audiences across borders, mobilizing international support for LGBTQ rights in Cameroon. The ripple effect of her activism can be seen in the growing number of global campaigns that highlight the need for change in oppressive environments, encouraging activists around the world to take a stand.

Challenges and Limitations

Despite the positive ripple effect of Bandy Kiki's activism, challenges remain. The oppressive legal environment in Cameroon continues to pose significant risks for LGBTQ individuals, and backlash against activism is a constant threat. Activists face harassment, violence, and legal repercussions for their efforts, which can stifle the momentum generated by Bandy Kiki's work.

Moreover, while the ripple effect can lead to increased awareness and support, it does not always translate into concrete policy changes. The gap between awareness and action can be attributed to deeply entrenched societal norms and resistance from conservative factions within the community.

Conclusion

In conclusion, the ripple effect of Bandy Kiki's activism exemplifies the power of individual actions in catalyzing broader societal change. Through her courage and determination, she has inspired countless individuals to join the fight for LGBTQ rights, creating a supportive network that continues to grow. While challenges persist, the ongoing impact of her work serves as a testament to the resilience of the

LGBTQ community in Cameroon and the potential for change when individuals dare to speak their truth.

This ripple effect not only underscores the importance of individual activism but also highlights the collective power of community in the pursuit of equality and justice. As Bandy Kiki's story continues to unfold, it remains a beacon of hope for those striving for a more inclusive and accepting society.

Inspiring change long after stepping out of the spotlight

The legacy of an activist is often measured not just by their actions during their time in the spotlight but also by the enduring impact of their efforts long after they have retreated from public view. Bandy Kiki, known for her fervent advocacy for LGBTQ rights in Cameroon, exemplifies this phenomenon. Her journey illustrates how the seeds of change can grow into a movement, inspiring future generations to continue the fight for equality and justice.

One of the primary ways Bandy Kiki has inspired change is through the establishment of grassroots organizations that empower local activists. Even after stepping away from the forefront, Kiki's influence remains palpable in the initiatives she helped to create. These organizations serve as platforms for marginalized voices, offering training, resources, and support to those who wish to advocate for LGBTQ rights. By fostering a sense of community and solidarity, Kiki has ensured that her vision for a more inclusive society persists, even in her absence.

The theory of social movement sustainability highlights the importance of institutionalizing activism. According to Tilly and Tarrow (2015), successful social movements often transition from charismatic leadership to collective action frameworks that empower individuals within the community. Kiki's work embodies this theory, as she has transitioned her activism into sustainable practices that allow others to carry on the struggle. The establishment of networks and coalitions has been critical in maintaining momentum and ensuring that the fight for LGBTQ rights continues.

Moreover, Kiki's story has been documented extensively, serving as a powerful narrative that inspires others. The role of storytelling in activism cannot be overstated; it humanizes issues and creates emotional connections that galvanize support. Bandy Kiki's journey, filled with trials and triumphs, resonates with many individuals facing similar struggles. Her biography, filled with vivid anecdotes and heartfelt reflections, serves as both a source of inspiration and a guide for those who seek to challenge the status quo.

An example of this can be seen in the emergence of young activists in Cameroon who cite Kiki as a pivotal influence in their decision to advocate for LGBTQ rights. These individuals have harnessed social media to amplify their voices, drawing on the strategies Kiki employed during her active years. By utilizing platforms like Twitter and Instagram, they share their stories and mobilize support, creating a ripple effect that extends beyond their immediate communities.

However, the challenges of sustaining activism in a hostile environment remain significant. The oppressive legal framework and societal stigma surrounding LGBTQ identities in Cameroon can stifle efforts to advocate for change. Yet, Kiki's legacy offers a framework for resilience. Activists inspired by her work have developed innovative strategies to navigate these challenges, such as using encrypted messaging apps to communicate safely and organizing covert support groups that provide resources and solidarity without drawing attention.

The concept of "transformative leadership" is also relevant here. Bandy Kiki's approach to activism emphasized empowerment and collaboration, allowing others to step into leadership roles. As noted by Allen (2017), transformative leaders create pathways for others to lead, ensuring that the movement does not rely solely on one individual. This decentralization of leadership has proven effective in sustaining activism, as it allows for a diversity of voices and perspectives to emerge.

In conclusion, Bandy Kiki's impact as an activist extends far beyond her time in the spotlight. Through the establishment of supportive networks, the power of storytelling, and the cultivation of transformative leadership, she has inspired a new generation of advocates committed to the fight for LGBTQ rights in Cameroon. Her legacy serves as a testament to the notion that true change is not merely a momentary phenomenon but a continual process, fueled by the passion and dedication of those who dare to dream of a more just and equitable world.

$$\text{Impact} = \text{Grassroots Organizations} + \text{Storytelling} + \text{Transformative Leadership} \tag{87}$$

The enduring influence on LGBTQ activism in Cameroon

The legacy of Bandy Kiki, the masked activist, resonates deeply within the fabric of LGBTQ activism in Cameroon. Her journey has not only illuminated the struggles faced by the community but has also catalyzed significant shifts in societal perceptions and advocacy efforts. The enduring influence of her activism can be analyzed through various lenses, including the theoretical frameworks of social movements, the challenges posed by local and international contexts, and the tangible impact of her work on subsequent generations of activists.

Theoretical Frameworks of Social Movements

To understand the impact of Bandy Kiki's activism, it is essential to engage with social movement theory. One relevant concept is the *resource mobilization theory*, which posits that the success of social movements hinges on the ability to gather resources—be it financial, human, or informational. Bandy Kiki's strategic use of social media platforms exemplifies this theory, as she leveraged online tools to mobilize support, raise awareness, and disseminate information about LGBTQ rights in a context where traditional avenues for activism are often stifled.

Moreover, the *framing theory* plays a crucial role in understanding her influence. By framing LGBTQ issues in ways that resonate with broader human rights narratives, Bandy Kiki was able to attract allies beyond the immediate community. For instance, her advocacy efforts often highlighted the intersections of LGBTQ rights with other social justice issues, such as gender equality and anti-discrimination, thereby creating a more inclusive movement that appealed to a wider audience.

Challenges in the Local Context

Despite the progress made, LGBTQ activism in Cameroon continues to face formidable challenges. The legal framework remains oppressive, with laws criminalizing same-sex relationships and fostering a culture of fear and discrimination. Bandy Kiki's work has shone a light on these issues, but the societal stigma surrounding LGBTQ identities persists. Activists often encounter hostility not only from the government but also from the communities they seek to educate and support.

One illustrative example is the case of the *LGBTQ Rights Cameroon* organization, which has faced numerous legal and social hurdles in its efforts to advocate for change. Following Bandy Kiki's rise to prominence, the organization has reported increased visibility and support but also heightened scrutiny and backlash. This duality reflects the complex landscape of activism in Cameroon, where progress can be met with resistance.

Tangible Impact on Future Activists

Bandy Kiki's influence extends beyond her immediate actions; it has inspired a new generation of activists who continue to build upon her work. Programs and initiatives aimed at youth empowerment and education about LGBTQ rights have emerged, often citing her as a pivotal figure in their motivation to engage in activism. For example, the *Queer Youth Initiative* has developed workshops that educate young people about their rights and the importance of advocacy, drawing directly from the frameworks established by Bandy Kiki.

Furthermore, the concept of *intersectionality* has gained traction within the Cameroonian LGBTQ movement, largely due to Bandy Kiki's emphasis on inclusivity. Activists today are more aware of the need to address the diverse identities and experiences within the LGBTQ community, acknowledging how factors such as race, gender, and socio-economic status intersect with sexual orientation.

International Solidarity and Support

Bandy Kiki's activism has also fostered international solidarity, connecting Cameroonian activists with global movements. This network has proven invaluable, as it provides resources, visibility, and a platform for Cameroonian voices on the international stage. For instance, collaborations with organizations such as *ILGA World* and *Human Rights Watch* have amplified the narratives of LGBTQ individuals in Cameroon, advocating for their rights within international human rights frameworks.

The impact of this solidarity is evident in the increased attention to Cameroonian LGBTQ issues in global forums. Bandy Kiki's participation in international conferences has opened doors for dialogue and advocacy, allowing local activists to share their experiences and challenges with a broader audience.

Conclusion

In conclusion, the enduring influence of Bandy Kiki on LGBTQ activism in Cameroon is multifaceted, encompassing theoretical frameworks, local challenges, and the empowerment of future activists. Her legacy is characterized by a commitment to resilience and authenticity, inspiring a movement that continues to evolve in the face of adversity. As activists build upon her foundation, they carry forward the torch of advocacy, aiming for a future where LGBTQ rights are recognized and upheld as fundamental human rights. The journey is far from over, but the spirit of Bandy Kiki lives on, igniting hope and courage in the hearts of those who dare to dream of a more inclusive and accepting society.

The legacy of courage and resilience

The legacy of Bandy Kiki is one that resonates deeply within the LGBTQ community in Cameroon and beyond. Her journey embodies the essence of courage and resilience, demonstrating how one individual's determination can ignite a movement and inspire countless others to stand up for their rights. This section delves into the foundational elements of her legacy, exploring the theoretical frameworks that underpin her activism, the societal challenges she faced, and the lasting impact of her work.

At its core, Bandy Kiki's legacy is rooted in the theory of resilience, which posits that individuals can overcome adversity through strength, adaptability, and support networks. According to Masten (2001), resilience is not merely about bouncing back from hardship; it involves significant personal growth and the ability to thrive despite challenges. Bandy Kiki exemplified this concept by transforming her struggles into a powerful platform for advocacy. Her ability to navigate the oppressive environment of Cameroon while maintaining her commitment to LGBTQ rights serves as a testament to her resilience.

$$R = f(A, S, N) \tag{88}$$

Where:

- R represents resilience,

- A denotes the individual's agency,

- S stands for social support, and

- N indicates the network of allies and resources available.

Bandy Kiki's agency was evident in her decision to adopt the pseudonym that allowed her to speak out without fear of persecution. This choice not only protected her identity but also empowered her to amplify the voices of those who were silenced. Her social support network, comprising friends, allies, and fellow activists, provided the emotional and logistical backing necessary to sustain her efforts. Furthermore, the connections she forged with international LGBTQ organizations expanded her resources and reach, allowing her to advocate for change on a global scale.

The societal challenges Bandy Kiki faced were immense. In Cameroon, LGBTQ individuals are often subjected to violence, discrimination, and legal repercussions. The oppressive legal system, characterized by laws that criminalize homosexuality, creates an environment of fear and hostility. Bandy Kiki's courage in confronting these realities head-on illustrates the significant risks involved in activism. Despite the potential for backlash, she organized protests, engaged in public speaking, and utilized social media to raise awareness about the plight of LGBTQ individuals in her country.

One poignant example of her resilience is the story of a young activist she mentored. This individual faced severe backlash from their family and community upon coming out. Inspired by Bandy Kiki's courage, they found the strength to advocate for LGBTQ rights in their own community, creating a ripple effect that inspired others to do the same. This mentorship not only empowered the young activist but also solidified Bandy Kiki's role as a leader and beacon of hope within the community.

Bandy Kiki's legacy is also marked by her ability to foster a sense of belonging among marginalized individuals. By creating safe spaces for dialogue and support, she helped many people come to terms with their identities and encouraged them to embrace their truths. This aspect of her activism aligns with the concept of intersectionality, which emphasizes the interconnected nature of social categorizations and the unique challenges faced by individuals at their intersections. Bandy Kiki understood that the fight for LGBTQ rights could not be isolated from broader issues of race, gender, and class, and she worked tirelessly to advocate for an inclusive movement that addressed these complexities.

$$I = \sum_{i=1}^{n}(C_i \cdot W_i) \qquad (89)$$

Where:

- I represents the impact of intersectional advocacy,

- C_i denotes the various categories of identity (e.g., race, gender),

- W_i indicates the weight or significance of each category in the context of activism, and

- n is the total number of categories considered.

Through her efforts, Bandy Kiki has left an indelible mark on the landscape of LGBTQ activism in Cameroon. Her legacy is not merely one of resistance but also of empowerment and transformation. She has inspired a new generation of activists to embrace their identities and fight for their rights, proving that courage can manifest in many forms.

In conclusion, the legacy of Bandy Kiki is characterized by her unwavering courage and resilience in the face of adversity. Her ability to navigate a hostile environment while advocating for change serves as a powerful reminder of the strength found within the LGBTQ community. As we reflect on her impact, it is clear that her story will continue to inspire future generations to rise up, embrace their identities, and advocate for a more inclusive and accepting society. The legacy of courage and resilience that Bandy Kiki has established will undoubtedly endure, lighting the way for those who follow in her footsteps.

The Evolution of LGBTQ Rights in Cameroon

Progress and setbacks in the fight for equality

The journey toward LGBTQ equality in Cameroon has been marked by significant progress as well as daunting setbacks. This duality reflects the complex interplay of cultural, social, and political factors that shape the experiences of LGBTQ individuals in the country.

Historical Context

Historically, homosexuality has been criminalized in Cameroon, with laws rooted in colonial-era statutes. Article 347 bis of the Cameroonian Penal Code, which punishes same-sex relations with up to five years in prison, exemplifies the legal framework that has perpetuated discrimination. However, the late 20th century and early 21st century saw a gradual emergence of LGBTQ activism, driven by both local and international pressures. Activists began to challenge these oppressive laws, advocating for decriminalization and greater acceptance of diverse sexual orientations and gender identities.

Progress Achieved

Despite these challenges, there have been notable advancements in the fight for LGBTQ rights in Cameroon:

- **Increased Visibility:** The rise of social media platforms has enabled activists to share their stories and experiences, fostering a sense of community and solidarity. Campaigns such as *#LoveIsLove* have garnered international attention, highlighting the struggles faced by LGBTQ individuals in Cameroon.

- **International Support:** Global organizations, such as Amnesty International and Human Rights Watch, have played a crucial role in amplifying the voices of Cameroonian activists. Their reports and advocacy efforts have pressured the Cameroonian government to reconsider its stance on LGBTQ rights.

- **Grassroots Movements:** Local organizations, such as *Alternatives-Cameroun*, have emerged to provide support, education, and resources for LGBTQ individuals. These grassroots movements have been instrumental in fostering resilience and empowerment within the community.

Setbacks Encountered

However, the fight for equality has not been without its setbacks:

- **Violence and Discrimination:** LGBTQ individuals in Cameroon continue to face violence, harassment, and discrimination. Reports of police brutality, mob violence, and societal ostracism remain prevalent, creating an environment of fear and insecurity.

- **Legal Obstacles:** Despite international pressure, the Cameroonian government has shown little willingness to amend or repeal discriminatory laws. Instead, authorities have intensified crackdowns on LGBTQ gatherings and organizations, leading to arrests and detentions of activists.

- **Cultural Resistance:** Deeply ingrained cultural norms and beliefs often perpetuate homophobia and transphobia. Many individuals face rejection from their families and communities upon coming out, leading to isolation and mental health challenges.

Theoretical Framework

To understand the progress and setbacks in the fight for LGBTQ equality in Cameroon, it is essential to consider several theoretical frameworks:

- **Social Movement Theory:** This theory posits that social movements arise in response to perceived injustices. In Cameroon, the LGBTQ movement has emerged as a reaction to systemic oppression, seeking to create change through collective action and solidarity.

- **Intersectionality:** Coined by Kimberlé Crenshaw, intersectionality emphasizes the interconnected nature of social categorizations such as race, class, and gender. The experiences of LGBTQ individuals in Cameroon cannot be understood in isolation from the broader socio-political context, which includes issues of poverty, gender inequality, and ethnic diversity.
- **Queer Theory:** This framework challenges normative definitions of gender and sexuality, advocating for the acceptance of diverse identities. Queer theory provides a lens through which to analyze the resistance faced by LGBTQ individuals in Cameroon, as they navigate a society that often seeks to marginalize them.

Conclusion

In conclusion, the fight for LGBTQ equality in Cameroon is characterized by a complex interplay of progress and setbacks. While significant strides have been made in terms of visibility and support, the persistent challenges of violence, legal discrimination, and cultural resistance continue to hinder the movement. Understanding this dynamic requires a multifaceted approach that considers historical context, theoretical frameworks, and the lived experiences of LGBTQ individuals. As activists like Bandy Kiki continue to advocate for change, the hope for a more inclusive and accepting society remains a driving force in the ongoing struggle for equality.

The role of activism in legal and social change

Activism plays a crucial role in shaping legal frameworks and social attitudes towards marginalized communities, particularly within the LGBTQ spectrum. The interplay between activism, legal reform, and social change is complex and multifaceted, often driven by grassroots movements and the relentless pursuit of equality. This section will explore the mechanisms through which activism influences legal systems and societal norms, highlighting key theories, challenges, and case studies that exemplify this dynamic.

Theoretical Frameworks

The relationship between activism and legal change can be understood through various theoretical lenses. One prominent theory is the *Social Movement Theory*, which posits that organized efforts by a group of people to promote or resist social change can lead to significant shifts in public policy and law. According to Charles

Tilly, social movements operate through a series of mechanisms, including *framing*, *mobilization*, and *political opportunity structures*.

$$\text{Social Change} = f(\text{Activism, Legal Frameworks, Cultural Attitudes}) \quad (90)$$

Where f represents the function that describes how activism interacts with existing legal frameworks and cultural attitudes to produce social change.

Legal Advocacy and Reform

Legal advocacy is a primary avenue through which activism can effect change. Activists often engage in strategic litigation, utilizing the courts to challenge discriminatory laws and practices. For instance, the landmark case of *Obergefell v. Hodges* (2015) in the United States exemplifies how legal activism can reshape societal norms. The Supreme Court's ruling that same-sex marriage is a constitutional right was the result of decades of advocacy, highlighting the power of legal frameworks in advancing social justice.

In Cameroon, however, the path to legal reform is fraught with challenges. The country's penal code criminalizes homosexuality, leading to widespread discrimination and violence against LGBTQ individuals. Activists like Bandy Kiki have worked tirelessly to challenge these oppressive laws, using both local and international platforms to bring attention to human rights abuses. Their efforts demonstrate the necessity of sustained activism in the face of legal barriers.

Social Movements and Cultural Change

While legal reforms are essential, they often do not translate into immediate social acceptance. Activism also plays a vital role in shifting cultural perceptions and combating stigma. The *Theory of Collective Identity* posits that shared experiences and struggles among marginalized groups foster a sense of belonging and solidarity, which can galvanize broader support for social change.

For example, the visibility of LGBTQ individuals in media and public discourse has significantly influenced public attitudes towards the community. Campaigns like *It Gets Better* have utilized personal storytelling to challenge stereotypes and promote acceptance, illustrating how activism can reshape cultural narratives.

Challenges and Barriers

Despite the potential for activism to drive legal and social change, numerous challenges persist. In many regions, including Cameroon, activists face severe repression, including violence, imprisonment, and social ostracism. The oppressive legal environment creates a chilling effect, discouraging individuals from openly advocating for their rights.

Moreover, the intersectionality of identities complicates the landscape of activism. LGBTQ individuals who also belong to other marginalized groups, such as racial or ethnic minorities, may experience compounded discrimination, making their fight for rights even more complex. This intersectionality underscores the importance of inclusive activism that addresses the diverse needs of all community members.

Case Studies and Examples

Several case studies illustrate the impact of activism on legal and social change within the LGBTQ context. In South Africa, the post-apartheid constitution enshrined LGBTQ rights, largely due to the efforts of activists who fought for inclusion during the transition to democracy. The recognition of same-sex marriage in 2006 further solidified South Africa's position as a leader in LGBTQ rights on the continent.

Conversely, in Uganda, the Anti-Homosexuality Act of 2014 exemplifies the backlash against LGBTQ activism. Despite international condemnation and advocacy efforts, the law reflects the challenges activists face in hostile environments. However, grassroots movements continue to challenge these oppressive measures, showcasing the resilience of activists in the face of adversity.

Conclusion

In conclusion, the role of activism in driving legal and social change is indispensable. Through strategic litigation, cultural advocacy, and grassroots mobilization, activists can challenge discriminatory laws and shift societal attitudes. While significant barriers remain, the ongoing efforts of individuals and organizations committed to LGBTQ rights demonstrate the power of activism to create a more just and equitable society. The journey toward equality is fraught with challenges, but the unwavering spirit of activists like Bandy Kiki continues to inspire hope and action in the fight for LGBTQ rights in Cameroon and beyond.

Building a more inclusive and accepting society

The journey towards a more inclusive and accepting society is not merely a linear path marked by victories; it is a complex interplay of cultural, social, and political forces that shape the environment in which marginalized communities exist. At the heart of this endeavor lies the necessity for systemic change, which involves dismantling entrenched prejudices and biases that have historically marginalized LGBTQ individuals.

One of the foundational theories that underscore the importance of inclusivity is **Intersectionality**, a term coined by Kimberlé Crenshaw. Intersectionality posits that individuals experience oppression in varying configurations and degrees of intensity based on their intersecting social identities, including race, gender, sexuality, and class. This framework allows us to understand that the fight for LGBTQ rights cannot be isolated from other social justice movements; rather, it must be viewed as part of a broader struggle against all forms of discrimination.

To build a more inclusive society, it is essential to address the **structural inequalities** that perpetuate discrimination. This includes advocating for policies that protect LGBTQ individuals in various sectors, such as employment, housing, and healthcare. For instance, the implementation of comprehensive anti-discrimination laws can provide legal protections that prevent discrimination based on sexual orientation and gender identity.

However, legislation alone is insufficient. Societal attitudes must also shift to foster acceptance and understanding. Education plays a pivotal role in this transformation. Incorporating LGBTQ history and issues into school curricula can help dismantle stereotypes and foster empathy among young people. Programs that promote diversity and inclusion, such as workshops and training sessions, can also be instrumental in educating individuals about the importance of acceptance.

Moreover, the role of media cannot be underestimated in shaping public perception. The representation of LGBTQ individuals in film, television, and literature can challenge stereotypes and promote positive narratives. For example, the success of shows like *Pose* and *Schitt's Creek* has not only provided visibility to LGBTQ characters but has also humanized their experiences, making them relatable to wider audiences.

Despite these efforts, significant challenges remain. Societal stigma still exists, fueled by misinformation and cultural beliefs that view LGBTQ identities as deviant. This stigma can manifest in various forms, including hate speech, violence, and social ostracism. According to the **Global Acceptance Index**, many countries still exhibit high levels of homophobia and transphobia, which directly impacts the mental health and well-being of LGBTQ individuals.

To combat these issues, community engagement is crucial. Grassroots movements that empower local LGBTQ organizations can create safe spaces for individuals to share their experiences and advocate for their rights. For example, initiatives like Pride marches and LGBTQ film festivals not only celebrate diversity but also serve as platforms for activism and awareness-raising.

Furthermore, building coalitions with allies from various sectors can amplify the message of inclusion. Collaborations between LGBTQ organizations and other social justice groups can create a unified front against discrimination. This solidarity is essential in advocating for comprehensive reforms that address the multifaceted nature of oppression.

In conclusion, building a more inclusive and accepting society requires a multifaceted approach that encompasses legal reforms, educational initiatives, media representation, and community engagement. By embracing intersectionality and recognizing the interconnectedness of various forms of discrimination, we can create a society that not only acknowledges but also celebrates diversity. The path may be fraught with challenges, but with resilience and collective action, a more inclusive future is attainable.

$$\text{Inclusivity} = \frac{\text{Diversity} + \text{Equity}}{\text{Resistance to Change}} \tag{91}$$

This equation symbolizes that true inclusivity is achieved when diversity and equity are prioritized, while the resistance to change is actively challenged. The journey is ongoing, and it requires the commitment of individuals, communities, and institutions to foster an environment where everyone, regardless of their identity, can thrive.

Celebrating milestones and breakthroughs

In the ongoing journey towards LGBTQ rights in Cameroon, recognizing and celebrating milestones and breakthroughs serves as a critical mechanism for motivation, solidarity, and progress. Each achievement, no matter how small, contributes to a larger narrative of resilience and hope within the community. This section explores significant milestones, their implications, and the transformative power they hold for activists and allies alike.

Legal Reforms and Policy Changes

One of the most significant milestones in the fight for LGBTQ rights in Cameroon has been the gradual shift in legal recognition and protections. While Cameroon remains one of the countries with the most oppressive laws against LGBTQ individuals, there have been instances where advocacy efforts have led to discussions around reform. For example, a notable breakthrough occurred when a local human rights organization successfully lobbied for the inclusion of sexual orientation as a protected category in anti-discrimination policies. This victory, albeit limited, marked a pivotal moment for activists, providing a framework for further advocacy efforts.

The theoretical underpinnings of such legal reforms can be traced back to the concept of *legal pluralism*, which recognizes the coexistence of multiple legal systems within a single state. According to Griffiths (1986), legal pluralism allows for the possibility of reform by acknowledging that not all laws are absolute. Activists have utilized this framework to argue for the recognition of LGBTQ rights as a fundamental aspect of human rights, thereby challenging existing legal structures.

Public Awareness Campaigns

Another crucial milestone has been the successful execution of public awareness campaigns that aim to educate the broader population about LGBTQ issues. These campaigns have utilized various media, including social media, community workshops, and art exhibitions, to challenge stereotypes and promote understanding. For instance, the "#LoveIsLove" campaign launched in 2020 saw a surge in public support, leading to increased visibility for LGBTQ individuals and their struggles.

The effectiveness of these campaigns can be analyzed through the lens of *social movement theory*, particularly the concept of *framing*. Snow and Benford (1988) argue that social movements must frame their issues in a way that resonates with the public's values and beliefs. The "#LoveIsLove" campaign successfully framed LGBTQ rights as a matter of love and acceptance, which resonated with many Cameroonians, thus fostering a more inclusive dialogue.

International Solidarity and Support

The role of international solidarity has also been a significant breakthrough in the LGBTQ rights movement in Cameroon. Global organizations, such as Amnesty International and Human Rights Watch, have amplified local voices by documenting human rights abuses and advocating for international pressure on the Cameroonian government. This support has led to increased visibility of the LGBTQ plight in international forums, contributing to a broader understanding of the issues at hand.

The concept of *transnational advocacy networks* (Keck and Sikkink, 1998) is crucial in understanding this dynamic. These networks facilitate the exchange of information and strategies across borders, allowing local activists to gain insights and support from their global counterparts. The impact of such networks can be seen in the increased attention to LGBTQ issues during international human rights reviews, leading to recommendations for the Cameroonian government to improve its human rights record.

Community Building and Support Networks

Milestones in community building have also emerged as vital breakthroughs in the LGBTQ movement. The establishment of safe spaces and support networks has provided individuals with the necessary resources to navigate the challenges of their identities. Organizations such as "Queer Cameroon" have created platforms for individuals to share their stories, seek legal assistance, and access mental health resources.

The theoretical framework of *community resilience* (Norris et al., 2008) is applicable here, as it emphasizes the capacity of communities to adapt and thrive despite adversity. By fostering a sense of belonging and support, these networks empower individuals to embrace their identities and advocate for their rights, ultimately contributing to the overall strength of the movement.

Cultural Representation and Visibility

Finally, the rise of cultural representation in media and the arts has marked a transformative milestone in the fight for LGBTQ rights. Artists, filmmakers, and writers have begun to portray LGBTQ experiences authentically, challenging prevailing narratives and stereotypes. For instance, the release of the documentary "Voices of the Silenced" in 2021 highlighted the stories of LGBTQ individuals in Cameroon, garnering international acclaim and sparking conversations about acceptance and diversity.

The significance of cultural representation can be understood through the lens of *cultural hegemony* (Gramsci, 1971), which posits that dominant cultures often marginalize alternative narratives. By elevating LGBTQ voices in mainstream media, activists are challenging this hegemony and creating space for diverse identities to be recognized and celebrated.

Conclusion

In conclusion, celebrating milestones and breakthroughs within the LGBTQ rights movement in Cameroon serves not only to acknowledge progress but also to inspire continued activism. Each achievement, whether legal reform, public awareness campaign, international solidarity, community building, or cultural representation, contributes to a collective narrative of resilience and hope. As the fight for equality continues, these milestones remind us of the power of perseverance and the importance of celebrating every step taken towards a more inclusive society.

Bibliography

[1] Gramsci, A. (1971). *Selections from the Prison Notebooks.* New York: International Publishers.

[2] Griffiths, J. (1986). *What is Legal Pluralism?* Journal of Legal Pluralism and Unofficial Law, 24(1), 1-55.

[3] Keck, M. E., & Sikkink, K. (1998). *Activists Beyond Borders: Advocacy Networks in International Politics.* Ithaca: Cornell University Press.

[4] Norris, F. H., Stevens, S. P., Pfefferbaum, B., Wyche, K. F., & Pfefferbaum, R. L. (2008). *Community Resilience as a Metaphor, Theory, Set of Capacities, and Strategy for Disaster Readiness.* American Journal of Community Psychology, 41(1-2), 127-150.

[5] Snow, D. A., & Benford, R. D. (1988). *Ideology, Frame Resonance, and Participant Mobilization.* In B. Klandermans, H. Kriesi, & S. T. Staggenborg (Eds.), *From Structure to Action: Comparing Social Movement Research across Cultures.*

Celebrating Diversity and Queerness

Embracing diverse identities within the LGBTQ community

In the vibrant tapestry of the LGBTQ community, diversity is not merely a characteristic; it is the very essence that enriches the movement for equality and justice. Embracing diverse identities within the LGBTQ spectrum is crucial for fostering a more inclusive society, as it recognizes the unique experiences and challenges faced by individuals across different sexual orientations, gender identities, and cultural backgrounds.

The Spectrum of Identities

The LGBTQ community encompasses a wide range of identities, including but not limited to lesbian, gay, bisexual, transgender, queer, intersex, and asexual individuals. Each identity brings its own narrative, shaped by cultural, social, and personal factors. For instance, the experiences of a Black transgender woman can differ significantly from those of a white gay man. This intersectionality is essential to understand, as highlighted by Kimberlé Crenshaw's theory of intersectionality, which emphasizes that individuals do not experience discrimination in isolation but rather through overlapping social identities.

$$\text{Intersectionality} = \sum_{i=1}^{n} \text{Identity}_i \qquad (92)$$

This equation illustrates that the impact of discrimination is compounded by the various identities one holds, necessitating a nuanced approach to advocacy and support within the LGBTQ community.

Challenges Faced by Diverse Identities

Despite the shared struggle for rights and recognition, members of the LGBTQ community often encounter unique challenges based on their identities. For example, LGBTQ individuals of color frequently face compounded discrimination due to both their sexual orientation and race, a phenomenon referred to as "double jeopardy." This can manifest in various ways, such as higher rates of violence, discrimination in employment, and social stigmatization.

Moreover, transgender individuals, particularly those of color, face alarming rates of violence and systemic barriers to healthcare. According to the Human Rights Campaign, in 2020, at least 44 transgender or gender non-conforming individuals were killed in the United States, the highest number recorded since the organization began tracking this data. This stark reality underscores the urgent need for intersectional advocacy that addresses the specific needs of marginalized identities within the LGBTQ community.

Cultural Representation and Visibility

Cultural representation plays a pivotal role in embracing diverse identities. Media representation of LGBTQ individuals has evolved, yet significant gaps remain. For example, while mainstream media has begun to include more LGBTQ characters, the representation of transgender and non-binary individuals is often limited or stereotypical. This lack of authentic representation can perpetuate harmful narratives and hinder societal acceptance.

The importance of visibility cannot be overstated. When diverse identities are represented in film, television, literature, and art, it fosters understanding and empathy among broader audiences. Initiatives like the "#TransIsBeautiful" campaign challenge stereotypes and celebrate the beauty of transgender identities, encouraging individuals to embrace their authentic selves.

Building Alliances and Solidarity

Embracing diverse identities within the LGBTQ community also involves building alliances across different social movements. The fight for LGBTQ rights intersects with racial justice, feminism, disability rights, and other social justice movements. By recognizing these intersections, activists can work collaboratively to address the systemic issues that affect multiple marginalized groups.

For instance, organizations like the Black LGBTQ+ Migrant Project focus on the unique challenges faced by LGBTQ migrants of color, advocating for their rights and providing resources tailored to their experiences. This approach not only amplifies marginalized voices but also fosters a sense of solidarity among diverse communities.

Education and Awareness

Education is a powerful tool in embracing diversity within the LGBTQ community. Initiatives aimed at increasing awareness about different identities and experiences can help dismantle prejudices and foster inclusivity. Schools and workplaces can implement training programs that focus on LGBTQ diversity, promoting understanding and acceptance among peers.

Furthermore, storytelling plays a critical role in this educational process. By sharing personal narratives, individuals can humanize their experiences, allowing others to connect with and understand the complexities of diverse identities. Platforms like social media provide an opportunity for individuals to share their stories, creating a sense of community and belonging.

Conclusion

In conclusion, embracing diverse identities within the LGBTQ community is essential for creating a more inclusive and equitable society. By recognizing the unique experiences and challenges faced by individuals across different identities, we can foster solidarity, understanding, and support. The journey toward equality is complex and multifaceted, but it is through the celebration of diversity that the LGBTQ movement can truly thrive. As we move forward, let us continue to amplify marginalized voices and advocate for a world where every individual, regardless of their identity, can live authentically and without fear.

The intersectionality of LGBTQ activism

Intersectionality, a term coined by legal scholar Kimberlé Crenshaw, refers to the ways in which various social identities—such as race, gender, sexuality, and class—interact to create unique modes of discrimination and privilege. Within the realm of LGBTQ activism, understanding intersectionality is crucial for addressing the diverse experiences of individuals who exist at the confluence of multiple marginalized identities. This section explores the significance of intersectionality in LGBTQ activism, the challenges it presents, and the ways in which it can enhance the movement's effectiveness.

Understanding Intersectionality

At its core, intersectionality posits that individuals do not experience oppression in isolation but rather through a complex interplay of their identities. For example, a Black transgender woman may face discrimination not only because she is transgender but also due to her race and gender. This multi-faceted oppression can manifest in various forms, including systemic inequality, social stigma, and economic disadvantage.

The mathematical representation of intersectionality can be expressed through the following equation:

$$O = f(I_1, I_2, I_3, \ldots, I_n) \tag{93}$$

where O represents the overall oppression an individual experiences, and $I_1, I_2, I_3, \ldots, I_n$ are the different intersecting identities (e.g., race, gender, sexuality). The function f illustrates how these identities interact, leading to a unique experience of oppression that cannot be understood by examining each identity in isolation.

Challenges of Intersectionality in LGBTQ Activism

Despite its importance, the concept of intersectionality has not always been fully embraced within LGBTQ activism. Historically, mainstream LGBTQ movements have predominantly centered on the experiences of white, cisgender, gay men, often sidelining the voices of those who identify as women, people of color, and individuals with disabilities. This lack of inclusivity can lead to a range of challenges:

- **Erasure of Voices:** Marginalized groups within the LGBTQ community often find their needs and experiences overlooked. For instance, issues specific to LGBTQ people of color, such as racial profiling and police violence, may not receive the same attention as those affecting white LGBTQ individuals.

- **Resource Allocation:** Funding and resources are frequently directed toward initiatives that cater to the dominant narratives within the LGBTQ movement, leaving intersectional activists struggling for support and visibility.

- **Fragmentation of the Movement:** The failure to address intersectionality can lead to divisions within the LGBTQ community, as individuals may feel alienated or unrepresented by mainstream activism. This fragmentation can hinder collective efforts to achieve equality and justice.

Examples of Intersectional Activism

Fortunately, many activists and organizations are recognizing the importance of intersectionality and are working to create a more inclusive movement. Here are a few notable examples:

- **The Black Lives Matter Movement:** This movement has made significant strides in addressing the intersectionality of race and LGBTQ identity. Founders Alicia Garza, Patrisse Cullors, and Opal Tometi have emphasized the importance of recognizing the unique struggles faced by Black LGBTQ individuals, advocating for both racial justice and LGBTQ rights.

- **Transgender People of Color Coalition (TPOCC):** TPOCC focuses specifically on the issues faced by transgender people of color, providing a platform for their voices and advocating for policies that address the systemic violence and discrimination they encounter.

- **Intersectional Feminism:** Many LGBTQ activists are integrating intersectional feminism into their work, recognizing that gender equality cannot be achieved without addressing the specific challenges faced by women within the LGBTQ community, particularly women of color and those with disabilities.

The Path Forward

To create a truly inclusive LGBTQ movement, it is essential to adopt an intersectional approach that prioritizes the voices and experiences of all marginalized identities. This can be achieved through:

- **Inclusive Leadership:** Ensuring that leadership positions within LGBTQ organizations reflect the diversity of the community, allowing for a broader range of experiences and perspectives to inform activism.
- **Collaborative Efforts:** Building coalitions with other social justice movements, such as those focused on racial justice, economic equality, and disability rights, can strengthen the fight for LGBTQ rights and promote a more holistic understanding of oppression.
- **Education and Awareness:** Promoting education around intersectionality within the LGBTQ community can foster greater understanding and empathy, encouraging allies to support marginalized voices and experiences.

In conclusion, the intersectionality of LGBTQ activism is not merely an academic concept but a vital framework for understanding and addressing the complexities of oppression. By embracing intersectionality, the LGBTQ movement can become more inclusive, effective, and powerful in its pursuit of equality and justice for all.

Empowering queer voices and experiences

The empowerment of queer voices and experiences is a critical aspect of LGBTQ activism, particularly in contexts where societal norms and legal frameworks often marginalize these identities. This empowerment not only fosters a sense of community and belonging but also drives systemic change by amplifying the narratives that challenge dominant cultural paradigms.

The Importance of Representation

Representation in media, politics, and social spheres plays a vital role in shaping public perceptions of queer identities. When queer individuals see themselves reflected in positive and diverse roles, it validates their experiences and encourages self-acceptance. For instance, the rise of LGBTQ characters in mainstream television series, such as *Pose* and *Sex Education*, showcases the richness of queer stories and highlights the struggles and triumphs of the community. These narratives not only entertain but also educate audiences, bridging the gap between ignorance and understanding.

Intersectionality in Queer Activism

To empower queer voices effectively, it is essential to adopt an intersectional approach. Intersectionality, a term coined by Kimberlé Crenshaw, refers to the interconnected nature of social categorizations such as race, class, and gender, which can create overlapping systems of discrimination or disadvantage. In the context of LGBTQ activism, recognizing the diverse experiences within the community is crucial. For example, the experiences of a queer Black woman may differ significantly from those of a white gay man. By acknowledging these differences, activists can create more inclusive spaces that honor the multifaceted identities within the queer community.

Challenges to Empowerment

Despite the progress made, many challenges persist in empowering queer voices. Discrimination, both systemic and interpersonal, continues to silence marginalized identities. In many regions, including parts of Africa, anti-LGBTQ laws create an environment of fear that stifles open expression. Activists like Bandy Kiki have faced threats and violence for their advocacy, illustrating the high stakes involved in amplifying queer voices. Furthermore, internalized homophobia can lead individuals to suppress their identities, further complicating the quest for empowerment.

Strategies for Empowerment

To combat these challenges, various strategies can be employed:

- **Community Building:** Establishing safe spaces where queer individuals can share their stories fosters a sense of belonging. Support groups and community centers provide platforms for dialogue and connection.

- **Education and Awareness:** Workshops and educational programs that focus on LGBTQ history and rights can help dismantle stereotypes and promote acceptance. For example, initiatives in schools that include LGBTQ topics in their curricula can significantly impact younger generations.

- **Advocacy and Policy Change:** Engaging with policymakers to advocate for inclusive laws and protections is essential. Grassroots movements that mobilize community members can exert pressure on governments to recognize and uphold LGBTQ rights.

- **Utilizing Digital Platforms:** Social media has become a powerful tool for empowerment. Platforms like Twitter and Instagram allow queer individuals to share their experiences, connect with others, and mobilize support for causes. The hashtag activism surrounding events like Pride Month exemplifies how digital spaces can amplify queer voices.

Real-World Examples

Numerous organizations and initiatives exemplify the empowerment of queer voices. The *Human Rights Campaign* works tirelessly to advocate for LGBTQ rights in the United States, providing resources and support for individuals navigating discrimination. Similarly, *OutRight Action International* focuses on global LGBTQ rights, emphasizing the need for intersectionality in their work.

In Cameroon, local activists have created networks that offer support and solidarity amidst adversity. The stories of individuals like Bandy Kiki resonate deeply, showcasing how personal narratives can inspire collective action. Her work has not only brought visibility to the struggles faced by LGBTQ individuals in Cameroon but has also empowered others to share their stories, fostering a culture of resilience and resistance.

Conclusion

Empowering queer voices and experiences is an ongoing journey that requires commitment, solidarity, and action. By prioritizing representation, embracing intersectionality, and confronting the challenges that silence marginalized identities, activists can create a more inclusive and equitable society. The fight for LGBTQ rights is not just about legal recognition; it is about ensuring that every individual has the right to express their identity freely and authentically. The power of storytelling, community, and activism can lead to profound change, inspiring future generations to continue the work of empowerment and advocacy.

$$\text{Empowerment} = \text{Representation} + \text{Intersectionality} + \text{Advocacy} + \text{Community}$$
$$(94)$$

The beauty of self-expression and individuality

In the vibrant tapestry of human experience, self-expression and individuality stand out as fundamental threads that weave together the diverse identities within the LGBTQ community. This section explores the profound significance of embracing one's unique identity, the challenges faced in doing so, and the transformative power of self-expression in fostering a more inclusive society.

At its core, self-expression is the act of conveying one's thoughts, feelings, and identity through various forms, such as art, language, fashion, and lifestyle choices. For LGBTQ individuals, self-expression often serves as a vital means of asserting their identity in a world that may not always be accepting. Judith Butler, a prominent gender theorist, posits that gender is performative, suggesting that individuals enact their gender identity through repeated behaviors and expressions. This perspective underscores the importance of visibility and representation in affirming one's identity and challenging societal norms.

$$\text{Self-Expression} = \text{Identity} + \text{Cultural Context} \tag{95}$$

This equation illustrates that self-expression is not merely a reflection of one's identity but is also influenced by the cultural and social environment in which an individual exists. In many societies, particularly those with conservative views on gender and sexuality, the act of self-expression can be fraught with danger. Individuals may face rejection, discrimination, and even violence for daring to live authentically. The fear of societal backlash can lead to internalized homophobia, where individuals struggle to accept their identity due to societal stigma.

For instance, consider the case of a young queer artist in Cameroon who uses her artwork to express her identity and experiences. Through vibrant colors and bold designs, she captures the struggles and joys of being a member of the LGBTQ community. However, her work is often met with hostility, leading to threats and censorship. This scenario highlights the duality of self-expression as both a source of empowerment and a potential risk.

The Role of Art in Self-Expression

Art has long served as a powerful vehicle for self-expression, particularly within marginalized communities. In the LGBTQ context, art provides a platform for individuals to share their stories, challenge stereotypes, and celebrate their identities. The late artist Keith Haring, for example, used his graffiti-inspired artwork to advocate for LGBTQ rights and raise awareness about the AIDS crisis.

His vibrant, accessible art resonated with many and became emblematic of the fight for visibility and acceptance.

Artistic expression can also foster a sense of belonging and community among LGBTQ individuals. Events such as Pride parades and LGBTQ film festivals celebrate diverse identities and provide safe spaces for self-expression. These gatherings create opportunities for individuals to connect with others who share similar experiences, reinforcing the notion that individuality is not only beautiful but also worthy of celebration.

Challenges to Self-Expression

Despite the beauty of self-expression, many LGBTQ individuals face significant challenges in their journey toward authenticity. Societal expectations often dictate how individuals should behave, dress, and love, leading to feelings of inadequacy and shame for those who do not conform. The pressure to fit into predefined molds can stifle creativity and hinder personal growth.

Moreover, the intersectionality of identity complicates the landscape of self-expression. Individuals who identify as LGBTQ and belong to other marginalized groups—such as people of color, those with disabilities, or those from lower socioeconomic backgrounds—may encounter compounded barriers to self-expression. For instance, a Black transgender woman may navigate not only the challenges of gender identity but also racial discrimination, which can further complicate her ability to express herself freely.

Celebrating Individuality and Diversity

In the face of these challenges, celebrating individuality and diversity within the LGBTQ community becomes essential. Initiatives that promote inclusivity and acceptance can help create environments where individuals feel safe to express themselves authentically. Educational programs that teach the importance of diversity and the value of self-expression can empower younger generations to embrace their identities without fear.

Furthermore, the rise of social media has transformed the landscape of self-expression, allowing LGBTQ individuals to connect with like-minded individuals across the globe. Platforms like Instagram and TikTok have given rise to a new wave of queer artists, activists, and influencers who use their platforms to showcase their identities and advocate for change. This digital revolution has democratized self-expression, enabling individuals to share their stories and experiences with a wider audience, thereby fostering empathy and understanding.

$$\text{Empathy} = \text{Exposure} + \text{Understanding} \tag{96}$$

This equation suggests that exposure to diverse identities and experiences can lead to greater empathy and acceptance. By amplifying the voices of LGBTQ individuals through various forms of media, society can begin to dismantle harmful stereotypes and foster a culture of inclusivity.

In conclusion, the beauty of self-expression and individuality lies in its ability to empower LGBTQ individuals to embrace their true selves and challenge societal norms. By celebrating diversity and fostering environments that promote self-expression, we can work towards a more inclusive society that values authenticity and individuality. The journey may be fraught with challenges, but the transformative power of self-expression remains a beacon of hope for future generations of activists and advocates.

The Fight Goes On

The ongoing battle for LGBTQ rights

The struggle for LGBTQ rights is a multifaceted and ongoing battle that transcends geographical, cultural, and social boundaries. It is a fight not only for legal recognition and protection but also for the basic dignity and humanity of individuals who identify as lesbian, gay, bisexual, transgender, queer, and other diverse sexual orientations and gender identities. This section will delve into the complexities of this ongoing battle, highlighting theoretical frameworks, prevalent issues, and real-world examples that exemplify the challenges faced by the LGBTQ community.

Theoretical Frameworks

At the core of LGBTQ rights activism lies a rich tapestry of theories that aim to explain and address the systemic injustices faced by queer individuals. One prominent framework is **Queer Theory**, which critiques the societal norms surrounding gender and sexuality. This theoretical lens posits that sexuality is not binary but exists on a spectrum, challenging heteronormative assumptions. Judith Butler, a key figure in queer theory, argues that gender is performative, suggesting that societal constructs of gender and sexuality are not innate but rather socially constructed.

$$G = P + S \tag{97}$$

Where G represents gender, P represents performance, and S signifies societal influence. This equation encapsulates the idea that gender identity is shaped by both personal expression and societal expectations.

Another important theoretical framework is **Intersectionality**, introduced by Kimberlé Crenshaw. This concept emphasizes that individuals experience overlapping systems of discrimination based on various identities, including race, gender, sexuality, and class. For LGBTQ individuals, intersectionality is crucial in understanding how different forms of oppression interact and exacerbate the challenges they face.

Prevalent Issues

Despite significant progress in many parts of the world, the LGBTQ community continues to face numerous challenges:

1. **Legal Discrimination:** In many countries, laws still exist that criminalize same-sex relationships or deny basic rights to LGBTQ individuals. For example, in Cameroon, homosexuality is punishable by up to five years in prison under Article 347 bis of the penal code. Such laws perpetuate a culture of fear and discrimination, making it difficult for individuals to live openly and authentically.

2. **Social Stigmatization:** Beyond legal challenges, societal attitudes towards LGBTQ individuals often remain hostile. Discrimination can manifest in various forms, including bullying, harassment, and exclusion from social and familial networks. A study conducted by the International Lesbian, Gay, Bisexual, Trans and Intersex Association (ILGA) found that 70% of LGBTQ individuals in Cameroon reported experiencing discrimination in their daily lives.

3. **Mental Health Challenges:** The constant threat of violence and discrimination can take a significant toll on the mental health of LGBTQ individuals. Studies indicate higher rates of anxiety, depression, and suicidal ideation among LGBTQ youth compared to their heterosexual peers. The Trevor Project's 2021 National Survey on LGBTQ Youth Mental Health found that 42% of LGBTQ youth seriously considered attempting suicide in the past year, highlighting the urgent need for mental health support and resources.

Real-World Examples

Several grassroots movements and organizations have emerged globally to combat these issues and advocate for LGBTQ rights:

- **The Black Lives Matter Movement:** While primarily focused on racial justice, BLM has also emphasized the importance of LGBTQ rights, particularly for Black queer individuals. The movement has brought attention to the intersectional struggles faced by LGBTQ people of color, advocating for a more inclusive approach to activism.

- **The Global Fund for Women:** This organization supports women's rights and gender equality, including LGBTQ rights. By providing funding and resources to grassroots organizations, the Global Fund for Women empowers local activists to address the unique challenges faced by LGBTQ women and non-binary individuals.

- **Pride Movements:** Pride events around the world serve as both celebrations of LGBTQ identity and as platforms for advocacy. For instance, the annual Pride March in New York City not only commemorates the Stonewall Riots but also highlights ongoing issues such as trans rights, racial justice, and healthcare access for LGBTQ individuals.

Conclusion

The ongoing battle for LGBTQ rights is a testament to the resilience and determination of individuals and communities fighting for equality. While significant strides have been made, the journey is far from over. By understanding the theoretical frameworks that underpin this struggle, recognizing the prevalent issues faced by the community, and supporting real-world initiatives, allies and advocates can contribute to a more inclusive and just society. The fight for LGBTQ rights is not only a fight for legal recognition but a broader struggle for human rights and dignity for all individuals, regardless of their sexual orientation or gender identity.

Continuing to Advocate for Change

Advocating for change is a continuous journey, one that requires unwavering commitment and resilience, especially within the LGBTQ community in Cameroon, where systemic barriers and societal prejudices persist. The fight for LGBTQ rights is not merely a series of events or campaigns; it is an ongoing dialogue that involves multiple stakeholders, including activists, policymakers, and the community at large. This section explores the theoretical frameworks, challenges, and examples of advocacy efforts that highlight the necessity of sustained activism.

Theoretical Frameworks of Advocacy

To understand the dynamics of ongoing advocacy, it is essential to consider several theoretical frameworks that inform activism. One such framework is the **Social**

Movement Theory, which posits that social movements arise in response to perceived injustices and seek to enact change through collective action. This theory emphasizes the role of grassroots mobilization and the importance of building coalitions to amplify voices that have been historically marginalized.

Another relevant framework is the **Intersectionality Theory**, which highlights how various forms of discrimination—based on race, gender, sexuality, and socioeconomic status—intersect and compound the challenges faced by individuals within the LGBTQ community. This theory serves as a guiding principle for advocates, reminding them that efforts to achieve equality must consider the diverse experiences of all community members.

Challenges in Advocacy

Despite the theoretical frameworks that guide LGBTQ advocacy, numerous challenges persist. The legal landscape in Cameroon remains hostile to LGBTQ rights, with laws that criminalize same-sex relationships and punish individuals for their sexual orientation. According to the *International Lesbian, Gay, Bisexual, Trans and Intersex Association (ILGA)*, Cameroon is one of the countries where homosexuality is punishable by imprisonment, creating an environment of fear and oppression.

Moreover, social stigmatization continues to hinder progress. Many individuals face discrimination not only from the government but also from their families and communities. This societal pressure can lead to internalized homophobia, where individuals struggle to accept their identities, further complicating advocacy efforts. The fear of violence and ostracism can deter individuals from participating in activism, creating a cycle of silence and repression.

Examples of Sustained Advocacy Efforts

Despite these challenges, various organizations and individuals have made significant strides in advocating for LGBTQ rights in Cameroon. One notable example is the work of **ADEFHO (Association for the Defense of Homosexuals)**, which has been at the forefront of advocating for LGBTQ rights in the country. Through legal aid, public awareness campaigns, and community support, ADEFHO has sought to challenge discriminatory laws and provide resources to those affected by such policies.

Another example is the rise of digital activism, which has become an essential tool for advocacy in the digital age. Social media platforms have allowed activists to connect, share their stories, and mobilize support on a global scale. Campaigns such as **#FreeTheLGBTQ** have garnered international attention, drawing awareness to the plight of LGBTQ individuals in Cameroon and pressuring governments to reconsider their stance on LGBTQ rights.

Additionally, the role of international organizations, such as **Human Rights Watch** and **Amnesty International,** cannot be understated. These organizations have documented human rights abuses against LGBTQ individuals in Cameroon and have called for accountability from the government. Their reports serve as critical tools for advocacy, providing evidence that can be used to lobby for change at both national and international levels.

The Importance of Collective Action

Continuing to advocate for change necessitates collective action. As the LGBTQ movement evolves, it is crucial to unite diverse groups under a common cause. Building alliances with other marginalized communities can strengthen the advocacy efforts and create a more inclusive movement. For instance, collaborating with women's rights organizations can amplify the voices of LGBTQ women, who often face unique challenges within both the LGBTQ community and society at large.

Moreover, engaging allies—individuals who may not identify as LGBTQ but support the cause—can broaden the reach of advocacy. Allies can use their privilege to challenge discriminatory practices and raise awareness within their networks, fostering a culture of acceptance and understanding.

The Path Forward

As we look to the future, the path of advocacy for LGBTQ rights in Cameroon must remain steadfast and innovative. This includes leveraging technology to create safe spaces for dialogue and support, utilizing digital platforms to disseminate information, and developing creative campaigns that resonate with the broader public.

In conclusion, the fight for LGBTQ rights in Cameroon is an ongoing endeavor that requires a multifaceted approach. By understanding the theoretical frameworks that underpin advocacy, recognizing the challenges faced, and learning from successful examples, activists can continue to push for change. The journey may be fraught with obstacles, but the resilience and determination of the LGBTQ community and its allies will pave the way for a more inclusive and equitable society. The fight is far from over, but with continued advocacy, hope for change remains alive and vibrant.

The importance of collective action

Collective action is a cornerstone of social movements, particularly in the fight for LGBTQ rights. It refers to the collaboration of individuals and groups towards a common goal, leveraging shared resources, knowledge, and experiences to create meaningful change. This section explores the significance of collective action, the theoretical frameworks that underpin it, the challenges it faces, and real-world examples that illustrate its impact.

Theoretical Frameworks

The theory of collective action is deeply rooted in social movement theory, which posits that individuals are more likely to engage in activism when they perceive that their actions can lead to significant social change. One foundational concept is the **Collective Action Problem**, which suggests that individuals may hesitate to contribute to a group effort due to concerns about personal costs, such as time and resources, versus the benefits that may accrue to the group as a whole. Mancur Olson, in his seminal work *The Logic of Collective Action*, argued that individuals will only participate in collective action if they believe their involvement will lead to tangible outcomes or if they are part of a community that values activism.

Another relevant framework is the **Resource Mobilization Theory**, which emphasizes the importance of resources—both tangible and intangible—in the success of social movements. This theory posits that movements require not only a shared grievance but also the ability to organize, mobilize, and sustain collective efforts. Resources can include financial support, organizational infrastructure, and social networks that facilitate communication and coordination among activists.

Challenges to Collective Action

Despite its importance, collective action is fraught with challenges. One major obstacle is **fragmentation** within the LGBTQ community itself. Diverse identities—such as race, gender, and socioeconomic status—can lead to differing priorities and strategies for activism. For instance, the concerns of transgender individuals may not always align with those of cisgender LGBTQ members, leading to potential rifts within the movement.

Additionally, **internalized oppression** can undermine collective action. Many individuals within marginalized communities may struggle with self-acceptance and fear of discrimination, which can inhibit their willingness to participate in public advocacy. This internal conflict can lead to a lack of visibility for certain identities, further complicating the quest for unity in activism.

Moreover, external pressures, such as **government repression** and societal stigma, can create an environment that discourages collective action. In many regions, including Cameroon, LGBTQ individuals face legal repercussions for their activism, leading to a chilling effect that stifles open collaboration. Activists may fear arrest, violence, or social ostracism, which can deter them from participating in collective efforts.

Examples of Successful Collective Action

Despite these challenges, there are numerous examples of successful collective action within the LGBTQ movement that demonstrate its power to effect change. One notable instance is the **Stonewall Riots** of 1969, which served as a catalyst for the modern LGBTQ rights movement. The riots, sparked by a police raid at the Stonewall Inn in New York City, were a collective response to systemic oppression and led to the formation of numerous activist organizations, including the Gay Liberation Front. This moment exemplified how collective outrage can galvanize a community and lead to sustained activism.

Another example is the **Marriage Equality Movement** in the United States, which saw a coalition of LGBTQ organizations, allies, and advocacy groups come together to fight for the right to marry. Through coordinated efforts, including grassroots mobilization, legal challenges, and public awareness campaigns, activists successfully shifted public opinion and ultimately achieved legal recognition of same-sex marriage in 2015 with the Supreme Court ruling in *Obergefell v. Hodges*.

Internationally, the **Global Fund for Women** has played a pivotal role in supporting LGBTQ rights through collective action. By funding grassroots organizations and providing resources for advocacy, the Global Fund has helped amplify marginalized voices and foster collaboration among activists worldwide. Their work highlights the importance of solidarity and resource-sharing in creating a more equitable society.

Conclusion

In conclusion, collective action is essential in the ongoing fight for LGBTQ rights. It enables individuals to unite their efforts, share resources, and amplify their voices in the face of adversity. While challenges such as fragmentation, internalized oppression, and external pressures persist, the power of collective action remains evident in historical and contemporary movements. By fostering a sense of community and shared purpose, activists can continue to push for change and advocate for a more inclusive and accepting society. As Bandy Kiki and others have demonstrated, the fight for equality is not just an individual endeavor but a collective journey towards justice and liberation.

Inspiring others to rise up and make a difference

In a world where the fight for LGBTQ rights continues to face significant challenges, the role of inspiration in activism cannot be overstated. The act of inspiring others to rise up and make a difference is a fundamental component of social movements, particularly within the LGBTQ community. This section delves into the theories of motivation and collective action, highlights ongoing problems faced by activists, and provides real-world examples of how individuals and groups have mobilized others in the pursuit of equality.

Theoretical Framework

One of the key theories relevant to inspiring activism is the Social Movement Theory (SMT), which posits that social movements arise in response to perceived injustices and seek to create social change. According to Tilly (2004), movements are characterized by three main components: *collective identity, resource mobilization,* and *political opportunity.* Each of these components plays a crucial role in inspiring individuals to participate in activism.

$$\text{Collective Identity} + \text{Resource Mobilization} + \text{Political Opportunity} = \text{Social Movement Su} \tag{98}$$

Collective Identity refers to the shared sense of belonging among individuals in a movement. This identity fosters solidarity and encourages members to take action. For LGBTQ activists, collective identity often manifests in pride, resilience, and a commitment to fight for rights and recognition.

Resource Mobilization involves the strategies and tools activists use to garner support and facilitate participation. This can include social media campaigns, fundraising efforts, and grassroots organizing. The effective use of resources not only amplifies the message but also inspires others to join the cause.

Political Opportunity highlights the external factors that can either facilitate or hinder a movement's progress. Activists must be aware of the political landscape and leverage opportunities to advocate for change. For example, shifts in public opinion or legal reforms can create a conducive environment for activism.

Challenges Faced by Activists

Despite the theoretical frameworks that guide activism, LGBTQ rights advocates encounter numerous challenges that can stifle inspiration and participation. Some of these challenges include:

- **Repression and Violence:** In many regions, LGBTQ individuals face violence, discrimination, and legal repercussions for their identities. This hostile environment can deter potential activists from joining the movement.

- **Internalized Homophobia:** Many individuals struggle with self-acceptance due to societal stigma. This internal conflict can inhibit their willingness to engage in activism, as they may fear rejection or ostracization.

- **Resource Scarcity:** Activists often operate with limited resources, which can hinder their ability to mobilize others. Lack of funding, access to technology, and inadequate training can create barriers to effective advocacy.

Real-World Examples

Despite these challenges, numerous activists and organizations have successfully inspired others to rise up and make a difference. Here are a few notable examples:

1. **The Stonewall Riots:** The 1969 Stonewall Riots in New York City serve as a seminal moment in LGBTQ history. The riots were sparked by a police raid at the Stonewall Inn, a gay bar, and led to six days of protests. Activists like Marsha P. Johnson and Sylvia Rivera became iconic figures, inspiring future generations to advocate for LGBTQ rights. The riots galvanized the community and marked the beginning of the modern LGBTQ rights movement.

2. **The It Gets Better Project:** Founded in 2010 by Dan Savage and Terry Miller, the It Gets Better Project aims to provide hope and support to LGBTQ youth facing bullying and discrimination. The campaign encourages individuals to share their stories of resilience, inspiring others to persevere through difficult times. By utilizing social media, the project has reached millions, creating a sense of solidarity and empowerment among LGBTQ youth.

3. **Global Pride Events:** Events like Pride parades and marches serve as powerful platforms for visibility and activism. They not only celebrate LGBTQ identities but also inspire individuals to take action. For example, the annual Sydney Gay and Lesbian Mardi Gras attracts thousands of participants and spectators, fostering a sense of community and encouraging involvement in advocacy efforts.

Conclusion

Inspiring others to rise up and make a difference is essential for the ongoing struggle for LGBTQ rights. Through the lens of Social Movement Theory, we understand the importance of collective identity, resource mobilization, and political opportunity in fostering activism. Despite the challenges faced by LGBTQ advocates, the examples of successful movements and campaigns demonstrate the power of inspiration. As individuals continue to share their stories and advocate for change, they pave the way for future generations to join the fight for equality, ensuring that the spirit of activism remains vibrant and unstoppable.

Bibliography

[1] Tilly, C. (2004). *Social Movements, 1760-2000*. Paradigm Publishers.

Index

-doubt, 53, 65, 99, 110, 202, 264, 266, 271

a, 1–17, 19–26, 28–33, 35, 37–39, 41–48, 50–59, 63–65, 67–82, 84–87, 89–99, 101–104, 106–108, 110, 113–118, 120, 122–128, 130–132, 134–137, 139–148, 150–157, 159, 161, 163, 165, 166, 168, 171–185, 187, 189, 190, 192, 193, 195, 197–202, 204–206, 208–219, 222–226, 228, 231, 233–241, 243–245, 247–249, 251–260, 262–265, 267–275, 277–289, 291, 293–295, 297–308, 310, 312–317, 319–329, 331–338
abandonment, 81
ability, 5, 13, 31, 38, 58, 81, 82, 94, 101, 110, 113, 116, 145, 157, 163, 171, 178, 188, 190, 198, 206, 210, 215, 222, 225, 226, 229, 233, 253, 254, 258, 272, 275, 277, 282, 289, 307, 308, 329
absence, 29, 302
abundance, 6
abuse, 124, 183
acceptance, 4, 6, 7, 9–11, 25, 30, 44, 48, 50, 53–55, 57, 61–63, 65, 67, 69, 72–75, 77, 80–82, 85–87, 89–92, 94–96, 101–104, 106, 108, 110, 115, 117, 120, 122, 128, 155, 166, 171, 172, 181, 184, 192, 193, 205, 206, 216, 217, 239, 240, 245, 253, 260–262, 264, 269–272, 279, 284, 286, 293, 297, 308, 313, 321, 328, 329
access, 41, 45, 79, 131, 140, 142, 163, 172, 225, 226, 279, 285
accessibility, 131
account, 211
accountability, 226
achievement, 22, 91, 110, 181, 314, 316
acknowledgment, 57, 73, 270
acquisition, 202

act, 8, 15, 19, 33, 73, 77, 90, 92, 94–96, 117, 120, 130, 132, 152, 179, 180, 198, 200, 204–206, 210, 212, 215, 217, 222, 223, 247, 248, 258, 260, 262, 327, 336

action, 5, 12, 31, 48, 50, 54, 93, 108, 125, 134, 142, 143, 148, 157, 159, 168, 174, 176, 180, 189, 217, 231, 235, 240, 249, 256, 258, 288, 289, 294, 295, 301, 312, 314, 326, 333–336

activism, 1–6, 11–17, 19–21, 23–25, 29, 30, 35, 37–39, 42, 44–48, 50–59, 65, 67, 77, 78, 81, 82, 89, 92–96, 98, 103, 104, 108, 110, 111, 118–120, 124, 127, 132, 136, 139, 141–143, 149–154, 157, 161, 163, 166, 168, 172–174, 178–180, 182–184, 187, 189, 190, 192, 193, 197–200, 202, 204–210, 212–217, 219, 222–224, 226, 228–231, 235, 237, 239, 242, 247–254, 256–258, 262, 264–266, 268, 269, 272, 274–277, 280–282, 284–286, 289, 291, 293–295, 297–308, 310–313, 316, 322, 324–326, 331, 332, 336–338

activist, 1, 3, 4, 12, 13, 19, 21, 52, 84, 91, 94, 101, 118, 150–152, 154, 185, 200, 202, 205, 206, 209, 213, 214, 217, 219, 231, 247–249, 252, 254, 255, 260, 264, 289, 302, 303, 307

activity, 47
actualization, 204
adaptability, 45, 253, 284
adaptation, 199, 282
addition, 45, 78, 96, 128
address, 38, 127, 155, 163, 199, 236, 237, 242, 243, 252, 280, 287, 301, 314, 321
advent, 277
adversity, 13, 31, 52, 67, 79, 84, 94, 101, 113, 115, 116, 154, 174, 180, 185, 198, 204, 207, 247–253, 256, 258–260, 282, 289, 305, 308, 312, 326, 335
advice, 209
advocacy, 3, 5, 6, 10, 11, 13, 19, 31–35, 39, 41, 45, 48, 82, 84–87, 92, 98, 106, 124, 125, 130, 132, 139, 141, 143, 145–151, 153, 154, 161, 163, 174, 175, 179, 181, 183, 189, 195, 199, 201, 208, 214, 217, 222, 224–226, 229, 236, 237, 239, 240, 243–245, 248, 249, 256, 257, 277–279, 281, 282, 294, 298, 300, 302, 303, 305, 312, 314, 315, 320, 325, 326, 331–333
advocate, 2–6, 10, 15, 20, 22, 24, 25, 30, 31, 41, 50, 58, 65, 70, 72, 79, 82, 84, 86, 91, 93–95, 101, 104, 108, 110, 113, 115, 118, 120, 126,

130, 134, 145, 149, 150, 152, 159, 171, 173, 176, 178, 187, 189, 197, 209, 210, 217, 225, 248, 249, 251, 254, 258, 260, 265, 268, 273, 277, 280, 282, 285, 286, 298, 300, 302, 303, 306–308, 310, 313, 322, 327, 328, 330, 333, 335, 338
affirmation, 75, 115–117
Africa, 125, 288, 325
age, 1, 3, 7, 15, 21, 22, 37, 39, 45, 48, 132, 178, 212, 225, 251, 257, 275, 277, 279, 280, 284
agency, 174, 189, 306
agender, 68
aid, 175
air, 5
Albert Bandura, 93
Alex, 72, 81, 89, 91, 101, 117
alienation, 242
alignment, 118, 120
allow, 225, 251, 262
allyship, 243, 245, 265, 268, 269, 271
Amina, 30
amplification, 125, 130–132
anger, 72
anonymity, 7, 13, 14, 17, 19–24, 29, 43, 47, 51, 135, 151, 152, 223, 225, 256, 279, 280
anti, 45, 143, 148, 154, 183, 237, 255, 288, 314, 325
anticipation, 77
Antonio Gramsci, 58
anxiety, 25, 74, 75, 89, 116, 149, 253
appearance, 76

approach, 16, 52, 54, 96, 101, 114, 118, 120, 130, 140, 145, 178, 184, 192, 209, 223, 224, 226, 235, 236, 238, 243, 249, 251–253, 256–258, 268, 279, 284, 286, 310, 314, 320, 324, 325, 333
aroma, 1
arrest, 23, 78, 123, 179, 225, 256
arsenal, 95
art, 3, 92, 96, 204, 205, 209, 210, 229–231, 271, 327, 328
artist, 327
artwork, 327
Asia, 288
aspect, 28, 43, 45, 47, 52, 87, 93, 95, 110, 124, 132, 150, 185, 192, 217, 226, 228, 248, 256, 265, 269, 272, 277, 307, 324
assault, 148
assertion, 270
assistance, 106
atmosphere, 28, 239
attention, 38, 57, 91, 124, 135, 142, 149, 154, 172, 226, 235, 257, 303, 305
attraction, 7
audience, 6, 41–43, 45, 94, 135, 142–145, 172, 178, 223, 224, 251, 256–258, 278, 279, 283, 305, 328
Audre Lorde, 223, 247
authenticity, 10, 11, 21, 29, 44, 61, 63–65, 70, 73, 76, 78–80, 89, 90, 92, 94, 95, 104, 108, 118, 120, 215, 217, 231, 247, 249, 267, 270,

289, 305, 328, 329
author, 210
avenue, 145, 205, 223
avoidance, 74
awakening, 3
awareness, 12, 15, 35, 38, 39, 42, 45, 54, 64, 82, 84, 103, 124, 126, 130, 132, 134, 135, 142, 143, 151, 172, 175, 176, 181, 183, 184, 200, 205, 210, 215, 225, 226, 234–236, 238, 240, 243, 248, 249, 251, 256–258, 265, 274, 275, 277, 279, 280, 285, 298–301, 307, 313, 316, 321, 327

backbone, 128, 254
backdrop, 29, 53, 171, 224, 255, 285
background, 10
backing, 258, 306
backlash, 3, 12, 20, 30, 34, 43, 57, 76, 78, 91, 96, 103, 144, 149, 153, 154, 172, 179, 212, 214, 223, 225, 231, 243, 247, 253, 255, 278–280, 301, 307, 312, 327
balance, 4, 21, 22, 43, 150–152, 207, 210, 213, 215, 248
balancing, 19, 21, 152, 209, 210, 282
Bandy, 1–12, 20, 21, 38, 51, 52, 58, 64–67, 74, 103, 104, 109, 110, 122, 143, 203–206, 215–217, 256
Bandy Kiki, 2–4, 6, 8, 10, 11, 13–16, 19–24, 28–30, 35, 37, 39–46, 48, 50–57, 59, 63, 65, 74, 77, 79, 80, 84, 93–96, 104, 108, 110, 113, 117, 120, 123, 125, 129, 130, 132–137, 139, 140, 142–145, 148, 151–154, 157, 161, 163, 166, 171–174, 180, 181, 185, 187, 192, 195, 198, 200–202, 204, 206, 208–217, 228, 231, 233, 235, 236, 238, 239, 247–258, 260, 264–266, 271, 280–282, 284–286, 289, 291, 293, 295, 297–299, 301–303, 305–308, 310, 312, 325, 326, 335
Bandy Kiki's, 5, 6, 8, 13, 23, 29, 38, 39, 52–54, 57–59, 64, 67, 78, 79, 93, 94, 102, 110, 122, 140, 141, 149, 154, 190, 205–210, 214, 217, 237, 248, 249, 251, 252, 254–257, 263–265, 297–302, 304–307
Bandy Kiki, 52
barrier, 4, 25, 38, 53, 77, 131, 144, 172, 183, 279
battle, 41, 125, 134, 150, 233, 235, 329, 331
beacon, 2, 8, 11, 13, 31, 44, 48, 55, 95, 122, 125, 173, 238, 249, 252, 256, 258, 264, 286, 291, 293, 297, 302, 307, 329
beauty, 10, 122, 270, 272, 328, 329
behavior, 53, 75, 76, 118
being, 3, 16, 21, 23, 25, 29, 31, 67, 77, 82, 86, 87, 89, 98, 106, 111–113, 116, 120, 149,

Index

152, 173, 193, 200, 207, 210, 226, 247, 252, 263, 265, 285, 327
belief, 12, 27, 77, 157, 299
bell, 247
belonging, 9, 16, 31, 46, 50, 77, 79, 81, 91, 92, 108, 175, 180, 193, 200, 204, 237, 269, 271, 307, 321, 324, 328
benefit, 209
betrayal, 234
bias, 240
binary, 8, 10, 66–70, 76, 90, 91, 95, 101, 117, 200, 268, 320
birth, 2
bisexual, 10, 30, 67, 69, 91, 320, 329
bisexuality, 7, 66, 70, 91, 200
blend, 6, 63, 206
blessing, 1
block, 182
blog, 31
blueprint, 22, 59
bond, 72
boundary, 21
brand, 14
bravery, 214
breakthrough, 314, 315
Brené Brown, 265
bridge, 192, 199, 205
buffer, 127
building, 35, 44, 45, 51, 57, 82, 107, 108, 115, 122, 124, 125, 128, 134, 136, 139, 141, 143, 150, 152, 154–157, 161, 163, 166, 168, 180, 182, 184, 192, 200, 202, 205, 210, 224, 231, 235–240, 253, 254, 258, 274, 285, 286, 289, 295, 313, 314, 316, 321
burden, 73, 75, 77, 202, 218
burnout, 20, 202, 218, 253, 281
Butler, 95

call, 12, 249, 265
Cameroon, 2–4, 6, 10–12, 15–17, 23–35, 37–39, 41–45, 47, 48, 50–55, 57–59, 64, 78, 82–85, 93, 94, 123, 125, 127, 128, 130, 132, 134–136, 139, 141–144, 148, 150–154, 156, 161, 171–173, 175, 177–185, 190, 204–206, 210, 211, 216, 217, 224–226, 233, 235, 239, 247–249, 252, 255, 256, 263, 264, 280, 281, 284–286, 293, 298–312, 314–316, 326, 327, 331, 333
campaign, 35, 45, 189, 316
campaigning, 218
canyon, 297
capacity, 139, 152, 161, 179, 201, 256
capital, 45, 58, 124
care, 20, 111–113, 120, 122, 154, 175, 203, 210, 215, 223, 253, 254
career, 210
Carl Rogers', 73
case, 63, 65, 96, 117, 138, 151, 163, 179, 204, 225, 226, 234, 277, 288, 310, 312, 327
catalyst, 52, 54, 57, 63, 72, 104, 153, 173, 202, 204
category, 314

cause, 2, 23, 44, 50, 94, 143, 150, 154, 163, 165, 166, 209, 248, 254, 333
celebration, 57, 73, 91, 92, 109, 110, 180, 249, 270–272, 295, 322, 328
censorship, 16, 29, 39–41, 43, 47, 48, 148, 214, 277, 280, 282, 294, 327
century, 308
chain, 300
challenge, 1, 2, 21, 25, 31, 32, 37, 52–54, 65, 67, 70, 84, 87, 95, 96, 99, 124, 125, 129, 134, 136, 152, 163, 173, 175, 176, 210, 214, 223, 224, 231, 233, 239–241, 243, 249, 252, 253, 266, 271, 280, 285, 286, 288, 289, 308, 312, 324, 327, 329
change, 3, 4, 6, 11–13, 15, 17, 24, 29, 31, 33–35, 37, 39, 41, 42, 48, 50, 52–54, 57, 72, 85, 87, 95–97, 99, 104, 108, 110, 113, 115, 120, 123, 130–132, 134, 136, 137, 141, 143, 145, 147, 150, 152, 154, 157, 159, 161, 168, 170, 173–176, 178, 180, 182, 189, 199, 202, 208, 210, 211, 216, 217, 224, 226, 228, 229, 231–233, 235–240, 244, 245, 247, 251, 254, 256, 258, 263, 265, 272, 274, 275, 277, 280, 282, 284, 286, 288, 289, 293, 295, 297, 298, 301–303, 306, 308, 310–312, 314, 324, 326, 328, 331, 333–335, 338
channel, 257
chaos, 5
chapter, 123, 185, 247, 249
character, 75
characteristic, 75, 152, 319
Charles Tilly, 288
child, 1, 3, 6
childhood, 4, 5
choice, 8, 11, 22, 151, 177, 306
choreography, 19
cinema, 96
circle, 20
citizenship, 273
city, 1, 3, 124
clarity, 3, 7
class, 5, 243, 287, 307, 325
Claude Steele, 53
climate, 24, 34, 57, 96, 135, 153, 179
clothing, 8, 95
co, 44, 45
coalition, 35, 44, 45, 52, 125, 134, 143, 154, 155, 157, 163, 166, 236, 237, 289
code, 125
coercion, 58
collaboration, 23, 44, 45, 47, 51, 124, 138–140, 155, 157, 161, 163, 168, 170, 171, 192, 199, 238, 245, 258, 294, 334
color, 95, 241, 242, 320, 323
combat, 45, 101, 110, 112, 124, 126, 167, 244, 253, 313, 325, 330
combination, 58, 67, 139, 205, 239, 260

comfort, 5
commentary, 223
commercialization, 231
commitment, 6, 13, 32, 33, 44, 52, 54, 59, 70, 94, 95, 118, 122, 141, 157, 168, 198, 206, 212, 215, 228, 240, 248, 252, 254, 282, 286, 289, 291, 295, 305, 314, 326, 331
communicating, 280
communication, 12, 21, 41, 48, 51, 133, 134, 140, 144, 155, 161, 199, 206, 222, 273, 282, 294
community, 3–5, 9–12, 15–17, 25, 28–33, 35, 37–39, 41–46, 48, 50–52, 54–59, 63, 64, 67, 72, 75–77, 79–81, 83, 84, 87–89, 91–99, 101, 103, 104, 106, 108, 110, 111, 114, 115, 117, 118, 122–124, 126, 132, 134, 136, 137, 142–144, 148–151, 157, 163, 166, 171–173, 175, 178, 180, 182–184, 187, 189, 193, 195, 197, 198, 200–202, 204–206, 208–210, 222, 224, 226, 231, 235–241, 243–245, 247–250, 252–254, 256–258, 260, 263, 264, 267–272, 274, 275, 277, 279–281, 283–287, 293, 294, 298–303, 306–308, 312–314, 316, 319–321, 324–331, 333, 335, 336
compassion, 75, 85, 101, 106, 115–117, 122, 207, 210
complexity, 70, 222
component, 44, 104, 115, 134, 161, 187, 195, 197, 205, 239, 249, 336
concept, 7, 12, 54, 59, 73, 80, 88, 93, 95, 115, 130, 157, 166, 178, 201, 243, 247, 256, 261, 271, 300, 307, 322, 324
conclusion, 2, 8, 10, 15, 21, 25, 28, 39, 45, 48, 52, 57, 59, 70, 77, 79, 82, 92, 95, 96, 104, 108, 110, 113, 120, 122, 125, 141, 145, 152, 154, 156, 161, 170, 173, 176, 179, 184, 192, 202, 205, 208, 210, 215, 217, 224, 226, 231, 233, 235, 240, 242, 245, 249, 254, 256, 258, 265, 272, 284, 286, 289, 291, 295, 299, 301, 305, 308, 310, 312, 314, 316, 321, 324, 329, 333, 335
condemnation, 312
confidence, 73, 74, 103, 187, 195
confine, 8
conflict, 25, 86, 118, 252
conformity, 3, 10, 215, 239, 270
confrontation, 3
confusion, 1, 3, 7, 63–65
connection, 29, 31, 72, 103, 106, 120, 183, 205, 215, 254, 262, 263, 265
connectivity, 15, 41, 48, 262
consciousness, 122
consent, 58
consideration, 22, 223

constitution, 179, 312
construct, 211
contagion, 300
content, 16, 46, 209, 273, 278, 281
context, 10, 19, 24, 53, 82, 93, 123, 136, 141, 142, 148, 152, 161, 171, 177, 179, 190, 199, 204, 222, 234, 244, 249, 250, 287, 310, 312, 325, 327
continent, 312
continuity, 200
contrast, 101, 116, 213
control, 24, 41
convergence, 144
conversation, 87
cooperation, 140, 141
core, 115, 118, 134, 241, 322, 327
cornerstone, 48, 82, 110, 139, 154, 157, 168, 270, 275, 334
cost, 210
counter, 58
countermeasure, 116
country, 33, 37, 123, 139, 248, 280, 307, 308
courage, 3, 4, 6, 10, 35, 59, 70, 72, 77, 79, 94–96, 104, 106, 124, 130, 180, 185, 187, 215, 226, 236, 247–249, 253, 259, 260, 262, 267, 285, 291, 297, 299, 301, 305–308
coverage, 134, 300
creation, 15, 16, 50, 52, 239
creativity, 35, 41, 130, 147, 229, 231, 328
credibility, 23, 45
criminalization, 128
crisis, 327
criticism, 116, 149
crowd, 248
crowdfunding, 253
crucible, 200, 217
culmination, 13
cultivation, 202
culture, 2, 11, 24, 54, 75, 95, 120, 122, 126, 171, 181, 183, 216, 229, 240, 253, 255, 260, 271, 272, 284–286, 304, 326, 329
cup, 214
curiosity, 5, 63
curricula, 313
cyberbullying, 278
cycle, 25, 26, 136, 182, 214, 255, 263, 266, 332

dance, 19, 213
danger, 12, 22, 28–30, 153, 219, 256, 327
data, 45, 225, 320
debate, 5
decision, 2, 4, 10–13, 15, 43, 77, 79, 94, 118, 149, 155, 216, 303, 306
declaration, 103
decriminalization, 135, 181, 225, 308
dedication, 94, 208, 238, 254, 299
defiance, 5, 8, 33, 73, 92, 120
degree, 21, 26, 29, 237
delight, 72
demand, 124, 247
democracy, 273, 312
demonstration, 123
denial, 76, 86
depression, 25, 74, 89, 116, 149
depth, 57

desire, 3, 13, 43, 64, 65, 78, 90, 172, 173
despair, 1, 28, 81, 83, 113, 257
determination, 2, 6, 115, 125, 136, 141, 154, 175, 184, 240, 248, 254–256, 293, 295, 301, 306, 331, 333
development, 200, 202, 237, 261
deviant, 27, 53
deviation, 3, 6
dialogue, 5, 42, 45, 86, 87, 96, 117, 126, 141, 163, 172, 253, 274, 285, 286, 298, 305, 307, 331, 333
dichotomy, 20, 252
difference, 13, 141, 187, 249, 336–338
difficulty, 153
dignity, 33, 128, 150, 286, 298, 329, 331
dilemma, 23
dilution, 44
disability, 321
disadvantage, 243, 322, 325
disappointment, 72
disapproval, 77
disclosure, 23
discomfort, 91
disconnect, 21, 142, 199
disconnection, 75
discourse, 53, 134, 142, 171, 286, 298
discovery, 1–4, 6, 10, 11, 63, 65, 70, 185, 193, 204, 208, 260, 271
discrimination, 4, 5, 10–12, 20, 24–33, 42, 44, 53, 64, 72, 73, 78, 81, 83, 86–88, 94, 102, 113, 115, 116, 122–126, 128, 135, 136, 148, 152, 153, 171, 172, 181, 183, 184, 201, 216, 223–226, 233, 236, 237, 239–243, 248, 252, 255, 263, 264, 270, 285–288, 300, 304, 306, 308, 310, 312, 314, 320, 322, 325, 327, 332
discussion, 54
disdain, 253
disenfranchisement, 128
dismantling, 12, 128, 226, 284, 286, 313
disparity, 38
display, 185
dissemination, 230
dissent, 16, 24, 34, 132, 148
dissonance, 118, 140, 214
distancing, 172
distress, 79, 149
diversity, 53, 73, 87, 89, 91, 118, 122, 131, 166, 175, 222, 240, 267, 269, 270, 272, 284, 286, 299, 313, 314, 319, 321, 322, 328, 329
divide, 38, 39, 277, 279
division, 166, 168
document, 124, 224
documentation, 135, 225, 226
Douala, 1, 3–6, 29, 63, 94, 163, 264
doubt, 53, 65, 99, 110, 202, 264, 266, 271
drag, 168
dream, 13, 130, 141, 240, 305
dress, 328
duality, 94, 135, 308, 327
dynamic, 81, 272, 284, 310

education, 35, 45, 87, 115, 126, 154, 174, 176, 183, 184, 210, 222, 224, 231, 235, 240, 244, 285, 286, 300
effect, 29, 89, 94, 189, 205, 225, 226, 231, 232, 239, 240, 249, 258, 259, 267, 297, 299–303, 307, 312
effectiveness, 24, 38, 41, 120, 161, 163, 189, 237, 275, 279, 281, 294
effort, 25, 54, 114, 184, 228, 286
element, 91, 120
Ellen DeGeneres, 267
embodiment, 95
embrace, 2–4, 8, 10, 58, 63, 66, 67, 74, 77, 80, 84, 87, 89–92, 94–96, 98, 99, 101, 106, 110, 117, 200, 204, 205, 216, 217, 249, 262, 264, 265, 267, 272, 289, 291, 295, 307, 308, 328, 329
emergence, 54, 171, 175, 300, 303, 308
emotion, 265
empathy, 5, 12, 30, 54, 72, 96, 118, 172, 175, 181, 184, 200–202, 205, 210, 222, 224, 226–229, 231, 233, 236, 239, 249, 259, 268, 279, 313, 328, 329
employment, 94
empower, 31, 58, 59, 84, 101, 108, 188, 195, 200, 237, 239, 256, 272, 302, 313, 325, 328, 329
empowerment, 8, 10, 15, 46, 48, 52, 56, 63, 81, 89, 92, 97–99, 102, 106, 108, 117, 174, 189, 192, 195, 197, 199, 205, 208, 215, 217, 231, 238, 239, 259, 265, 266, 269, 271, 285, 286, 291, 305, 307, 324–327
encourage, 54, 180
encouragement, 80, 98
encryption, 43
endeavor, 22, 24, 52, 85, 113, 127, 143, 154, 166, 208, 215, 258, 260, 286, 312, 333, 336
energy, 214
enforcement, 25, 226
engagement, 15, 45–47, 56, 57, 67, 85, 94, 95, 101, 122, 131, 138, 142, 143, 152, 153, 161, 163, 172, 173, 199, 202, 206, 236, 249, 268, 273, 276–279, 281, 283, 313, 314
environment, 6, 11–13, 23, 25, 26, 29, 33, 39, 43, 45, 51, 53, 57, 63, 70, 72–74, 77–80, 82, 83, 85, 87, 89, 91, 94, 101, 123, 125, 127, 135, 142–144, 150, 151, 153, 171, 172, 183, 193, 195, 196, 200, 213, 224, 235, 240, 249, 250, 252, 255, 257, 259, 268, 271, 272, 281, 285, 289, 299–301, 303, 306, 308, 312, 314, 325, 327
equality, 2, 4, 5, 11–13, 22, 25, 30, 33, 35, 39, 41, 42, 44, 47, 48, 52, 55, 57, 85, 87, 95, 98, 108, 110, 113, 118, 123–125, 127, 128, 130,

Index   351

    134, 136, 137, 140–142,
    145, 154, 157, 159, 166,
    168, 171–174, 176, 180,
    182, 184, 187, 190, 192,
    195, 197, 198, 200, 202,
    206, 208–210, 212, 216,
    217, 231, 233, 235, 243,
    245, 247–249, 254, 262,
    265, 269, 272, 274, 279,
    284, 286, 289, 291, 294,
    295, 299, 302, 308–310,
    312, 316, 319, 321, 324,
    331, 336, 338
equation, 2, 4, 13, 24–26, 42, 43, 46,
    48, 56, 58, 69, 114, 118,
    139, 144, 152, 180, 182,
    199, 204–206, 209, 218,
    219, 238–241, 247, 249,
    259, 278–280, 286, 293,
    300, 314, 320, 322, 327,
    329
equity, 314
era, 24, 41, 308
Eric, 226
Eric Ohena Lembembe, 148
Erik Erikson's, 200
Erikson, 261
error, 39
Erving Goffman's, 75
essence, 2, 48, 64, 94, 130, 206, 240,
    247, 291, 293, 306, 319
establishment, 173, 179, 237, 239,
    285, 300, 302
esteem, 53, 101, 238
estrangement, 72, 149
event, 124, 172, 248
evolution, 200, 206, 274, 298
example, 10, 16, 27, 35, 38, 44, 45,
    47, 51, 53, 75, 77, 78, 80,
    87, 90–96, 118, 124, 126,
    135, 142, 148, 149, 155,
    163, 199, 209, 226, 237,
    241, 244, 248, 256, 257,
    264, 272, 278–281, 283,
    285, 287, 294, 300, 301,
    303, 307, 313, 314, 320,
    322, 325, 327
exception, 77, 252
exchange, 294
exclusion, 5, 76, 242
existence, 22, 90, 96, 126
expansion, 177–179, 279
expectancy, 180
expectation, 76, 180, 252
experience, 4, 10, 12, 20, 62, 68, 72,
    75, 76, 78, 88, 90, 95, 101,
    106, 116, 117, 149, 166,
    202, 205, 214, 222, 224,
    226, 241, 253, 263, 264,
    267, 272, 312, 320, 322,
    327
exploration, 1, 7, 8, 65, 67, 91,
    204–206
exposure, 5, 7, 11, 20, 23, 24, 64,
    281, 329
expression, 8, 13, 25, 37, 39, 75, 96,
    122, 124, 204, 209, 210,
    216, 223, 229–231, 270,
    325, 327–329
extent, 231

fabric, 303
facade, 102
face, 4, 11, 13, 16, 17, 20, 23, 26,
    28–31, 33, 39, 41, 43, 47,
    52, 53, 67, 69, 71, 72, 76,
    78, 79, 81, 84, 94, 95, 97,
    99, 102, 113, 115, 116,

118, 120, 123, 135, 138, 140, 142, 144, 149, 152–154, 172–174, 179, 180, 185, 187, 188, 190, 198, 200, 207, 212, 216, 219, 220, 225, 226, 230, 231, 239, 241, 243, 247–250, 252, 253, 256–258, 260, 263, 270, 276, 278, 280, 282, 287, 289, 301, 304, 305, 308, 311, 312, 320, 322, 327, 328, 330, 332, 333, 335, 336
failing, 155
failure, 25
fairness, 5
family, 1, 2, 20, 28, 30, 70, 72–74, 77, 80–82, 86, 87, 101, 106, 149, 203, 226, 248, 253, 258, 270, 307
fashion, 8, 92, 327
father, 72
fear, 2, 4, 6, 9–12, 20, 23–25, 28–30, 33, 34, 63, 64, 74, 76, 77, 79–81, 83, 86, 94, 96, 117, 126, 134, 135, 140, 142, 144, 148, 153, 171, 183, 214, 215, 224, 225, 243, 244, 247, 253, 255, 263, 265, 270, 281, 285, 286, 304, 306, 322, 325, 327, 328, 332
feat, 2
feeling, 29, 69, 239, 264, 265
female, 68, 91
feminism, 321
fight, 2–6, 10–13, 24, 35, 39, 41–44, 48, 52, 55, 57, 59, 85, 95, 104, 108, 110, 113, 120, 123–125, 128, 130, 134–136, 140, 141, 145, 147, 150, 152, 154, 156, 159, 161, 163, 168, 171–173, 176, 177, 180, 184, 185, 190, 192, 195, 198, 200, 208, 210, 212, 216, 217, 226, 231, 235, 236, 240, 243, 245, 248, 249, 252, 254, 256, 258, 265, 274, 277, 279, 284, 286, 289, 291, 294, 299, 301, 302, 307–310, 312, 314, 316, 321, 326, 328, 329, 331, 333–336, 338
fighting, 12, 132, 204–206, 253, 331
figure, 57, 139, 198, 210, 252
film, 181, 223, 269, 313, 328
finding, 67, 104, 254
fine, 57
fire, 4, 5
firsthand, 29, 211, 212, 216
flexibility, 120
fluidity, 95
focus, 175, 209, 241, 253, 294, 321
food, 5
force, 2, 6, 44, 76, 154, 159, 176, 231, 238, 284, 310
forefront, 135, 302
form, 8, 25, 37, 152, 254, 257, 272
formation, 23, 95, 140, 154, 200, 202
forum, 94
foster, 5, 15, 23, 31, 39, 52, 58, 73, 77, 83, 87, 103, 114, 124, 126, 132, 136, 137, 141, 143, 157, 166, 168, 171, 175, 183, 184, 192, 199,

Index 353

205, 212, 222, 224, 226, 227, 231, 233, 236, 237, 239, 240, 242, 259, 260, 263, 268, 269, 271, 275, 279, 281, 285, 307, 313, 314, 321, 328, 329
fostering, 9, 12, 28, 30, 45, 46, 48, 51, 53, 54, 57, 64, 69, 72, 75, 77, 79, 82, 83, 85, 87, 91, 92, 96, 101, 108, 111, 113, 115, 117, 120, 127, 134, 139, 143, 157, 159, 172, 174–176, 178, 179, 187, 189, 195, 198, 200, 202, 205, 209, 216, 223, 224, 226, 235, 239, 240, 244, 245, 248, 249, 251, 253, 260, 269, 271, 273, 282, 284–286, 289, 302, 304, 319, 326–329, 335, 338
foundation, 59, 65, 108, 113, 185, 243, 284, 305
fragmentation, 159, 166, 335
frame, 234
framework, 2, 4, 11, 24, 28, 29, 33, 62, 67, 73, 78, 83, 123, 125, 135, 143, 148, 166, 167, 171, 174, 183, 224, 237–239, 242, 248, 255, 285, 288, 303, 304, 308, 315, 324
framing, 87, 136, 142, 143, 286
freedom, 5, 39, 148, 214
friend, 29
front, 44, 45, 142, 154, 157, 166, 184, 236, 245, 285, 314
frustration, 118
fulfillment, 81, 205, 209, 210

function, 2, 118, 236, 238, 241, 259
funding, 35, 142, 225, 253
future, 3–6, 22, 28, 32, 46, 55, 57, 59, 63, 65, 67, 89, 92, 106, 136, 139, 141, 148, 168, 173, 175, 176, 180, 182, 184, 190, 199, 200, 224, 228, 233, 238, 240, 252, 254, 256, 271, 274, 286, 289, 291, 293–295, 302, 305, 308, 314, 326, 329, 333, 338

gain, 11, 131, 195, 249
gap, 301
gathering, 25, 72
gay, 77, 168, 225, 226, 241, 242, 287, 320, 322, 325, 329
gender, 1, 3, 5, 7, 8, 24, 25, 29, 31, 52, 61, 65, 66, 68–70, 73–77, 81, 90, 91, 95, 96, 127, 134, 136, 137, 166, 176, 183, 226, 241, 243, 245, 248, 252, 267, 268, 286, 287, 307, 308, 319, 320, 322, 325, 327, 329, 331
genderqueer, 68, 90, 268
generation, 35, 50, 173, 187, 188, 190, 195, 197, 198, 205, 294, 307
glimmer, 173
globalization, 171, 286
globe, 140, 328
goal, 73, 240, 249, 293, 334
Goffman, 75
government, 16, 38, 130, 143, 154, 225, 280, 286, 304, 315, 332

graffiti, 327
gravity, 11
ground, 65, 173, 235
groundwork, 4, 6, 65, 168, 237, 238, 289, 291
group, 12, 16, 25, 30, 52, 53, 75, 80, 81, 87, 89, 124, 155, 168, 180, 238
growth, 55, 63, 73, 79, 85, 99, 101, 106, 108, 110, 182, 192, 195, 197, 202, 204–209, 213, 215, 254, 259, 263, 266, 328
guidance, 195, 207, 237, 294
guide, 125, 142, 184, 198, 337

hand, 17, 72, 273, 315
harassment, 22, 25, 29, 33, 47, 48, 76, 78, 142, 148, 153, 172, 179, 212, 224, 248, 254, 277–282, 294, 301
hardship, 30
harm, 94, 152
hate, 25
hatred, 74, 89
haven, 79, 80
head, 28, 168, 198, 245, 254, 258, 307
healing, 122, 213, 231
health, 16, 20, 22, 25, 44, 72, 79, 86, 106, 111–113, 149, 163, 173, 175, 202, 207, 219, 237, 244, 253, 279, 281, 285
healthcare, 163, 172, 320
heart, 4, 312
hegemony, 58, 126, 128
help, 71, 75, 82, 86, 111, 118, 175, 179, 183, 240, 244, 245, 271, 313, 321, 328
Henri Tajfel, 53
hesitation, 247
hiding, 77
hierarchy, 241
highlight, 8, 41, 42, 62, 96, 116, 141, 142, 178, 248, 264, 269, 272, 285, 301, 331
history, 16, 19, 168, 189, 199, 224, 272, 294, 313
holiday, 72
home, 5, 87, 139
homophobia, 4, 11, 25, 53, 66, 74, 86, 88, 89, 94, 96, 131, 136, 172, 239, 263, 270, 325, 327, 332
homosexuality, 4, 11, 24, 29, 125, 148, 171, 181, 183, 224, 234, 248, 255, 280, 285, 298, 306, 308
honesty, 264
hope, 2, 8, 11, 13, 15, 31, 32, 44, 48, 54, 55, 59, 85, 95, 106, 122, 125, 136, 141, 143, 173–176, 180, 184, 231, 235, 238–240, 248, 249, 252, 256, 258, 259, 261, 264, 285, 286, 293, 295, 297, 302, 305, 307, 310, 312, 314, 316, 329, 333
hopelessness, 83
hostility, 15, 24, 26, 27, 31, 72, 81, 152, 225, 252, 257, 270, 304, 306, 327
human, 6, 10, 11, 30, 32, 33, 38, 39, 44, 70, 117, 123, 124, 127, 128, 134–136, 142, 143, 161, 163, 171, 172, 175, 178, 181, 184, 224, 226,

Index

236, 256, 272, 285, 286, 294, 298, 301, 305, 314, 315, 327, 331
humanity, 126, 226, 329
humor, 6
hurdle, 225

idea, 5, 73, 204, 247, 257
ideal, 168
identification, 44, 238
identifying, 201
identity, 1–10, 12, 15, 19–21, 23–26, 29, 31, 43, 48, 52, 53, 57, 61, 64–67, 69, 70, 73–75, 77, 78, 80, 81, 85, 87, 90–93, 95, 96, 99, 101, 108, 110, 111, 117, 120, 125, 134, 137, 149, 151, 176, 181, 183, 200–202, 204–206, 208, 215–217, 240, 241, 245, 247–249, 253, 255, 260, 262, 267, 270, 286, 297, 306, 314, 320, 322, 326, 327, 331, 338
image, 21, 98
imitation, 93
immediacy, 42
impact, 4, 6, 26, 28, 46–48, 53, 55, 57, 59, 78, 86, 87, 89, 93–95, 99, 101, 104, 106, 120, 122, 147, 161, 173, 174, 177, 180, 184, 185, 192, 193, 202, 210, 215, 216, 243, 245, 249, 264, 269, 280, 281, 284, 289, 291, 299, 301, 302, 304–306, 308, 312, 320, 334

imperative, 126, 141, 166, 235, 294
imperialism, 178
implementation, 130
import, 234
importance, 4, 8, 10, 41, 44–46, 51, 57–59, 73, 79, 82, 86, 93, 97, 106, 110, 111, 116, 122, 125, 130, 134, 136–138, 145, 152, 154, 159, 166, 168, 171, 181, 192, 196, 199, 202, 205, 207, 212, 226, 237, 240, 242, 247, 252, 253, 258, 267, 272, 279, 302, 312, 313, 317, 322, 323, 327, 328, 338
imprisonment, 11, 24, 135, 148, 153, 171, 183, 224, 288, 312
inadequacy, 69, 81, 90, 96, 110, 115, 202, 263, 270, 328
inauthenticity, 69
incident, 29, 225
inclination, 3, 5
inclusion, 179, 269, 312–314
inclusivity, 45, 52, 95, 118, 141, 166–168, 173–176, 216, 238, 240, 267, 284–286, 295, 314, 321, 323, 328, 329
increase, 244
individual, 10, 32, 52–54, 63, 69, 72, 76, 79, 81, 91, 94, 95, 101, 114, 115, 117, 118, 122, 141, 153, 180, 181, 200, 208, 231, 237, 259, 260, 262, 299, 301, 302, 306, 307, 322, 326, 327, 336
individuality, 12, 91, 270–272, 327–329

inequality, 322
influence, 53, 94, 172, 225, 291, 297, 302, 303, 305
information, 14, 41, 42, 54, 163, 236, 257, 280, 282, 333
ingenuity, 253
initiative, 35, 87, 189, 285
injustice, 3
innovation, 134, 192
inquiry, 67
insight, 62, 192
inspiration, 43, 59, 75, 179, 254, 258, 261, 336–338
instance, 5, 25, 42, 44, 45, 53, 54, 56, 72, 74, 76, 78, 84, 86, 87, 91, 94–96, 103, 118, 123, 127, 133, 140, 142, 148, 149, 153, 154, 163, 179, 181, 198, 200, 209, 210, 223, 226, 237, 239, 241, 242, 248, 251, 255, 257, 264, 268, 270, 280, 281, 285, 300, 320, 327, 333
integration, 181, 198, 209, 229
integrity, 22, 118
intent, 231
intentionality, 22, 45, 210
interaction, 241, 283
interconnectedness, 46, 47, 122, 128, 178, 184, 241, 314
interdependence, 48
interest, 5
internalization, 74, 88
internet, 11, 37–39, 41, 64, 279, 280
interpersonal, 108, 325
interplay, 25, 30, 65, 69, 125, 171, 174, 208, 241, 308, 310, 312, 322
intersect, 243, 287

intersection, 39, 111, 204, 208, 231, 239, 274
intersectionality, 35, 67, 85, 95, 96, 118, 136, 137, 142, 159, 166, 168, 189, 240–243, 248, 269, 286, 287, 289, 295, 307, 312, 314, 320, 322–324, 326
intersex, 320
intimidation, 172, 212
introspection, 65
invalidation, 268
investing, 195
investment, 190
invisibility, 142
involvement, 5, 51, 54, 130, 237, 240, 283
invulnerability, 94, 102
Iran, 41
isolation, 11, 25, 28, 33, 51, 75, 81, 83, 89, 90, 99, 113, 134, 149, 166, 218, 236, 254, 256, 257, 263, 265, 268, 285, 320, 322
issue, 16, 69, 96, 131, 178, 199, 222, 241, 278

James Baldwin, 223
Jamie, 91, 101
Janet Mock, 210
job, 78
John Turner, 53
journaling, 75, 117
journey, 1–4, 6–8, 10, 11, 13, 15, 22, 24, 25, 31, 50, 52, 55, 57, 59, 61–63, 65, 67, 69, 70, 73–75, 79–82, 85, 89–92, 94–97, 99, 101, 102, 104, 106, 108, 110, 111, 113,

115, 117, 120, 125, 130, 143, 144, 147, 154, 166, 168, 171, 173, 180, 182, 184, 185, 192, 193, 198, 202, 204–208, 210–213, 215, 217, 224, 228, 235, 240, 245, 247–249, 251, 252, 254–258, 260–266, 269, 270, 272, 282, 284, 286, 289, 291, 293, 295, 297, 299, 302, 303, 305, 306, 308, 312, 314, 321, 326, 328, 329, 331, 333, 336

joy, 1, 57, 72, 180

judgment, 9, 80, 86, 99, 101, 115, 214, 244, 265

Judith Butler, 327

Judith Butler's, 95

justice, 2, 3, 5, 6, 12, 13, 22, 25, 32, 35, 39, 41, 59, 118, 120, 124, 127, 128, 130, 132, 136, 150, 152, 157, 159, 166, 171, 173, 178, 179, 184, 187, 190, 197, 202, 205, 208, 210, 231, 243, 245, 247, 265, 269, 272, 273, 285, 291, 295, 302, 314, 319, 321, 324, 336

Keith Haring, 327

Kiki, 94, 95, 212, 219, 252–254, 259, 298, 299, 302, 303

Kimberlé Crenshaw, 95, 166, 243, 287, 325

Kimberlé Crenshaw's, 320

kindness, 115

knack, 3

knowledge, 59, 67, 187, 189, 192, 198, 273, 334

Kristin Neff, 115

label, 53, 67

labor, 96, 253

lack, 25, 28, 33, 38, 64, 131, 142, 199, 225, 241, 268, 285, 321, 323

landscape, 11, 23, 30, 39, 41, 43, 46, 48, 103, 123, 128, 135, 139, 142, 143, 148, 152, 163, 166, 171, 172, 179, 181, 183, 184, 189, 223, 224, 248, 252, 262, 263, 272, 274, 277, 281, 282, 284, 291, 294, 298, 307, 312, 328

language, 144, 229, 327

latter, 75

laughter, 1, 5

law, 25, 134, 148, 226, 312

layer, 23, 153

lead, 3, 21, 23, 25, 27, 34, 37, 38, 42, 44, 50, 53, 57, 69, 74–77, 81, 86, 88, 90, 93, 96, 99, 102, 110, 111, 113, 116, 120, 130, 136, 139, 145, 148, 149, 155, 179, 189, 199, 202, 209, 212, 214, 217, 219, 254, 257, 259, 263, 265, 268, 279, 281, 288, 301, 323, 325–327, 329, 332

leader, 307, 312

leadership, 93, 94, 161, 173, 189, 195–199, 206

learning, 157, 177, 179, 180, 192, 200, 248, 333

legacy, 52, 57–59, 95, 185, 200, 208, 217, 226, 231, 252, 286, 289, 291, 295, 302, 303, 305–308
legalization, 244
legislation, 313
legitimacy, 52
lens, 12, 24, 57, 58, 67, 95, 145, 166, 204, 241, 299, 338
lesbian, 320, 329
lesson, 5
level, 26, 118, 152, 184, 204, 219, 236, 237, 278, 279, 300
leverage, 12, 39, 142, 257, 259, 283, 286, 294
lexicon, 7
liberation, 12, 132, 336
lie, 182, 293, 295
life, 1–5, 13, 19–21, 28, 79, 87, 94, 113, 116, 148, 150, 153, 185, 202, 205, 208, 210, 213–215, 248, 253, 254
lifeline, 4, 11, 15, 50
lifestyle, 327
light, 13, 291, 304
like, 3, 9, 11, 13–17, 19, 21, 22, 28, 35, 39–41, 45–48, 65, 75, 77–79, 93–96, 104, 113, 120, 123, 125, 129, 130, 134–137, 142, 144, 145, 148, 150, 152, 154, 156, 161, 171–174, 179–181, 192, 201, 202, 210, 212, 215, 223, 225, 231, 233, 235, 238, 239, 247–252, 256–258, 271, 280, 282–286, 293, 297, 303, 310, 312, 313, 321, 325, 326, 328

likelihood, 56
limit, 79, 279
line, 57
listening, 72
literacy, 41, 199, 294
literature, 4, 5, 74, 91, 96, 223, 269, 271, 272
litigation, 312
living, 20, 74, 96, 219, 220, 262
lobbying, 135
location, 226
loneliness, 28
loss, 44, 78, 94
love, 10, 63, 72, 73, 75, 80, 97–99, 120, 122, 140, 217, 240, 295, 328

mainstream, 142, 181, 218, 241, 320, 322
making, 23, 34, 43, 47, 73, 90, 110, 118, 126, 128, 131, 133, 142, 155, 171, 180, 183, 222, 224, 257, 263, 278, 279, 312
man, 77, 226, 241, 287, 320, 325
management, 21
mantra, 12
marginalization, 26, 38, 122, 241
marginalize, 24, 52, 92, 96, 324
Marie, 31
mark, 223, 307
market, 1
marriage, 47, 244, 312
Marsha P. Johnson, 12
Maslow, 204
matter, 13, 19, 125, 213, 269, 314
means, 43, 93, 132, 142, 224, 231, 247, 257, 280, 327
measure, 184

Index 359

mechanism, 314
media, 5, 14–16, 21, 23, 27, 29, 37,
    38, 41, 42, 45, 47, 48, 51,
    53, 56, 57, 84, 96, 103,
    122, 124, 134–136, 142,
    149, 159, 172, 174, 178,
    181, 183, 189, 198, 212,
    223, 225, 226, 236, 239,
    248, 249, 251, 255, 257,
    258, 262, 264, 268, 269,
    271–275, 277, 279, 280,
    282, 284, 285, 300, 301,
    303, 307, 314, 320, 321,
    328, 329
meditation, 75, 117
melting, 1
member, 28, 226, 327
membership, 201
memory, 124
mentor, 194
mentoring, 192, 198
mentorship, 190, 192–194, 198,
    200, 205, 207, 307
message, 38, 52, 135, 144, 181, 231,
    251, 264, 278, 283, 294,
    301, 314
messaging, 16, 24, 280, 303
method, 54, 236
methodology, 93
microcosm, 64
milestone, 57, 73, 108
mind, 1, 4
mindfulness, 117, 253
mindset, 85
minority, 261
misconception, 91
mission, 15, 44, 141, 209, 248
misstep, 23
mistrust, 23

mob, 29
mobilization, 35, 135, 142, 143, 183,
    231, 274, 277, 312, 338
model, 45, 93, 236
modeling, 87, 264
moment, 2, 7, 11, 57, 72, 73, 91,
    168, 172, 180, 315
momentum, 190, 254, 294, 301
motivation, 43, 180, 209, 314, 336
motivator, 108, 180
mouth, 277
movement, 2, 23, 24, 31, 39, 46, 52,
    57, 58, 75, 87, 95, 98, 103,
    118, 120, 122, 127, 128,
    130, 132, 137, 140, 141,
    143, 152, 154, 159, 163,
    167, 168, 170, 171, 173,
    175–180, 184, 185, 187,
    189, 190, 192, 195,
    198–200, 205, 208, 209,
    217, 224, 226, 229, 231,
    236, 238, 240, 242–245,
    248, 249, 254, 256, 258,
    260, 262, 265, 268, 270,
    272, 284, 286, 288, 289,
    291, 294, 295, 299, 302,
    305–307, 310, 315, 316,
    319, 322–324, 333
multimedia, 281
multitude, 267, 269
murder, 29, 148
music, 271
myriad, 71, 77, 148, 224, 255

name, 13, 15, 297
narrative, 6, 8, 32, 42, 54, 74, 106,
    124, 143, 180, 205, 208,
    211, 217, 223, 224, 268,

279, 285, 298, 314, 316, 320
nation, 189
nature, 24, 28, 70, 102, 104, 182, 208, 215, 220, 243, 285, 307, 314, 325
navigation, 48
necessity, 11, 13, 19, 22, 46, 113, 131, 141, 163, 168, 177, 209, 213, 312, 331
need, 15, 21, 29, 41, 43, 47, 118, 125, 127, 135, 143, 149, 187, 189, 207, 225, 235, 238, 239, 298, 301, 320
negotiation, 215
net, 38
network, 30, 42, 46, 50–52, 81, 87, 95, 106, 108, 110, 127, 140, 206, 210, 249, 252, 256, 258, 301, 306
newfound, 4, 117
night, 87
non, 3, 8, 10, 11, 33, 53, 66–70, 76, 90, 91, 95, 96, 101, 117, 172, 183, 200, 268, 270, 320
norm, 77
normalization, 272
notion, 57, 102, 163, 173, 182, 202, 207, 271, 328
number, 56, 134, 237, 301, 320

observation, 5, 93
obstacle, 155
offering, 41, 79, 80, 211, 302
on, 1, 4–6, 10, 12, 13, 15–17, 23, 24, 26, 28, 29, 31, 37, 38, 42, 44, 45, 47, 53–55, 59, 61, 62, 75, 81, 86, 89, 93–95, 103, 106, 110, 117, 120, 122, 126, 130, 140, 145–150, 155, 166, 168, 172, 173, 175, 178, 180, 182, 184, 187, 189, 198–200, 202, 208, 209, 214, 215, 217, 223, 225, 226, 235, 241, 243, 245, 249, 250, 252–255, 258, 265, 273, 277, 281, 283, 285, 286, 289, 294, 299, 301, 303–308, 312, 315, 321, 322, 327
one, 7, 8, 11, 17, 21, 23, 47, 54, 58, 59, 67, 72–75, 77, 80, 90–95, 99, 101, 102, 116, 117, 120, 125, 150, 166, 187, 204, 205, 207, 210, 220, 231, 238, 241, 247, 251, 260, 262, 264, 268–270, 289, 291, 295, 299, 300, 306, 307, 314, 320, 327, 331
openness, 72, 263, 265
opportunity, 6, 101, 179, 269, 321, 338
oppression, 24, 25, 30, 41, 42, 93, 95, 136, 141, 148, 154, 166, 168, 184, 241, 243, 244, 255, 285, 314, 322, 324, 335
optation, 44, 45
option, 46
organization, 48, 81, 155, 256, 314, 320
organizing, 5, 6, 54, 132, 135, 143, 237, 245, 303
orientation, 1, 7, 10, 24, 25, 29, 37, 52, 61, 69, 73–75, 77, 90,

95, 126, 134, 137, 166, 176, 183, 241, 243, 245, 248, 286, 298, 314, 331
ostracism, 3, 12, 22, 78, 94, 96, 123, 135, 149, 183, 216, 244, 248, 263, 285, 312, 332
ostracization, 212, 234
other, 1, 2, 4, 17, 23, 53, 72, 179, 184, 198, 236, 273, 275, 285, 295, 312, 314, 321, 329, 333
out, 11, 16, 29–31, 41–44, 70–74, 76–81, 86, 87, 91, 94, 101, 108, 148, 149, 151, 153, 212, 213, 234, 253, 264, 267, 297, 306, 307, 327
outlook, 174, 176
outrage, 225
outreach, 31, 51, 98, 142
overlap, 287
oversimplification, 222
ownership, 294

pace, 199
pain, 31, 65
pandemic, 172, 173
paradigm, 102
paradox, 219, 280
part, 2, 12, 24, 42, 57, 75, 82, 87, 128, 178, 182, 201, 252
participation, 50, 131, 136, 180, 181, 281, 305, 337
partnership, 163, 271
passion, 3, 4, 67, 195, 198, 206, 209, 210, 214
past, 182, 274, 277
path, 3, 5, 13, 22, 32, 35, 51, 62, 67, 74, 94, 109, 128, 140, 157, 215, 217, 235, 252, 254, 258, 285, 297, 312, 314, 333
pathway, 132
patience, 86, 99
pattern, 86
peer, 79, 173, 203
people, 1, 172, 199, 241, 242, 271, 294, 307, 313, 323
perception, 2, 52, 89, 117, 134, 149, 181, 240, 285
performance, 52, 53, 95, 210
performativity, 95, 96
period, 154, 248
persecution, 17, 25, 28, 35, 94, 123, 140, 225, 231, 253, 285, 286, 306
perseverance, 240, 254, 317
persistence, 248, 254–256
person, 5, 95, 272, 300
persona, 20, 21, 94, 202, 213
perspective, 4, 68, 95, 327
petition, 38
phase, 65, 90
phenomenon, 29, 44, 74, 155, 270, 299, 302
phrase, 93
place, 1, 6, 8, 15, 120, 223, 288, 298
planning, 24, 124, 134, 143, 206
platform, 6, 15, 29, 37–39, 41, 44, 50, 56, 84, 92, 124, 135, 137, 143, 200, 210, 258, 327
play, 73, 82, 91, 101, 131, 136, 137, 139, 240, 243, 271
plight, 35, 42, 135, 171, 235, 252, 301, 307, 315
poetry, 209
point, 4, 7
police, 25, 168, 234

policy, 30, 42, 45, 115, 130, 172, 225, 245, 301
population, 12, 236, 272
portrayal, 27, 53, 269
position, 312
possibility, 235, 239, 299
post, 103, 264, 312
pot, 1
potential, 12, 13, 20, 22, 23, 39, 103, 130, 142, 143, 150–152, 155–157, 159, 161, 168, 173, 175, 182, 190, 199, 204, 212, 216, 223, 225, 244, 247, 248, 263, 265, 274, 276, 279, 280, 286, 293, 302, 307, 311, 327
poverty, 79
power, 6, 10, 11, 17, 24, 31, 41, 42, 44, 45, 48, 54, 62, 67, 74, 77, 79, 81, 94, 120, 131, 132, 141, 143, 154, 155, 157, 159, 161, 163, 166, 171, 175, 180, 195, 202, 205, 206, 210, 222, 224, 230, 233, 237, 239, 242, 255, 258, 264, 265, 267, 270, 274, 277, 281, 284, 288, 289, 295, 299, 301, 302, 312, 314, 317, 326, 327, 329, 335, 338
practice, 47, 115, 116, 130, 132, 167
precursor, 5
preference, 19, 213
prejudice, 102, 128, 240, 297
presence, 21, 43, 72, 91, 234, 244, 251, 253, 258, 264
preservation, 19
pressure, 5, 21, 23, 38, 42, 69, 75, 76, 81, 90, 94, 110, 130, 136, 142, 172, 202, 214, 252, 270, 286, 301, 315, 328, 332
prevalence, 131, 278
pride, 12, 31, 54, 56, 72, 89, 92, 172, 241, 299
principle, 130, 168, 175
prison, 29, 125, 308
privilege, 95, 240, 243
problem, 44
process, 3, 6, 8, 15, 45, 52, 65, 67, 70, 71, 73, 74, 76, 85, 90, 95, 96, 99, 104, 108, 115, 131, 155, 195, 198, 200, 206, 211, 215, 226, 236, 238, 248, 249, 252, 253, 260, 262, 272, 321
product, 180
professional, 79, 206–208, 248, 252–254
profile, 149
profit, 231
program, 189
progress, 25, 34, 46, 55, 157, 171–173, 175, 180, 182–184, 188, 217, 225, 233, 235, 237, 239, 268, 285, 288, 298, 304, 308–310, 314, 316, 325, 330, 332
promise, 180, 184, 217, 269
promotion, 122
protection, 13, 23, 43, 135, 181, 329
protest, 45, 124, 133, 234, 248
pseudonym, 13–15, 19–21, 23, 135, 151, 255, 280, 306
public, 6, 19–21, 25, 45, 53, 54, 57, 92, 94, 96, 124, 126, 130, 134, 136, 148–150, 154,

Index 363

172, 181, 183, 189, 202, 204, 213–215, 226, 236, 240, 249, 252, 285, 286, 301, 302, 307, 316, 333
pulse, 3
punishment, 125
purpose, 51, 103, 115, 143, 155, 157, 178, 200, 204, 205, 209, 256, 294, 335
pursuit, 17, 32, 33, 52, 57, 63, 95, 123, 132, 134, 143, 150, 161, 166, 171, 173, 206, 215, 217, 247, 284, 291, 302, 310, 324, 336
push, 47, 147, 282, 289, 333, 335
pushback, 6

quality, 79, 95, 152
queer, 7, 95, 96, 118, 242, 271, 287, 320, 324–329
quest, 22, 61, 104, 125, 128, 248, 270, 325
question, 5, 66
quo, 1, 5, 52, 54, 123, 143, 173, 240

race, 166, 241, 243, 287, 307, 322, 325
racism, 131
raid, 168
raising, 42, 45, 132, 135, 143, 181, 183, 238, 257, 258, 301, 313
rallying, 256
range, 68, 76, 320, 323
re, 223
reach, 45, 51, 85, 172, 177, 204, 236, 256, 258, 277–279, 281, 306
reaction, 300

reality, 16, 20, 23, 28, 29, 78, 96, 217, 285, 320
realization, 3, 4, 7, 10, 11, 65, 90, 167, 204
realm, 19, 50, 93, 141, 143, 150, 154, 157, 190, 202, 210, 222, 226, 254
rebellion, 95
recognition, 30, 50, 58, 65, 69, 150, 181, 226, 284, 312, 314, 326, 329, 331
recourse, 25
reflection, 65–67, 118, 120, 182, 202, 213, 244, 327
reform, 44, 126, 225, 235, 286, 310, 314, 316
refuge, 29, 77
refugee, 35
refusal, 94, 247
regard, 73
rejection, 2, 4, 30, 72–74, 77, 81, 86, 88, 99, 101, 116, 149, 153, 216, 248, 253, 270, 327
relatability, 6
relationship, 42, 72, 75, 152, 280, 281, 293
relevance, 294
reliance, 29
relief, 7
reluctance, 74, 86, 253, 263, 270
remain, 22, 40, 48, 57, 110, 124, 136, 140, 145, 149, 173, 198, 239, 268, 274, 279, 284, 288, 293, 295, 298, 301, 303, 312, 320, 333
reminder, 10, 29, 75, 79, 104, 141, 208, 249, 295, 308
repeal, 38, 181
report, 69, 79, 123, 239

representation, 4, 8, 15, 64, 96, 131, 134, 136, 142, 241, 268, 269, 301, 314, 316, 320–322, 326, 327
representative, 45
repression, 15, 76, 224, 263, 312, 332
requirement, 177
research, 45, 65, 67, 225
researcher, 265
resilience, 2, 3, 6, 10, 13, 15, 24, 30–32, 35, 41, 48, 50, 54–56, 59, 70, 72, 77, 79, 82–85, 92, 94–96, 99, 101, 102, 104, 106, 108, 110, 111, 113–117, 120, 122, 125, 130, 132, 134, 136, 141, 143, 147, 152–154, 157, 166, 171–175, 180, 184, 192, 195, 198, 202, 205, 207, 208, 215, 226, 231, 233, 235–240, 244, 248–252, 254, 256–260, 262, 264, 281, 285, 289, 291, 295, 297, 299, 301, 303, 305–308, 312, 314, 316, 326, 331, 333
resistance, 31, 42, 86, 123, 231, 248, 257, 298, 301, 307, 310, 314, 326
resolve, 10, 12
resource, 139, 161, 338
respect, 118, 128, 179, 240, 286, 298
response, 79, 141, 143, 224, 279, 288, 300
responsibility, 12, 19, 202, 213, 294
result, 25, 77, 78, 94, 163, 179, 212, 241
retribution, 12, 183, 225

revolution, 328
rhetoric, 93
richness, 267, 272
ridicule, 3, 244
rift, 72
right, 30, 90, 140, 326
rise, 96, 99, 172, 183, 199, 249, 260, 277, 279, 308, 328, 336–338
risk, 13, 16, 43, 44, 78, 114, 131, 148, 149, 151, 153, 166, 178, 183, 212, 222, 231, 234, 256, 280, 282, 327
ritual, 117
road, 35, 104, 235
roadmap, 271
role, 15, 19, 21, 23, 45, 46, 52, 53, 72, 77, 79–82, 86, 91, 93, 96, 130, 131, 136, 137, 139, 145, 172, 175, 178, 181, 183, 192, 198, 229, 231, 239, 240, 243, 245, 249, 256, 269, 271–273, 301, 307, 310, 312, 313, 315, 320, 321, 336
room, 3
routine, 20
rule, 224
Russia, 41

s, 1–8, 10–13, 21, 23, 25, 29–31, 38, 39, 51–54, 57–59, 64, 67, 69, 73–75, 77–79, 90–95, 99, 102, 109, 110, 116–118, 122, 127, 140, 141, 149, 150, 154, 172, 178, 179, 189, 190, 199, 200, 204–210, 214, 215, 217, 219, 220, 224, 225,

237, 238, 247–249, 251, 252, 254–257, 260–265, 268, 270, 285, 297–307, 312, 320, 327, 333
sacrifice, 219
safety, 13, 15, 23, 29, 38, 43, 57, 127, 133, 148, 150–152, 172, 204, 223, 225, 251, 280, 282, 294
sanctuary, 52, 213
Sarah, 72, 87
satisfaction, 116, 209
scale, 31, 47, 145–147, 300, 301, 306
scenario, 239, 327
scent, 5
scholar, 166
school, 5, 101, 189, 313
scope, 148
scrutiny, 57, 179, 212, 213, 280
secrecy, 172, 225, 265
section, 3, 4, 6, 17, 28, 46, 48, 61, 70, 77, 82, 85, 93, 104, 111, 123, 125, 130, 132, 134, 141, 145, 148, 150, 152, 154, 157, 163, 166, 168, 171, 173, 180, 187, 190, 192, 208, 210, 215, 224, 229, 233, 235, 243, 250, 252, 258, 263, 267, 270, 272, 275, 277, 306, 310, 314, 327, 329, 331, 334, 336
self, 1–4, 6, 8, 10–12, 19–21, 25, 29, 52, 53, 61–63, 65, 67, 69, 70, 72–75, 77, 80–82, 85, 89–92, 94, 95, 97–99, 101–104, 106, 108, 110–113, 115–118, 120, 122, 148, 154, 185, 189, 193, 200–205, 207, 208, 210, 213–216, 231, 238, 244, 247, 253, 254, 260, 261, 264, 266, 270–272, 327–329
sensationalism, 136
sense, 3, 5, 7, 9, 11, 12, 16, 25, 31, 46–48, 50–52, 54, 55, 57, 63, 64, 74, 77, 79, 81, 82, 84, 91, 92, 94, 99, 103, 108, 110, 115, 117, 134, 143, 157, 173, 175, 178, 180, 189, 193, 195, 199–201, 204, 205, 209, 237, 248, 252, 256, 257, 264, 269–271, 279, 283, 285, 294, 302, 307, 321, 324, 328, 335
sensitivity, 179, 224
sentiment, 154
series, 63, 95, 154, 163, 301, 331
set, 3, 4, 20, 22, 174
setting, 5, 20, 120, 209, 214
sex, 2, 11, 24, 28, 29, 33, 53, 74, 78, 83, 123, 125, 128, 135, 153, 171, 181, 183, 224, 239, 244, 255, 285, 298, 304, 308, 312
sexism, 131
sexuality, 1, 5, 65, 69, 70, 75, 268, 287, 327
shame, 74, 75, 77, 89, 96, 117, 263, 265–267, 328
share, 7, 14, 16, 21, 23, 29, 31, 37, 38, 41, 44, 45, 47, 51, 54, 72, 87, 91, 94, 98, 103, 124, 136, 142, 145, 174, 178, 181, 183, 193, 198,

205, 223, 225, 236, 237, 239, 249, 251, 257, 262, 263, 269, 280, 285, 299, 300, 303, 305, 313, 321, 326–328, 335, 338
sharing, 5, 12, 16, 23, 42, 47, 53, 56, 59, 86, 91, 94, 96, 104, 139, 141, 161, 172, 177, 198, 205, 210–212, 217, 222–225, 231, 233, 239, 249, 252, 257, 264, 265, 278, 279, 281, 321
shield, 3, 17, 22, 279
shift, 52, 54, 91, 102, 117, 134, 173, 200, 205, 223, 226, 240, 279, 282, 285, 298, 301, 312–314
shoestring, 225
side, 69
significance, 11, 53, 59, 82, 144, 161, 180, 210, 270, 327, 334
silence, 4, 24, 65, 79, 126, 131, 136, 148, 247, 255, 263, 265, 285, 325, 326, 332
simplicity, 67
situation, 78, 135
size, 278
skepticism, 6
skill, 82, 202
societal, 2–6, 8, 10–12, 24, 25, 27, 29–31, 33, 52–54, 57, 63, 65–67, 69, 70, 73–77, 81, 82, 85, 86, 88–92, 94–97, 99, 102, 104, 106, 110, 111, 113, 115–118, 120, 123, 125, 128, 131, 134–136, 142, 153, 161, 171, 172, 181, 183, 184, 200, 202, 204, 208, 216, 217, 229, 233, 239, 240, 247–249, 252, 254, 260, 263, 266, 267, 269, 271, 272, 285, 286, 289, 293–295, 300, 301, 303, 304, 306, 310, 312, 321, 324, 327, 329, 331, 332
society, 1–3, 5, 8, 10, 13, 15, 16, 20, 24–26, 28, 32, 35, 54, 57, 66, 67, 75, 77, 82, 87, 89, 92, 96, 97, 113, 115, 125, 130, 134, 161, 173, 176, 181, 184, 212, 218, 226, 228, 231, 233, 237–240, 243, 245, 253, 258, 260, 262, 269, 272, 274, 286, 293, 295, 300, 302, 305, 308, 310, 312, 314, 317, 319, 321, 326, 327, 329, 331, 333, 335
socio, 11
solace, 2, 4, 7, 29, 30, 64, 77, 79, 80, 252
solidarity, 5, 12, 31, 39, 41, 42, 44, 45, 47, 54, 58, 79, 82, 84, 92, 94–96, 103, 124, 130, 132, 136, 137, 140–143, 145, 147, 150, 166, 171–174, 178, 180, 184, 198, 205, 235, 237–240, 243, 248, 252, 256, 257, 262, 263, 265, 269, 271, 275, 279, 285, 286, 289, 294, 301–303, 305, 314–316, 321, 326
source, 2, 4, 24, 43, 56, 79, 101, 102, 327
South Africa, 179, 312
South Africa's, 312

Index

space, 5, 7, 9, 16, 21, 23, 41, 45, 57, 124, 213, 231, 252, 257, 264, 273, 274
speaking, 6, 29, 143, 145, 189, 204, 245, 249, 307
spectrum, 198, 267, 268, 270, 310, 319
sphere, 205
spirit, 2, 3, 10, 13, 30, 32, 35, 59, 110, 130, 184, 198, 235, 247, 249, 284, 293, 295, 297, 299, 305, 312, 338
spotlight, 171, 297, 302
spread, 300
stability, 78
stage, 2, 5, 9
stake, 148
stance, 130, 143
stand, 1, 3, 4, 13, 31, 108, 168, 172, 239, 249, 260, 265, 291, 295, 301, 306, 327
standard, 47
state, 25, 171, 219
statement, 8, 206, 257
status, 1, 5, 10, 52, 54, 123, 143, 166, 173, 226, 240
step, 5, 10, 11, 15, 44, 57, 67, 81, 89, 92, 94, 108, 180, 182, 198, 214, 236, 237, 317
stereotype, 52, 53
stigma, 4, 6, 11, 26, 28, 32, 33, 53, 69, 72–75, 81, 83, 88, 89, 91, 113, 115, 123, 128, 136, 149, 181, 183, 225, 234, 252, 263, 272, 285, 288, 300, 303, 304, 322, 327
Stigmatization, 26

stigmatization, 25, 27, 28, 110, 142, 153, 239, 332
sting, 5
stoicism, 102
storm, 253
story, 3, 10–12, 23, 24, 30, 31, 39, 54, 59, 72, 77, 79, 81, 87, 89, 91, 94, 101, 103, 104, 187, 206, 217, 226, 248, 249, 259, 267, 298, 300, 302, 307, 308
storytelling, 3, 5, 31, 96, 122, 143, 205, 210, 222–224, 226, 233, 249, 257, 260, 265, 279, 281, 321, 326
strain, 81, 111
strategy, 41, 51, 93, 135, 137, 156, 209, 236, 253
streaming, 283
street, 5
strength, 2, 4, 30, 32, 48, 50, 52, 72, 79, 80, 82, 94, 101, 102, 104, 115, 152, 154, 157, 166, 180, 190, 202, 203, 217, 247, 248, 252, 254–256, 259, 262, 263, 307, 308
stress, 20, 81, 149, 248, 253, 261
struggle, 2–4, 8, 11, 12, 21, 24, 30, 35, 48, 54, 65, 86, 90, 91, 96, 97, 117, 118, 123, 125, 128, 130, 134, 136, 150, 152, 154, 166, 173, 179, 181, 202, 208, 224–226, 231, 233, 235, 236, 238, 245, 249, 252, 263, 268, 270, 293, 294, 310, 327, 329, 331, 332, 338
style, 8, 94

submission, 247
success, 134, 180, 181, 190, 288
suffering, 115
summary, 6, 67
sun, 3
support, 5, 8, 9, 12, 14–16, 21, 28, 30–33, 35, 37, 38, 41, 42, 44–47, 50–52, 58, 69, 72, 77–82, 84–86, 89, 94, 96, 98, 99, 101, 103, 106–108, 110, 115, 124, 130–132, 136, 137, 140–143, 148, 150, 152, 163, 168, 171–175, 179, 189, 194, 202–204, 206, 207, 209, 210, 223, 225, 226, 234–240, 244, 249–253, 256, 258, 260, 262, 268, 277, 279, 281, 282, 285, 286, 294, 300–304, 306, 307, 310, 315, 320, 321, 326, 333
surface, 1
surrounding, 4, 6, 11, 24, 33, 52, 65, 75, 78, 134, 135, 183, 234, 255, 259, 263, 285, 303, 304
surveillance, 16, 29, 39–41, 43, 47, 280, 294
survival, 30, 32, 46, 249, 258
sustainability, 161, 190, 192, 198, 199, 253
sword, 17, 22, 41, 64
symbol, 15
system, 24, 25, 53, 80, 90, 106–108, 136, 142, 207, 258, 306

taboo, 3, 24, 285, 298
tale, 2

tapestry, 5, 59, 173, 178, 181, 198, 206, 223, 224, 267, 270, 297, 319, 327
task, 2, 50, 94, 135, 144, 253
technology, 21, 31, 39, 45–48, 52, 140, 178, 180, 251, 274, 279, 281, 282, 294, 295, 333
television, 269
tenacity, 233
tendency, 241
tension, 231
ter, 24, 33
term, 166, 190, 199, 237, 253, 287, 325
terrain, 99, 274
test, 153, 255
testament, 10, 67, 70, 120, 154, 206, 235, 248, 251, 254, 255, 289, 299, 301, 331
the Atlantic Ocean, 3
the Middle East, 288
the United States, 47, 244, 320
theme, 2, 254
theorist, 327
theory, 52, 53, 57, 58, 75, 85, 88, 93, 95, 132, 134, 143, 180, 200, 211, 286, 288, 299, 300, 320
therapy, 89, 101, 253
thinking, 250
thirst, 6
thought, 144
threat, 16, 25, 29, 52, 53, 57, 96, 137, 148, 149, 219, 253, 301
time, 7, 42, 87, 89, 117, 168, 181, 190, 209, 214, 283, 302
today, 59

Index

tokenism, 155
tokenization, 131
toll, 20, 74, 94, 149, 252, 253
tomorrow, 59
tool, 5, 13, 15, 24, 31, 37, 45, 51, 87, 95, 98, 124, 132, 139, 142, 148, 174, 180, 211, 222, 224, 225, 231, 248, 251, 257, 272, 273, 279, 280, 283, 321
toolkit, 206
torch, 55, 187, 198–200, 205, 238, 305
toy, 1
traction, 31, 131
tragedy, 248
training, 179, 189, 205, 239, 286, 302, 313, 321
trait, 82, 113
transfer, 192, 198
transformation, 122, 269, 307, 313
transgender, 31, 81, 168, 210, 241, 242, 268, 320, 322, 329
transition, 7, 198, 282, 312
transnationalism, 286, 289
transphobia, 239
transportation, 54
trauma, 218, 248
traumatization, 223
triumph, 56, 240
trolling, 281
trust, 161
truth, 2, 4, 8, 10, 94, 104, 220, 263–265, 291, 302
turn, 25
turning, 4, 7

Uganda, 143, 312
uncertainty, 1, 255
understanding, 4, 5, 7, 8, 10–13, 21, 39, 41, 45, 48, 53, 54, 59, 66–70, 73, 75, 77, 86, 87, 89, 96, 99, 101–103, 106, 108, 113, 126–128, 134, 143, 147, 152, 157, 166, 172, 175, 184, 189, 199, 200, 204, 205, 222, 224, 226–229, 231, 235, 239, 240, 243–245, 249, 253, 259, 262, 268, 271, 274, 279, 282, 285, 288, 313, 315, 321, 324, 328, 331, 333
uniqueness, 10, 73, 117, 271, 272
unity, 51, 55, 154, 157, 159, 166, 168, 289, 294
unworthiness, 74, 265
up, 1, 3, 11, 24, 29, 31, 89, 93, 99, 125, 224, 239, 249, 306, 308, 336–338
uplift, 243
urgency, 33, 150, 173, 199, 283
use, 13, 16, 31, 37, 38, 46, 48, 52, 53, 68, 135, 142, 143, 224, 226, 236, 248, 256, 257, 271, 279–281, 283, 300, 328
utilization, 45

validation, 5, 72, 73, 96, 98, 122, 262
value, 45, 75, 118, 122, 180, 199, 328
vehicle, 327
victimization, 183
victory, 172, 181, 314
view, 24, 67, 222, 254, 285, 302
vigilance, 24, 94
vigor, 184

violence, 4, 6, 11, 12, 20, 22–25, 29, 30, 33, 42, 64, 78, 79, 83, 94, 96, 123–126, 142, 148, 149, 153, 172, 179, 183, 212, 216, 224, 234, 239, 242, 248, 253, 255, 256, 263, 285, 288, 301, 306, 310, 312, 320, 325, 327, 332
visibility, 4, 12, 13, 23, 43, 45, 46, 52, 57, 64, 77, 91, 124, 142, 143, 152, 171, 172, 181, 183, 212, 213, 219, 236, 242, 247, 257, 268, 269, 280, 282, 286, 300, 310, 315, 326–328
vision, 12, 206, 238, 248, 286, 289, 295, 302
voice, 2, 4, 6, 13, 21, 24, 37, 94, 140, 144, 205, 247, 255, 294
void, 81
volunteer, 142, 225
vulnerability, 21, 94, 102–104, 110, 154, 202, 215–217, 252, 253, 263–265

wave, 103, 190, 328
way, 46, 54, 63, 89, 97, 106, 125, 173, 184, 206–208, 233, 235–238, 240, 243, 254, 262, 271, 282, 287, 289, 295, 300, 308, 333, 338
weakness, 102, 202, 263
wedding, 225
weight, 75–77, 252, 260
well, 5, 21, 25, 30, 45, 57, 61, 82, 86, 98, 99, 106, 111–113, 116, 120, 152, 173, 193, 205, 207, 210, 248, 308
wellbeing, 79
wellness, 253
whim, 5
whole, 25, 120, 132, 284
willingness, 65, 264
win, 180
wisdom, 199
wish, 187, 238, 263, 302
woman, 30, 31, 72, 87, 241, 287, 320, 322, 325
word, 277
work, 6, 10, 21, 48, 54, 57, 59, 67, 77, 86, 120, 122, 148, 150, 152, 168, 173, 180, 190, 195, 208, 209, 215, 219, 223, 228, 231, 256, 271, 289, 291, 299, 301, 303, 304, 306, 321, 326, 327, 329
workplace, 31, 78
workshop, 54
world, 8, 10, 13, 37, 73, 77, 82, 87, 92, 120, 122, 124, 130, 139, 141, 147, 148, 150, 152, 168, 173, 179, 190, 215, 224, 233, 239, 240, 245, 249, 260, 273, 289, 297, 299, 301, 322, 327, 329–331, 334, 336
worth, 73, 74, 99, 108, 116, 117, 270
writer, 209
writing, 204, 205, 209, 210

Yaoundé, 30, 124, 225, 234
youth, 6, 16, 86, 173, 184, 187–190, 199, 237, 272, 294